The Beginner's Guitar Mn

Three Books in One! – Master Chords, Progre

How to Learn and Play Guitar for Beginners

The Beginner's Guitar Method Compilation

Three Books in One! – Master Chords, Progressions and Soloing on Guitar

How to Learn and Play Guitar for Beginners

ISBN: 978-1-911267-70-6

Published by **www.fundamental-changes.com**

Copyright © 2017 Joseph Alexander and Simon Pratt

The moral right of this author has been asserted.

All rights reserved. No part of this publication may be reproduced, stored in a retrieval system, or transmitted in any form or by any means, without the prior permission in writing from the publisher.

The publisher is not responsible for websites (or their content) that are not owned by the publisher.

www.fundamental-changes.com

Twitter: **@guitar_joseph**

Over 9000 fans on Facebook: **FundamentalChangesInGuitar**

Instagram: **FundamentalChanges**

For over 250 Free Guitar Lessons with Videos Check Out

www.fundamental-changes.com

Cover Image Copyright: Shutterstock: By Labutin.Art

Contents

Foreword to the Compilation 5
Get the Audio 7

The First 100 Chords for Guitar 8
Introduction 9
How to Read Chord Diagrams 11
Chapter One: Open Position Chords 12
Chapter Two: Dominant 7 Open Chords 20
Chapter Three: Barre Chords 24
Chapter Four: A Little (Non-Scary) Music Theory 33
Chapter Five: More Open Chords 40
Chapter Six: More Barre Chords 47
Chapter Seven: Bass Note Movements 51
Chapter Eight: Basic Piano Voicings 53
Chapter Nine: Fourth-String Barres 56
Chapter Ten: Diatonic Extensions to Dominant 7 Chords 60
Chapter Eleven: Chromatic Alterations to Dominant Chords 67
Chapter Twelve: How to Practice 73
Chapter Thirteen: Adding Rhythm 76
Conclusion and Practice Directions 83

First Chord Progressions for Guitar 84
Introduction 85
Before You Get Started 86
Chapter One: Common Rhythmic Patterns 87
Chapter Two – Open Chords Part 1 95
Chapter Three – Open Blues Chords 108
Chapter Four – Barre Chords 119
Chapter Five – Extended Barre Chords 126
Chapter Six – Lush Open Chords 136
Chapter Seven – Extended Barre Chords 145
Chapter Eight – Creative Application 156

Chapter Nine – The Big List of Chord Progressions 160
Chapter Ten – Practice Workouts 175
Conclusion 179

The Beginner Lead Guitar Method 180

Introduction 181
Tips 182
Chapter One – The A Minor Pentatonic Scale 183
Chapter Two – Building Melodies 190
Chapter Three – Slides 198
Chapter Four – Bends 204
Chapter Five – Legato 215
Chapter Six – A Minor Pentatonic Licks 226
Chapter Seven – A Minor Pentatonic Full Solo 232
Chapter Eight – Moving to E Minor 236
Chapter Nine – E Minor Solo 243
Chapter Ten – The A Blues Scale 247
Chapter Eleven – A Blues Scale Licks 254
Chapter Twelve – A Blues Scale Solo 259
Chapter Thirteen – The A Major Pentatonic Scale 263
Chapter Fourteen – A Major Pentatonic Licks 269
Chapter Fifteen – A Major Pentatonic Solo 274
Chapter Sixteen – The Four Note Soloing Challenge 277
Chapter Seventeen – 'In The Style of' Licks 282
Conclusion 287
Discography 288
Quiz Answers 290

Foreword to the Compilation

Welcome to the Beginner's Guitar Method Compilation, it's great to have you with us.

This book is about helping beginners to improve quickly and efficiently. We set out to provide the most comprehensive beginner's guitar guide in the world by combining three of our best-selling books, *The First 100 Chords for Guitar, First Chord Progressions for Guitar*, and *The Beginner Lead Guitar Method*.

This compilation will provide you with the perfect foundations of chord knowledge, rhythm playing, and soloing on both electric and acoustic guitar.

You will:

- Discover *every* essential chord on guitar
- Build chord progressions and master strumming
- Discover how to play your first solos on guitar
- Develop picking, strumming and arpeggio patterns for every style of music.
- Instantly apply and use chords to make songs!
- Master soloing techniques such as bends, slides, picking, legato and so much more…

There's no rush to plough through all the content contained within these pages. This book contains a wealth of information that's equivalent to more than a year of private lessons.

Aim to practice for ten to fifteen minutes a day, rather than one hour once a week, and ensure you keep on track by keeping a practice journal. You can also record videos or audio to help you measure your progress.

About each book:

The First 100 Chords for Guitar.

The guitar is a *harmonic* instrument (just like the piano) and capable of playing many notes at the same time. Most instruments, such as the trumpet or flute, can only play one note at a time. By playing multiple notes together, guitarists and pianists create chords and provide a bed of harmony to accompany other instruments or singers.

Chords are the essential building blocks of music, and therefore the starting point for our study of the guitar. A vocabulary of chords and an understanding of how they are combined are fundamental goals of all guitarists, whether they are beginners or professional musicians.

The First 100 Chords for Guitar teaches you how to play and apply *every* chord you'll ever use on the guitar (and a couple you probably won't!).

These chords are combined into short phrases that form songs you will definitely know.

First Chord Progressions for Guitar.

This book builds on the foundations laid out in book one and teaches you how to combine chords into meaningful music. Chord progressions are the foundation of every song you have ever heard, and when you understand the logic used in their construction, you'll have an instant creative resource to use when writing your own music.

First Chord Progressions for Guitar covers *every* common chord sequence used in popular music and is an essential resource for the guitarist.

With a comprehensive understanding of the "formulas" of music, you will learn to instantly recognize any chord sequence in any song played on the radio, and play it on the guitar without a second thought. This sounds like witchcraft, but it is actually a skill that is fairly easy to develop.

Once you can lay down some chord progressions it's time to look at the most glamorous part of guitar; soloing and you'll learn how to solo in book three:

The Beginner Lead Guitar Method

The Beginner Lead Guitar Method is our exciting, creative soloing school. You'll quickly get to grips with the scales, techniques and musical approaches that'll have you wailing on the guitar in no time!

It contains a detailed overview of every skill you need to play awesome guitar solos immediately, with plenty of licks, tips and tricks to build you into a devastating lead guitarist.

There are complete solos for you to learn, and hundreds of musical examples that will develop your style, personality and vocabulary on the guitar.

This step-by-step guide takes you from zero to hero as a soloist and helps you build a comprehensive set of musical skills that will wow any audience.

Ready to dive in?

Download the audio and let's get started with The First 100 Chords for Guitar

Have fun!

Joseph and Simon

Get the Audio

The audio files for this book are available to download for free from **www.fundamental-changes.com.** The link is in the top right-hand corner. Simply select this book title from the drop-down menu and follow the instructions to get the audio.

We recommend that you download the files directly to your computer, not to your tablet, and extract them there before adding them to your media library. You can then put them on your tablet, iPod or burn them to CD. On the download page there is a help PDF, and we also provide technical support via the contact form.

For over 250 Free Guitar Lessons with Videos Check out:

www.fundamental-changes.com

Twitter: **@guitar_joseph**

Over 9000 fans on Facebook: **FundamentalChangesInGuitar**

Instagram: **FundamentalChanges**

Get your audio now for free:

It makes the book come alive, and you'll learn much more!

www.fundamental-changes.com/download-audio

The First 100 Chords for Guitar

Introduction

The first chords you learn on guitar may take you some time. Not only are you learning to use your fingers in a completely new way, you also have to learn some intricate muscle movements and commit those to subconscious memory. If you're a musician, or have ever played a sport, you may have heard the term 'muscle memory'.

Muscle memory is the name for something that is so automated that we no longer have to think about it. Walking, riding a bike, throwing a ball and swimming are all examples of processes where we need to develop muscle memory to do them well. They are all *learned* processed which may have taken some time for you to develop (probably when you were very young), but once you know them, the movements go to a very deep part of your brain and you don't need to actively think about them to make them work.

In fact, if you tried to think about the exact sequence of muscles you need to trigger in order to walk, then you would never get anywhere at all!

Walking probably took you a good few months to figure out, but now you probably never think about having to do it at all. Remember this fact while you're taking your first steps on guitar. For many people, playing chords isn't an instant skill and it will take a while before their precise movements are committed muscle memory. To put chords firmly into muscle memory we need to do a bit of structured (yet fun!) practice, where we train our brains exactly how to form each chord, and how to move from one chord to another.

Chords need to be locked into our muscle memory because we don't have a lot of time to form, or change between them when playing songs. If we change too slowly there will be a big hole in the rhythm and flow of the song. To use a sporting analogy again; imagine what would happen if you had to actually think about blocking every time someone threw a punch in a boxing match. We need to build chords to the point where they become a reflex reaction.

Developing this skill isn't as hard as it may seem… It just takes a bit of commitment, regular practice and a structured approach to learning. As adults, we sometimes don't like to learn new things. It's easy to feel that learning finished when we left school or college, so we can sometimes shy away from new challenges or experiences. Music, however, is a really fun habit to get into. The results can be quick and effortless, or sometimes slow and challenging. Either way, the end result; playing music, is one of the most rewarding experiences you can have.

If you want to use this book as a reference, you can dive straight in now. However, in the final chapters I have included some really useful tips on how to practice efficiently, develop some great playing habits that will stay with you for life, and move from learning chords to playing songs by adding rhythm. These sections will teach you to learn and memorise chords more quickly, make you into a better musician, and help you develop a healthy approach to the guitar.

Two questions that guitar teachers get asked regularly are:

How long will it take to learn to play the guitar?

And,

How many chords are there?

Both are quite difficult to answer.

The first is difficult to answer because it has a lot of variables. For example, how much will you practice? Will you focus on the right things? *How* will you practice? How do you define 'being able to play the guitar'? – Do you just want to strum a few chords around a campfire or is it your goal to become the next Eddie Van Halen?

With all these variables and more, it is almost impossible to give a straight answer or time frame. But, if you practice for about twenty minutes every day, practice efficiently and are aiming to play some chord-based pop music, then it normally takes a few months to get fairly competent.

In answer to the second question, the answer is simply 'lots, but as a guitarist you will probably use relatively few of them'. Luckily for us, once you've learned a few 'open' chords and a few 'barre' chords, you can play pretty much any chord or song on the guitar.

Let's get started and look at the *open position* chords available to us. If you're a beginner, I highly recommend working through Chapter One in conjunction with the How to Practice section at the end of the book.

A Final Note!

PLEASE download and listen to the audio along with each example. It will really help you develop as a player. It takes a lot longer to reach a goal if you don't know what that goal looks (or sounds) like.

Get the audio examples from **www.fundamental-changes.com** and follow the instructions. The Download Audio tab is in the top right.

How to Read Chord Diagrams

The following images show how the written notation of a chord diagram relates to where you place your fingers on the neck of a guitar to play a chord. Pay careful attention to which strings are played and which fingers are use.

The first diagram shows the notes on each of the open strings of the guitar.

The second diagram shows you how to number the fingers of the fretting hand. If you are left-handed, the same numbers apply to your right hand

The third diagram shows the standard way chords are notated on chord *girds*. Each dot represents where you place a finger.

The final diagram shows how the notation relates to where you place your fingers on the guitar neck.

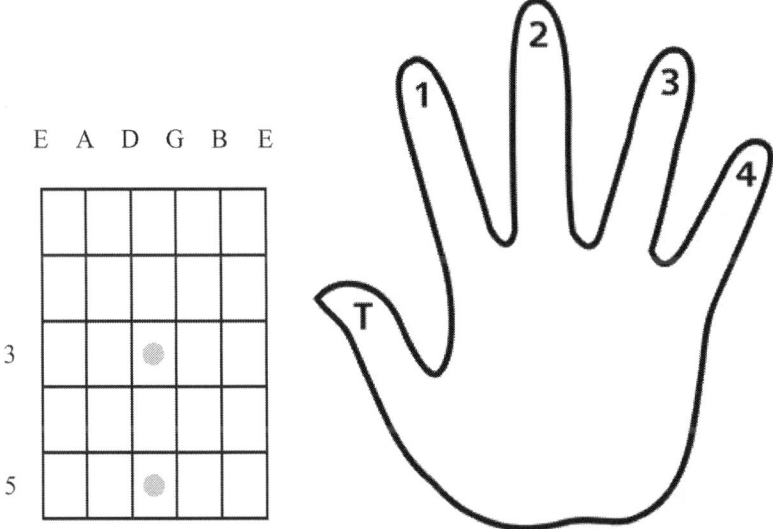

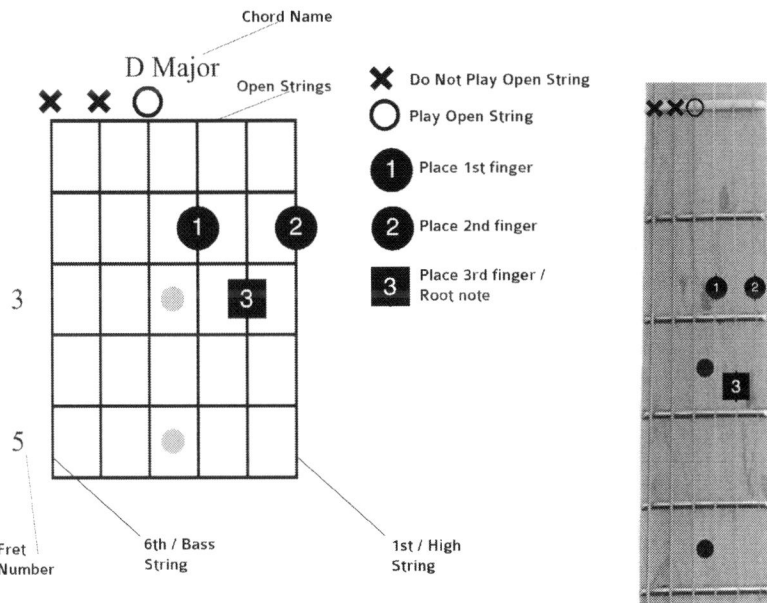

Chapter One: Open Position Chords

Open position chords are normally the first chords people learn on the guitar. They are named 'open position' chords because they often use open strings as notes within the chord. As you will see later, there are many chords which do not use open strings.

Open position chords can be used to play the majority of songs that you hear on the radio (depending on your taste in music!). They are great to use while songwriting because they are relatively easy to play, and provide a 'full-sounding' harmony to accompany vocals or other instruments.

Not all chords are easily accessible in the open position, but songs are written by guitarists are normally in easy 'guitar keys', so you will find that the chords in this chapter cover most situations.

The first chord I teach my students is normally E Minor, or 'Em' for short. It looks like this as a chord diagram:

Example 1a:

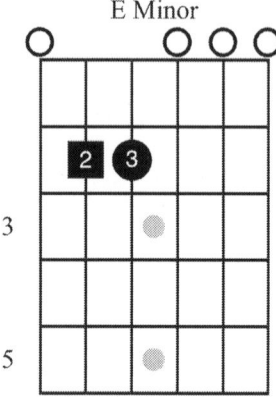

The root of the E Minor chord is the note 'E' and is played on the lowest open string (the thickest bass string). Look at how the above diagram relates to the neck image on the previous page.

Place your second finger on the 2nd fret of the 5th string, and then place your third finger on the 2nd fret of the 4th string, right next to it.

Make sure you use the correct fingers; it's tempting to use the first and second finger, but they will be needed a little later. Refer to the hand diagram on the previous page if you're not sure.

Now flick to the **How to Practice** section and work through the first set of exercises for learning new chords. Apply these steps to the Em chord.

Let's learn our second chord: A Minor, or Am.

Am is played like this.

Example 1b:

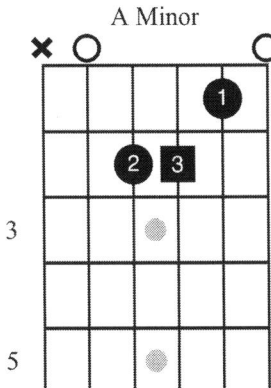

Notice that there is an 'x' on the bottom string of the guitar, so do *not* play it. Strum the guitar from the 5th string downwards.

Compare the notes and fingering of Am to Em. Can you see that the second and third fingers both move across one string as a single unit and then the first finger is added on the second string?

Complete the steps in the **How to Practice** section and work with a metronome up to the target speed.

A Quick Note about your Thumb

The thumb of the fretting hand should be placed on the back of the neck, roughly in line with the fingers but not necessarily directly behind them. This placement isn't a precise science, but the thumb provides support for the fretting fingers to squeeze against. Sometimes, the thumb may be closer to the head of the guitar than the fingers and it will normally find a slightly different position for each chord. As long as the hand is comfortable and each note rings clearly you should be fine.

Be aware though, if you're just starting out playing guitar, you'll probably have a tendency to 'over-squeeze' the neck when playing chords. Experiment with the smallest possible pressure you can use to play the chord cleanly. Fret the chord, and make sure that when you strum it, each note rings. Then simply relax the pressure gradually in your hand to find the minimum pressure needed to make the chord ring out.

When you feel confident playing both Em and Am separately, work through the steps in the **Learning Chords in Context section** of the **How to Practice** chapter, and learn how to combine the two chords together as a short piece of music.

Next, add some strumming to the chord progression using steps in Chapter Thirteen.

Listen for any buzzes and muted notes while you play each chord and try to minimise these as much as possible.

The next chord to learn is C Major. Notice that it has two fretted notes in common with Am. All you need to do to move from Am to C Major is move your third finger off the 3rd string, and on to the 3rd fret on the 5th string. This is a bit of a stretch at first, but adjust your thumb position on the back of the neck, and you will soon find a comfortable way to play the chord. Start your strum from the fifth string and avoid the sixth.

Example 1c:

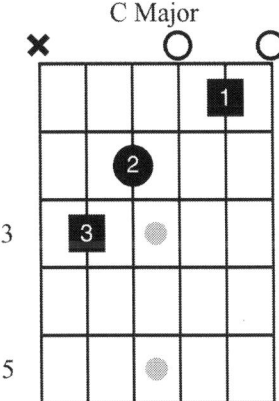

Compare the chords of Am and C Major to see how much they have in common. Use the steps in the **How to Practice** section learn the chord of C Major and then link it with the chord of Am.

The next chord to learn is D Major. Pay attention to the fingering and listen to the audio track so you can hear how it should sound.

Example 1d:

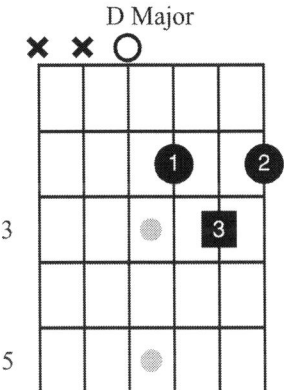

Learn D Major just as you learnt the previous three chords. First tackle it individually and build your muscle memory, then work through the steps to combine it with another chord. I recommend you combine it with Em to begin with.

G Major is a little harder because it uses all four fingers. Listen to the audio and practice matching the sound you hear. Be careful to pay attention to any buzzes or muted noted you create.

Example 1e:

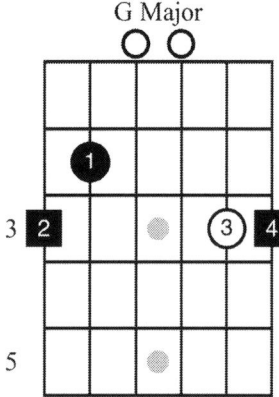

The white note is optional. If you decide not to play it, that's fine, but it's good to know it is an option.

Work through the steps to incorporate this chord into your vocabulary. I recommend that you pair G Major with Em for now. G Major is a challenging chord and Em is less difficult. If you really can't manage to play between G Major and Em in rhythm, simply strum on the open strings instead of the Em. It won't sound great, but it will help you build muscle memory on the G Major before adding the Em back into the sequence.

Our brains work best when learning new information in context, so practicing pairs of chords helps us learn the muscle memory of the chord change, as well as the chord's sound, feel, and how it works in relation to other chords.

The following sets of chords are good to learn in pairs. Learn each one individually at first and then use the steps in the **How to Practice** section to build your muscle memory and fluency as you combine them. Some new chords are paired with chords you already know.

Example 1f:

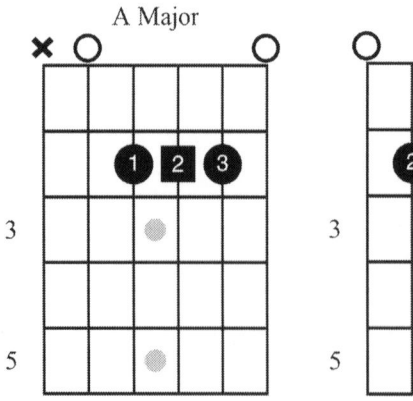 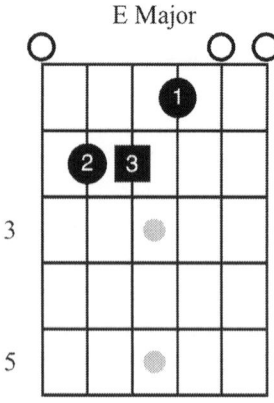

16

Example 1g:

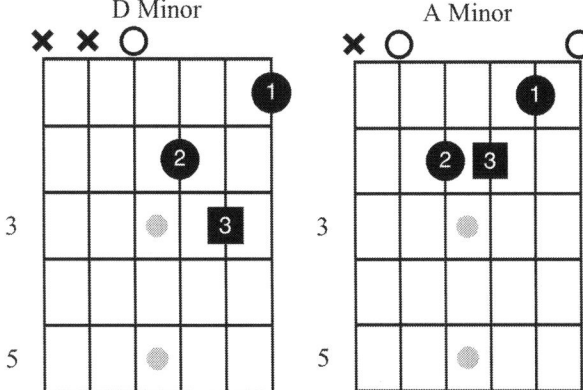

The next chord, F Major, is challenging as it uses a small *barre* to play two notes on the 1st fret. Getting a barre right is all about the position of your *thumb* (believe it or not!). Until now, your thumb has been placed towards the top of half of the neck and used to squeeze against the fretting fingers. With the F Major chord, experiment by allowing your thumb to drop right down to the bottom half of the guitar neck. This movement will rotate your wrist slightly and make it easier to get your first finger parallel to the fret wire to play the barre.

Learn F Major in conjunction with A Minor.

Example 1h:

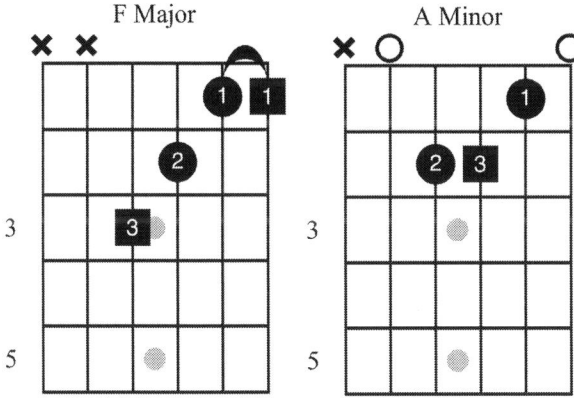

F Major is one of the more difficult chords, so if you are struggling it's ok to play the easier chord of F Major 7 (FMaj7). Instead of the barre, you can play the first string open.

Example 1i:

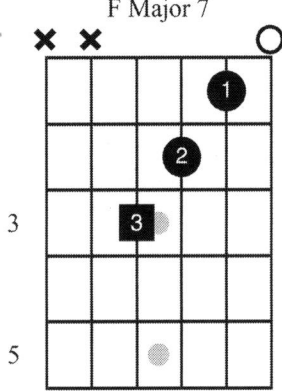

Test yourself and make some music!

After you have worked through the steps in the **How to Practice** section, try the following short chord progressions. You don't have to know all the chords in this chapter before you begin… just work with what you have. Add new chords as you learn them and get creative with your practice. Some chords sound better together than others, and trial and error is a great way to discover new and exciting sounds.

Example 1j:

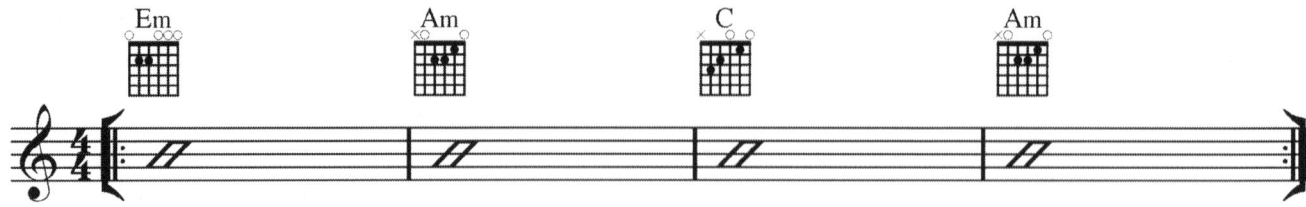

Example 1k:

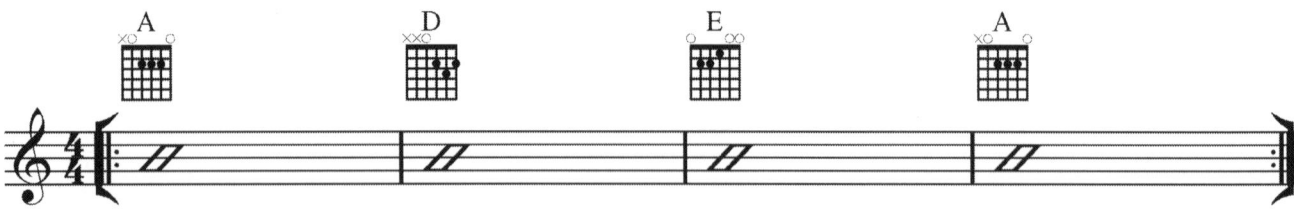

Example 1l:

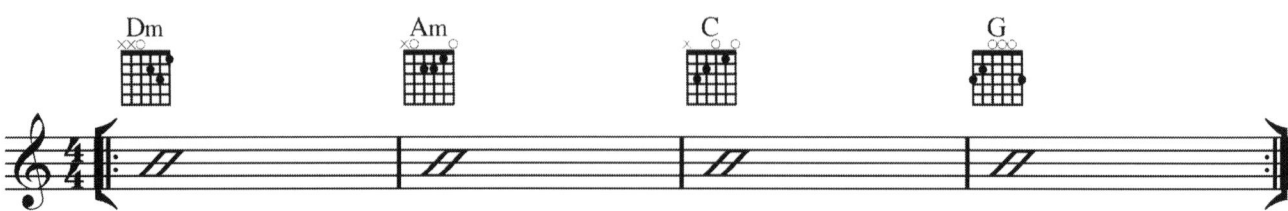

18

Example 1m:

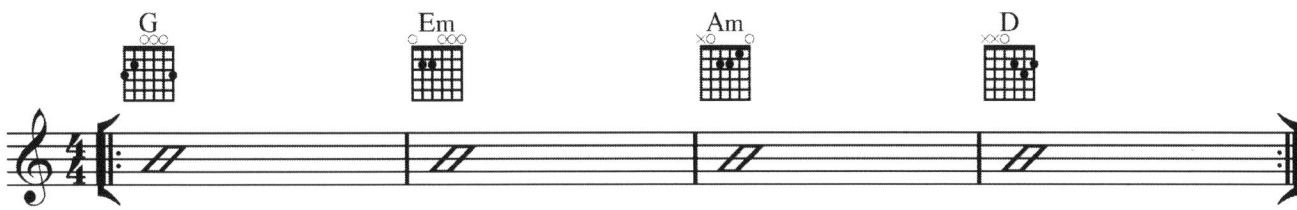

Example 1n:

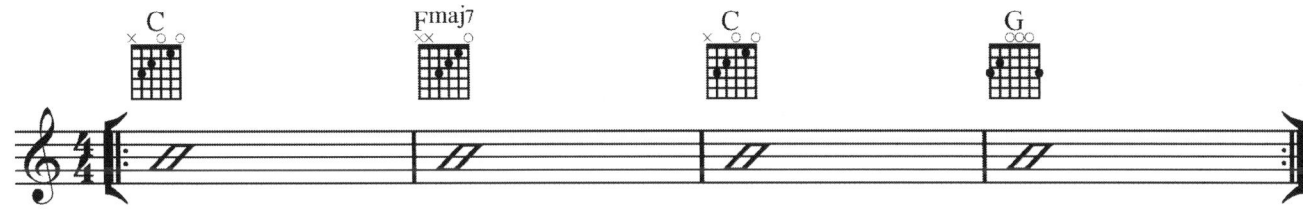

You'll probably begin by just strumming one chord per bar of music, but as you work further through the **How to Practice** section, start adding more rhythms and strumming patterns. There's a breakdown of how to strum rhythms on the guitar in **Chapter Thirteen**.

Think about *how* you play each chord… loud or soft? Gentle or Aggressive? Pick or no pick?

The most important thing to do is listen carefully to what you play. Don't accept any muted notes or buzzes! Keep adjusting your fingers and thumb until each chord is clean! If you need to, go back to the muscle memory exercises on individual chords and make sure you are placing your fingers correctly

If your fingers get sore, take a break and come back later.

Have fun! – You're making music.

Chapter Two: Dominant 7 Open Chords

The chords in this section are named *Dominant 7* chords. They have a slightly tense sound and often want to *resolve* that *tension* to another chord. These chords will expand your musical horizons and teach you some great new sounds.

As always, learn these chords in pairs. Combine a chord you don't know with one that you do, then practice moving between them. Each new chord is listed with a suggested friend you learnt in Chapter One.

Example 2a:

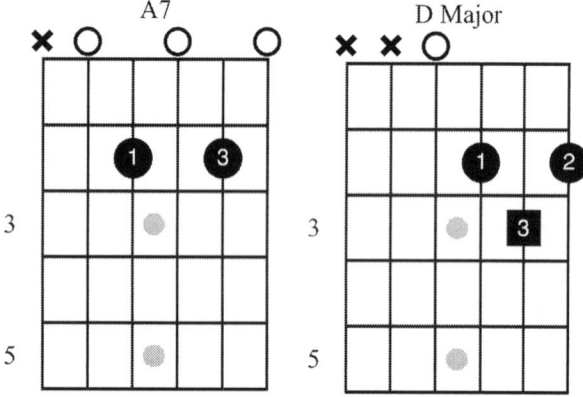

Example 2b:

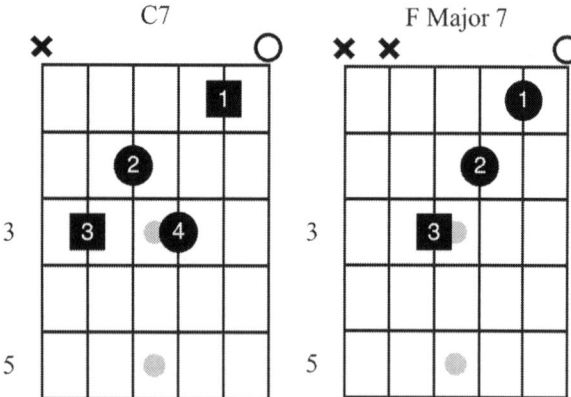

Example 2c:

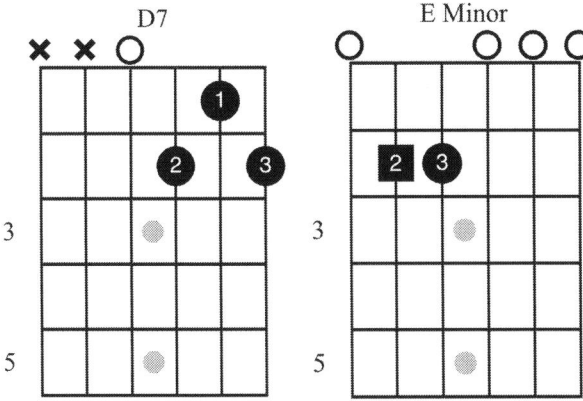

Example 2d:

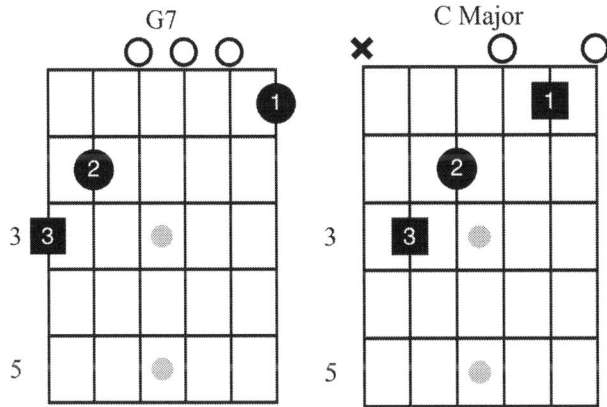

Example 2e: ** On the B7, the second string can also be played open.*

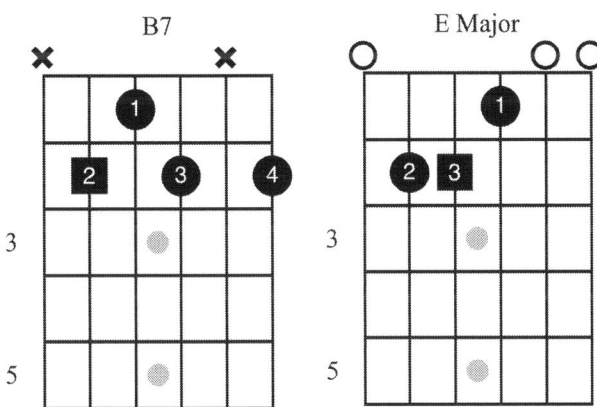

Example 2f:

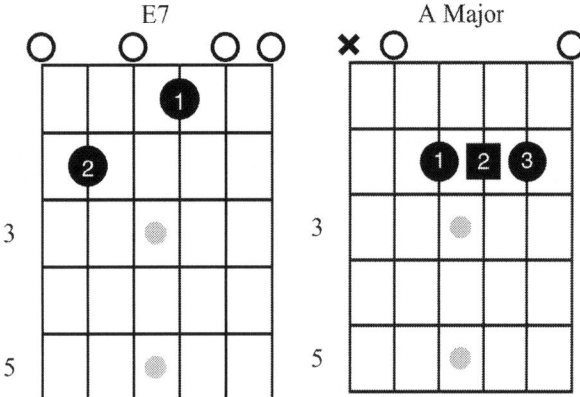

Test yourself!

Once you have introduced each new chord into your vocabulary by using the steps in the **How to Practice** section, work towards building the following short chord progressions. Begin by strumming one chord per bar and gradually add more interesting rhythms by working through **Chapter Thirteen.**

Example 2g:

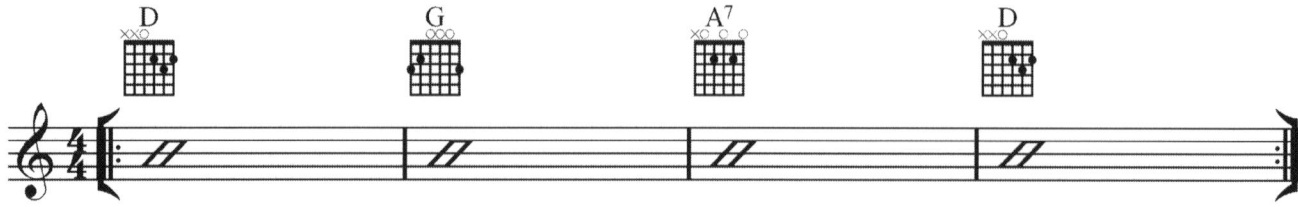

Example 2h:

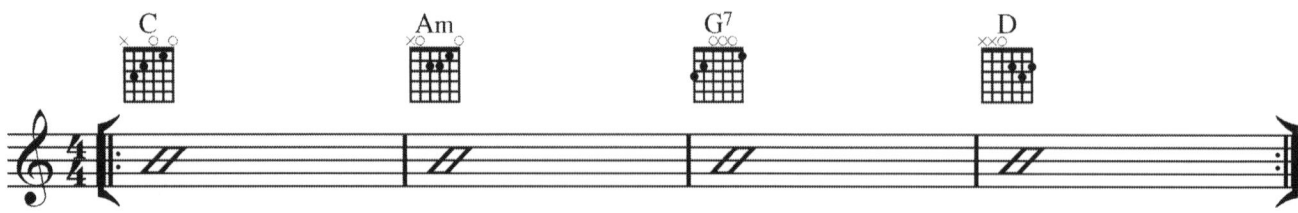

Example 2i:

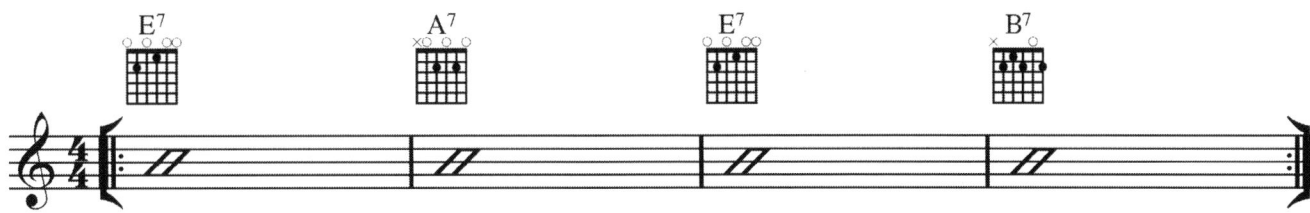

Example 2j:

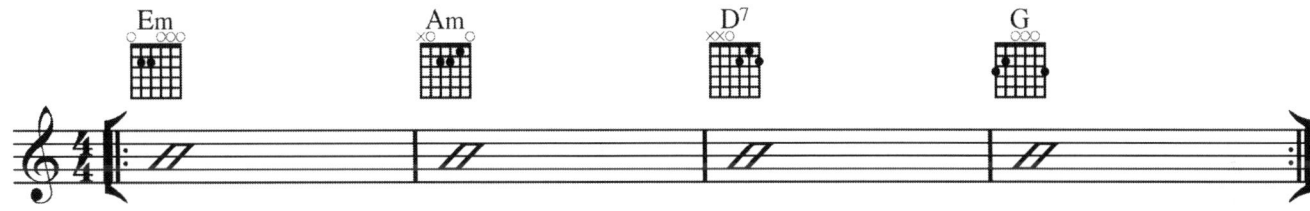

Example 2k:

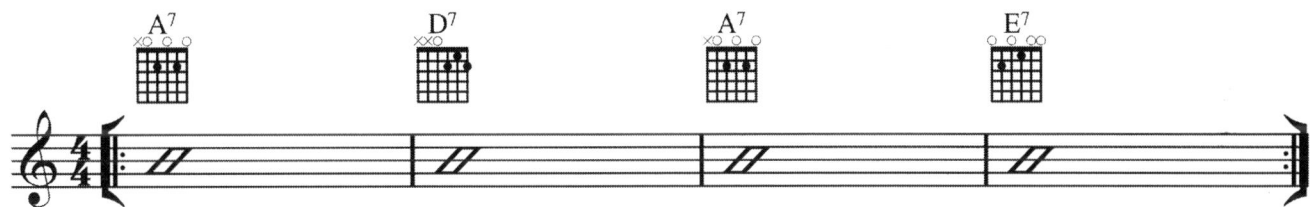

Chapter Three: Barre Chords

We will look at some more open chords in Chapter Five, but first it's time to learn some essential *barre* chords.

A barre chord uses a finger to make a bar (*barre* in Spanish, the birthplace of the guitar) across multiple strings. You saw a mini-barre in Chapter One in the chord of F Major. Now, however, we will learn to use a full-barre to form some new and important chord shapes.

Barre chords have an advantage over open chords: They're movable. It is possible to slide a barre chord up and down the strings to play different chords because barre chords don't contain any open strings.

For example, play an E Minor chord, then slide your fingers up one fret and strum the chord again. It sounds wrong because you moved some of the notes (the fretted ones) up the neck, but the notes on the open strings stayed put. If we could bring the open string with us when we move the chord up the neck, we could keep the relationship between all the notes the same and 'not leave any notes behind'.

Barre chords allow us to bring the open strings with us as we move chord shapes around the neck.

The first barre chord to learn is the 'minor' barre. Compare the barre chord version of Bm below, with the open position chord of Em.

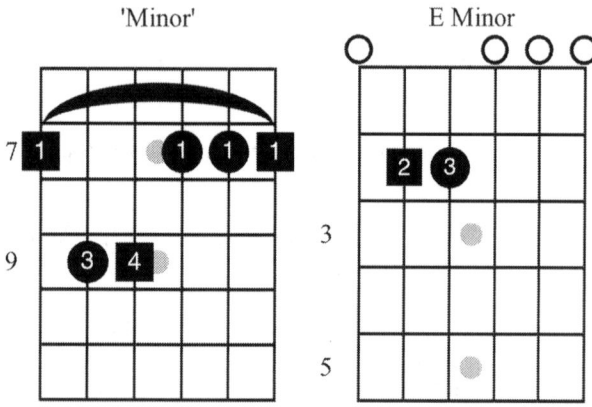

Can you see that these two chords are formed identically? The barre in the first diagram replaces the open strings in the second Em diagram.

The first chord hasn't been named, although when you place the barre at the 7th fret this just happens to be a Bm because the note at the 7th fret of the sixth string is B. We will look at this in more detail soon.

For now, practice forming the chord of Bm by placing your first finger across the strings at the 7th fret and using your third and fourth fingers to play the other notes.

Example 3a:

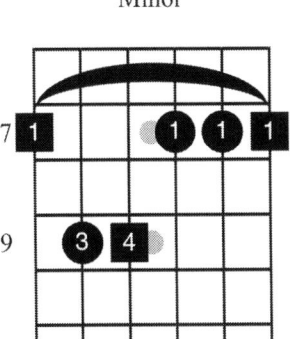

'Minor'

Playing a barre is tricky at first. Just as with the F Major chord in Chapter One, a big part of the secret is to move your thumb to the lower half of the neck. However, it is also important to place the barre finger on its *side* so that the nail of the finger *points towards the head of the guitar.*

If you place the finger so the nail points in the same direction as the fret wire, you will find that the strings fall into the little folds of your finger joints and become muted. By using the *bony side* of the finger, you will make a better contact with the strings and your chords will sound much cleaner.

Barre chords are always a challenge for beginners, but with a little perseverance and some analytic practice, you will get the knack of it in no time.

Work through the **How to Practice** steps to commit the barre chord to muscle memory. Don't worry if this takes a few days or weeks! Try combining it with an Em or a strum on open strings to help you master the movement.

The shape you have just learnt is a Minor barre chord with its root on the *sixth* string. Notice that the square root marker is on the lowest string of the guitar. The chord written above is a B Minor chord because the root has been placed on the note B. If you know the names of the notes on the bottom string of the guitar, you can place this chord shape anywhere and play *any* minor chord.

Here are the notes on the bottom string of the guitar:

Notes on the Sixth String

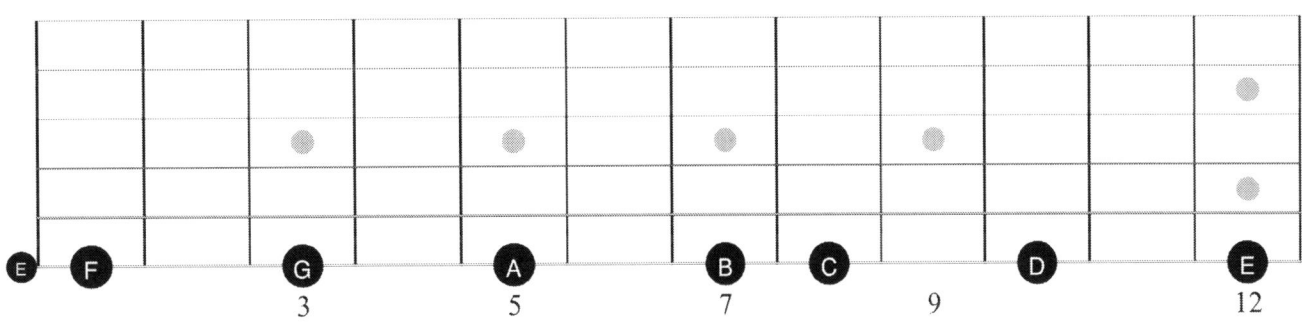

So, by placing the minor barre on the 5th fret, you will create an Am chord:

Example 3b:

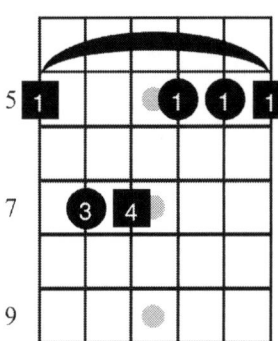

A Minor

If you place the minor barre shape on the 10th fret, you will play a Dm chord.

Example 3c:

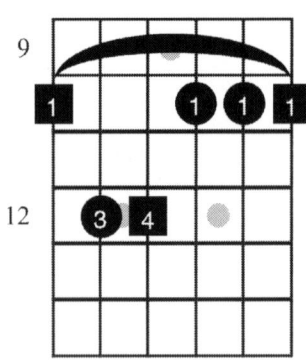

D Minor

Check that these chords sound similar to their open string versions by first playing the barre chord and then playing the open string chord. The *voicing* of the chord is different, but they both have the same overall sound or *tonality*.

Example 3d:

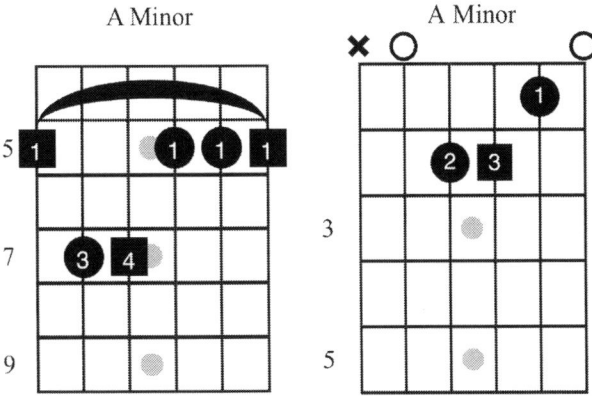

Use the map of the notes on the sixth string above to play the following chord progression. All you need to do is use the minor barre shape and slide to the correct location for each chord. Listen to the audio to hear how this works.

Example 3e:

The note Bb is located on the 6th fret between A and B

Now you have learnt the Minor barre chord voicing for the sixth string, let's learn the *Major* barre chord voicing.

Example 3f:

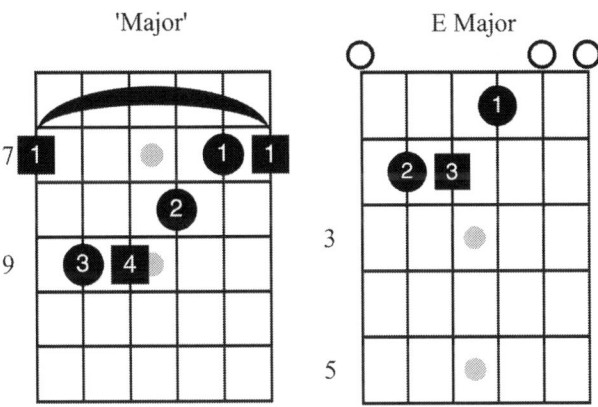

As you can see, this barre chord has the same shape as the open E Major chord from Chapter One, but it uses a first finger barre instead of playing the open strings:

Barre chords allow us to move all the notes in a chord up the neck while keeping their relationship with the root intact. Everything moves in the same amount because there are no open strings.

All we need, is to know a barre shape for each chord *type* (major, minor '7' etc.), and where to place it.

Repeat example 3e, but this time use major barres instead of minor barres.

Example 3g:

We can also play barre chords on the fifth string using the A Major, and A Minor shapes from Chapter One.

Here is a movable Minor barre chord shape with the root on the fifth string.

Example 3h:

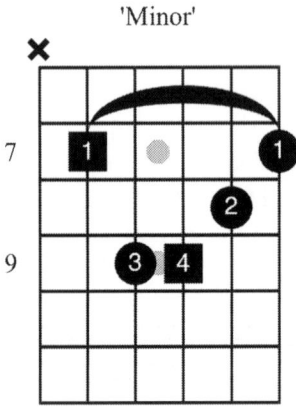

Here is the movable Major barre chord shape with the root on the fifth string.

Example 3i:

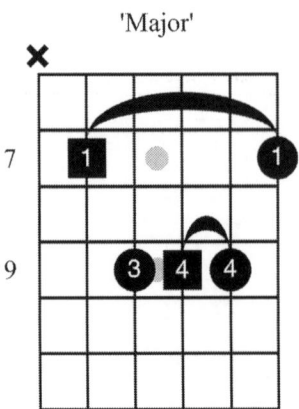

The major barre on the 5th string is quite challenging because the barre is not played with the first finger. In fact, there are various ways to finger this chord; some people even play all three notes on the 9th fret with a third finger barre. Either way, you don't need to worry about hitting the note on the 1st (thinnest) string. It's a bit awkward and doesn't add much to the sound of the chord so don't worry if it is muted for now.

Once you know how to play the Major and Minor barre chord shapes on the fifth string, all you need to know is where to find the root notes to be able to access *any* major or minor chord. The following diagram shows the location of each note on the fifth string. Notes like D#/Eb are located between the notes D and E.

Notes on the Fifth String

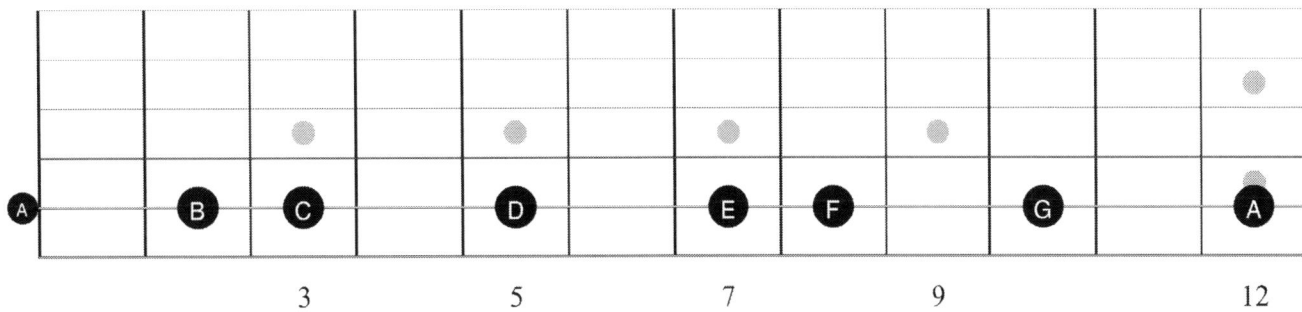

Play through the following sequence using only minor barre chords on the fifth string.

Example 3j:

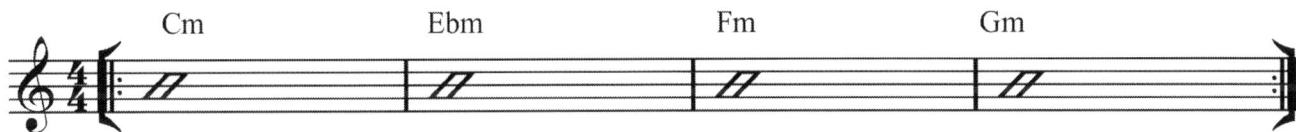

Play through the following sequence using only major barre chords on the fifth string.

Example 3k:

Play through the following sequence but this time combine major and minor barre chords on the fifth string.

Example 3l:

Next, play through this progression that combines major and minor barres on both the 5th and the 6th strings. There are a few ways to play this progression depending on where you choose to play the barres. You could play any chord with a root on either the 5th or 6th string.

Example 3m:

Try playing through some of the progressions in Chapters One and Two but this time play them with barre chords.

The placement of barre chords can be limited by the type of guitar you are playing. It is more difficult to play barres on an acoustic guitar as the strings are normally thicker. Also, acoustic guitars often only tend to give access to around the 10th fret where the guitar neck joins the body.

Electric guitars usually have a greater available range and thinner strings, making barre chords easier to play.

There are barre chord shapes for every type of chord *quality*. We will talk more about chord qualities and look at a little theory in the next chapter, but for now, simply learn the following barre chord shapes.

Example 3n:

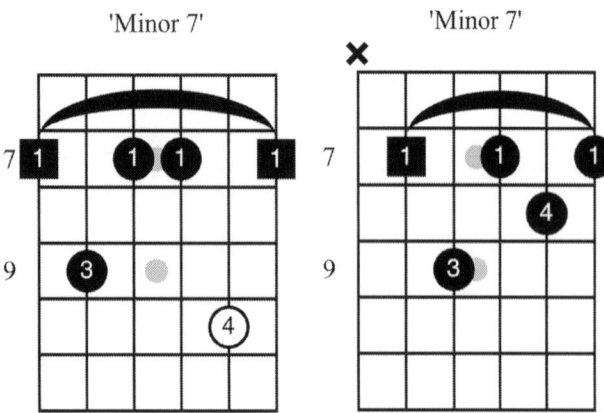

Example 3o:

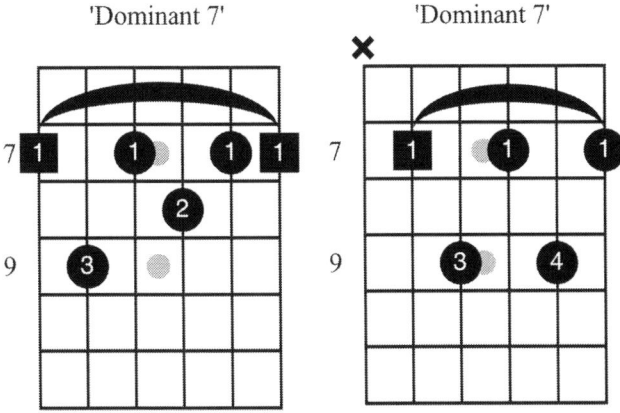

Example 3p:

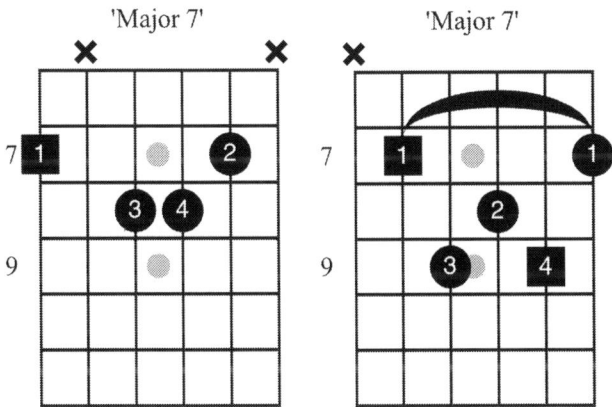

Even though the Major 7 barre on the sixth string isn't technically a barre chord, the underside of the first finger is used to mute the unfretted fifth string as shown by the 'x'. As there are no ringing strings, the shape is movable.

As always, learn each barre chord individually using the steps in the **How to Practice** chapter, before combining different chords into sequences.

Here are some ideas to get you started. It doesn't matter whether you use a 6th string, or a 5th string barre to play each chord so there are many ways to play through each sequence. Try to keep the chords close together to avoid big movements up and down the neck. For example, it is normally preferable to play Am to Dm by moving a barre chord from the 6th to the 5th string, than by sliding the same shape from the 5th to the 10th fret on the sixth string.

Example 3q:

Example 3r:

Example 3s:

Try altering sequences from the previous two chapters to use these new 7th chords. Try turning a Major chord into a Dominant 7 or a Major 7th. Try turning a Minor chord into a m7 chord or a Dominant 7th. You can create some great results.

Write down your favourite ideas and you'll be well on your way to some serious song writing.

Chapter Four: A Little (Non-Scary) Music Theory

If you're *not* interested in learning the theory of how music works, and just want to learn some more chords then you are allowed to skip this chapter! I do suggest you use this section as a little 'light' night time reading though because it's good to understand what you are playing; it will help you to be more creative.

In previous chapters, we came across some '7th' chords so let's now learn how they are formed.

Chord construction begins with scales.

What is a scale?

As far as we need to know for this book, a scale is a sequence of notes that begins and ends in the same place. For example, the scale of C Major is

C D E F G A B C

Scales are very important, so if you want more information about how they work, I highly recommend my two books, The Circle of Fifths for Guitarists and **The Practical Guide to Modern Music Theory for Guitarists**.

What is a chord?

A chord, technically, is the combination of three or more notes. A major or minor chord has only three individual notes. Often, major or minor chords on the guitar *look* like they have more than three notes. However, even though we play notes on four, five, or even six strings, we are only actually playing three separate individual notes which are doubled in different octaves.

For example, in the following chord of C Major, the names of the notes are labelled... You can see that even though we play six strings, there are only three unique notes.

C Major Chord

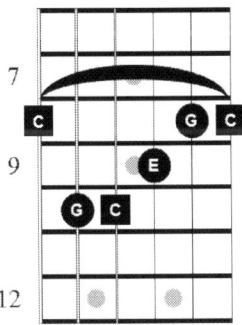

In this voicing, the note C appears three times, and the note G appears twice. The only note to appear once is the E.

33

Where do these notes come from?

To find out which notes go together to form each individual chord, we must learn how to *harmonise* the major scale.

Chords are formed when we 'stack' specific notes from a scale on top of each other. Look again at the previous example. The chord of C Major contains *only* the notes, C, E and G. In the context of the major scale, we have taken the notes 1, 3 and 5:

C	D	E	F	G	A	B	C
1	2	3	4	5	6	7	8/1

This can be seen as 'jumping over', or 'leapfrogging' every other note in the scale. For example, we formed this chord by starting on C, Jumping D and landing on E, jumping F and landing on G. This is how most simple, three-note chords are formed.

C E G

D F A

E G B

F A C

G B D

A C E

B D F

If we view the notes of C Major spaced out on the fretboard, we can establish what pattern of notes is required to form A Major chord.

Example 4a:

C Major

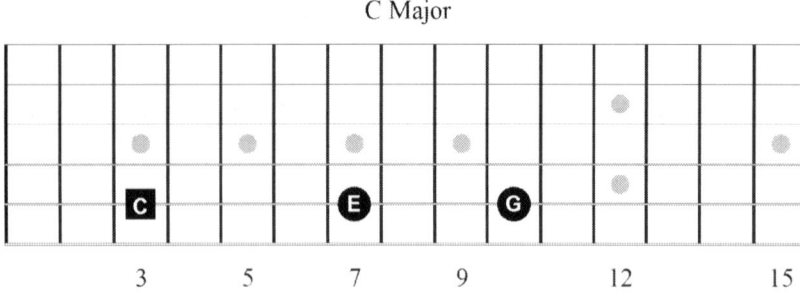

The distance between the notes C and E is *two tones*.

Any chord with a distance of two tones between the first two notes can be classed as a 'major-type' chord. This distance in music is called a *'major 3rd'*.

The distance between the 3rd and 5th (the notes E and G), is *one-and-a-half tones*. This is *one semitone smaller* than the major 3rd, so we call it a *minor* 3rd.

When measured from the *root*, any major chord *must* consist of two tones between the root and 3rd, and three-and-a-half tones between the root and 5th.

It is the convention in music to describe the notes in a chord in terms of their relationship to the major scale formula, **1 2 3 4 5 6 7**.

So, in simple terms, a Major chord has the formula 1 3 5, and **the first chord of any major scale is always major.**

Moving on to the second note in the C Major scale, (D) and repeating the previous process we generate:

C	D	E	F	G	A	B	C
1	2	3	4	5	6	7	8/1

As we harmonise up from the second note of the scale, we get the notes D, F and A. On the guitar, these look and sounds like:

Example 4b:

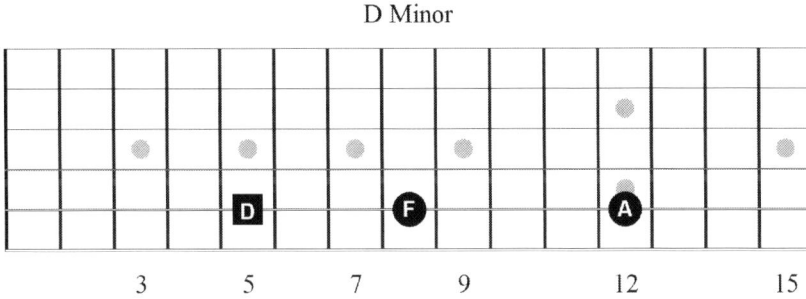

D Minor

The distance between the notes D and F is one-and-a-half tones or a '*minor 3rd*' which means that the chord is *minor*.

However; the distance between the notes D and A is still three-and-a-half tones, which is the correct spacing for a *perfect* 5th.

With a minor 3rd and a perfect 5th, this chord is classified as a minor chord built on the note D, or simply 'D minor' for short.

As a formula, a minor chord is expressed as 1 b3 5 and **the second chord in any major key is always minor.**

All the notes of the major scale can be harmonised in this way, and with the exception of the 7th note, B, they are all major or minor chords.

To save space, I will not show the construction of every chord (although do try this by yourself). The harmonised chords of the C Major scale are:

Chord I	C Major
Chord ii	D Minor
Chord iii	E Minor
Chord IV	F Major
Chord V	G Major
Chord vi	A Minor
Chord vii	B Minor (b5) or B *Diminished*

It is quite rare to play a Diminished chord, so we won't cover them here. In the table above, you will see that instead of listing each chord 1, 2, 3, etc., they are listed by Roman numerals. This may seem strange but actually saves a lot of confusion later. Major chords are shown with capital letters, and Minor chords are shown with lower case letters.

Chords I, IV, and V are Major

Chords ii, iii, vi and vii are Minor.

7th Chords

In Chapter Three, we studied Dominant 7 chords.

In music, you will sometimes see chords with names like 'G7', 'A minor 7', 'C Major 7' or even 'B minor 7b5'. All these '7th' chords can be formed from the major scale. In fact, they are simply *extensions* to the original process we used to construct chords in the harmonisation chapters.

Look back at how we formed major and minor chords from the major scale. We took the first, third and fifth notes by leapfrogging adjacent scale tones. If we continue to jump notes to land on the seventh note, i.e., 1 3 5 7 we would have created a '7th' chord. For example:

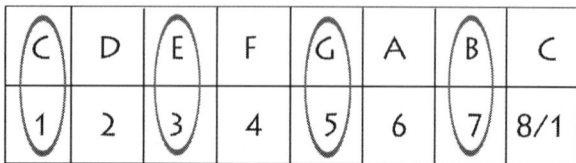

In addition to the notes C, E, and G, we have now introduced the note B. This chord is a C Major *triad* with an added *natural 7th* and is named C Major 7. Notice how the 7th note, (B) is *one semitone* below the root, (C). The chord can be played like this:

Example 4c:

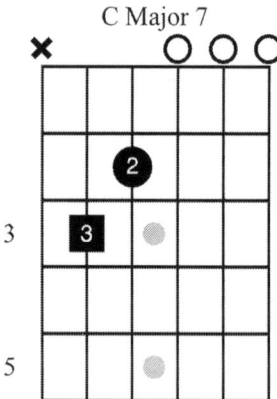

The added note, B is played on the open 2nd string. Play and listen to this chord. Notice how it has a richness compared to an ordinary C Major chord. The formula for a Major 7th chord is 1 3 5 7.

When we add the 7th note to chord ii (D minor), we get the following notes:

D F A C.

This time, the 7th note (C) is a *whole tone* below the root, (D). This 7th note, therefore, is a *b7* not a *natural 7* as in the previous example of C Major.

When we add a b7 note to a minor chord, the chord is named 'minor 7'. In this case, we have formed the chord of D minor 7. It can be played like this:

Example 4d:

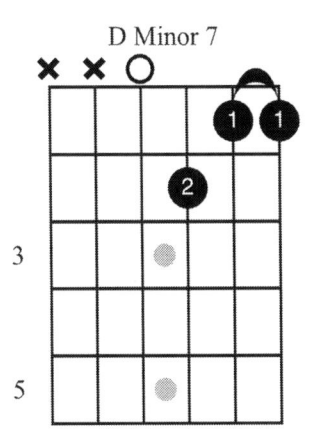

I hear this as a kind of *softened* minor chord. Still sad, but not as sad as a straight minor chord. Any minor 7 chord has the formula 1 b3 5 b7.

The previous two chord types, major 7 and minor 7, account for five of the harmonised scale tones:

Chord 1 (Imaj7)	C Major 7
Chord 2 (iim7)	D Minor 7
Chord 3 (iiim7)	E Minor 7
Chord 4 (IVmaj7)	F Major 7
Chord 5	
Chord 6 (vim7)	A Minor 7
Chord 7	

As you can see, I have missed out chords V and vii. This is because they are slightly different. As you now know, when we harmonise the major scale, chord V (G) is always A Major chord. However, the added the 7th note *not* a natural 7th. Here is the harmonised V chord in the Key of C:

G B D **F**.

The note F is a whole tone below the root, (G). This is similar to the b7th note in a minor 7 chord. What we now have is a major chord with an added *b7*.

This chord is called a *dominant* 7 and is simply written as a '7' after the chord root, e.g., *G7* or *A7*. It has the formula 1 3 5 b7. G7 can be played like this:

37

Example 4e:

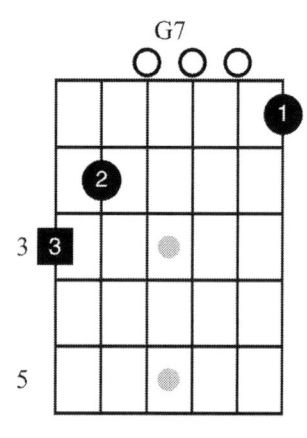

Dominant 7 chords have a tense, unresolved sound, and often move to tonic (home) chord the key, in this case, C Major.

Finally, when we harmonise the 7th note of the major scale, we generate a chord which is fairly uncommon in pop or rock music but is often used in jazz.

Chord vii forms a *minor b5* or *diminished* chord. When we harmonise this chord up to four notes from the key of C, we get

B D F **A**

Again, we are adding a flattened 7th (b7), and so the chord is now described as a 'minor 7b5'. It is often written as *m7b5*. In this case, you would see Bm7b5. This type of chord has the formula 1 b3 b5 b7.

It is played like this and has a dark, brooding quality:

Example 4f:

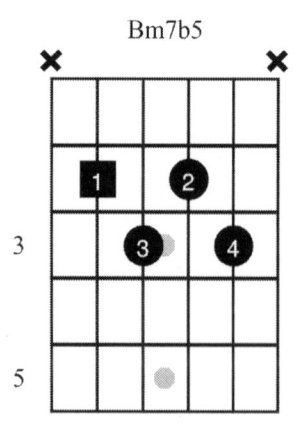

We can now complete the chart of the harmonised major scale.

Chord Imaj7	C Major 7
Chord iim7	D Minor 7
Chord iiim7	E Minor 7
Chord IVmaj7	F Major 7
Chord V7	G7 or G *Dominant* 7
Chord vim7	A Minor 7
Chord viim7b5	B Minor 7 b5 or Bm7b5

You will be very pleased to know there is a simple shorthand way to describe and write any type of 7th chord.

Each has a special formula that describes the way they are formed.

Remember that a major chord has the formula 1 3 5.

A minor chord (with that smaller distance between the 1 and 3) has the formula 1 b3 5.

The following table shows the construction and naming convention of all 7th chords.

Chord	**Formula**
Major 7 (Maj7)	1 3 5 7
Dominant 7 (7)	1 3 5 b7
Minor 7 (m7)	1 b3 5 b7
Minor 7 flat 5 (m7b5)	1 b3 b5 b7

Major 7 chords are the only chords to have a 'natural' 7th. All other chords (at least for the purposes of this book) have b7s.

To see this process in action, we can simply compare some of the notes in different 'C' chords.

Chord	**Formula**	**Notes**
C Major 7	1 3 5 7	C E G B
C7	1 3 5 b7	C E G Bb
Cm7	1 b3 5 b7	C Eb G Bb
Cm7b5	1 b3 b5 b7	C Eb Gb Bb

That's definitely enough theory for now! Let's move on and learn some new chords.

Chapter Five: More Open Chords

We have looked at the most important 7th chords in barre chord form, but there are some really beautiful '7th' voicings you can play in the open position.

Learn the following chords just as you did in the earlier chapters.

Example 5a:

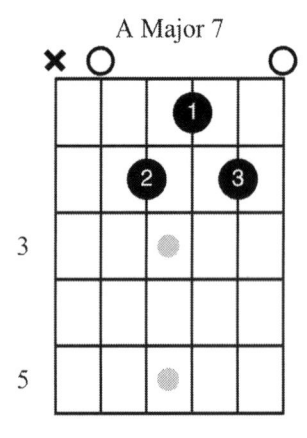

A Major 7

Example 5b:

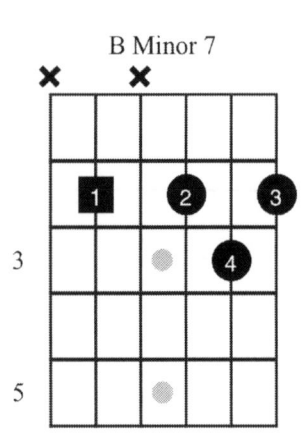

B Minor 7

Example 5c:

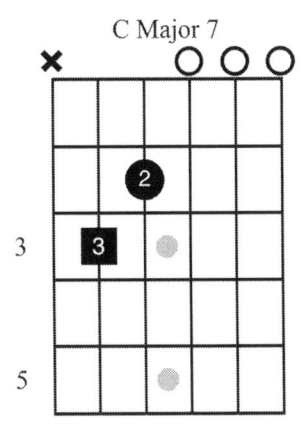

C Major 7

Example 5d:

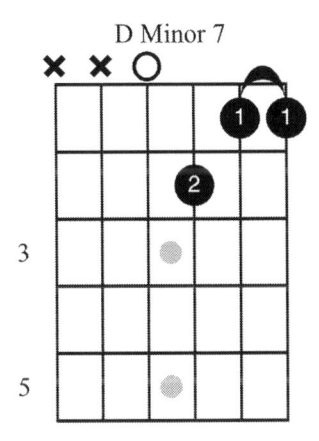

D Minor 7

Example 5e:

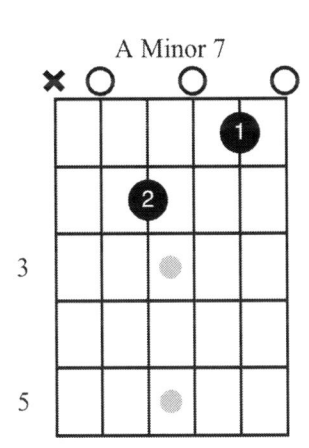

A Minor 7

Example 5f:

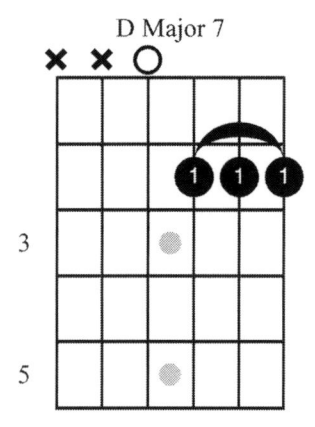

D Major 7

Example 5g:

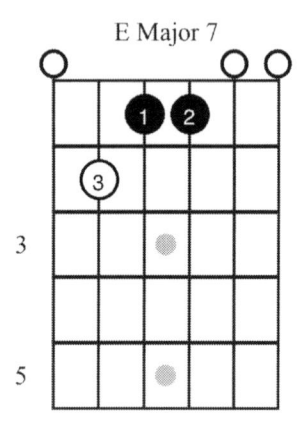

E Major 7

Example 5h:

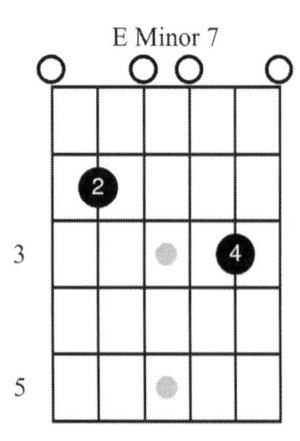

E Minor 7

Example 5i:

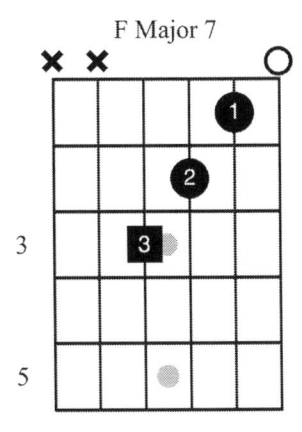

F Major 7

Example 5j:

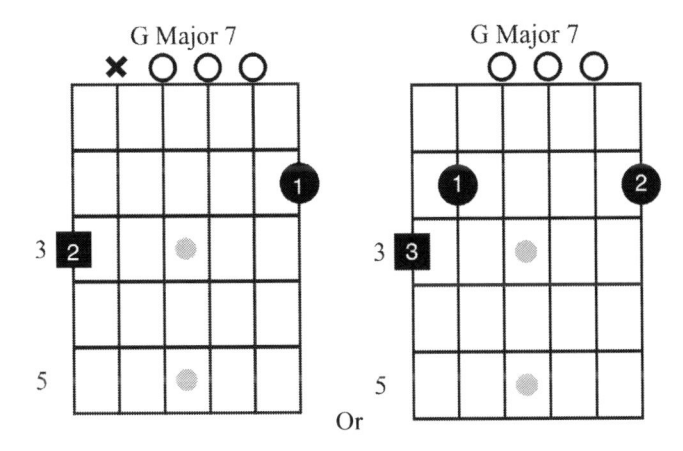

G Major 7   G Major 7

Or

There are also a few chord types we haven't covered yet.

A *suspended or 'sus'* chord is one that replaces the 3rd with either the 2nd or the 4th.

Instead of 1 3 5, the formula is 1 2 5 or 1 4 5.

Instead of C E G, the notes are C D G or C F G.

If the 3rd is replaced with the 2nd, the chord is named 'sus2'. If the 3rd is replaced with the 4th, then the chord is named 'sus4'.

Here are some suspended open chords. Play them and you will hear why they are named 'suspended'.

Example 5k:

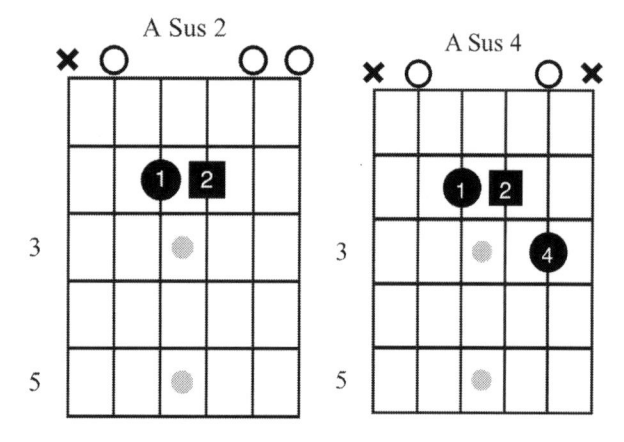

A Sus 2   A Sus 4

Example 5l:

D Sus 2   D Sus 4

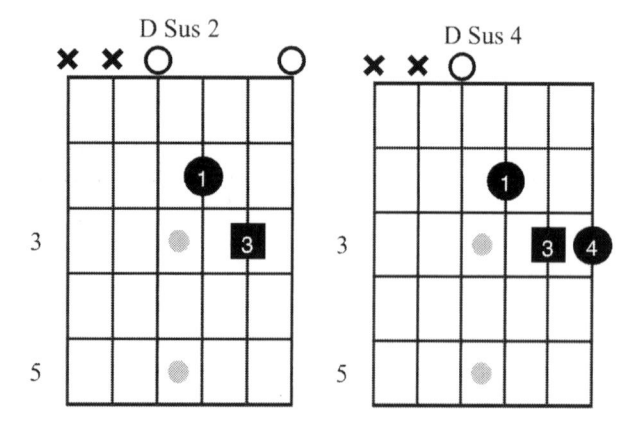

'6' chords have the formula 1 3 5 6. They are quite rich-sounding and a little bit 'jazz'. Often they are used quite sparsely in music as they can quickly overpower a pop-type chord progression.

Example 5m:

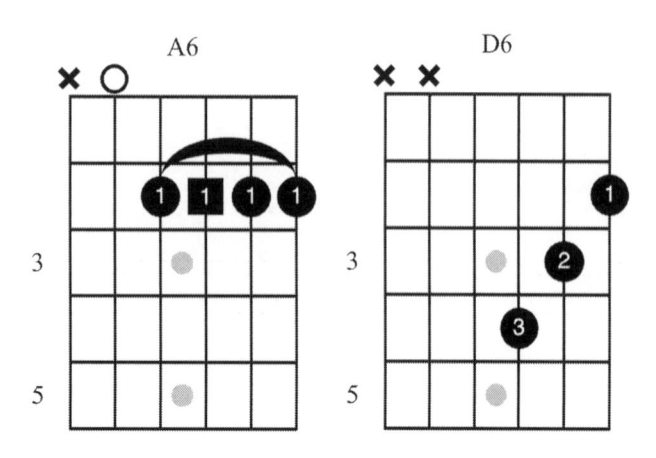

A6   D6

44

Example 5n:

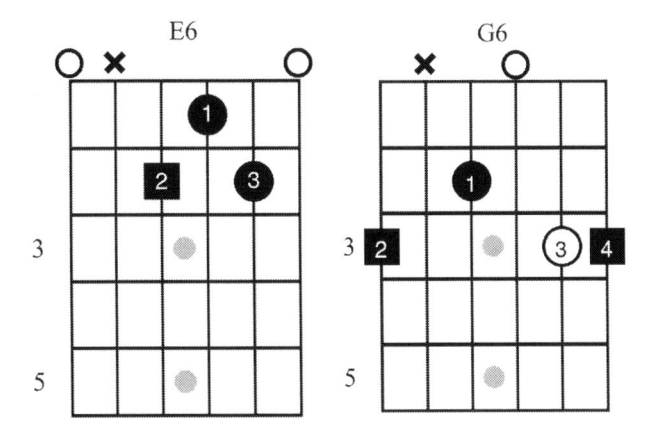

E6   G6

* On the E6, be careful to avoid the fifth string. Try playing the sixth string by itself, then jumping over the fifth string to strum the rest of the chord.

Test Yourself!

Use the following progressions to test your knowledge of the chords in this chapter. Combine these chords with chords that you already know to create new music.

You can also 'substitute' one chord for another. For example, if you see a D Major chord in an earlier chord sequence, try substituting it for a Dsus2, Dsus4, DMaj7 or D7. Not every chord substitution will work, and some might sound kind of weird, but you'll never know until you experiment. Try it; it's fun!

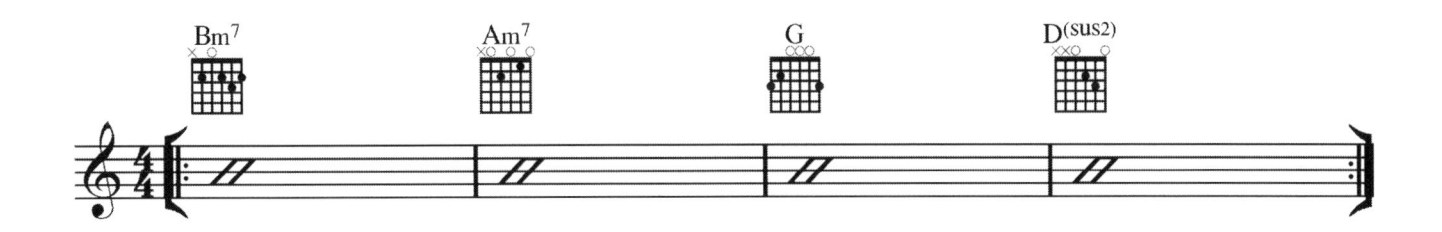

Example 5o:

| Bm7 | Am7 | G | D(sus2) |

Example 5p:

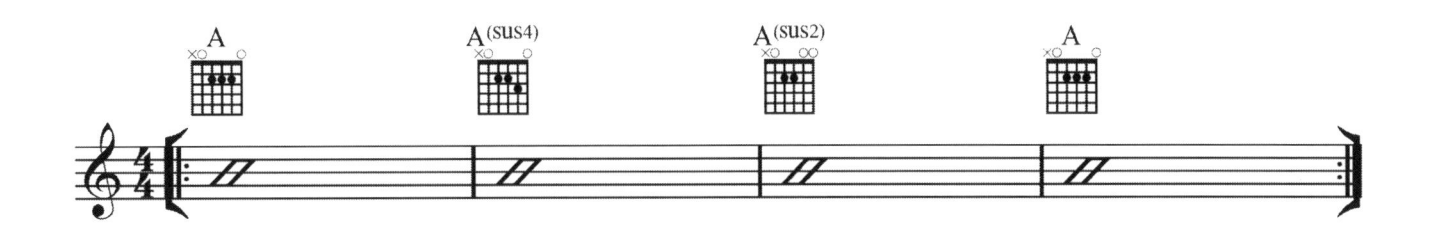

| A | A(sus4) | A(sus2) | A |

45

Example 5q:

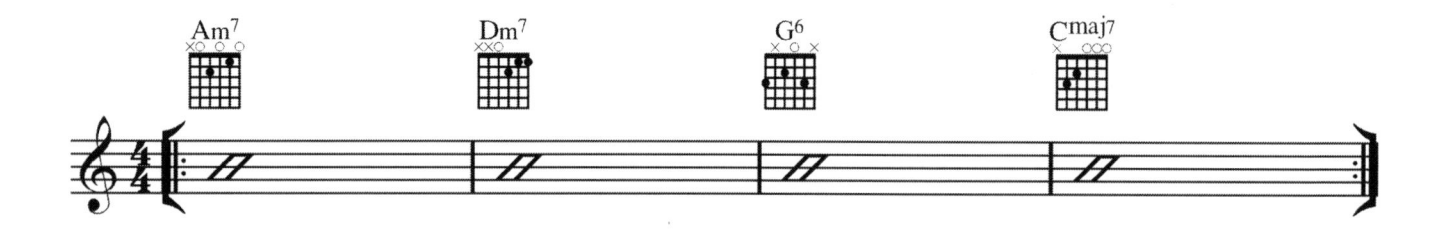

Example 5r:

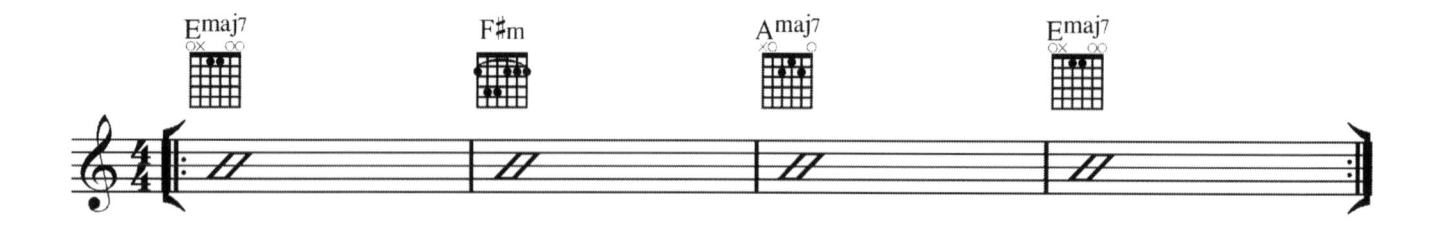

Example 5s:

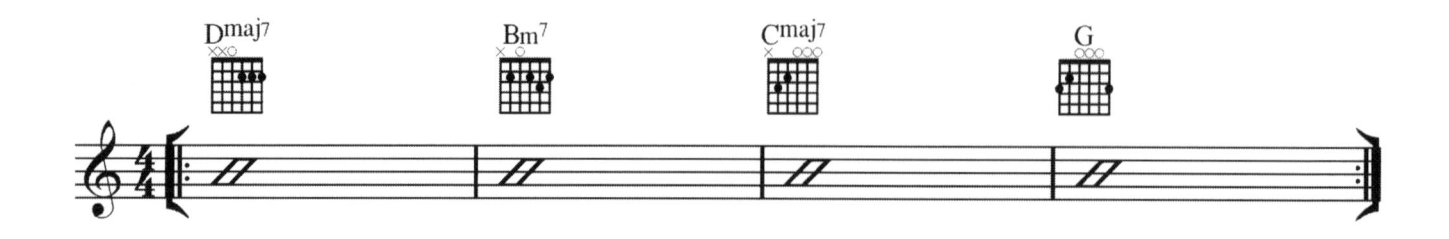

Chapter Six: More Barre Chords

The chords in this chapter are mainly barre chord versions of the Suspended and '6' open chords in Chapter Five. However, we will explore a couple of important '9' chords.

Here are the barre chord voicings of the suspended chords that you should know.

Example 6a: - sixth string root

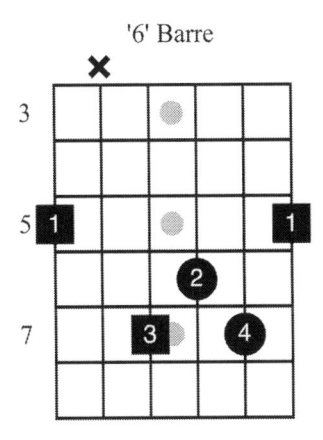

'6' Barre

* Be careful to avoid the fifth string

Example 6b: fifth string root

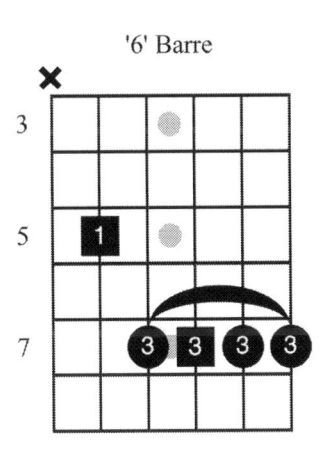

'6' Barre

Notice how these barre chord shapes are once again based around the open position versions of the chords.

Next, here are the sus2 and sus 4 voicings you should know. These are normally played as barres on the fifth string.

Example 6c:

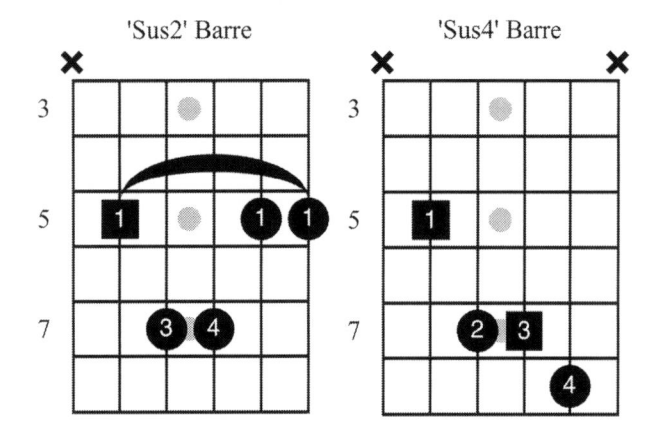

'Sus2' Barre   'Sus4' Barre

Experiment with the fingering of the Sus4 barre. Many guitarists use a third-finger barre to play the notes on the 3rd and 4th strings.

Next, let's take a quick look at a few common 'Dominant 9' chord voicings.

A Dominant 9 chord is an extension of a Dominant 7 chord and can normally be used as a straight substitution: For example, anywhere you could play a D7 you could play a D9 instead[1].

Building on the ideas in Chapter Four, a Dominant 9 chord is built by extending a Dominant 7 chord by one note.

A Dominant 7 chord is 1 3 5 b7

A Dominant 9 chord is 1 3 5 b7 9

However, we don't normally have to play all the notes of a chord to convey its unique quality. Quite often we will miss out notes like the 5th as they don't really add much to the character of the sound.

Dominant 9 chords are the backbone of most funk tunes, especially anything James Brown-esque. The most common barre chord voicing is this one.

Example 6d:

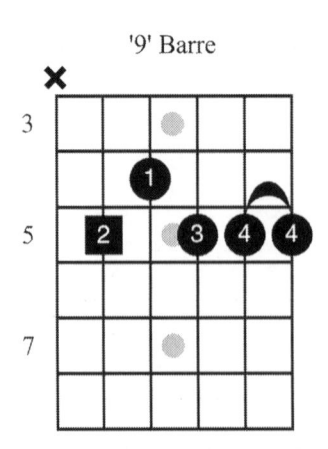

'9' Barre

---

[1] Handle with care!

48

There are a variety of ways to finger the above chord voicing. Many players will barre with their third finger across all three of the top strings.

It's also possible to play a '9' barre chord with a root on the 6th string, but it's a bit awkward and less common.

Example 6e:

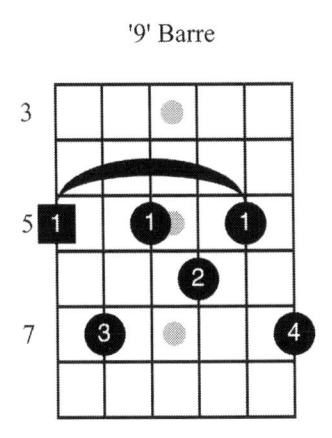

'9' Barre

Personally, I'd avoid playing the notes on the 5th and 6th strings, and just aim to hit the top four strings as much as possible. Often, it's OK to let the bass player take care of the root notes so that the guitar doesn't take up too much sonic space in the band. A lot depends on context though. If it's just you and a singer, you'll normally need to play the root notes.

Test yourself!

Work through the following chord progressions using barre chords. To refresh your memory, the root notes on the 6th and 5th strings are given below.

Notes on the Sixth String

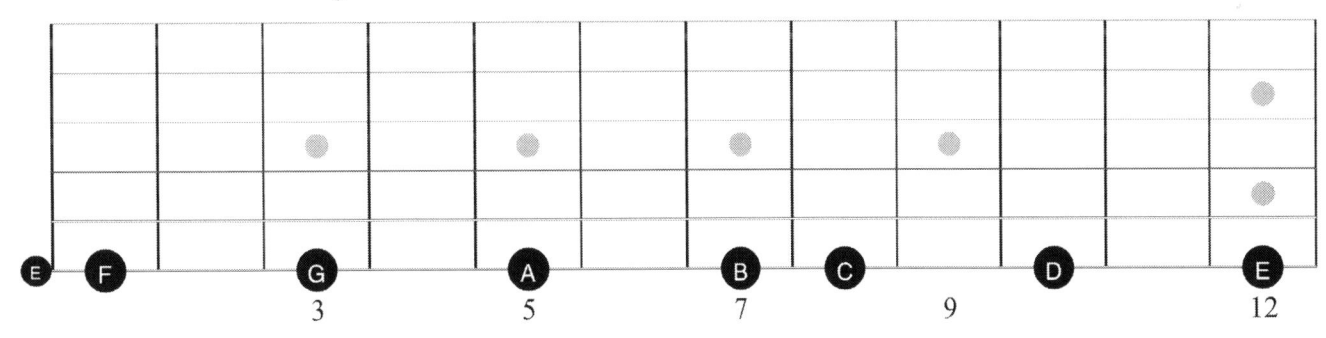

Notes on the Fifth String

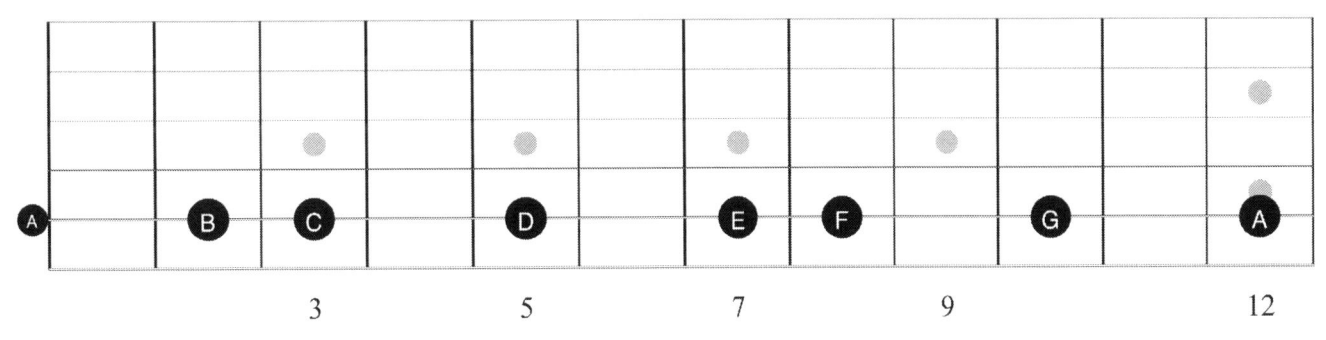

Example 6f:

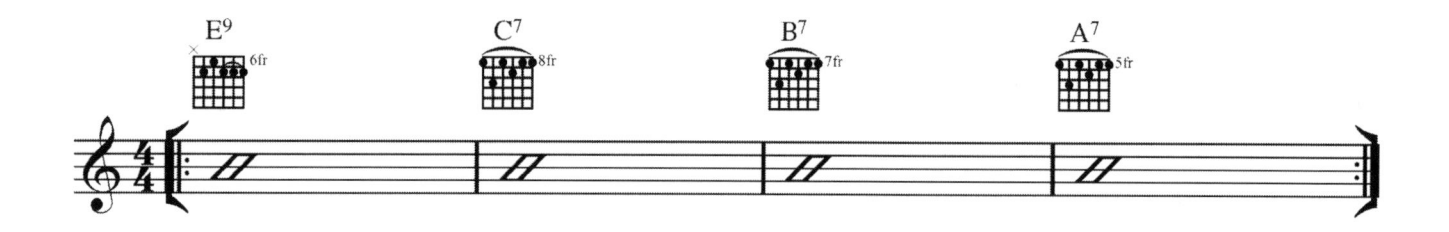

Example 6g:

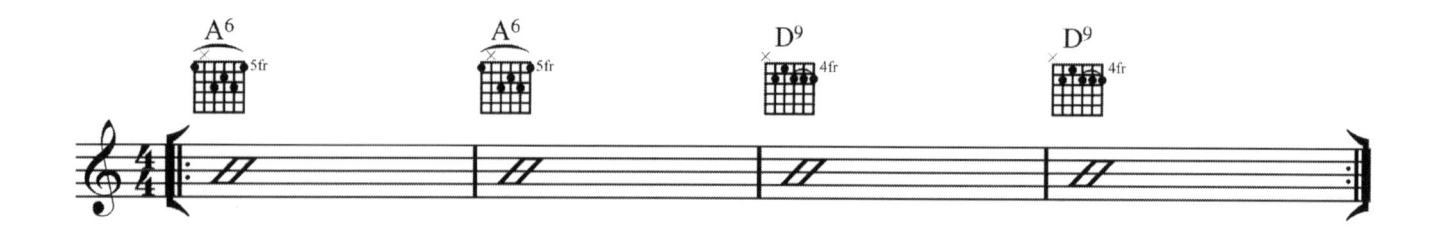

Chapter Seven: Bass Note Movements

When playing open chords, it is common to use small movements in the bass to help link chords smoothly together. The 'top' part of the chord stays the same, but the lowest notes of the chord will often descend or ascend by step. This type of movement is called a *descending bassline*.

It is easy to move between C Major and A Minor by using a descending bassline.

Example 7a:

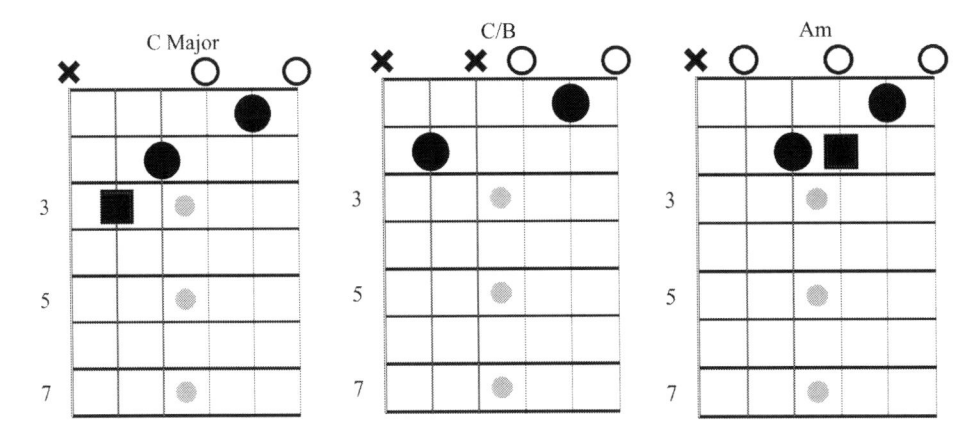

Be careful with the muted strings on these chords. It can work well to pick the bass note in each chord before strumming the rest of the strings.

The name C/B simply means that the C Major chord is being played over a B bass note. These *slash* chords normally sound a little strange out of context, but great when moving between two strong chords.

The same idea can be applied to the movement between G Major and Em7.

Example 7b:

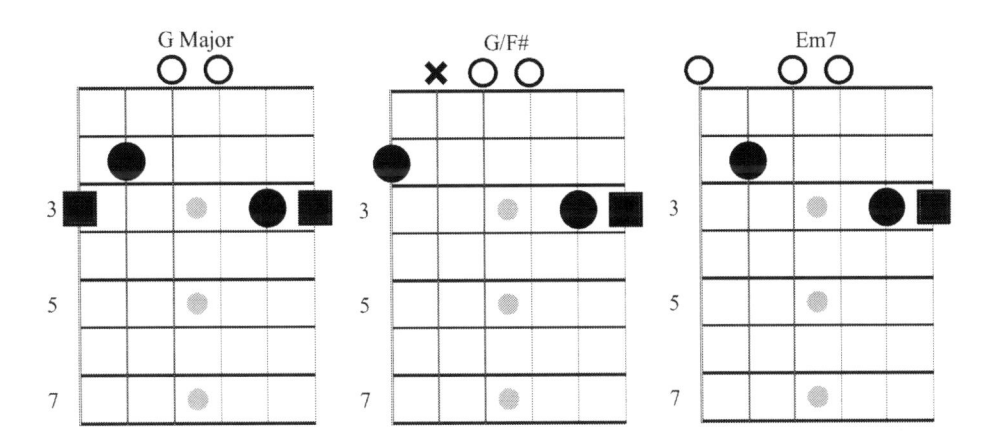

Check out the following examples to learn how you can use these slash chords to create moving basslines of your own. Experiment with other chord types.

Example 7c:

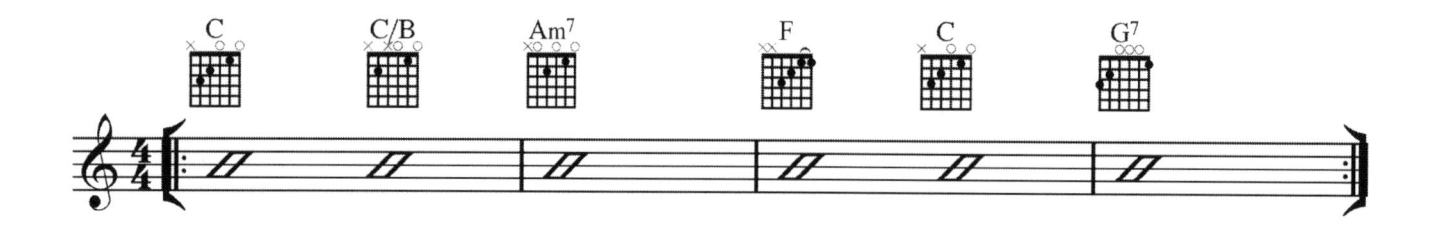

Example 7d:

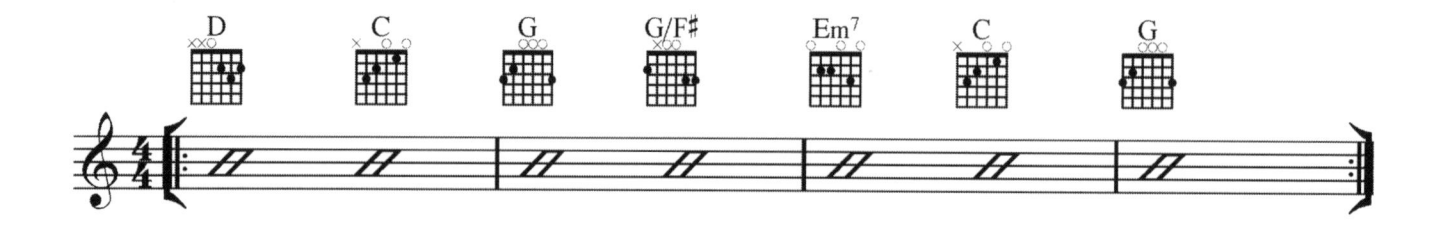

Chapter Eight: Basic Piano Voicings

The chords in the chapter are a little more suited for jazz guitar playing. This may not be your thing, but the rich texture of these chords is great to experiment with.

These voicings are called 'piano' voicings because they mimic the way many pianists voice chords on the piano. Notice that there is a one-string 'gap' between the bass note (sixth string) and the first upper-chord note (fourth string).

The underside of the first finger will be able to easily mute the unwanted string in the middle of the chord.

As always, use the steps in the **How to Practice** section to build your muscle memory and fluency with these chords. Then, add rhythm and start to combine them. Apply these voicings to the sequences at the end of this chapter, and also use them on the sequences in earlier chapters.

Example 8a:

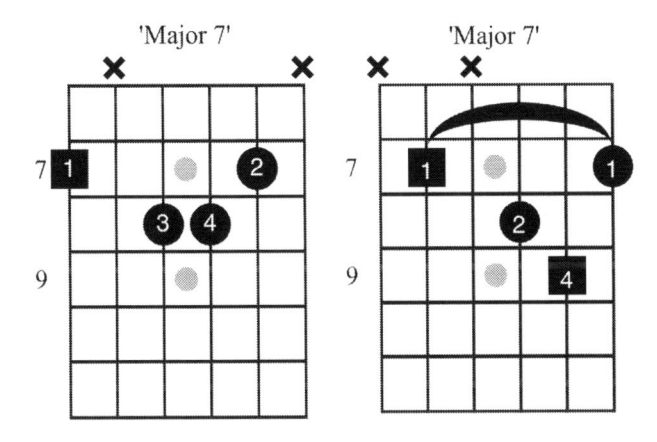

Example 8b:

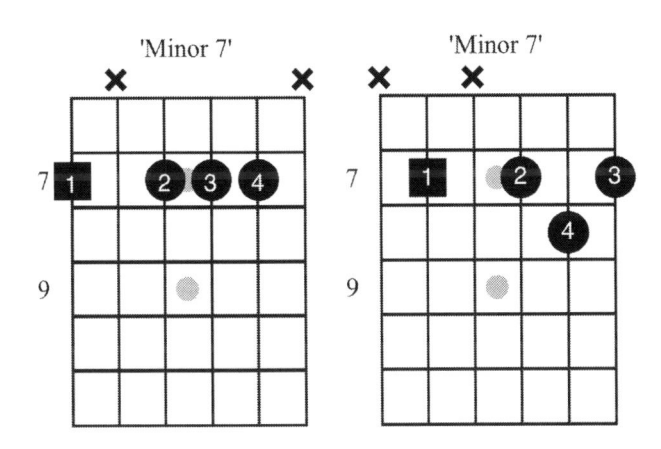

Example 8c:

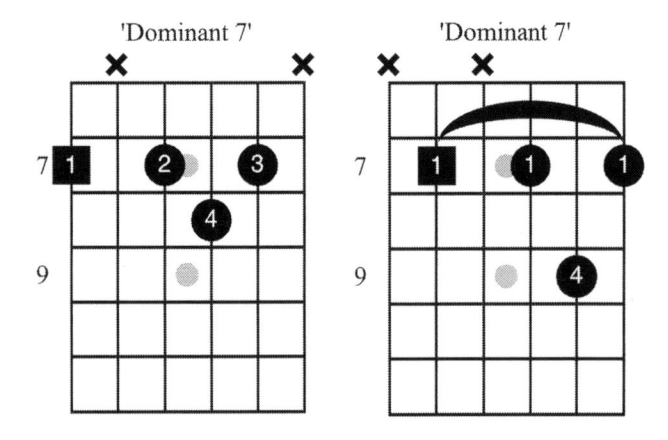

'Dominant 7'   'Dominant 7'

Example 8d:

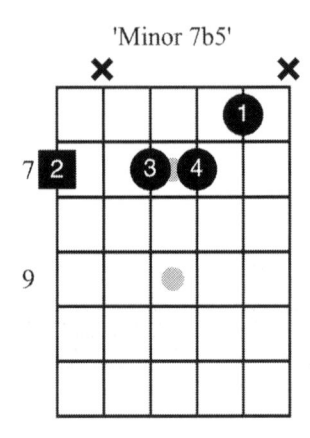

'Minor 7b5'

The following m7b5 shape is *technically* correct, but most guitarists will automatically reach for the second, easier voicing.

Example 8e:

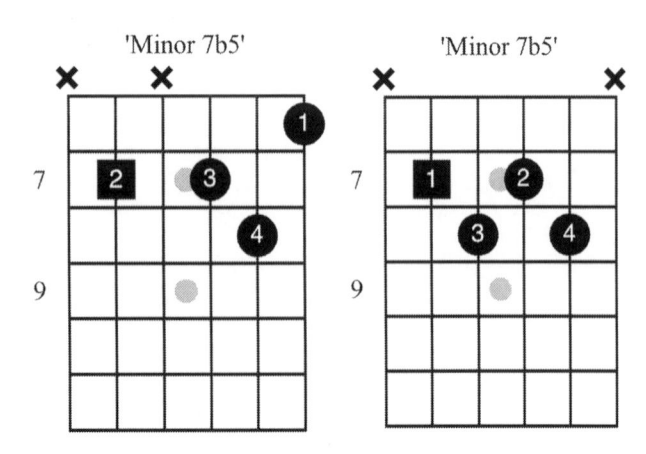

'Minor 7b5'   'Minor 7b5'

Test Yourself!

Play through the following progressions using piano voicing barre chords.

Example 8f:

| Bm7 | Em7 | A7 | DMaj7 |

Example 8g

| Dm7 | Bb7 | Em7b5 | A7 |

Example 8h:

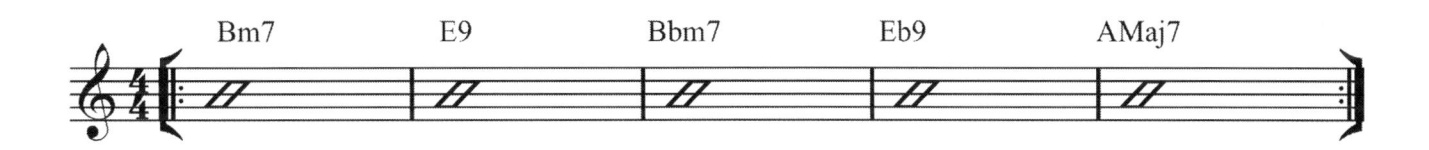

| Bm7 | E9 | Bbm7 | Eb9 | AMaj7 |

Example 8i:

| Am7b5 | Ab7 | Am7 | Cm7 |

Chapter Nine: Fourth-String Barres

In this short section, we will quickly look at how to play the most important chord-types on the top four strings. These voicings are used often in Motown and R&B music.

The first major voicing is a barre chord version of an open D Major chord. It's quite tricky to play, so most guitarists will miss out the root and play the chord with the same fingering as D Major.

Example 9a:

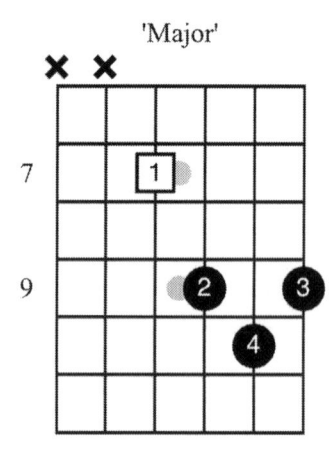

Once again, the Dm voicing is quite challenging, so try playing it without the root.

Example 9b:

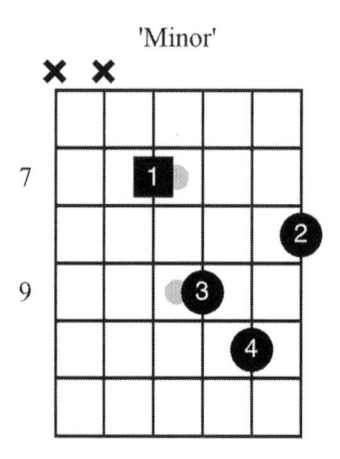

Example 9c:

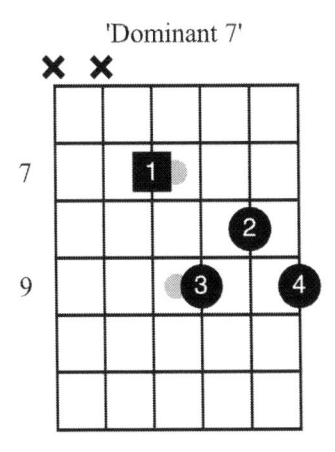

'Dominant 7'

Example 9d:

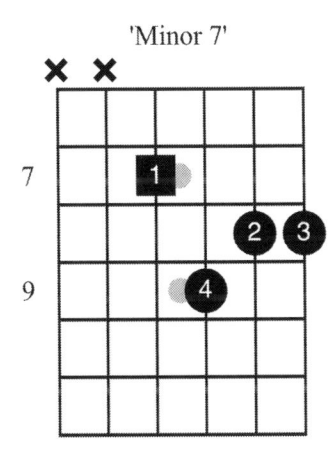

'Minor 7'

Some guitarists just use fingers one and three to play the following Maj7 barre chord. It's never worked for me, but it's a great option if you can manage it!

Example 9e:

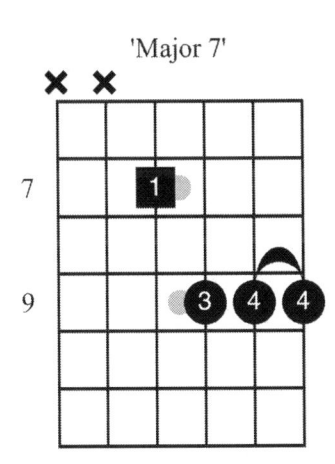

'Major 7'

Notice how the following m7b5 chord is just like the top four notes of a '9' chord.

Example 9f:

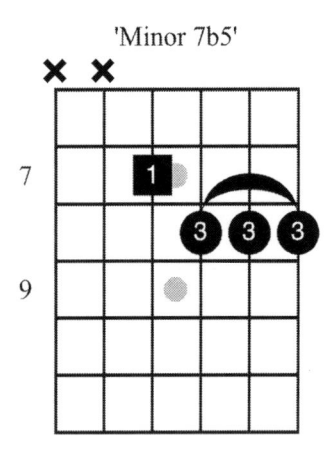

'Minor 7b5'

You'll need to know the notes on the fourth string so that you can place these movable voicings on the correct note.

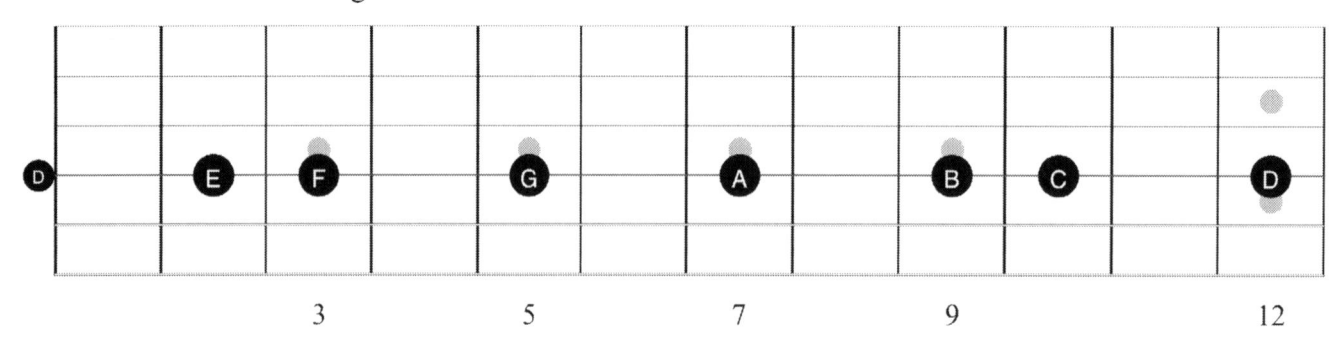

Notes on the Fourth String

Test yourself!

Combine the chord voicings in this chapter with the ones from previous chapters to play through the following chord sequences.

Example 9g:

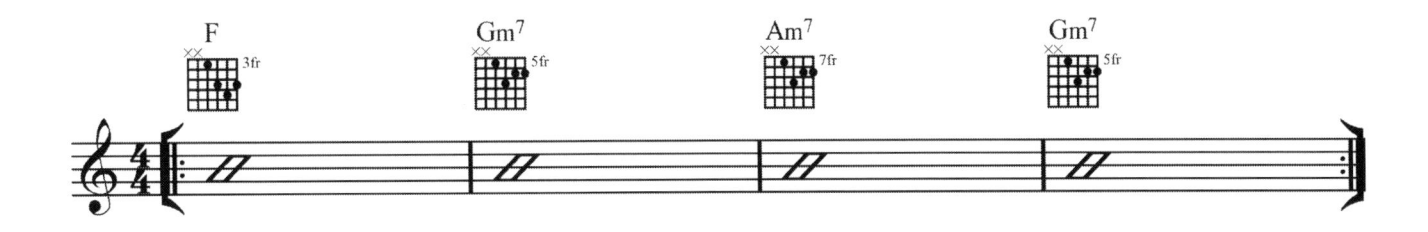

Example 9h:

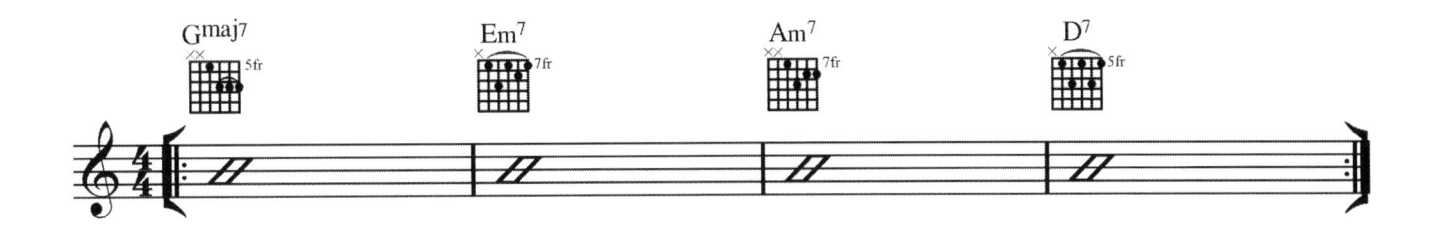

Example 9i:

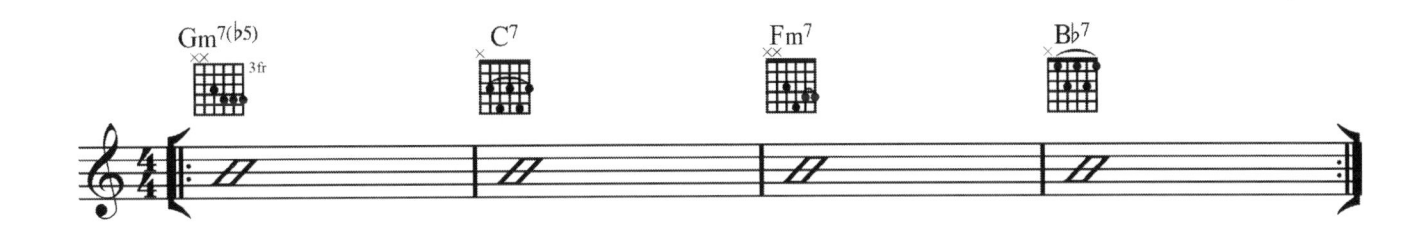

Come up with your own examples and use the four-string barres to play other sequences from earlier chapters.

Chapter Ten: Diatonic Extensions to Dominant 7 Chords

OK, I'll be honest… you probably don't need to work through the following two chapters unless you're really inquisitive about music, or you know that you definitely want to play jazz. If you want to strum out some pop songs, I recommend that you focus your time on the previous nine chapters and apply everything there to as many songs as you can. Spending time in the **How to Practice** and **Strumming** sections of this book will be much more beneficial to you than struggling through this section if you're not ready.

Find some band mates, rehearse, get a gig and have some fun.

However, if you want to peek into the murky underbelly of jazz, you may find the next two chapters interesting. They are advanced, so I really don't recommend them for beginners. Get out while you still can and come back later!

Still here?

OK then… The following section is taken from my best-selling book **Guitar Chords in Context**. It's a constant best seller on Amazon and goes way beyond being a simple chord dictionary. There's loads of stuff that we haven't covered in this book so I highly recommend it if you're interested in becoming a great guitarist.

In jazz, it is common to add diatonic 'extensions' and chromatic 'alterations' to dominant 7 chords. A natural or 'diatonic' extension is a note that is added to the basic 1 3 5 b7 chord but lies within the original parent scale of the dominant chord. In other words, to form an extended dominant chord we continue skipping notes in the scale, just as we did when we originally learnt to form a chord.

We can extend the basic 1 3 5 b7 chord formula to include the 9th, 11th and 13th scale tones.

These extensions occur when we extend a scale beyond the first octave. For example, here is the parent scale of a C7 chord (C Mixolydian):

C	D	E	F	G	A	Bb	C	D	E	F	G	A	Bb	C
1	2	3	4	5	6	b7	1/8	9	3	11	5	13	**b7**	1

Notice that in the second octave, if a note is included in the original chord it is still referred to as 1, 3, 5, or b7. This is because the function of these notes never changes in the chord: A 3rd will always define whether a chord is major or minor and the b7 will always be an essential part of a m7 or 7 chord.

The notes *between* the chord tones are the notes that have changed their names. Instead of 2, 4 and 6, they are now 9, 11, and 13. These are called *compound* intervals

In very simple terms you could say that a C13 chord could contain *all* the intervals up until the 13th:

1 3 5 b7 9 11 and 13 – C E G Bb D F and A

In practice though, this is a huge amount of notes (we only have six strings), and playing that many notes at the same time produces an extremely heavy, undesirable sound where many of the notes clash with one another.

The answer to this problem is to remove some of the notes from the chord, but how do we know which ones?

There are no set rules about which notes to leave out in an extended chord, however, there *are* some guidelines about how to define a chord sound and what *does* need to be included.

To define a chord as major or minor, you must include some kind of 3rd.

To define a chord as dominant 7, major 7 or minor 7, you must include some kind of 7th.

These notes; the 3rds and 7ths, are called guide tones, and they are the most essential notes in any chord. It may surprise you, but these notes are more important than even the root of the chord and quite often in jazz rhythm guitar playing, the root of the chord is dropped entirely.

We will look more closely at guide tone or 'shell' chord voicings in the next chapter, but for now, we will examine common ways to play the extensions that regularly occur on dominant chords in jazz progressions.

To name a dominant chord, we always look to the highest extension that is included, so if the notes were 1, 3, b7, and 13, we would call this a dominant 13, or just '13' chord. Notice that it doesn't include the 5th, the 9th or the 11th, but it is still called a '13' chord.

As long as we have the 3rd and b7th, a chord will always be a dominant voicing.

We will begin by looking at a fairly common voicing of a D7 chord. In the following example, each *interval* of the chord is labelled in the diagram.

In D7 the intervals 1 3 5 b7 are the notes D, F#, A and C.

Example 10a:

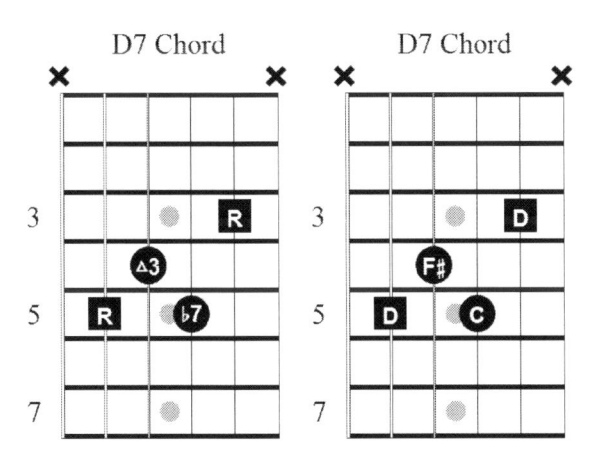

The 'triangle 3' symbol is shorthand for 'major 3rd'.

As you can see, this voicing of D7 doesn't include the 5th of the chord (A).

Here is the extended scale of D Mixolydian (the parent scale of D7).

D	E	F#	G	A	B	C	D	E	F#	G	A	B	C	D
1	2	3	4	5	6	b7	1/8	9	3	11	5	13	b7	1

We can use this voicing of D7 to form a dominant 9 or '9' chord. All we need to do is add the 9th of the scale (E) to the chord. The easiest way to do this is to move the higher-octave root (D) up by one tone and replace it with an E.

Example 10b:

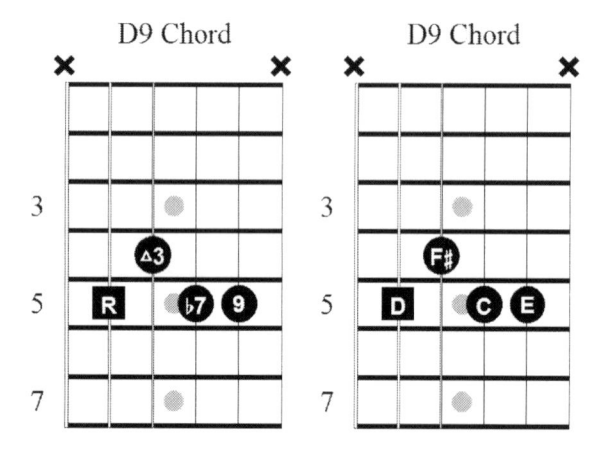

Look carefully to make sure you understand how I replaced the root of the chord with the 9th of the chord to form a dominant 9 or '9' chord.

The intervals contained in this chord voicing are now 1, 3, b7 and 9. We have the 1, 3 and b7 defining the chord as dominant and the 9th (E) creating the *extended* dominant 9th chord.

Dominant 11th or '11' chords are less common and need some special care because the major 3rd of the chord (F#) can easily clash with the 11th (G).

We will gloss over 11th chords for now and come back to them later, although the most common way to form an 11 chord it to lower the 5th of a dominant chord by a tone. The lowering of the 5th is generally voiced one octave above the 3rd, otherwise a semitone clash between the 3rd and 11th can occur.

Here is another voicing of a D7 chord, this time it does contain the 5th:

Example 10c:

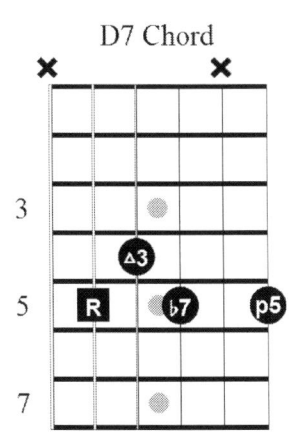

D7 Chord

By lowering the 5th (A) by a tone to the 11th (G), we form a dominant 11 or '11' chord.

Example 10d:

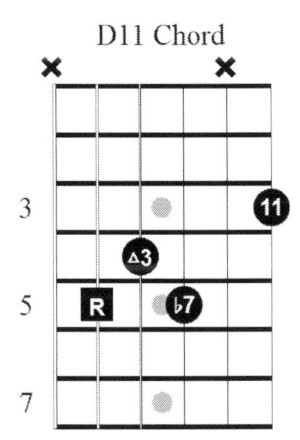

D11 Chord

Dominant 13 chords are much more common in jazz than dominant 11 chords. They are normally created by raising the 5th of a dominant 7 chord by one tone so that it becomes the 13th (6th). It is common to include the 9th of the scale in a 13th chord, but it is by no means necessary.

By combining the last two ideas we can form a D9 chord with the fifth on the 1st string of the guitar:

Example 10e:

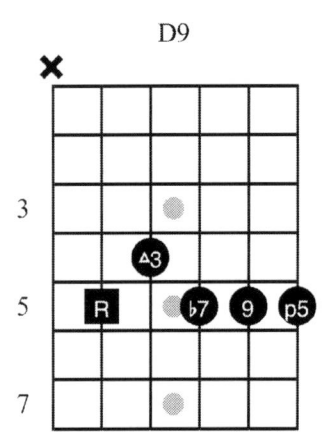

[Chord diagram: D9 chord, showing R at 5th fret, △3, ♭7, 9, p5]

By raising the 5th by one tone, we can reach the 13th degree (interval) of the scale. The chord is given first with the intervals shown, and then with the recommended fingering:

Example 10f:

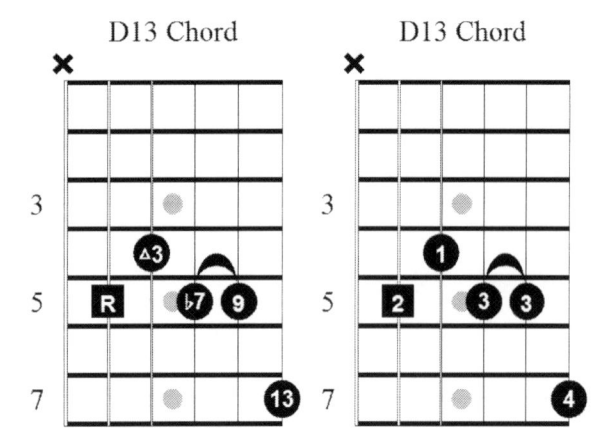

[Two chord diagrams: D13 Chord with intervals (R, △3, ♭7, 9, 13) and D13 Chord with fingering (1, 2, 3, 3, 4)]

As I'm sure you're starting to see, adding extensions to dominant chords is simply a case of knowing where the desired extension is located on the fretboard and then moving a nonessential chord tone to that location.

The previous '13' chord can also be voiced slightly differently to achieve a subtly different flavour. We could replace the 9th with the 3rd:

64

Example 10g:

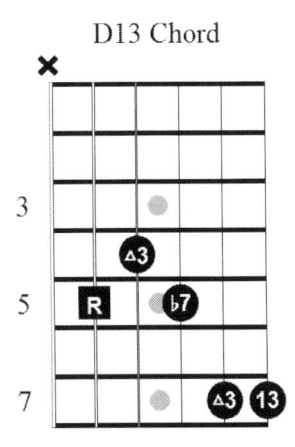

D13 Chord

In this voicing, there are two 3rds which is completely acceptable. You will probably find the preceding version with the 9th included to be a slightly richer sound. This approach can also be applied to a dominant 7 chord voiced from the 6th string of the guitar. Here is the root, 3 and b7 of a D7 chord with a 6th string root:

Example 10h:

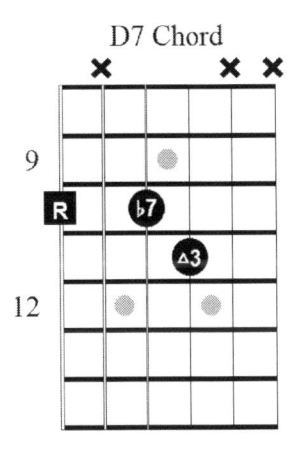

D7 Chord

The 5th and higher octave root of this chord are located here

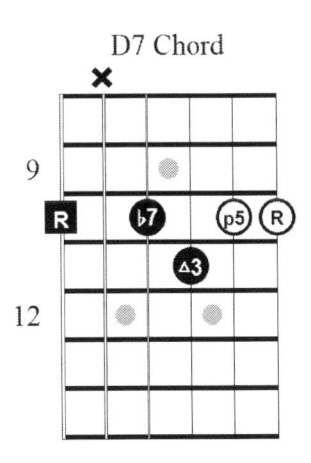

D7 Chord

If you remember, we can raise the 5th by a tone to play the 13th of the chord, and we can raise the root of the chord by a tone to target the 9th.

Example 10i:

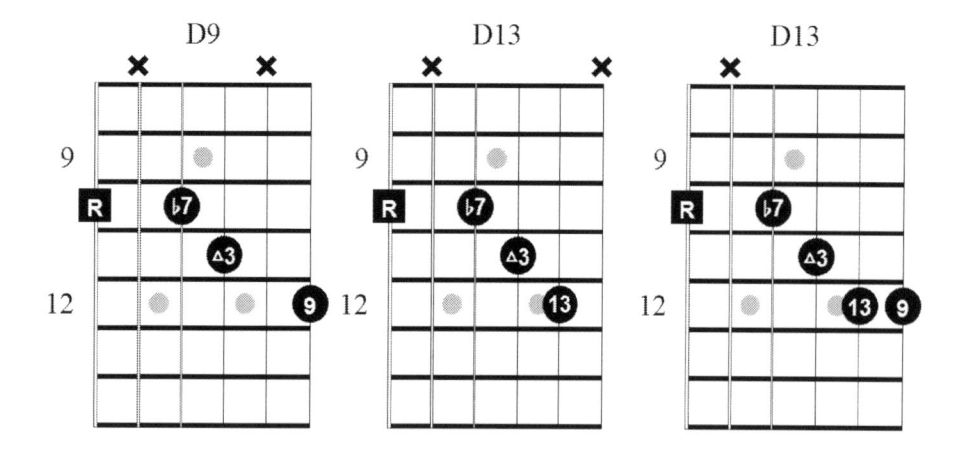

The third diagram shows a 13 chord which includes the 9th. It is still a 13th chord whether or not the 9th is present.

The following two 'shell' voicings are extremely useful fingerings to know, as it is easy to add extensions to them while keeping the root of the chord in the bass. However, as you will learn in chapter fourteen, diatonic extensions are often added by the clever use of chord *substitutions* that replace the original chord.

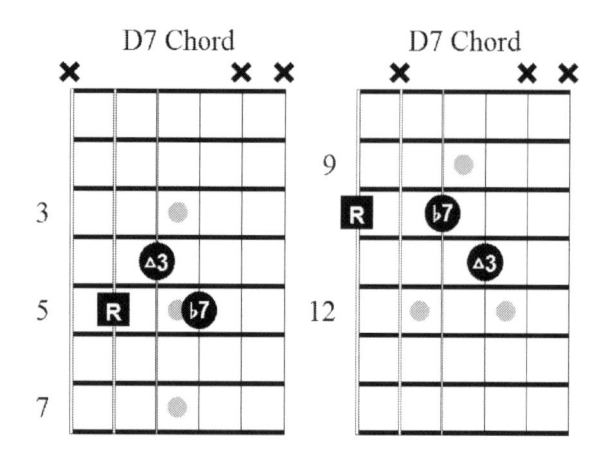

Chapter Eleven: Chromatic Alterations to Dominant Chords

While diatonic extensions (9, 11 and 13) are added to a dominant chord, it is also extremely common to add *altered* or *chromatic* extensions to a dominant chord. These alterations occur mainly at points of tension in a jazz progression, such as the dominant chord in a ii V I (two, five, one) sequence.

A chromatic alteration is a note that is added to a dominant chord that is not a 9, 11 or 13. We can account for *every* possible chromatic alteration by simply raising or flattening the 9th or 5th of the chord. In fact, there are only really four possible altered extensions; b5, #5, b9 and #9.

To see why this is true, let's look at a little bit of theory. Here is the two-octave scale of C Mixolydian, the parent scale of C7:

C	D	E	F	G	A	Bb	C	D	E	F	G	A	Bb	C
1	2	3	4	5	6	b7	1/8	9	3	11	5	13	b7	1

And here it is laid out on the guitar neck:

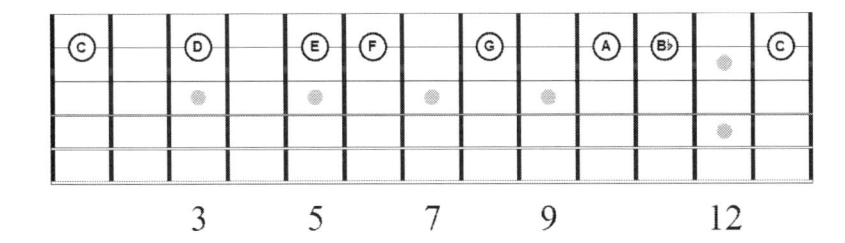

The 5th of the scale is the note G, and the 9th is the note D.

I can sharpen the 5th (G) to become a G# to create a #5 tension. I could also achieve the same result by flattening the 6th or 13th note (A) to become an Ab/G#.

For this reason, a b13 interval is exactly the same as a #5. The chords C7#5 and C7b13 are the same.

If you look at the fretboard again, you will see that a #11 (F#) is identical to a b5 (Gb).

A similar thing happens with the 9th of the scale however in any dominant chord you would *never* flatten the 3rd because it would change the quality of the chord from dominant to minor 7.

Remember dominant = 1 3 5 b7, and minor 7 = 1 b3 5 b7. By flattening the 3rd of a dominant chord, we change the chord quality so it is no longer dominant unless there is *another* major 3rd sounding in the chord.

I can sharpen the 9th (D) to become a D# and create a C7#9 sound. I can also flatten the 9th to Db to create a 7b9 sound.

Unlike the 3rd however, it is acceptable to remove the root note from any chord, so as you will see in chapter 9, it is possible to raise the root by a semitone to create a b9 sound.

We cannot raise the b7 of the chord because it would change the chord quality from dominant 7 to major 7.

In summary: b5 = #11 and #5 = b13 so the only true altered extensions to a dominant chord are b5, #5, b9 and #9. You will see chords written down like C7#11b13. This isn't wrong; it's just a question of terminology. The key is to realise that C7#9b13 is the same as C7#9#5.

The reason I teach b5, #5, b9, #9 is because it makes the chords much easier to understand and play on the fretboard.

We will work with a D7 chord to make these examples easier to play.

Here is a fretboard diagram showing the 1 3 b7 shell voicing of a dominant chord in black, and the 5th and 9th intervals marked in white:

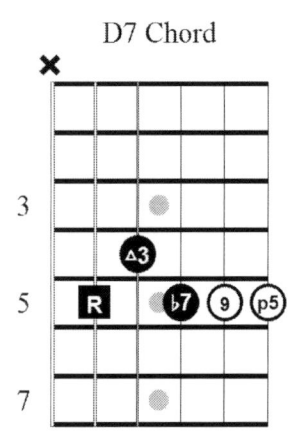

I can create *any* altered extension by simply moving the white notes up or down by one semitone.

Example 11a:

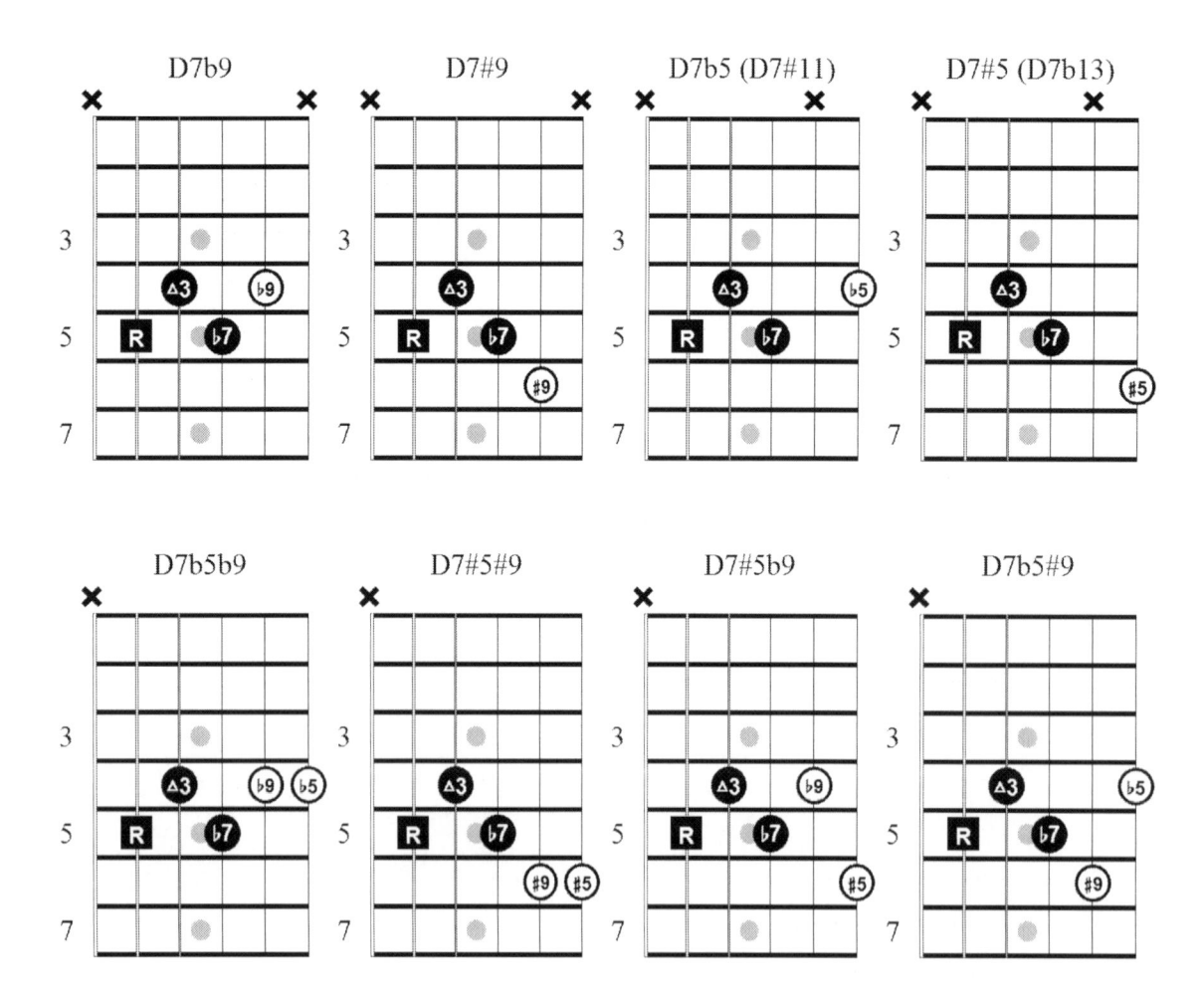

The same is true when we use the dominant 7 shell voicing with a root on the 6th string:

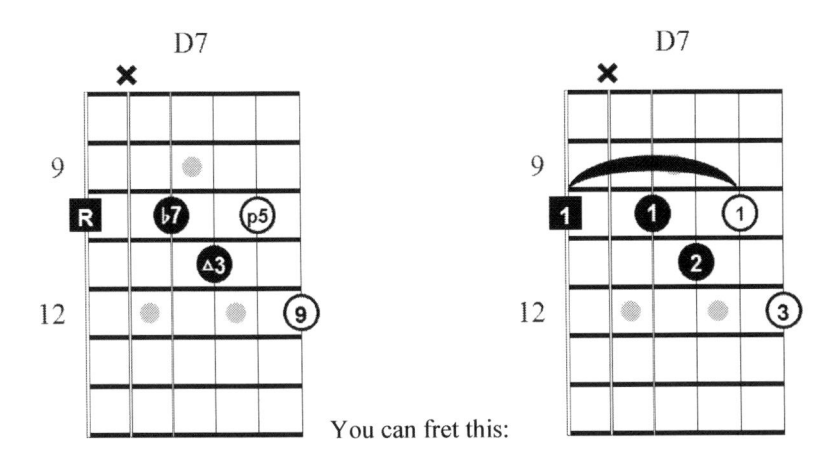

You can fret this:

Some of the altered extensions in this position can be a little hard to reach so quite often these voicings are played rootless. Here are a few of the altered extension permutations available in this position.

Example 11b:

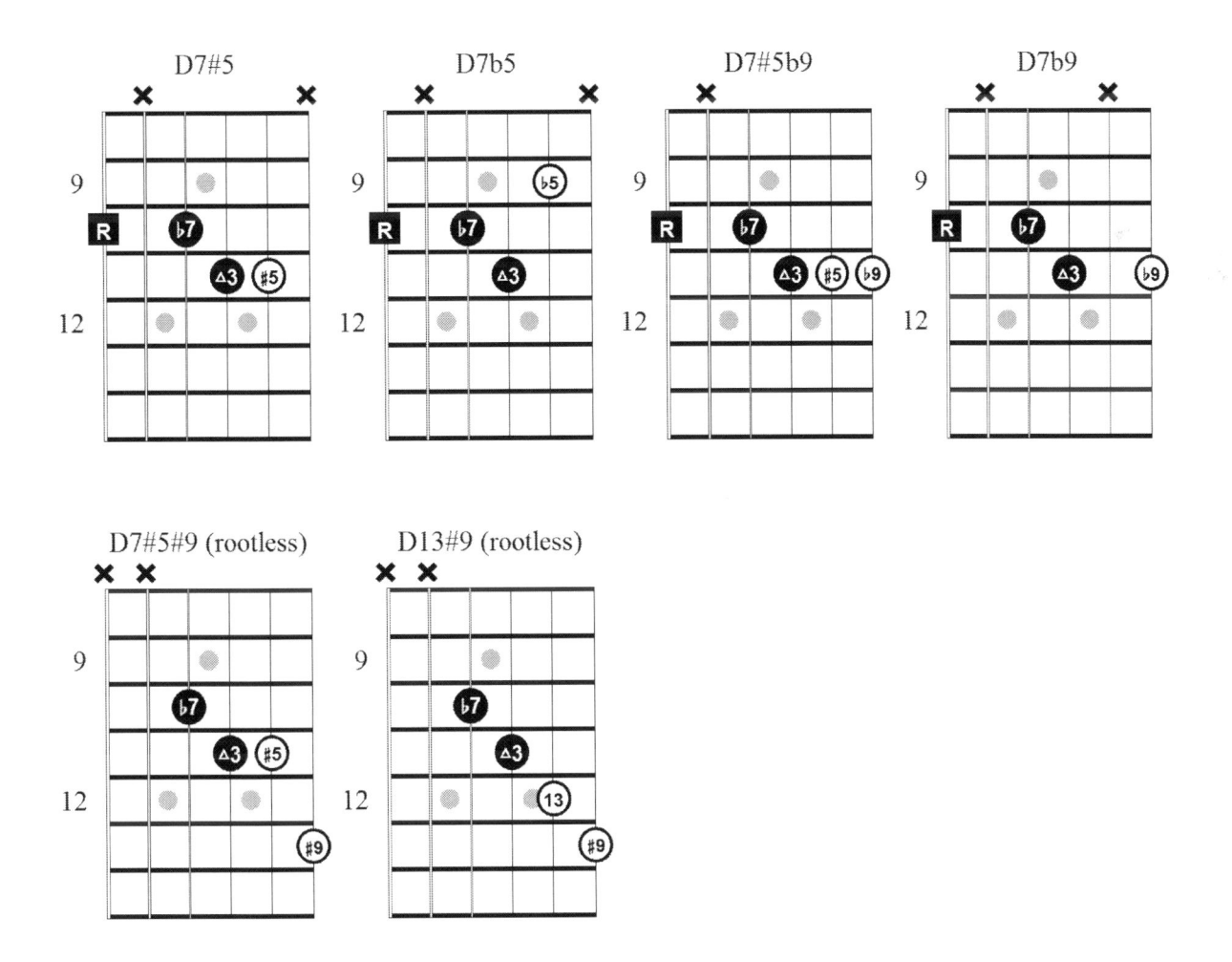

These approaches can be taken with a dominant 7 chord with the root on the 4th string too, although, in the basic root-position voicing we learnt earlier, we must omit the root when adding a #9 or b9.

The following example uses a G7 chord as the basis for the alterations.

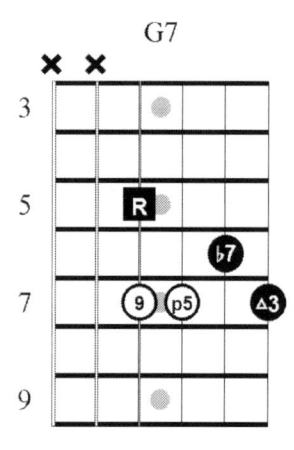

The easiest alterations to add are the #5 and b5, although often the root note will be raised a semitone to create a rootless 7b9 chord.

Example 11c:

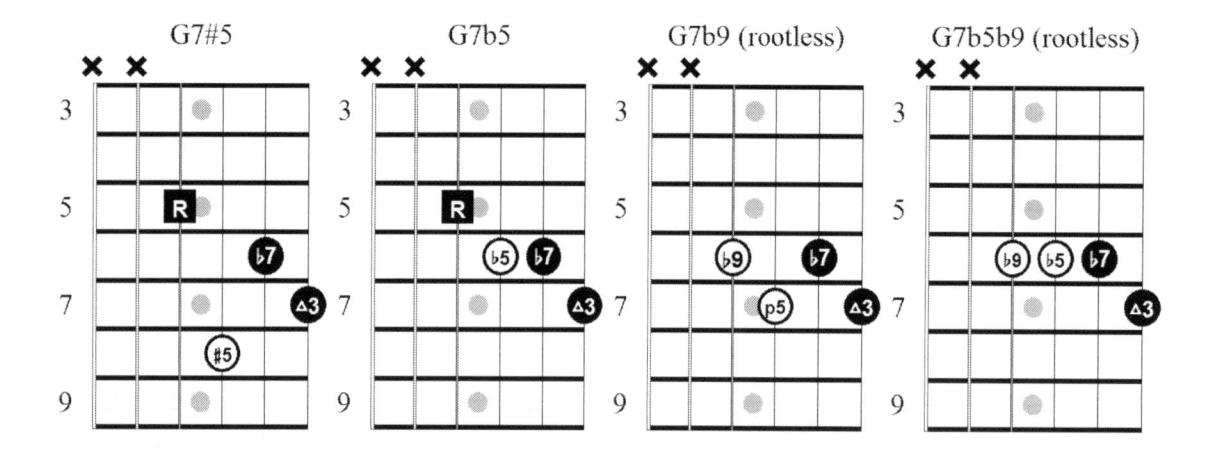

Quite often in jazz chord charts, you will simply see the symbol 'alt'. For example 'D7alt'. This means that the composer has not specified a particular altered extension for a dominant 7 chord and so you can use whichever one you feel works best with the music.

It is also important to know that just because a chord chart says '7' it doesn't mean that the chord must be played as a 'straight' 7 chord. If the dominant chord is *static* (not moving), it is normally fine to add in as many natural extensions as you like. For example, four bars of D7 could be played like this:

Example 11d:

| D13 | D9 | D13 | D7 |

If a dominant 7 chord is *functional* (resolving to another chord), then a basic '7' chord can normally be substituted for any dominant chord with a natural extension *or* chromatic alteration.

A chord progression like this:

Example 11e:

| Am7 | D7 | GMaj7 | E7 |

Could be played in any or more of the following ways:

Example 11f:

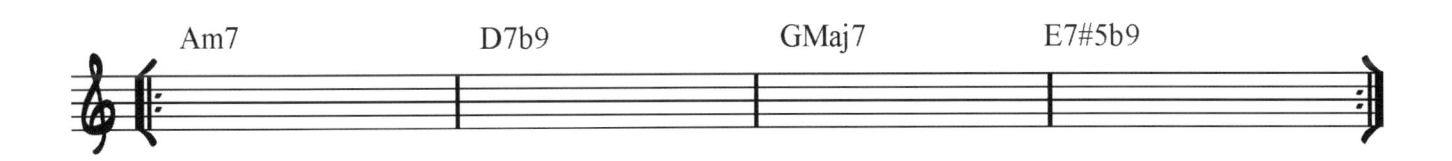

| Am7 | D7b9 | GMaj7 | E7#5b9 |

Example 11g:

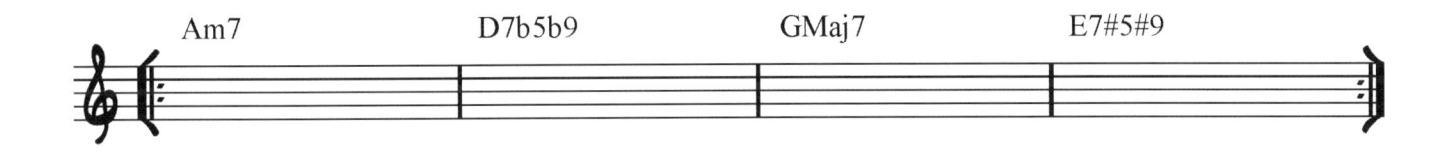

| Am7 | D7b5b9 | GMaj7 | E7#5#9 |

Example 11h:

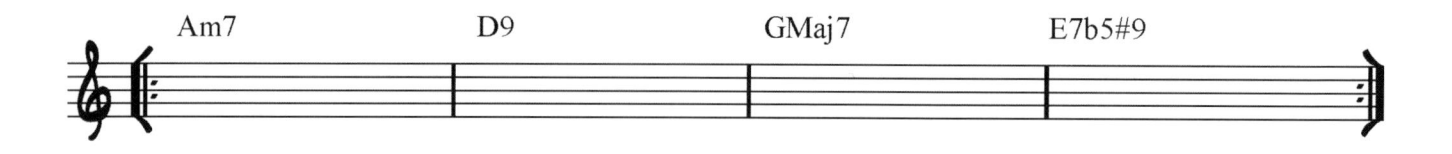

| Am7 | D9 | GMaj7 | E7b5#9 |

Try playing through the following examples beginning from different root notes, and substitute any diatonic or chromatic extensions you like for the dominant chords you have learnt already.

1)

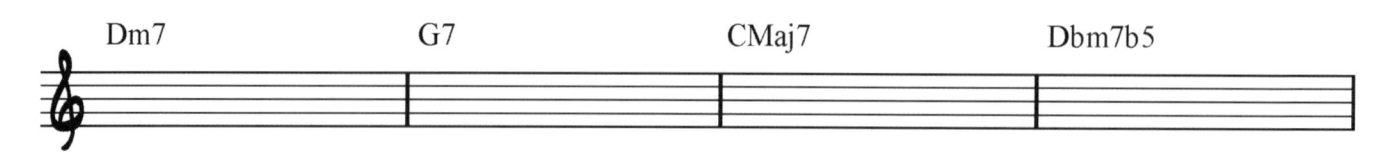

| Dm7 | G7 | CMaj7 | Dbm7b5 |

2)

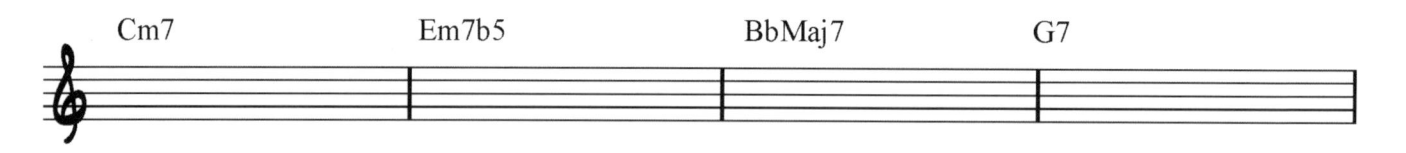

| Cm7 | Em7b5 | BbMaj7 | G7 |

3)

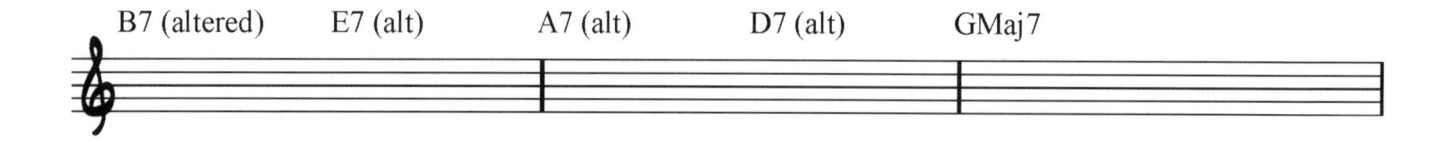

| B7 (altered) | E7 (alt) | A7 (alt) | D7 (alt) | GMaj7 |

We can take the same approach when adding chromatic alterations to major 7, minor 7 and m7b5 chords; the secret is simply to know where the alterations are on the fretboard.

Chapter Twelve: How to Practice

In this section, I share my favourite techniques for learning and mastering new chords. I've been teaching these methods for years and I have broken them down into bullet point steps for you.

Learning New Open Chords.

The following set of steps is designed to help you quickly build the muscle memory that you need to memorise, recall and play any new open chord.

1) Read the chord diagram carefully! Ensure you're using the correct fingers on each note.

2) Place the tips of your fingers on the correct notes and strum the guitar once. Don't worry about the sound too much for now. Don't even worry too much about hitting the correct strings with the pick.

3) Remove your fretting hand from the guitar neck. Right off! Touch your leg with your fingertips.

4) Replace the fretting hand and fret the chord correctly. Strum the guitar. Don't worry about the sound.

5) Remove your hand again, right away from the guitar. Touch your leg again!

6) Replace your hand on the chord, and this time pick the correct strings one by one. Listen for any buzzes or muted notes and try adjusting your hand or thumb position until you can pick each note and it sounds clean. You may still get small buzzes at this stage, especially if you're a complete beginner. Don't worry! As your hand gets stronger, these buzzes will gradually disappear.

7) Lift your hand slightly from the guitar neck and replace the chord. You don't need to strum this time. Remove and replace the chord.

8) Remove and replace the chord.

9) Repeat steps 7 and 8.

10) Now try strumming the chord and check for buzzes.

11) If this is one of the first chords you're learning, then take a break. Get up, walk around and grab a drink.

12) Sit down again and repeat steps 1 – 11.

13) Finally, replace the chord on the neck and strum the strings. Listen. Remove, replace and strum the chord. Listen. Do this about ten times. If you know a few other chords, move on to the next set of steps immediately. If you don't know any other chords yet, repeat the above steps with a new chord. The first four chords I suggest you learn are Em, Am, C Major, then F Major 7.

Once you have a few (two or more) chords under your belt, the best thing you can do is to link them together. Our brains work well be learning information and movements in context. Want proof? What's easier to memorise, the words, "Quail, lemon, 78.4, Delhi," or the sentence, "The quail was drinking lemon in the 78.4-degree heat in Delhi."?

Most people would say the second sentence is more memorable because they can easily form a picture in their minds by linking up the words. All we did was add a little useful context.

When we learn chords individually, we are just creating a list of random words. When we link chords together, we learn the sounds and movements in context, so our brains will absorb them much more quickly.

Before you start, get a metronome. It's really important that you add an element of time keeping, and even a little 'time pressure' to get you moving more quickly. In music, rhythm is always king. Your audience will always notice a bad rhythm before noticing a bad note, so it pays to play in time from day one.

I recommend these metronomes.

Metrotimer for iPhone

Mobile Metronome for Android.

They both offer free versions, and it's great to finally be able to do something useful with a cell phone.

I'll use the chords of Em and Am for example, but you can pick any two chords you like. The best approach is to combine the new chord you are trying to learn with a simple chord you already know.

Learning Chords in Context

1) Complete steps 1 – 13 of the *Learning New Open Chords* method for each of the chords you wish to learn.

2) Set your metronome to 60 beats per minute (60 bpm).

3) Tap your foot and count "1, 2, 3, 4, 1, 2, 3, 4' in time with the click.

4) On a "1" strum an Em. Don't hold the chord! Immediately start moving to the next chord in the sequence (Am in this case). You are aiming to arrive there before the next "1", so you have four beats in which to get your fingers organised. If you get there early, just wait.

5) On the next "1" strum the Am.

Example 12a:

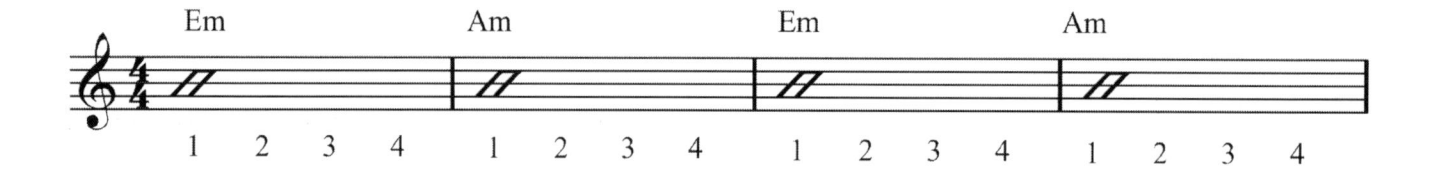

6) If you didn't make it, try again. If it's still tough, give yourself eight beats to get to the Am.

7) As soon as you strum the Am, start moving back to the Em so you can play it on the next "1". You don't need to let the chords ring. Just get moving!

8) If you arrive early at Em, wait and strum the chord on the next "1".

9) Don't worry about the sound of the chord, muted strings, buzzes, etc. These will improve with time. All you are concerned about is getting to the next chord by the next "1".

10) As you start to improve, repeat steps 4 – 8, but *keep moving!* Strum the guitar on the "1", and play whatever you have managed to get down in the fretting hand. It might sound terrible but that's not important right now. As soon as you have played one chord on beat one, immediately start moving to the next chord.

11) Take a break for two minutes.

12) Repeat step 10. If you're starting to get the idea, increase the metronome speed by 8bpm. Repeat.

13) As you improve, increase the metronome speed incrementally by around 8bpm until you get to around 120 bpm. Continue playing a down-strum on each chord on beat 1.

14) When you reach 120, stop, congratulate yourself, and set the metronome back on 60bpm. Repeat all the previous steps, but now allow each chord to last for just two beats. It will *feel* different, but you are playing the same speed as you were before. Two strums per bar at 60 bpm = one strum at 120 bpm.

You should now be playing Em on beat 1 and 3 and then Am on beats 1 and 3. Again, if this is too difficult then slow the metronome down slightly. As ever, don't worry too much about the sound of the chords, the goal is to be in the right place at the right time.

Example 12b:

| Em | Am | Em | Am |

1 2 3 4   1 2 3 4   1 2 3 4   1 2 3 4

16) Once again, gradually increase the metronome speed, but this time by 4bpm until you reach 120bpm, or wherever you simply can't make it anymore.

Repeat the previous process but now play four strums on each chord. It's OK if you slow right down for this but keep the metronome ticking.

Example 12c:

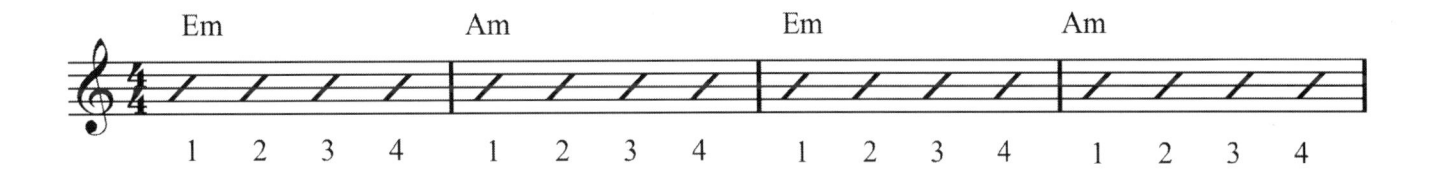

| Em | Am | Em | Am |

1 2 3 4   1 2 3 4   1 2 3 4   1 2 3 4

17) Introduce some rhythms using the method in the next chapter. Ensure that whatever rhythm you choose has a 1/4 note on beat four so that you have time to change between chords.

The above process can be used to learn, and also introduce any new chord into your vocabulary. Don't worry too much about the way each chord sounds; the idea is to build confident muscle memory first and then hone the movement a little later once you can confidently finger the chord.

Chapter Thirteen: Adding Rhythm

I make clear to all my private students that I am not a 'theory first' teacher. I prefer to get hands-on and have them making music as soon as possible. The one exception to this is in the way I teach rhythm and strumming.

Your strumming hand (normally your right if you're right-handed) only has two useful directions to hit the strings; *up* and *down*. When you understand why certain strums are *ups* and others are *downs,* you build a fundamental security with rhythm. In fact, if you practice the following method, quite soon you'll never wonder how to play a rhythm again. You'll simply hear it and replicate it instantly and unconsciously.

When we talk about rhythm in music, what we're essentially doing is breaking down a song into little chunks. That song might be a 3 minute Beatles tune or a 17 minute Rachmaninov symphony. Either way, we always arrange the chunks of rhythm the same way.

You may have heard the words *bars* and *beats* before. A beat is one pulse of a song: the distance from one click to the next on your metronome. Think of the beat as a one-syllable word.

One beat of a piece of music looks like this:

♩

This note is called a **'Quarter Note'** as you can fit four of them in a bar, i.e., four ¼ notes = 1 bar.

A bar is a *container* for the beats, and at this stage, we will normally have four beats in each bar**.** An empty bar of music looks like this:

The 4/4 at the start tells us that there are 4 beats in the bar.

If we fill the bar with quarter notes it looks like this:

This is a whole load of preamble to get to one very simple rule:

Every time you see a ♩, you play a down strum.

Down strums are always on the beat, so if you're counting 1, 2, 3, 4 as in previous chapters, every time you say a number you strum downwards on guitar.

Look at and listen to **Example 13a**:

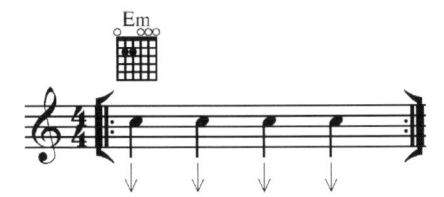

[Musical notation: Em chord, 4/4 time, four quarter note down strums]

Set your metronome to play at 60 beats per minute, then play a down strum on each click while holding down the chord of E minor.

Try the same idea with A minor:

Example 13b:

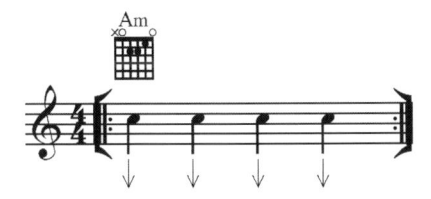

[Musical notation: Am chord, 4/4 time, four quarter note down strums]

While this is a great method for developing good solid rhythm, music would be extremely dull if all our rhythms were like this.

One way to add interest is to double up on each quarter (1/4) note. In other words, imagine splitting each 1/4 note in half. This gives us 8 notes in the bar, and these are imaginatively called *1/8* or *eighth* notes.

On its own, an 1/8th note looks like this:

♪

But when we put two of them next to each other, we join up their tails:

♫

In other words, in music, instead of seeing two 1/8th notes written like this:

♪ ♪ , you would always see them written like this: ♫ .

You can see that two 1/8th notes take the same amount of time to play as one 1/4 note.

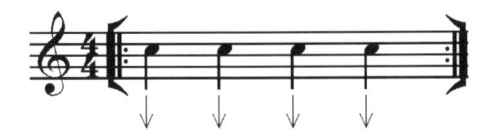

[Musical notation: 4/4 time, four quarter note down strums]

So it takes the same amount of time to play as,

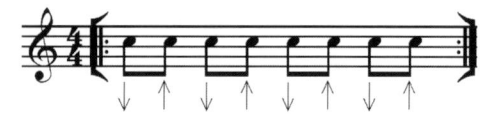

That is the end of the mathematics; I promise!

As you can see in the previous example, when we play 1/8th notes, our down strum is still in exactly the same place. All we need to do is squeeze in an up strum between each one. This up-strum should be *exactly* in the middle of each down.

On paper it looks like this:

Example 13c:

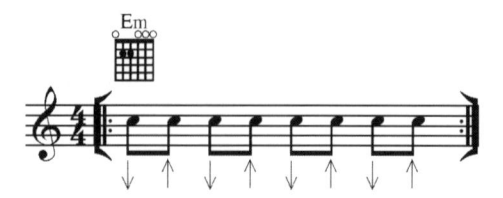

Set your metronome to 60 beats per minute and begin by playing just a down strum on each click. When you're ready, add up strums in the middle of each down. Count out loud '1 and 2 and 3 and 4 and ', etc.

Listen to the audio example to help you.

Try the same idea with other chords like D Major, shown below.

Example 13d:

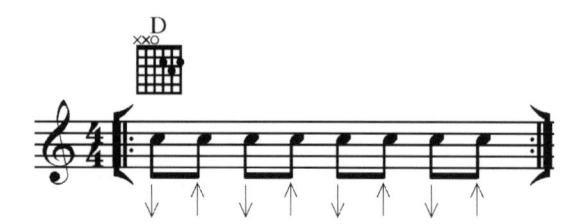

While we have added interest to our playing by adding more strums, music would be very repetitive if this was the only rhythm we ever played. To add interest, let's learn to combine 1/4 notes and 1/8th notes to add variety.

Look at **Example 13e:**

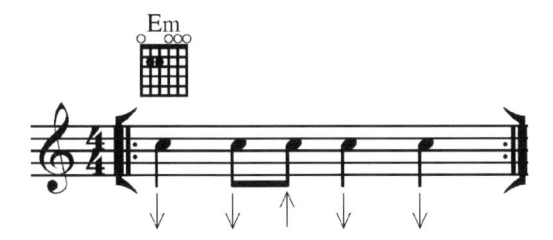

[Musical notation: Em chord, 4/4 time, strumming pattern with down, down-up, down, down arrows]

Beat 1 is a down strum, **beat 2** is a 'down-up', **beat 3** is a down strum, as is **beat 4.**

Before you play, set the metronome on 60 bpm and say out loud:

One. Two and Three. Four. Down. Down-Up Down. Down.

Say it in time, rhythmically and confidently. Saying the rhythm out loud really helps your brain to process what it needs to do to strum the rhythm in time.

When you're ready, strum the rhythm confidently. Don't worry about any buzzes in your fretting hand. Ignore them; we're only focusing on strumming.

When you're happy with the above, try the next idea.

Example 13f:

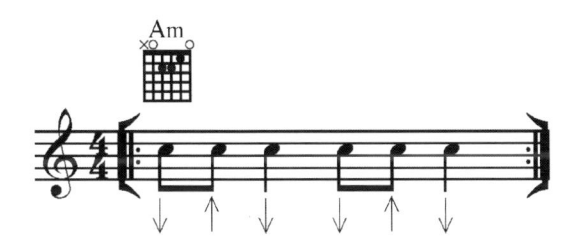

[Musical notation: Am chord, 4/4 time, strumming pattern with down, up, down, down, up, down arrows]

Say out loud *"One and Two. Three and Four. Down Up Down. Down Up Down."*

If it helps, you might want to think *jin gle bells jin gle bells.*

Throughout any rhythm you play on the guitar, the strumming hand never stops moving. It is constantly moving up and down in time. Downward movements are on the beats, upward movements are between the beats. This keeps you in time; like a little built-in conductor. To create rhythms, all we do is sometimes hit the strings and sometimes miss them.

Here are some other rhythms to practice:

Example 13g:

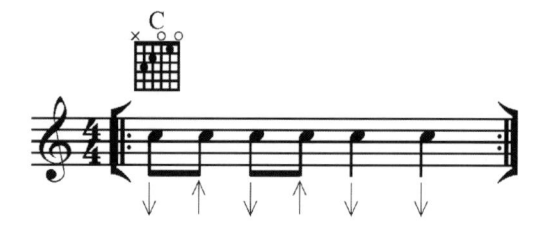

Down-Up Down-Up Down. Down.

Example 13h:

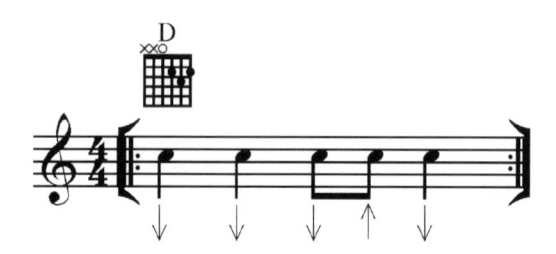

Down. Down. Down-Up Down.

With each rhythm, remember to keep your strumming hand moving down and up all the time. To play a 1/4 note, simply don't strike the guitar on the up-strum.

More Interesting Rhythms

The simplest and most common way to add energy to your rhythm playing is to miss out strumming some down beats. To teach you this idea, we need to introduce a new musical symbol. It is an 1/8th note *rest* and looks like this:

This rest simply means *silence* or 'don't strum.' It will always be seen in combination with a strummed quarter note so that together they add up to **one beat,** like this:

Before, when we played the rhythm, the strumming pattern was **Down Up.** With the rhythm, we *miss out the down strum* but *still play the up strum*.

To make this easier, always keep moving the strumming hand as if you are going to play the down strum, but simply *miss the strings.* This will keeps you in time.

In other words, the strumming hand is going up and down constantly, but *does not make contact* with the strings on the down strum. This is shown in the notation below by the brackets around the arrow.

To practice this idea, study the following.

Example 13i:

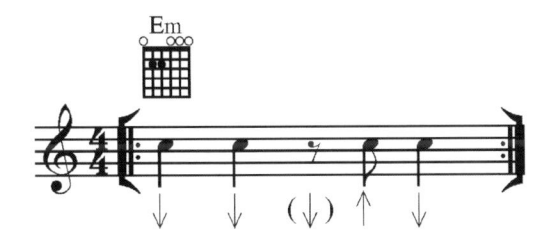

Count out loud: "Down. Down. Miss Up Down".

Next, try holding down an E minor chord while you strum this rhythm. Remember to keep the strumming hand moving all the time, miss the strings on the down strum of **beat 3** but make contact on up strum of **beat '3 and'**.

This is tricky at first, but incredibly important.

Once you have this idea under your fingers, try the next rhythm:

Example 13j:

Down. Down Up Miss Up Down.

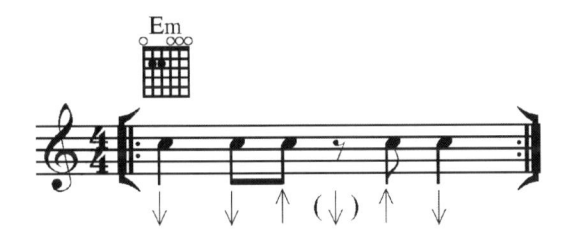

81

Finally, strum this:

Example 13k:

Down. Miss Up Miss Up Down.

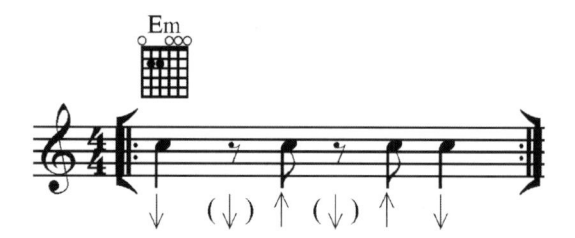

When you're comfortable with the idea of missing a down strum, transfer these rhythms to some of the chord changes given in the early chapters. There is no need to make the tasks difficult for both hands at the same time.

Try the following at 60 beats per minute.

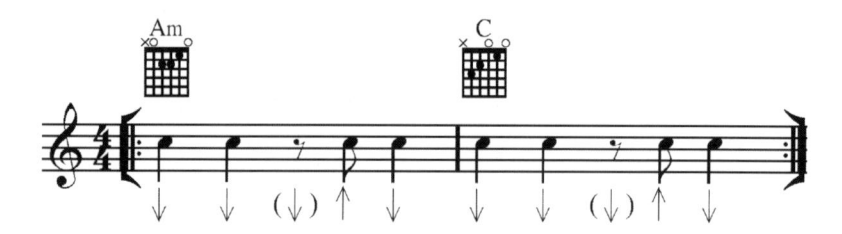

Example 3l:

Here's one more example to spur your imagination. Spend as much time as you can mixing and matching chord changes and rhythms.

Example 13m:

Down Up Miss Up Miss Up Down.

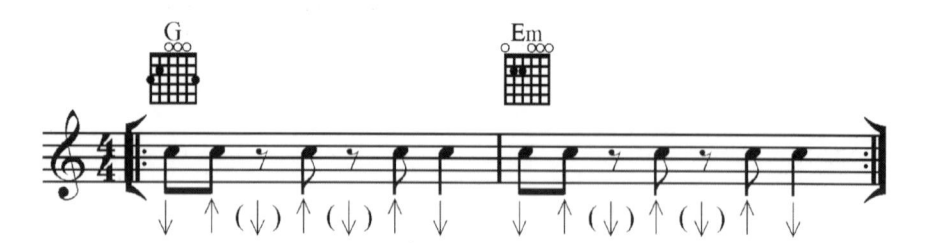

Now try making up some of your own rhythms and apply them to simple chord changes.

Conclusion and Practice Directions

There's a huge amount of information in this book, and there is probably a temptation to try to memorise it all at once. I strongly advise against this, and instead suggest you try to learn just one or two chords a day (or even a week). Spend the majority of your practice time exploring and actually using these chords and voicings.

Remember, context is everything. There's no point learning a long list of information if you're never going to figure out when to play it or what effect it has on the music. While chords can easily be substituted (a Dominant 9 for a Dominant 7, for example), the effect caused by these small changes can be quite dramatic.

In theory, '6' chords function in exactly the same way as straight-ahead Major chords, but you're really going to want to know what that substitution will do to the song. Experimentation is the key (and rehearsal with your band too), because the last thing they need is to hear a 'strange' note appear while they're playing. Sometimes risks are good, but normally it's best to try out these ideas with your band *before* you get on stage!

My biggest piece of advice is that there's no massive hurry to learn everything, especially the information in Chapters Ten and Eleven. Those ideas really are quite advanced and I've only included them here for completeness and to give you a deeper understanding of how chord theory works.

If you're interested in what my first guitar lesson looks like for the average beginner, in an hour I would normally have expected to cover five or six chords (Em, Am, C Major, F Major7, D Major and G Major), taught them the steps in Chapter Twelve, and taught them how to strum the first basic rhythms in Chapter Thirteen.

The real work, however, begins once they get home.

I insist that my students practice for a minimum of 20 minutes a day, ideally 20 minutes twice a day because the physical repetition is important to build muscle memory. Their homework is to practice the steps I've given in Chapters Twelve and Thirteen.

If the student practices every day, then normally they come back to me the following week to get some more chords, a few songs, and some more rhythms to work on.

Often, my students develop an effortless command of the chords in Chapters One and Two after about four weeks.

If they've practiced well, the continuing improvement in their ability is exponential because they've covered the basics so thoroughly. At this point, I can write down almost any new chord and they will grasp it quickly. The muscle memory work has paid off by this stage, so all I need to do to teach them an actual song is to write down the chord sequence and strumming pattern (rhythm).

There's no great secret to learning how to play a musical instrument; it's simply a case of committing yourself and practicing regularly. The hardest part is making a lifestyle change to fit in some quality guitar practice time.

Add up all the time you spend on Facebook, Twitter, Instagram, playing video games, watching cat videos on YouTube etc. Reduce that time by 20 minutes and play your guitar instead. I promise you, it's much more rewarding than worrying what Kim and Kanye are up to. Your soul will thank you.

If you need any further help with learning guitar, there are loads of good resources out there.

JustinGuitar is an amazing resource for beginners and improvers alike. He's got a lesson on pretty much any song you care to learn, and his patient, upbeat style is a joy to learn from.

Chords are a huge subject and I go into great detail in Guitar Chords in Context. In this book you'll learn much more about voicings and how to use chords to open up the guitar neck. Three voicings of each chord type are given and you'll learn everything about how chords are created, used and applied.

I really hope you enjoy your journey as a guitarist.

Have fun, and keep rocking!

Joseph

First Chord Progressions for Guitar

Introduction

You sit down at a jam session surrounded by a room full of expectant musicians. You are down to play rhythm guitar and the vocalist looks over and says, "Play me some different chord progressions." How would you react?

I have seen this situation countless times at gigs, band rehearsals, and in my private teaching where even good guitarists are daunted by the prospect of remembering chord progressions.

In this book, I will provide you with a guide to overcoming that apprehension and teach you to feel confident playing a wide variety of patterns and progressions. Open chord progressions, barre chords, and extended chords will be covered and applied in different genres including pop, blues, rock, jazz, and funk.

I like to think of chord progressions as the foundation on which a good guitar career can be built. Although playing riffs, licks, and solos may seem more attractive, spending time developing a good knowledge of chord progressions will set you apart from the crowd.

The exercises featured in this book suit both electric and acoustic guitar. Whether you are a beginner, intermediate, or an advanced player, you will benefit from this book.

For beginners, I recommend starting at the first chapter and working your way through the book. More advanced players can pick specific exercises and techniques they want to focus on and dedicate their practice time to mastering those.

At the end of the book, I have provided sample workouts. These workouts are divided up into 10, 15, 30, and 60-minute sessions. They will help you create a balanced practice routine that combines the elements covered in each chapter.

The audio for this book is available from **www.fundamental-changes.com/download-audio** so you can hear how I play and phrase each example. The backing tracks for the final chapter are also available.

This book will improve your rhythm guitar prowess, but remember that the most fundamental principle is to always enjoy yourself and have fun playing music.

Once you have finished this book I recommend checking out my book **Beyond Rhythm Guitar** for an in-depth guide to blending rhythm and lead guitar.

Happy Playing!

Simon

Before You Get Started

Throughout this book there are many examples for you to learn and commit to memory. To do so, it is useful to practice them in a variety of ways.

Using a Metronome

When you are developing your chord progression knowledge, always use a metronome.

Begin by playing each example very slowly with the metronome set at 50 beats per minute (bpm) and make sure that every note is clean and audible. Watch your picking hand and make sure you are applying the strict 'down, up' alternate picking pattern required.

When you can play an example correctly three times in a row at 50 bpm, raise the metronome up to 53 bpm. Continue to increase the metronome speed in increments of 3 bpm up to the target speed of 90 bpm.

This form of structured practice means that you will only increase your speed once the lick is played accurately.

I use the Tempo app (made by Frozen Ape) on my phone. I know I will always have my phone with me, so I never have an excuse to practice without a metronome.

Using a Drum Track

Drum tracks make for a more musical approach to practicing than using a click track/metronome. They will also help you to improve your knowledge of how to sync your guitar parts to a drummer and get you used to the feel of playing live from the comfort of your own home.

I recommend checking out the app Drum Loops HD and Drum Loops HD 2 for an extensive selection of drum tracks. Alternatively, you can go to YouTube and search for the required genre and tempo you need.

Using a Backing Track

Backing tracks are the closest thing you can get to playing with other musicians when you're your own. As well as the backing tracks I have provided with this book, I recommend collecting a wide selection for both rhythm, and lead guitar practice.

If you feel like creating your own backing tracks I highly recommend the program Band in a Box. This software gives you access to hundreds of live recorded loops on a wide range of instruments that you can easily instruct to play different chords, tempos and genres.

Playing in a Duo

If you feel nervous playing in a full band, I recommend first playing with just one other musician. It could be another guitarist to help gain confidence and skills, a vocalist to form a group, or a drummer to learn to sync up with a groove.

My main advice when learning to play with other musicians is to try to play with people who are better than you. That way you will be inspired to propel your playing forward instead of becoming complacent with your abilities.

Playing in a Band

The ultimate goal when learning and playing music is to play with other musicians. Whether it is just rehearsing in someone's garage, or playing a gig at a local pub, the joy that comes from being around like-minded musicians is difficult to achieve playing on your own.

If you are struggling to find musicians in your area to play with, ask your guitar teacher, check on internet forums, and start regularly going to open mic nights and gigs in your area.

Chapter One: Common Rhythmic Patterns

Before we look closely at specific chord progressions, I want to show you some common rhythmic patterns that you can use on any chord progression. I have split this chapter into three sections: strumming, arpeggios, and strumming and arpeggios combined.

Start by learning the examples in this chapter and committing your favourites to memory. Then, when you are comfortable with those patterns, create your own with the techniques shown.

Follow the picking directions I have included in each example. Make sure you listen to all the audio examples before playing them.

Strumming

In example 1a, strum an open E minor chord four times using down-strokes.

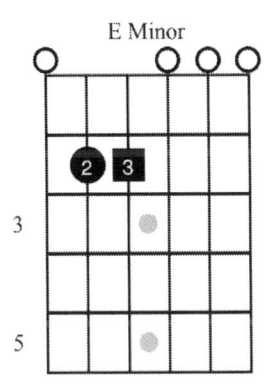

Example 1a

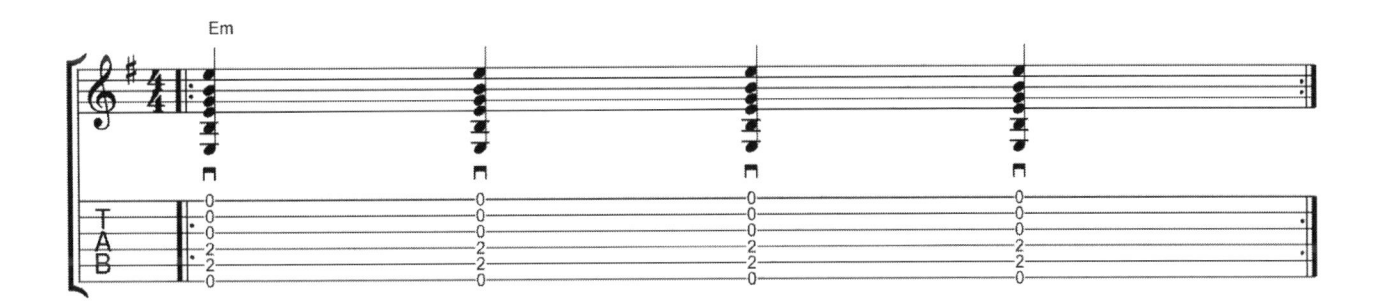

Now add a down-up strum on beat two of the bar before introducing this movement to other beats of the bar.

Example 1b

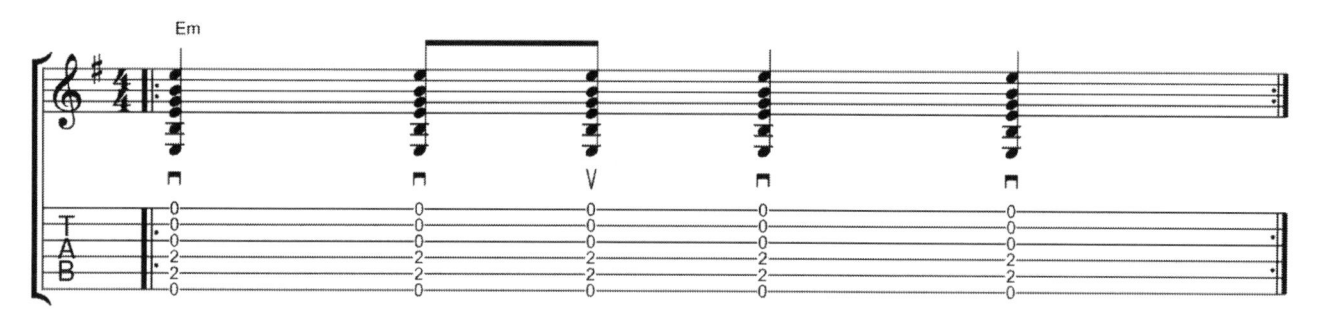

Example 1c

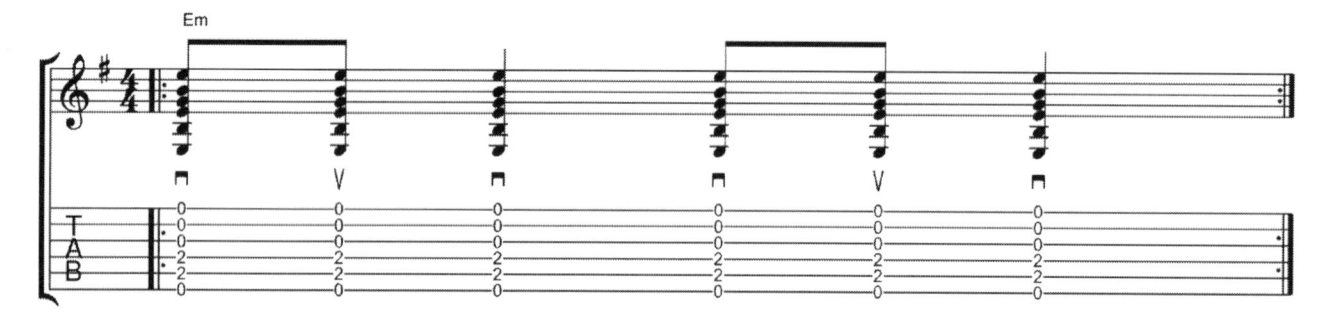

Example 1d

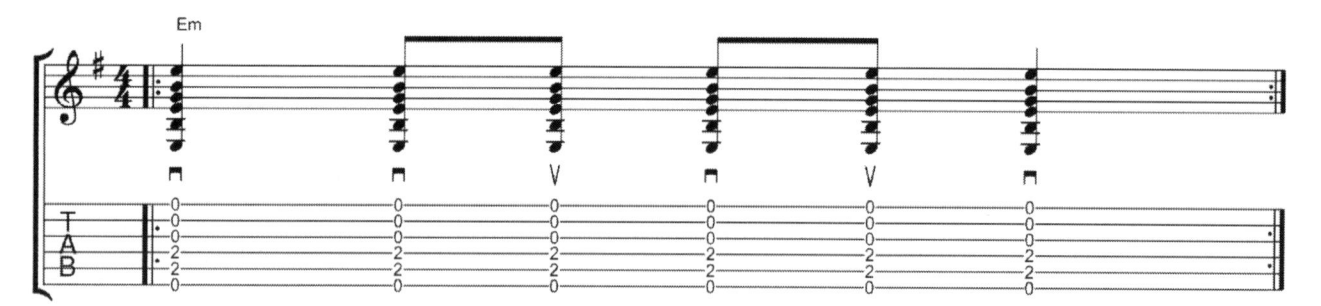

Example 1e introduces a tied or held note. This forces you to use two up-strokes in a row. This pattern is very common in pop guitar playing.

Example 1e

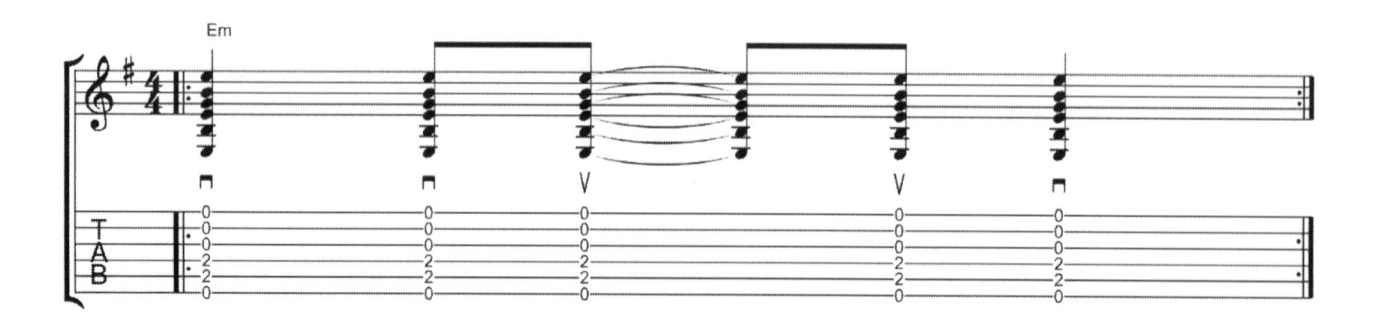

Now the tied note comes earlier on in the bar (at the end of beat one).

Example 1f

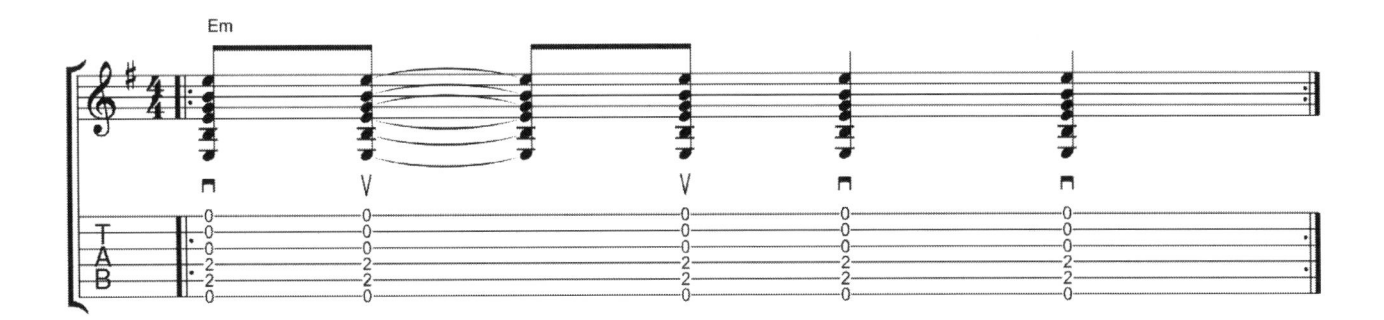

Triplets are an important rhythm found in many genres of music, especially blues. The aim is to play three strums to each beat. I recommend saying a three-syllable word, such as el-e-phant, to keep in time.

You can pick triplets using two different strumming patterns:

Down up down, up down up.

Down up down, down up down.

Play both and see which is more comfortable to you.

Example 1g

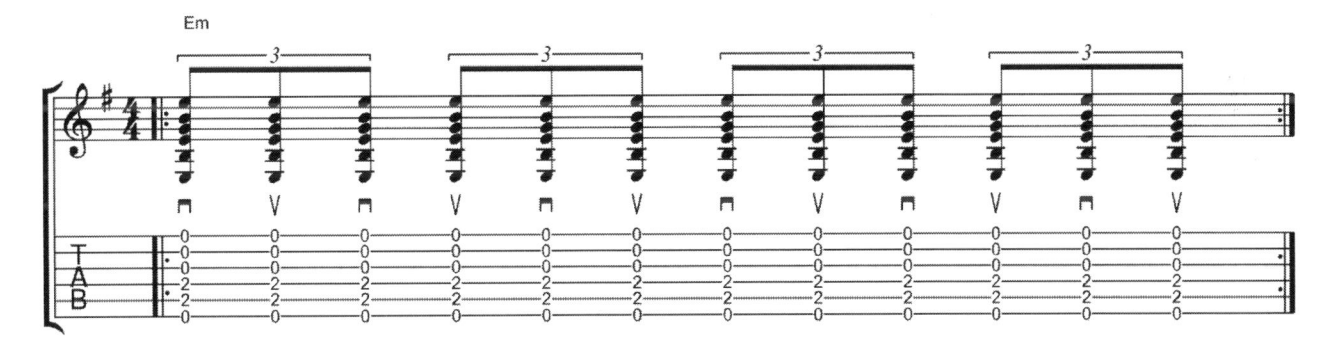

A typical shuffle pattern misses out the middle strum of the triplet.

Example 1h

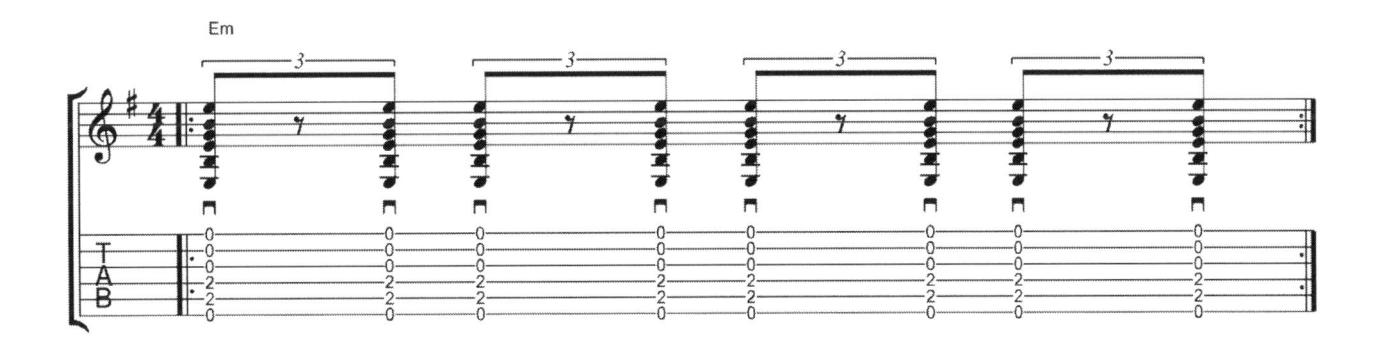

Example 1i shows a standard jazz rhythm. This pattern is great for the jazzier chords featured towards the end of the book.

Example 1i

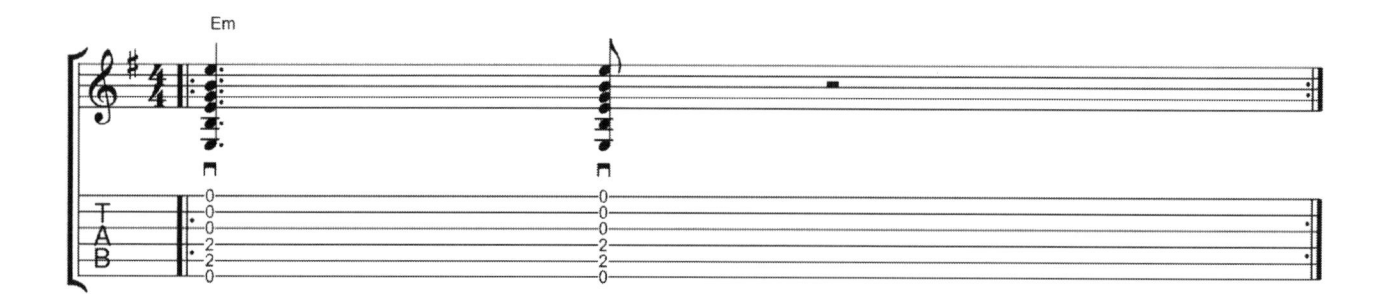

1/16th note patterns are very widespread in funk music. Combining them with 1/4 notes, as seen in example 1j, is a good way to build stamina in your picking hand.

Example 1j

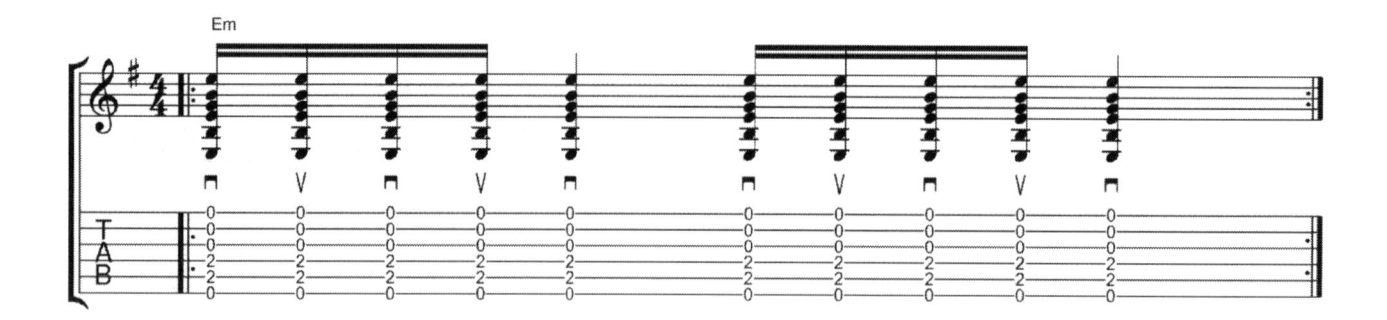

To vary the texture of your strumming patterns, practice alternating between picking the root note of the chord and strumming. This is demonstrated using an E Minor chord in example 1k.

Example 1k

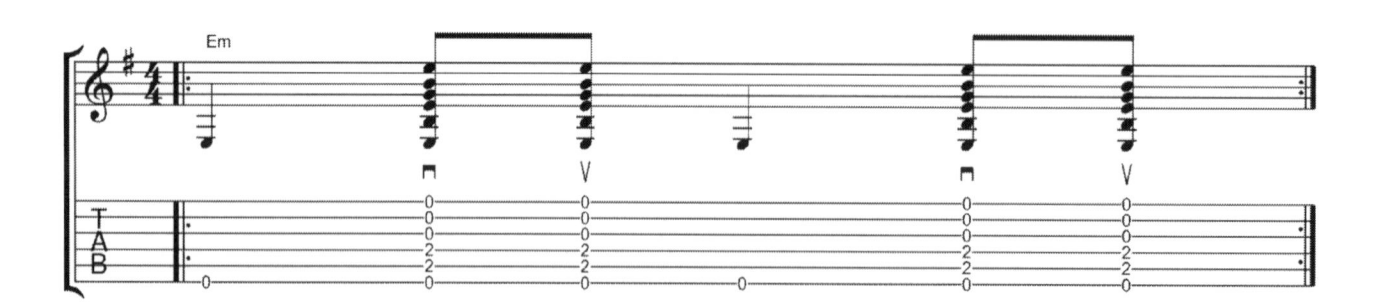

Arpeggios

When learning new arpeggio patterns, it is important to recognise songs that include them. Learning the song Everybody Hurts by REM will show you an example of an arpeggio pattern in a song context.

One way to break up the traditional strumming patterns is to arpeggiate a chord. In example 1l, pick from strings six to one and back again.

Example 1l

Example 1m is an arpeggio pattern that you can apply to any of the chord sequences featured throughout this book.

Example 1m

Example 1n demonstrates an arpeggio pattern frequently seen in pop and rock songs.

Example 1n

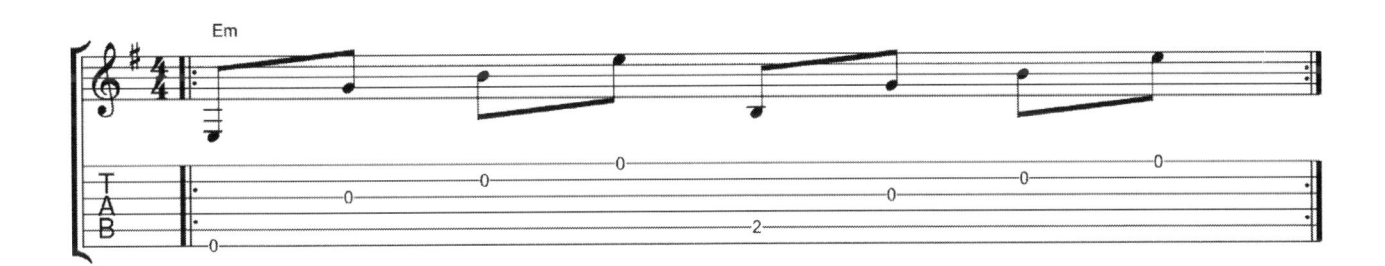

Example 1o

Example 1p

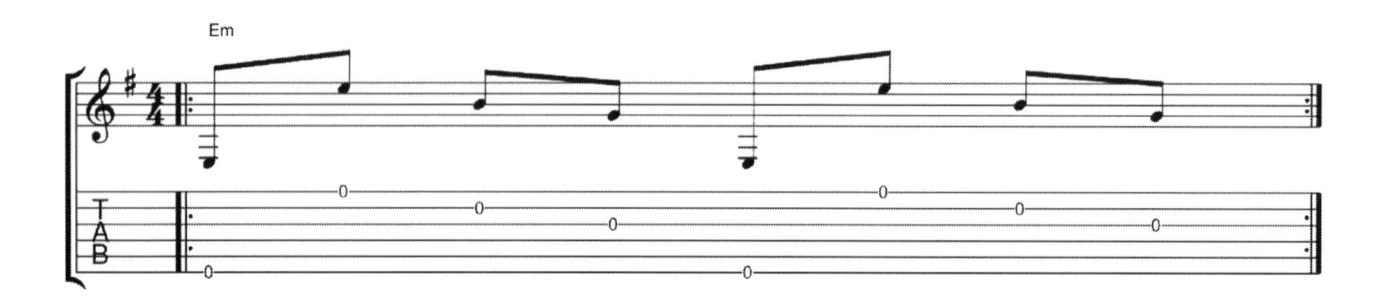

The final arpeggio pattern uses triplets and will require a bit more practice. Use whatever picking pattern you find comfortable.

Example 1q

Combining Strums and Arpeggios

These examples combine strums and mini arpeggios to create slightly more sophisticated rhythm patterns.

Example 1r

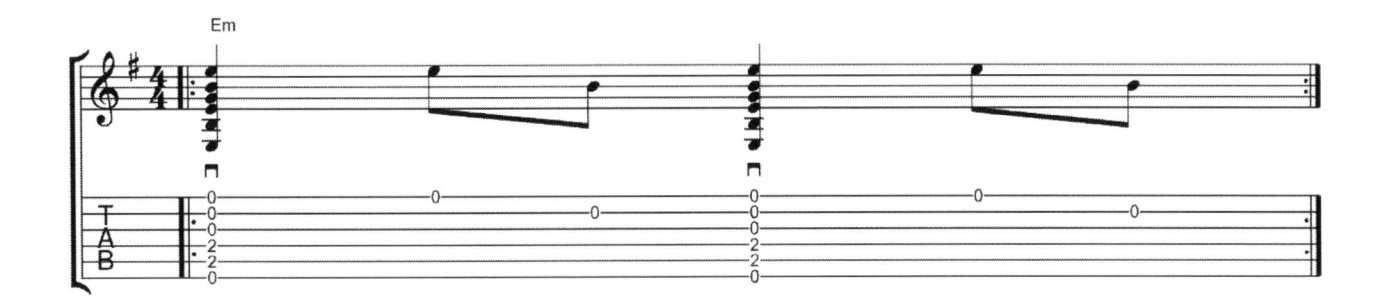

Example 1s

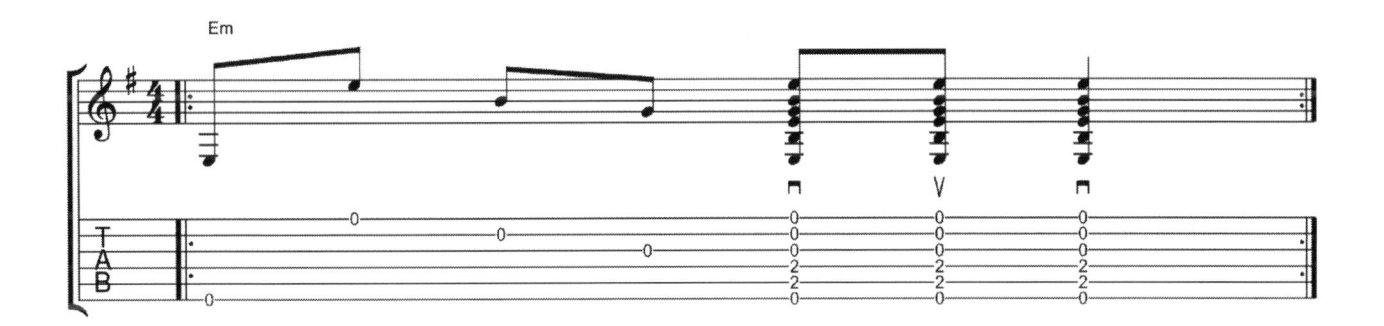

Example 1t

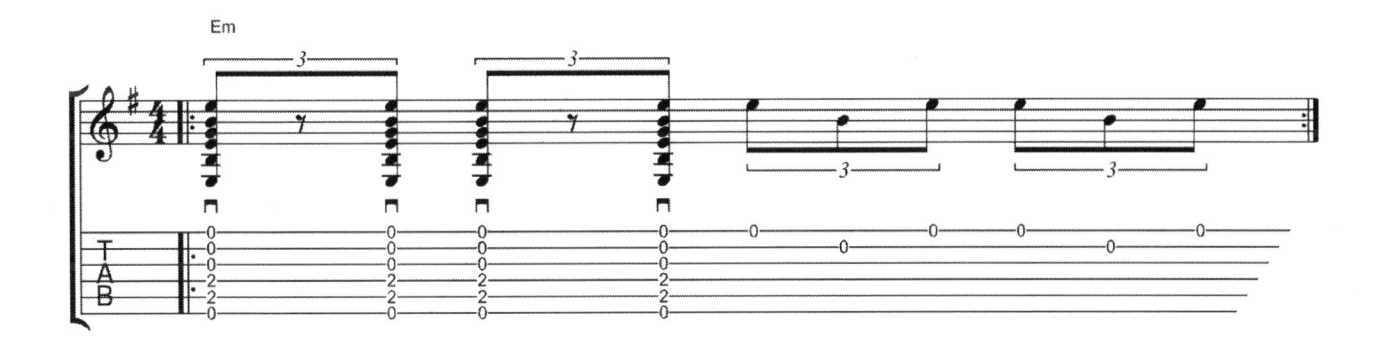

Now that you have completed the chapter, go through the following checklist before moving on. Remember, there is no race to finish this book, it is far better that you master each chapter than rush through without memorising any of it.

Bring these patterns into your playing as quickly as possible by using them on songs you already know.

Checklist

Can you comfortably play strumming patterns, arpeggio patterns, and combine the two?

Have you committed at least five of the examples of this chapter to memory?

Chapter Two – Open Chords Part 1

An 'open' chord is simply one that contains one or more open strings. They have a distinctive ringing quality and are used across multiple genres including pop, folk, rock, and country.

Although studying open chords may seem basic, the concepts in this chapter are the building blocks for all future chapters. By studying how each example is created you will be able to apply the ideas into your own playing and compositions, which is the aim of this entire book!

I recommend that you listen to the audio examples before playing through the ideas featured in this chapter. Take your time to learn and digest all the material: there is no rush!

If you are unfamiliar with open chord shapes, or would like a reminder, I recommend Joseph Alexander's book **The First 100 Chords for Guitar**.

Remember that even though open chords are restricted by their inclusion of an open string, you can move them into any key by using a capo.

Check out this video lesson I created to learn more about using a capo.

www.fundamental-changes.com/creative-capo-chords

In example 2a play the A, D, and E with a light, soft strum and concentrate on getting the movement between the chords as smooth as possible.

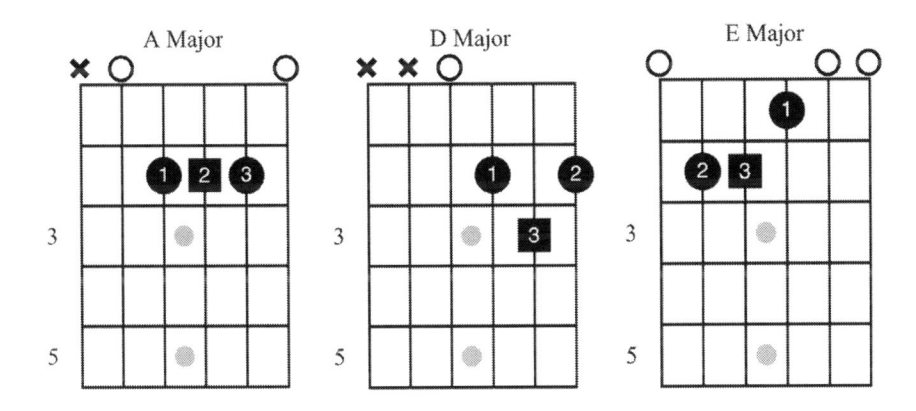

Example 2a

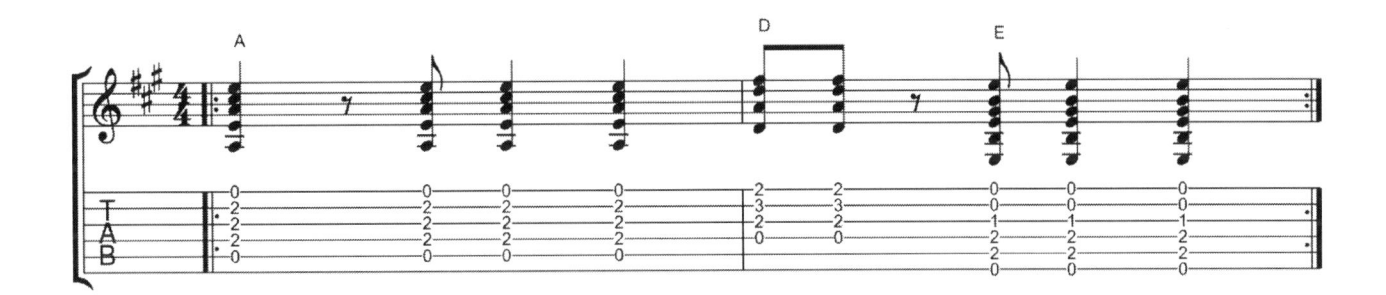

When composing a rhythm guitar part for a track, I aim to build up to a chorus. I often favour using arpeggio patterns, such as that in example 2b, for the verses and a strumming pattern for the chorus. This means that your guitar part is not static throughout a song, even if it only uses three chords.

Some songs that can be played using the chords of A, D, and E (not necessarily in that order) include Wild Thing by The Troggs, Chasing Cars by Snow Patrol, and I Have a Dream by Abba.

Example 2b

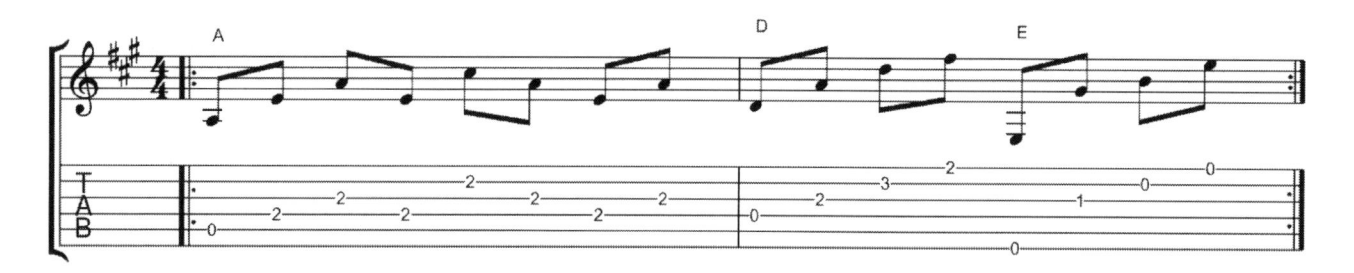

Next, we will look an extremely common pop chord progression in the key of G Major. Although it may look more complicated than the previous examples, it uses the same strumming pattern in all four bars.

The new chord shapes are shown in diagram form.

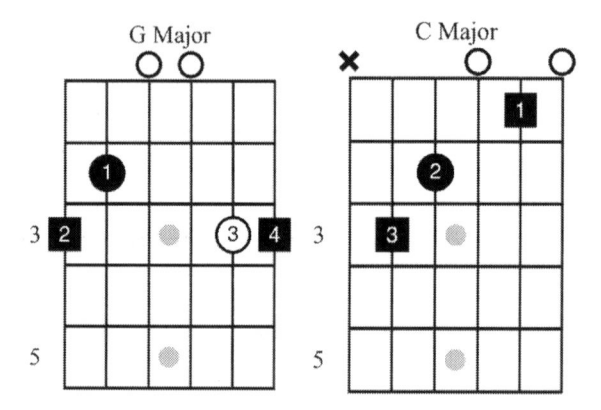

Example 2c

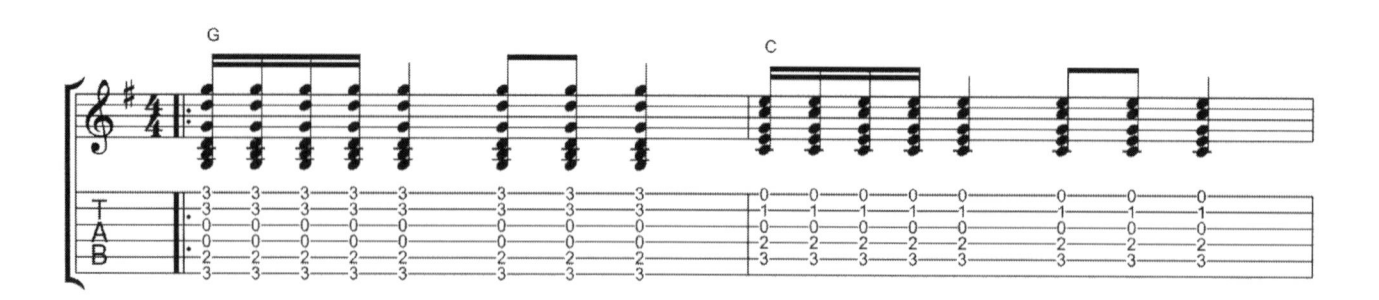

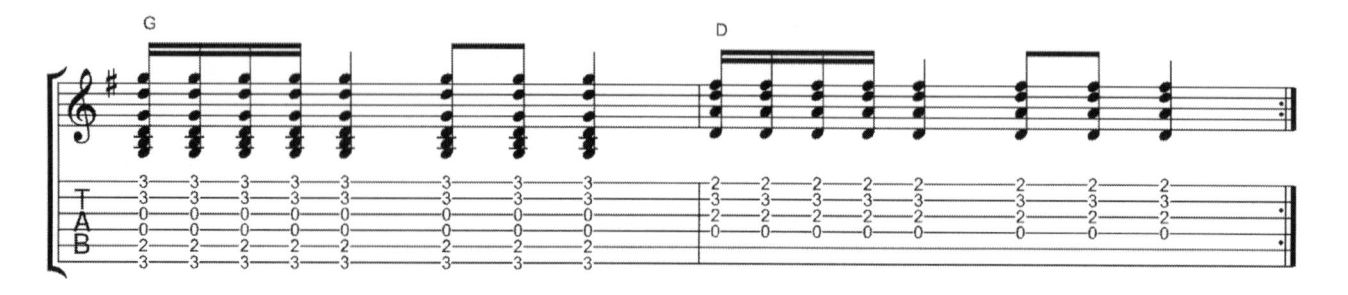

A useful way to break up the sound of strumming patterns is to pick the root note of the chord and then play the G, B, and E strings altogether. An excellent example of a song that uses this technique is Extreme's More Than Words.

Example 2d

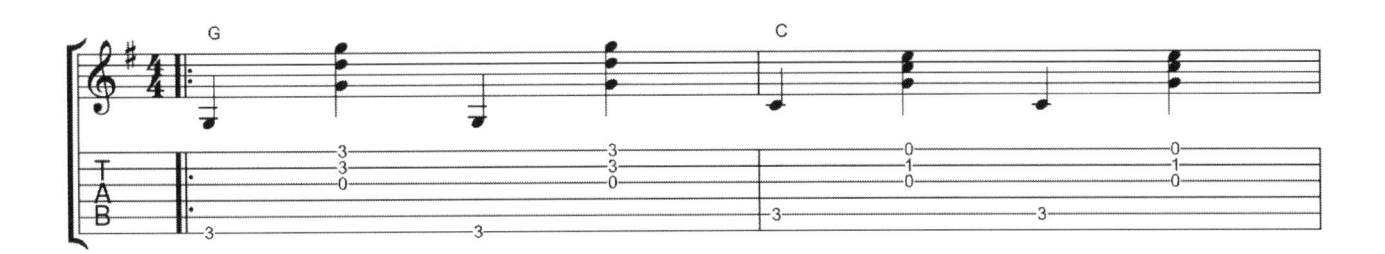

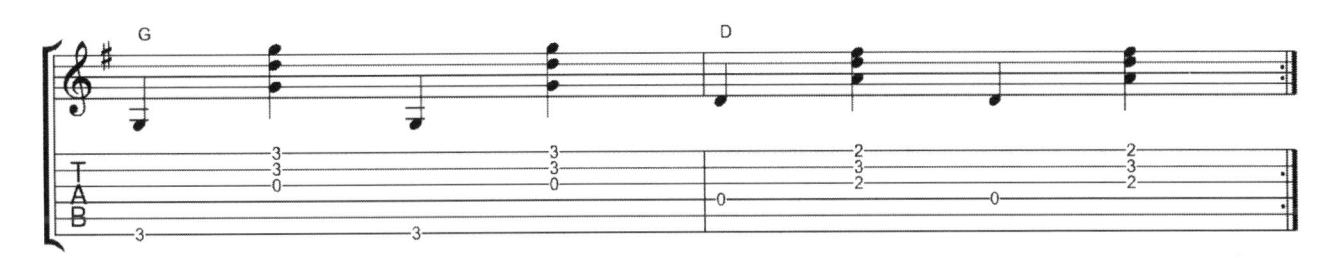

Now add in an F Major chord. There are many ways to play an F on the guitar, but they normally involve using a barre shape. A barre shape is where you lie your first finger across multiple strings at once. This may feel uncomfortable at first, but stick with it and the rewards far outweigh the effort.

If you want more information on how to play barre chords, check out Joseph Alexander's book **Beginner Guitar Lessons: The Essential Guide**.

Example 2e shows how to play a bar of arpeggios followed by a bar of strumming using the chord progression of C, F, and G.

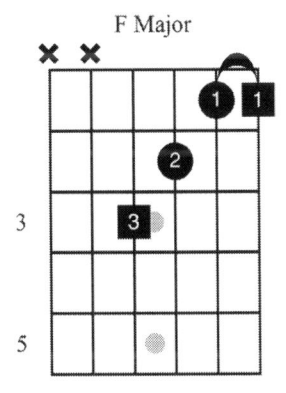

Example 2e

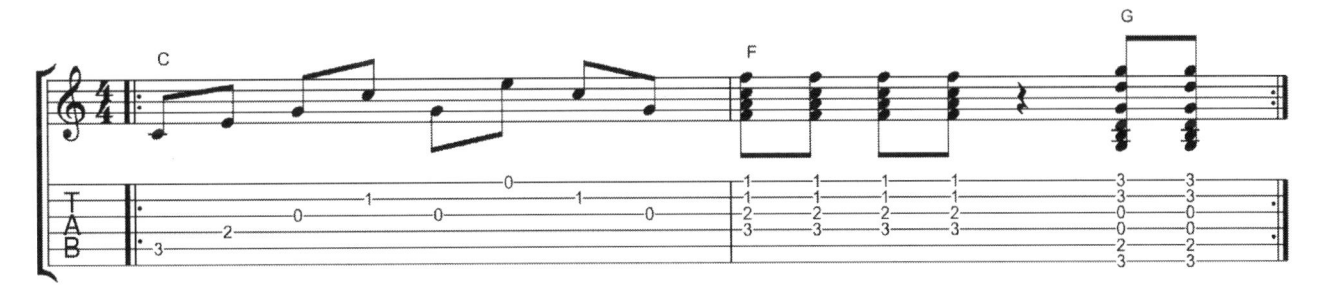

Songs that can be played using the chords of C, F, and G include All the Small Things by Blink 182 and Hound Dog by Elvis Presley.

Example 2f

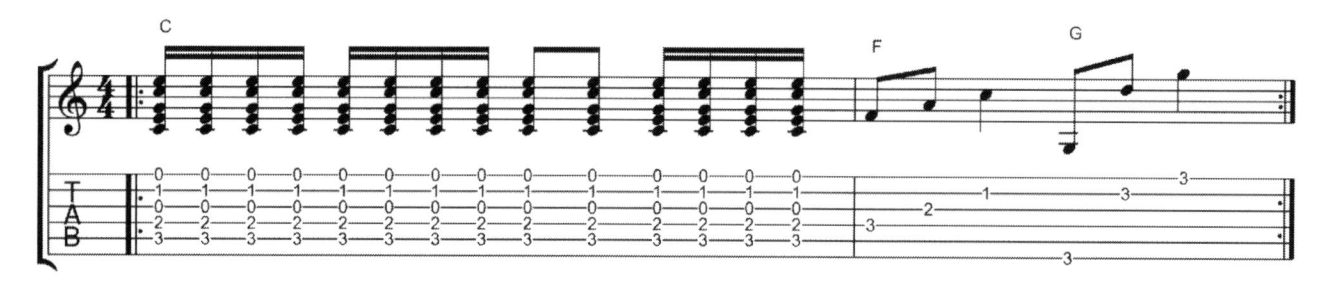

Another 'must learn' chord progression uses the chords of D, G, and A. This can be heard in in Breakfast at Tiffany's by Deep Blue Something.

Example 2g

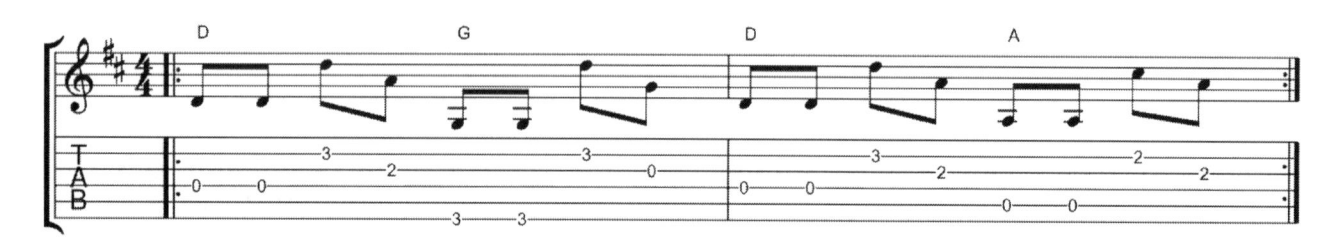

In example 2h, I created an off-beat pattern commonly used in reggae and ska music.

Example 2h

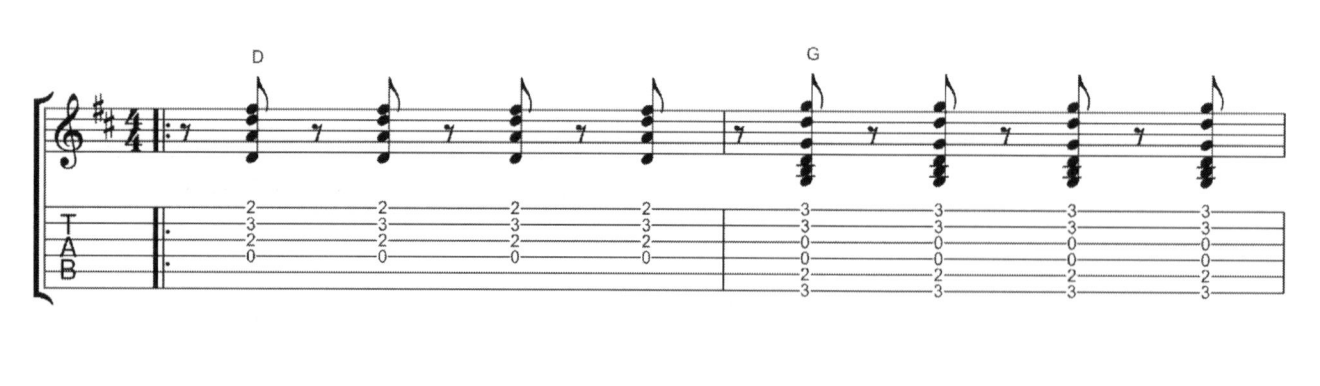

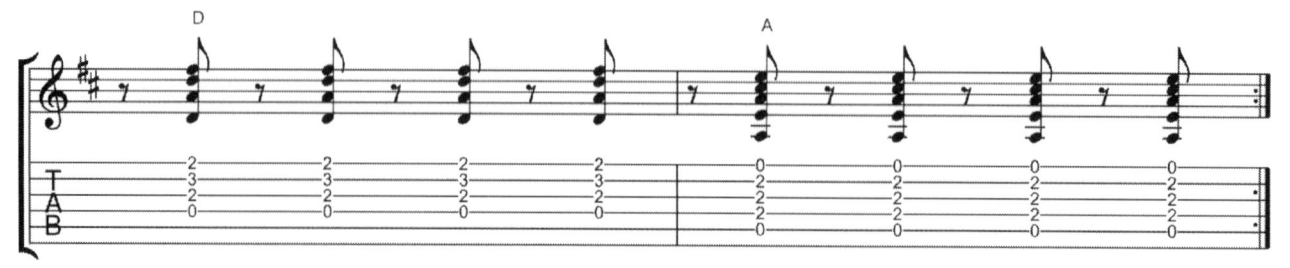

By adding in the chord of A minor (shown in the neck diagram), another pop-rock chord progression can be created using the chords of G, E Minor, A Minor, and D.

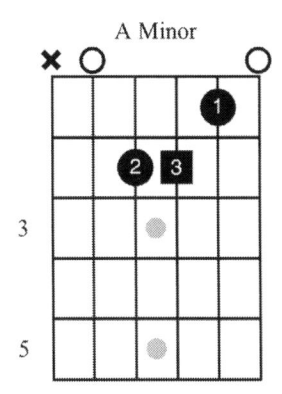

Example 2i

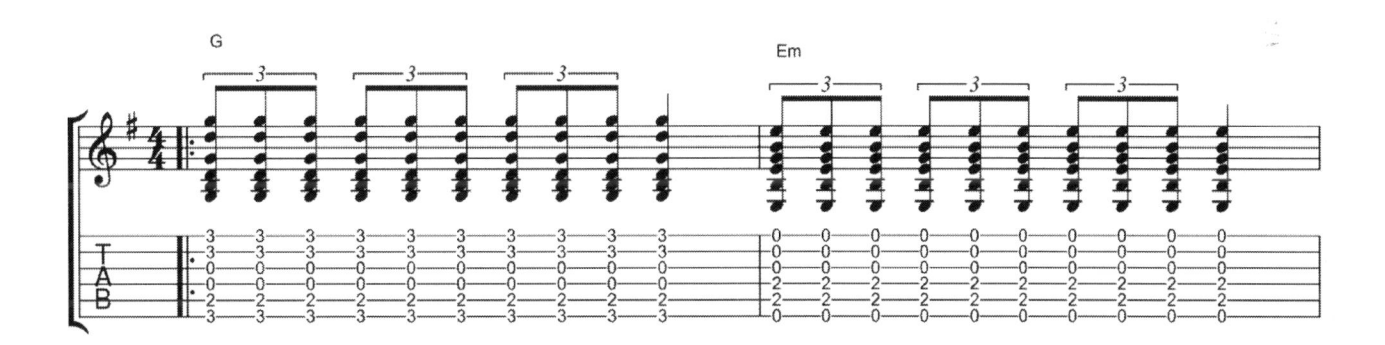

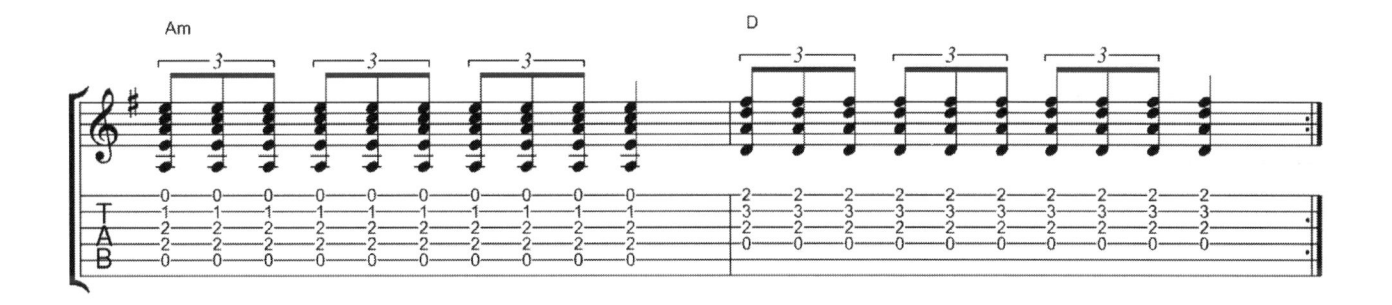

Now alternate between strumming and picking the high E and B strings.

Example 2j

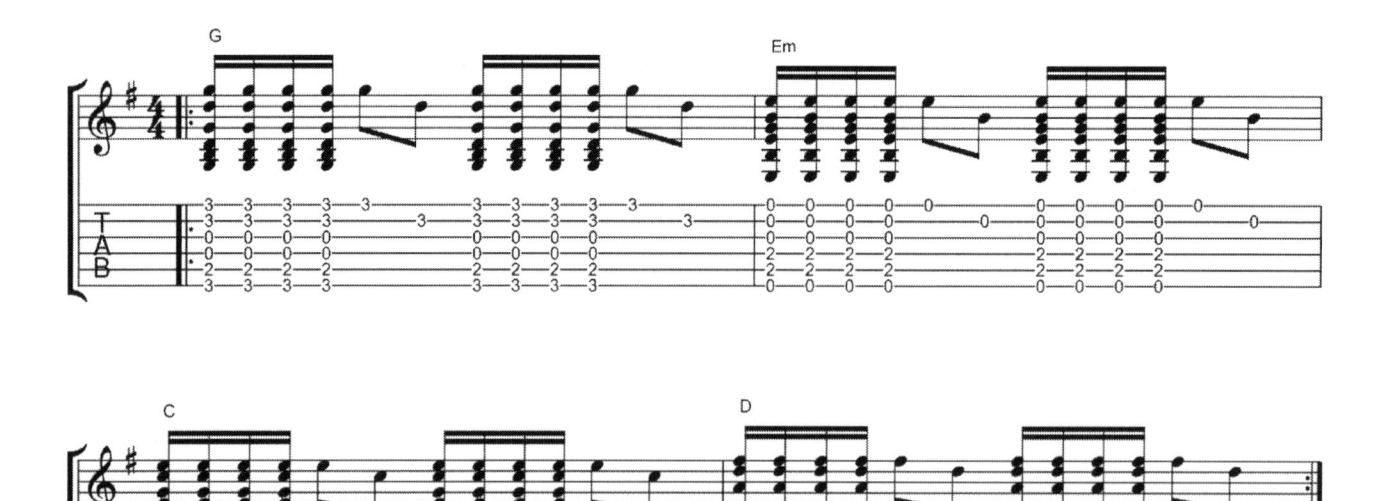

Example 2k shows a common picking pattern used in pop/folk songs. Pick the root note of each chord and then strum the rest of the chord minus the root note.

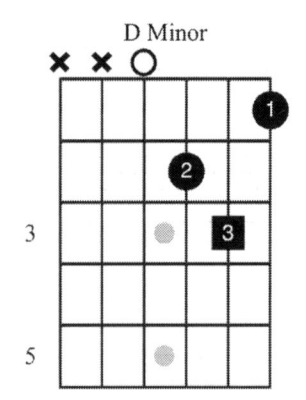

D Minor

Example 2k

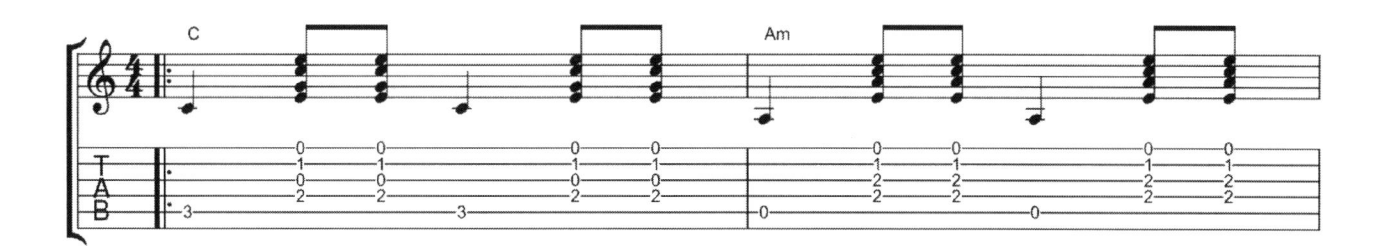

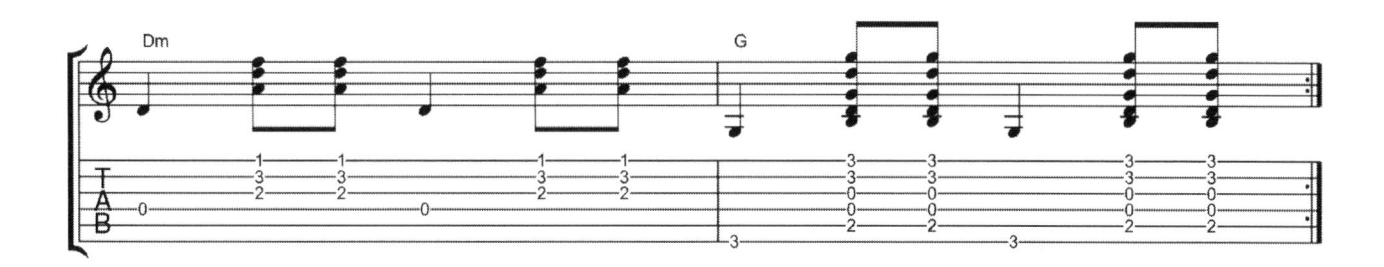

Next, play this tied rhythmic pattern on the same chord progression.

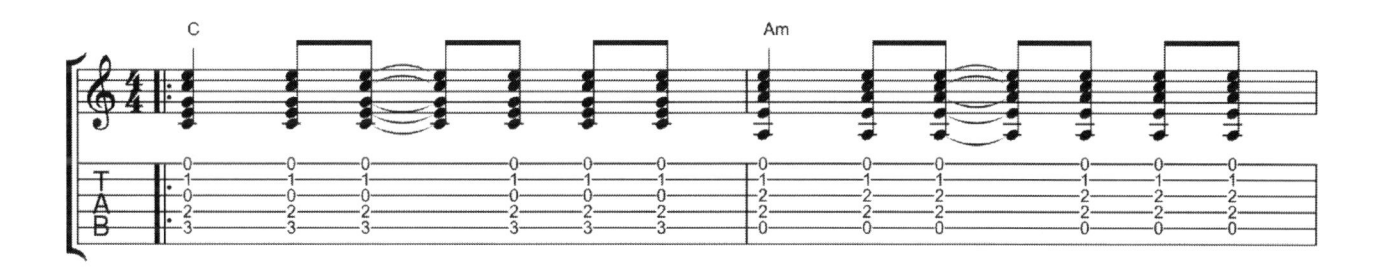

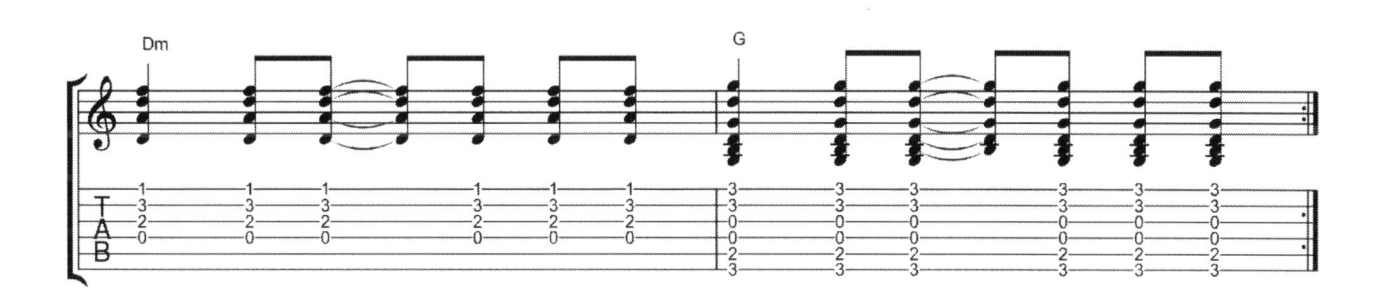

Example 2l

The first thing I get my students to do after they become proficient strummers, is to pick through each chord using arpeggios. This helps you break away from playing constant strumming patterns, and means that each chord has to be fretted perfectly, otherwise there may be an unwanted muted string or buzzy fret.

Arpeggiate a chord whenever you learn a new shape. Check that each fret is ringing out as it should be, and if it isn't, make sure you take the time to correct it. Remember, it is far easier to learn something correctly in the first place than it is to have to re-learn something you thought you already knew.

Example 2m

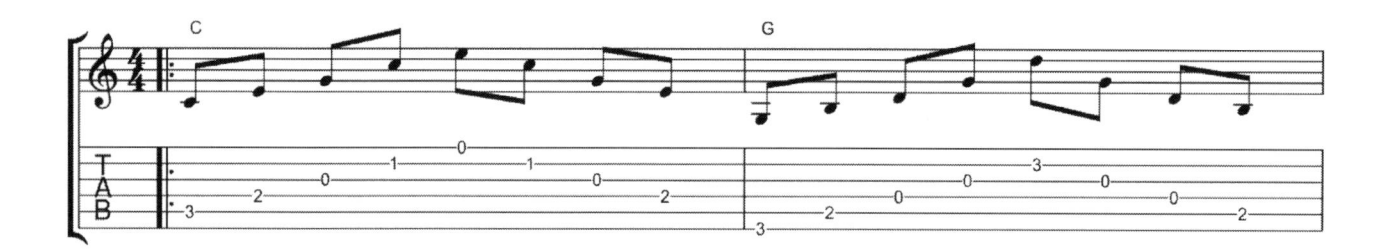

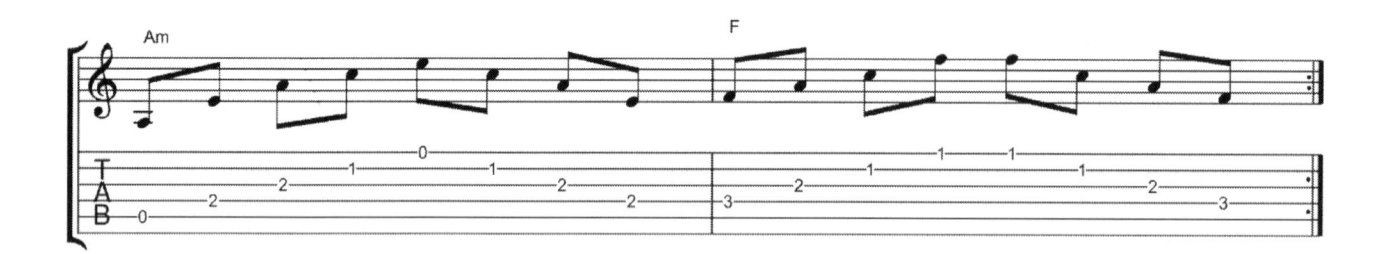

Rests between strums can create a more syncopated strumming pattern.

Example 2n

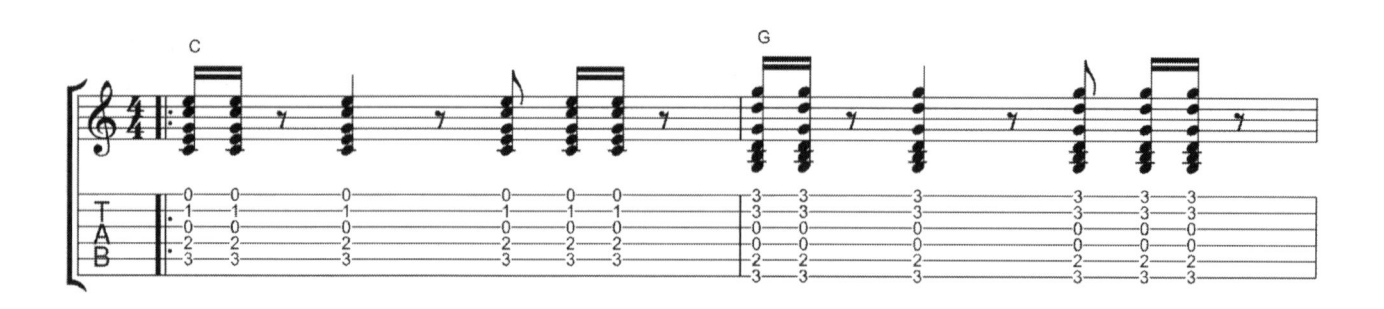

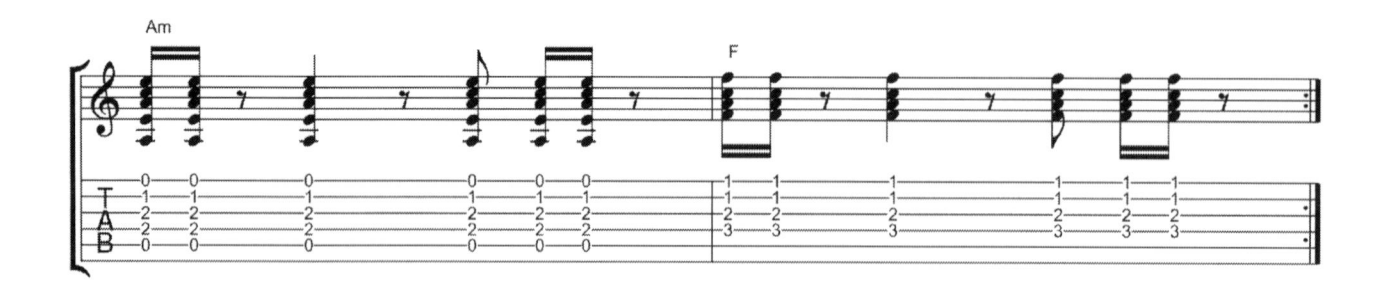

Example 2o is perhaps the most common chord progression in pop music. After you have learnt the chord sequence, create your own rhythmic pattern using any of the examples seen in Chapter One.

Example 2o

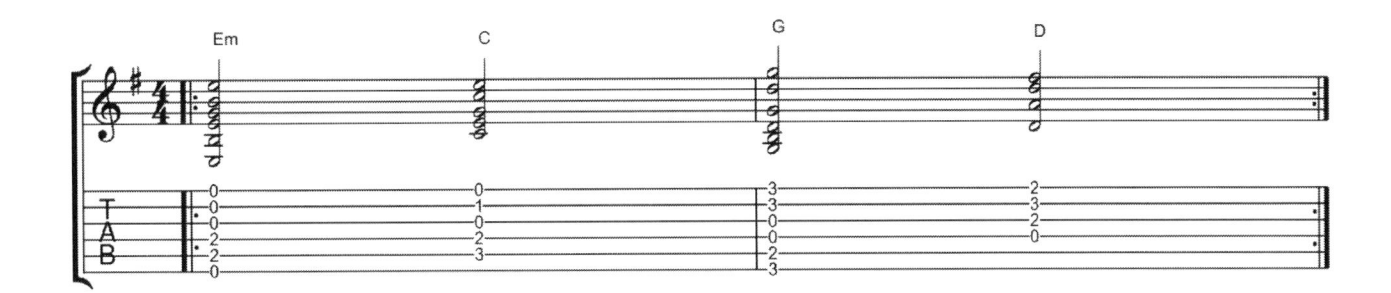

Muted strums add a percussive feel to your playing. Before you play them in a chord sequence, get used to strumming them on their own. Lay your fretting hand down very gently over the strings and strum. If you can hear anything but a deadened mute, you are pushing down too hard.

Listen to the attached audio and copy how I play this example.

Example 2p

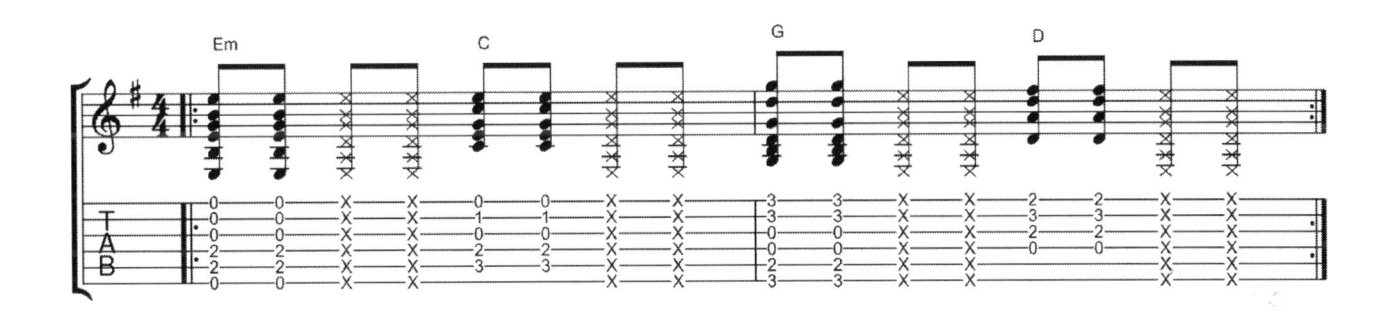

Combine picking root notes with 1/16th note strums for a sparse yet exciting rhythm pattern.

Example 2q

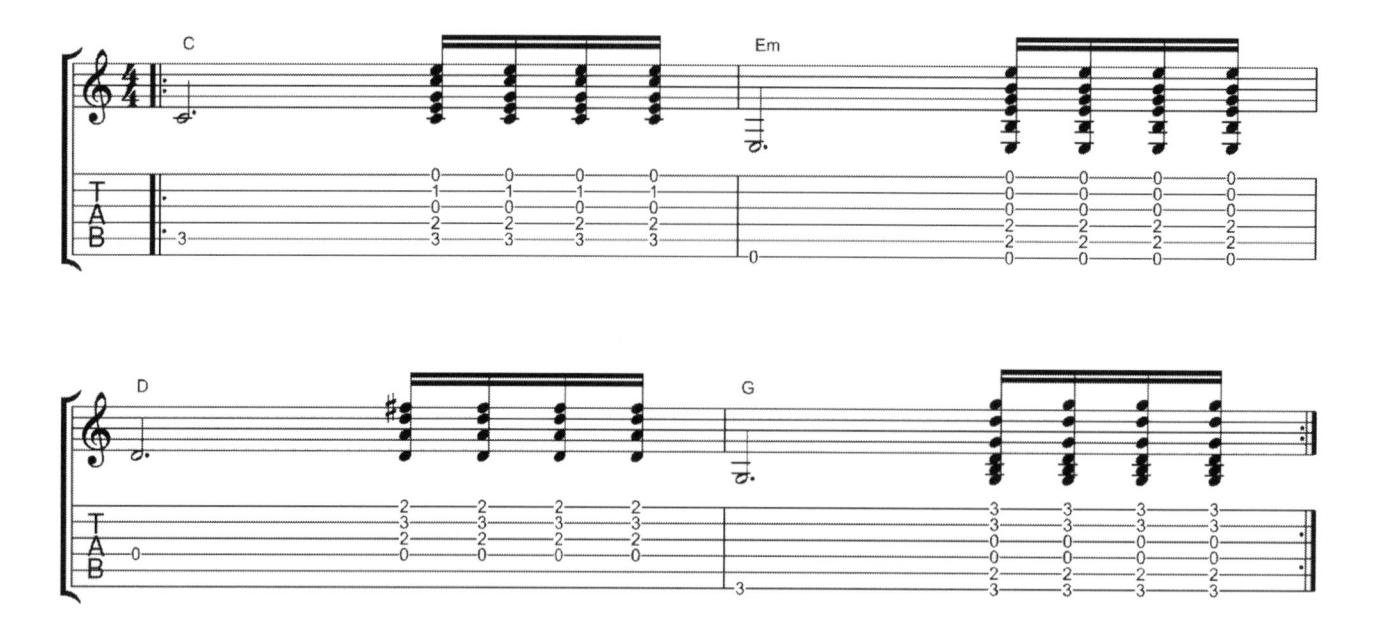

Learn this chord progression in the key of C Major, and then apply the patterns you learnt in Chapter One. By this stage you should have a handful of favourite strumming and picking patterns you can play anytime. If not, don't panic! Just go back through Chapter One and pick out your favourites.

Example 2r

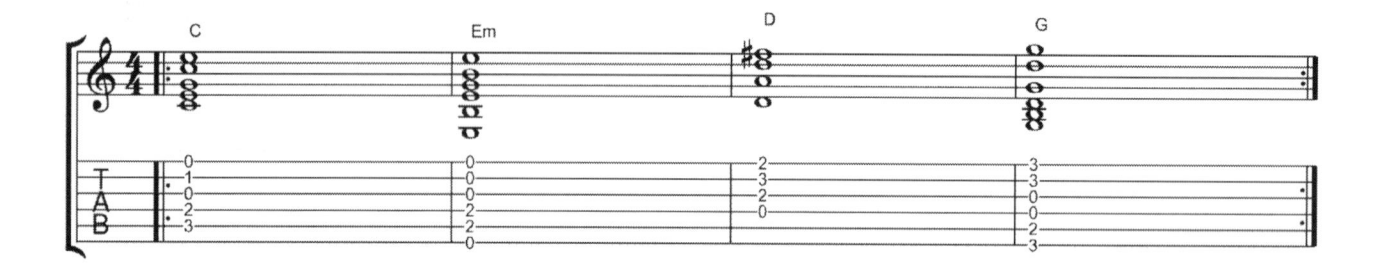

Your ear is the most valuable thing you possess as a musician and transcribing (figuring out music and writing it down) is the best skill you can have. Whenever you hear something you like, transcribe it, even if it is one bar or a couple of notes. In time, transcribing will become easier and is far more rewarding than just reading a tab and then forgetting it.

Example 2s is a chord progression I've been playing since I heard it in a pop song and transcribed it when I was 14.

Example 2s

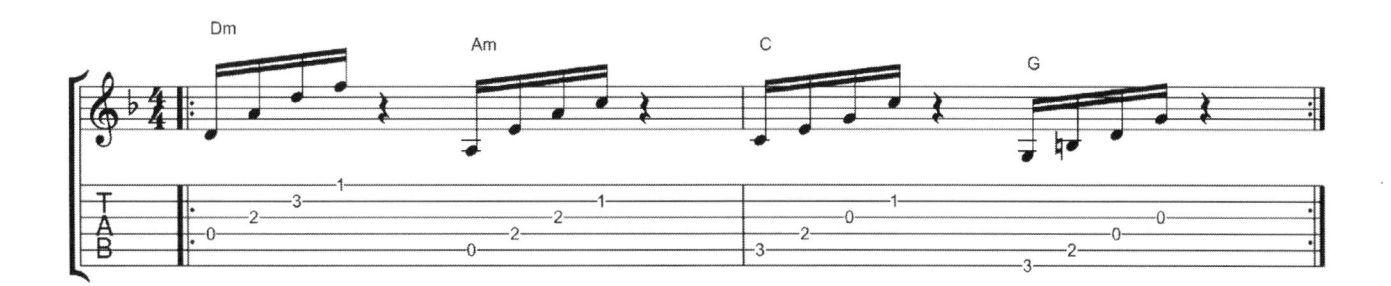

Another skill I want to introduce is the art of recognising a chord by sight as well as by sound. See if you can name the chords in bar two before playing them.

Answers on the final page!

Example 2t

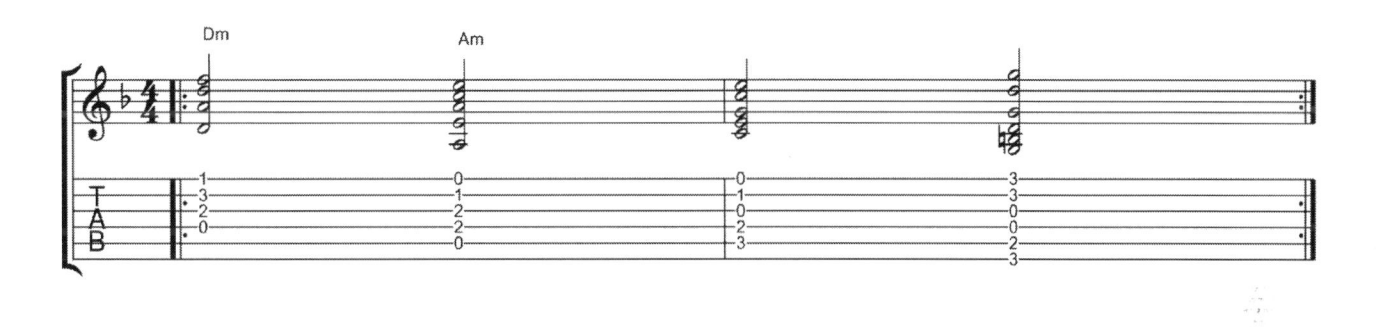

Example 2u uses the jazz rhythm first seen in Chapter One. Sometimes all you need for a jam is a two-chord sequence.

Example 2u

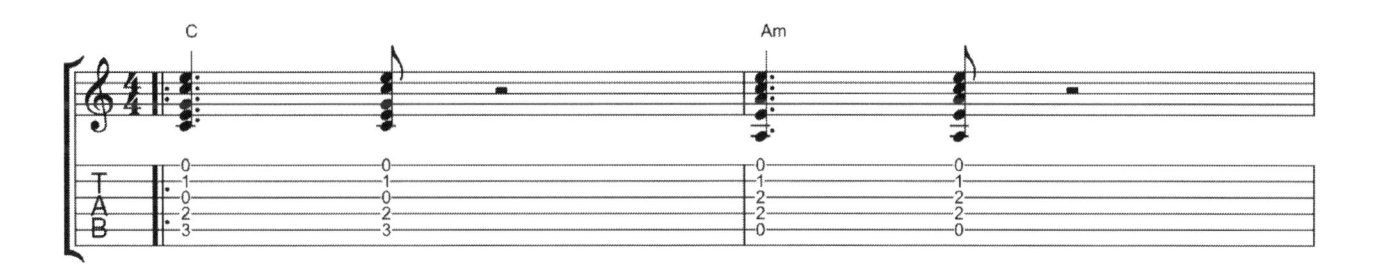

How many different strumming and picking patterns can you apply to example 2v from memory?

Example 2v

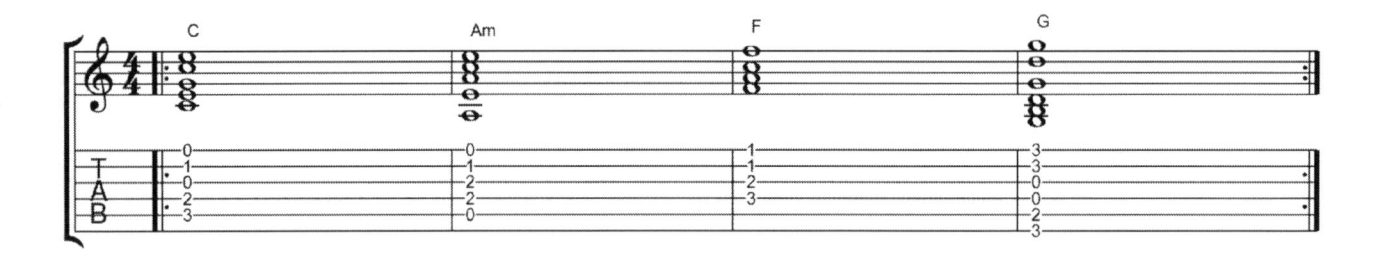

Based on the main chord progression in Sweet Home Alabama by Lynyrd Skynyrd, example 2w is a great jam sequence.

Example 2w

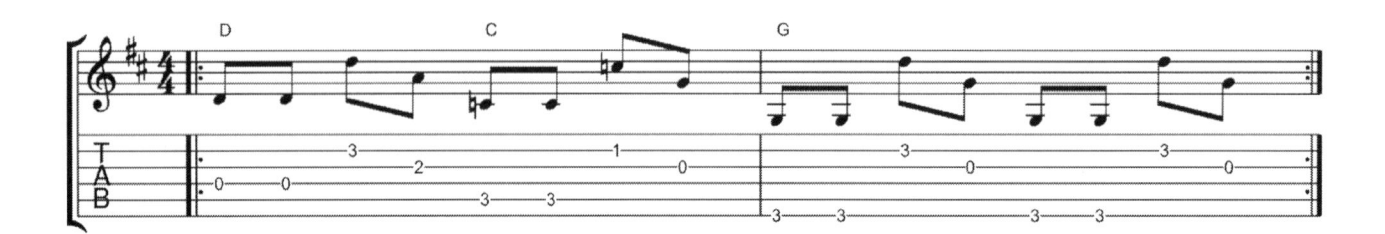

Finally, take example 2x and create your own rhythm pattern for it. Then record yourself playing it and add a second rhythm guitar part over the top. This will prepare you for playing in a band where there are two guitarists playing the same chords.

Example 2x

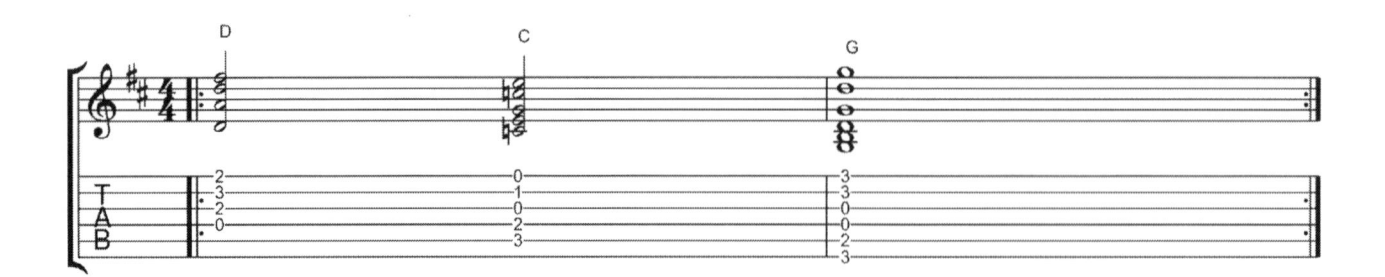

I think that being a proficient open chord player is the most crucial element to rhythm guitar playing. Everything can be built on this foundation, so avoid any temptation to skip on to the following chapters too quickly.

Building a good repertoire of songs is as important as learning great technique and chord progressions. I have put together a few of my favourite songs below. Remember, you may need a capo to play some of these songs in the original key.

Open Chord Songs to Learn

- Bob Marley – Three Little Birds
- The Beatles – Love Me Do
- Noah and The Whale – 5 Years' Time
- Blondie – The Tide is High
- Van Morrison – Brown Eyed Girl
- Lynyrd Skynyrd – Sweet Home Alabama
- Green Day – Time of Your Life
- Tom Petty – Free Fallin'
- Enrique Inglesias – Hero
- Ed Sheeran – Thinking Out Loud

Chapter Three – Open Blues Chords

Now that you have mastered rhythmic patterns and some essential open chord sequences, it is time to get bluesy. Throughout my teaching career, I have found that the twelve-bar blues progression is the most useful structure to teach and get students to jam along to. Take your time working through this chapter as it will prove invaluable at your next jam night.

In this chapter, you will learn how to:

- Play dominant 7th open chord voicings.
- Play twelve-bar blues progressions in the keys of A, E, and G.
- Play common rhythms and techniques used in these patterns.
- Play pop chord progressions that feature dominant 7th chords.

The Twelve-Bar Blues

When I get a group of students together for a jam session, there are always nerves present. The first thing I get people to do is to jam a twelve-bar blues sequence.

For more information on the construction of a twelve-bar blues check out Joseph Alexander's book **The Complete Guide to Playing Blues Guitar Part One: Rhythm Guitar.**

Example 3a demonstrates a twelve-bar blues in the key of A using the chords of A7, D7, and E7. Memorising the sequence of chords is the most important thing, and don't worry that it is only one strum per bar for now. Jam along with the audio example until you can play this progression by heart.

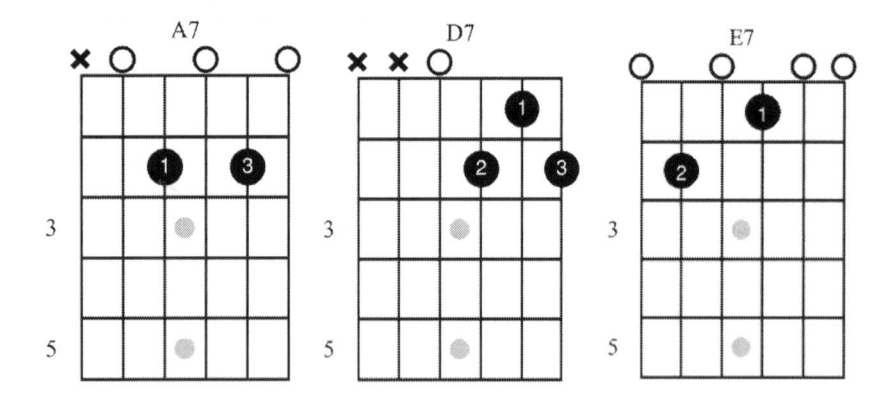

Example 3a

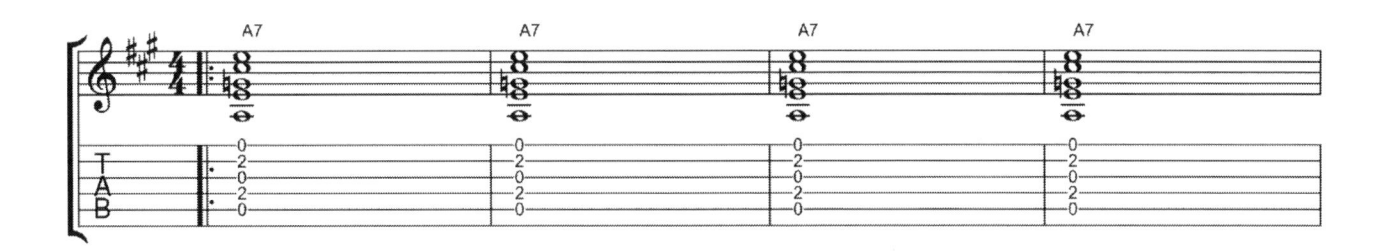

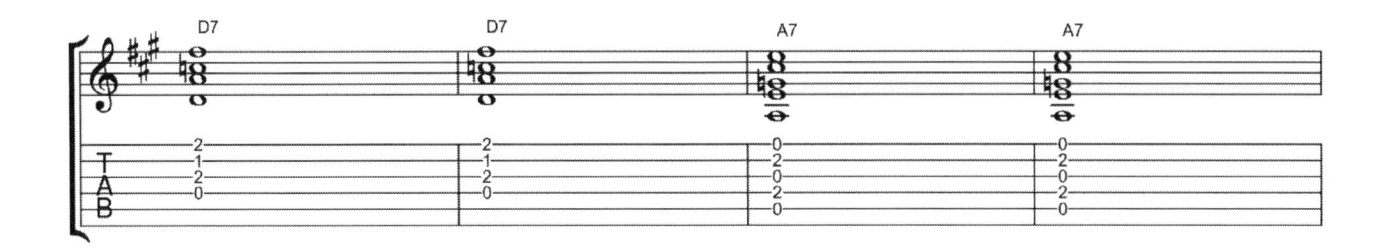

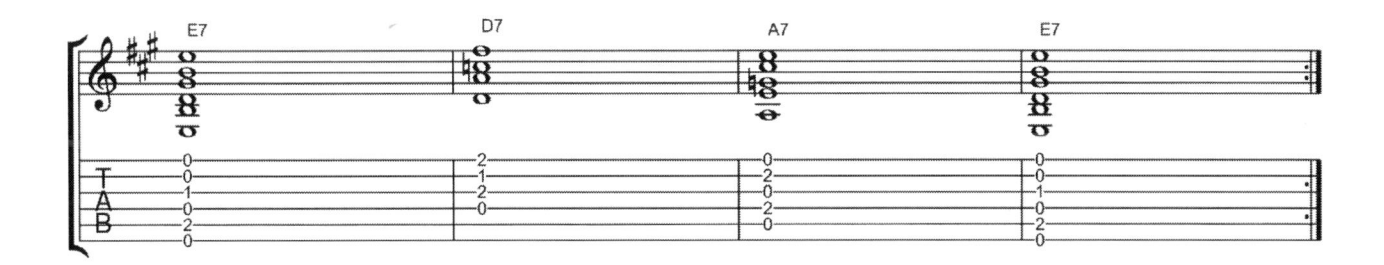

Next, add this common jazz-blues rhythm to the twelve-bar chord sequence.

Example 3b

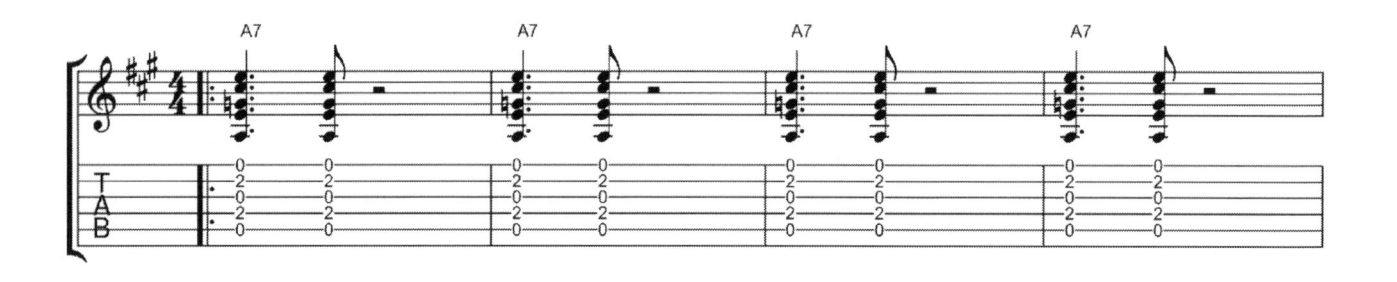

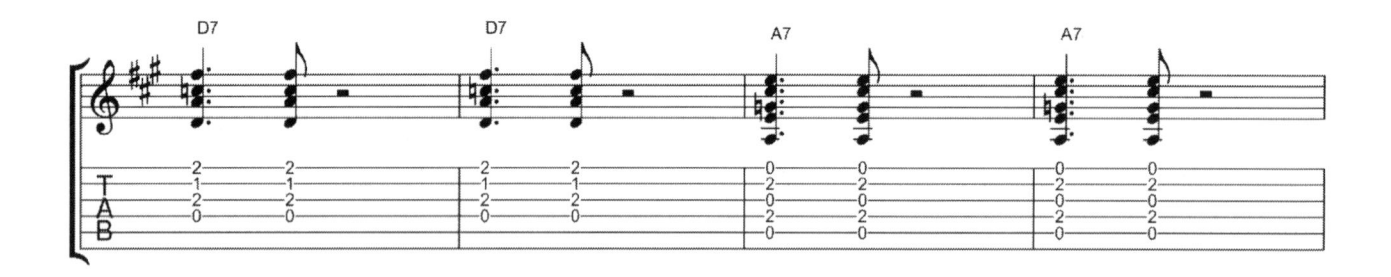

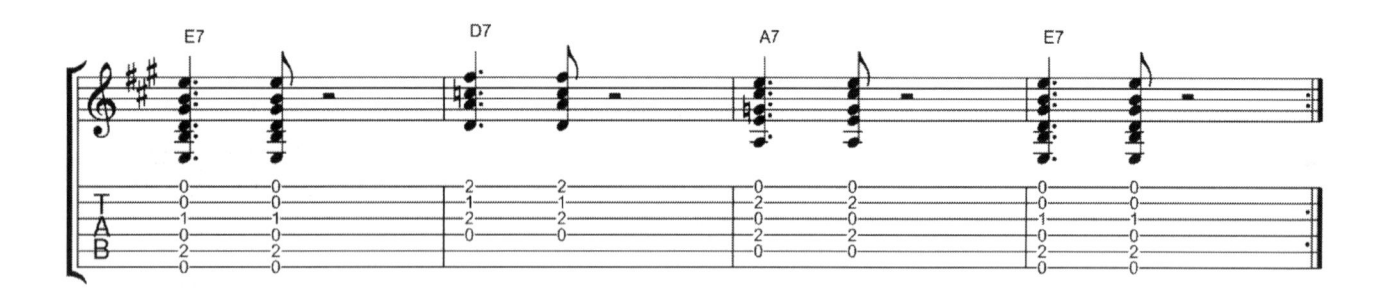

Triplets are essential in blues music. Example 3c is an arpeggio pattern based around continuous triplets. I recommend starting this one very slowly, at around 50 bpm, before speeding it up to the required speed.

Example 3c

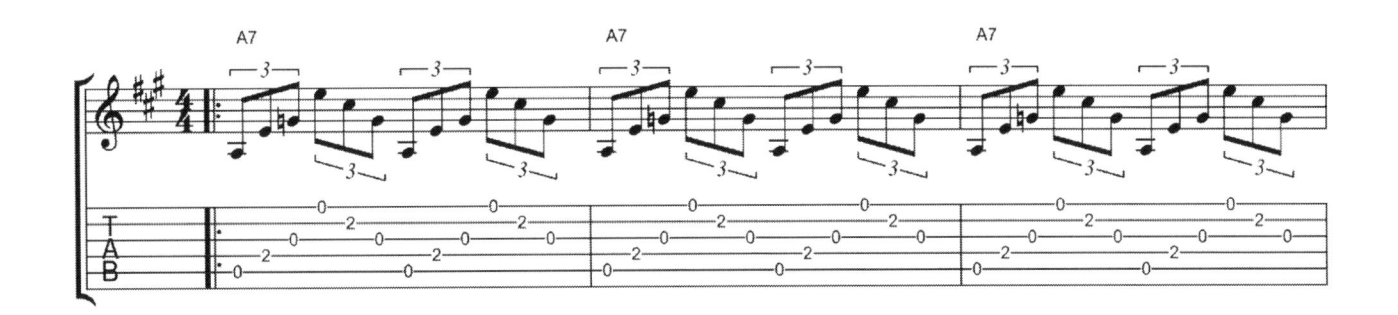

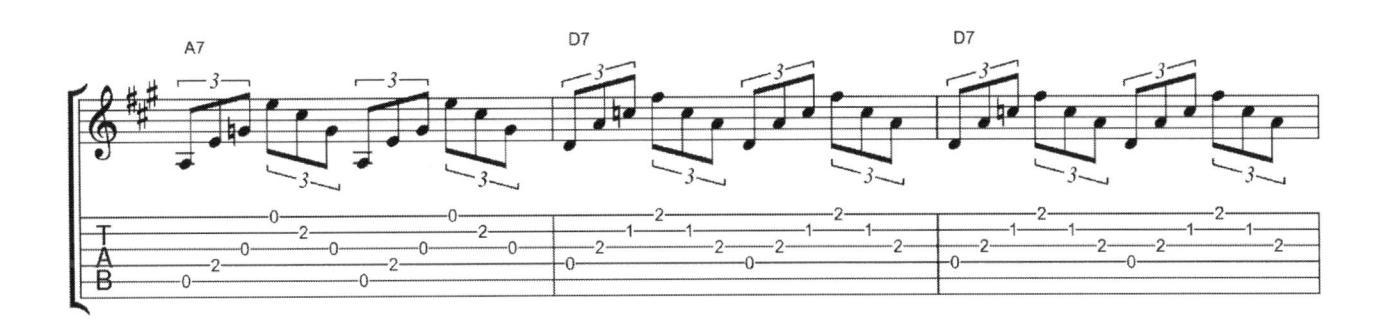

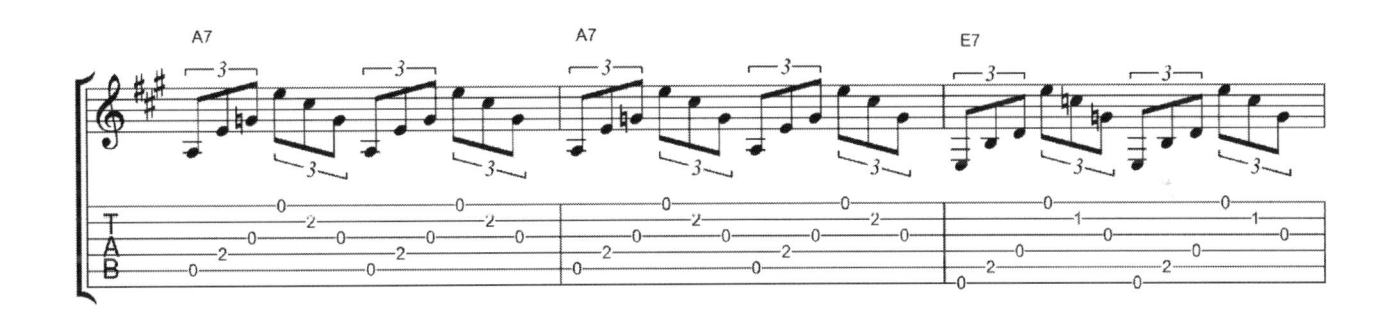

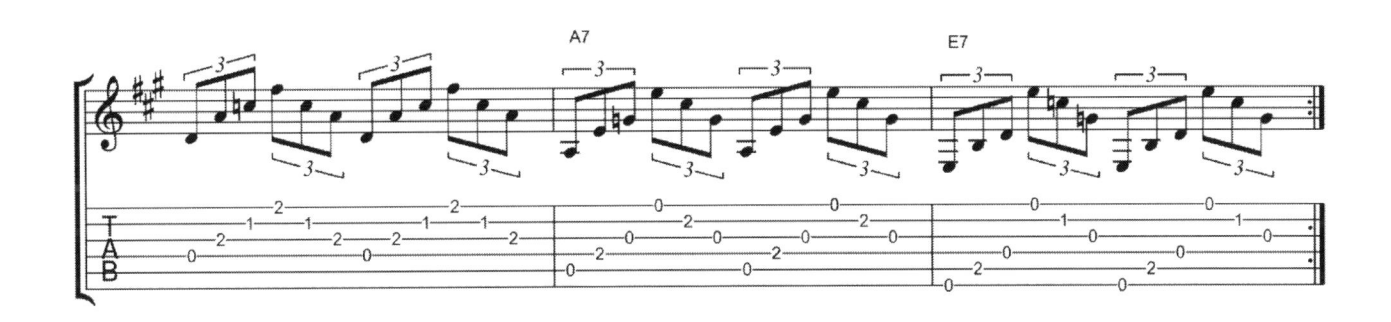

Now that you have mastered the twelve-bar blues in A, check it out in the key of E. You'll need the chord of B7 shown in the neck diagram.

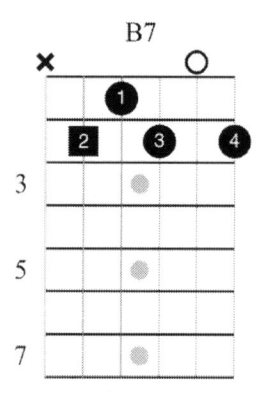

Example 3d

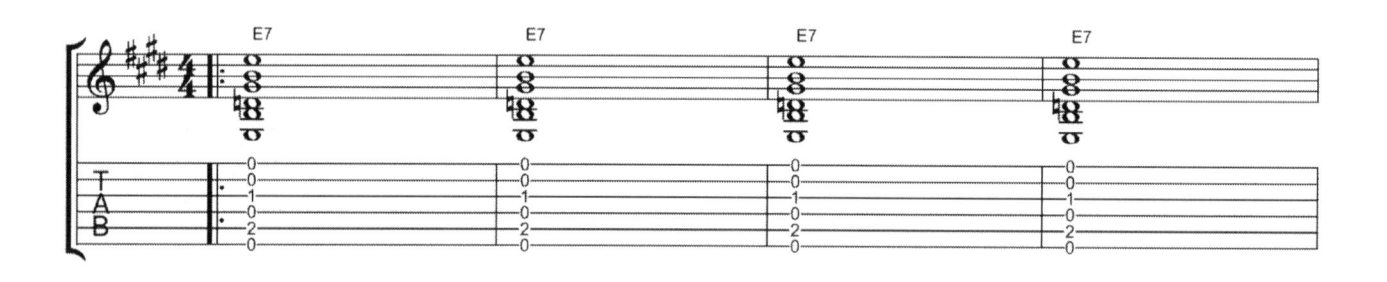

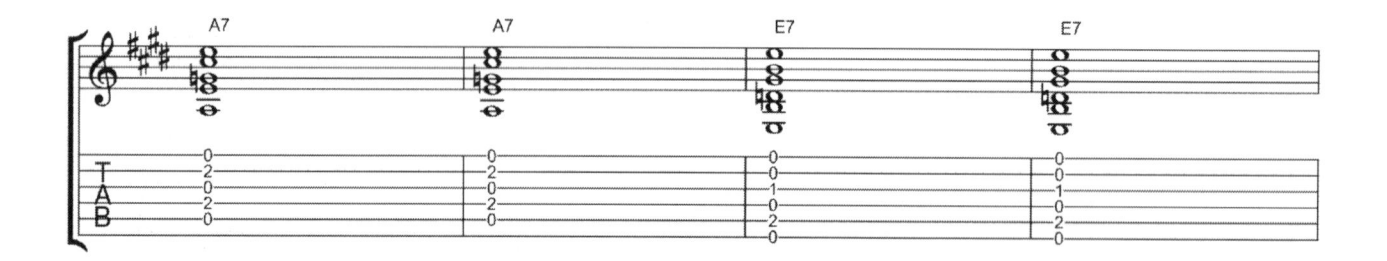

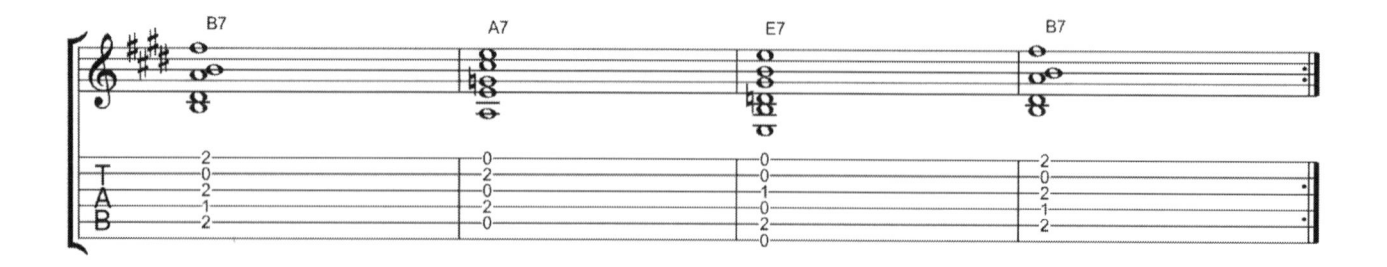

Don't forget you can download all the audio examples from **www.fundamental-changes.com**

Add a mini blues 'curl' bend on the low E string, and this twelve-bar chord progression gains an extra bluesy feel. A curl is the smallest audible distance you can bend a string on the guitar. For more information on bending and blues curls check out my book Melodic Rock Soloing for Guitar.

Example 3e

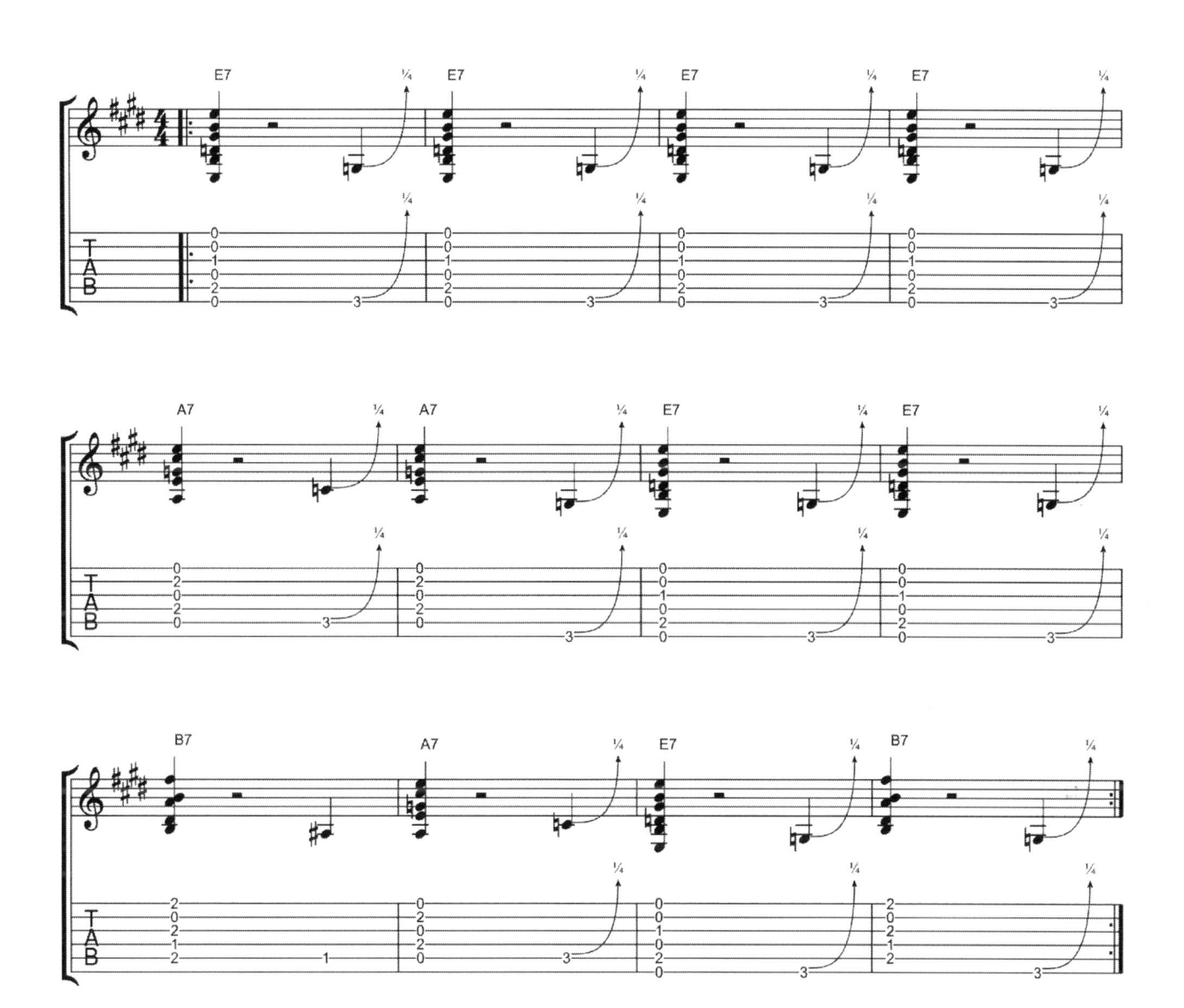

The final twelve-bar blues sequence to master is in the key of G and uses the chords of G7, C7, and D7.

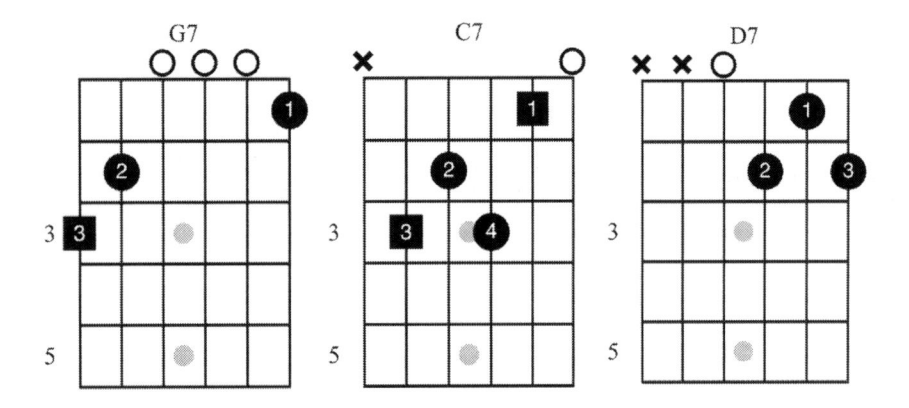

Example 3f

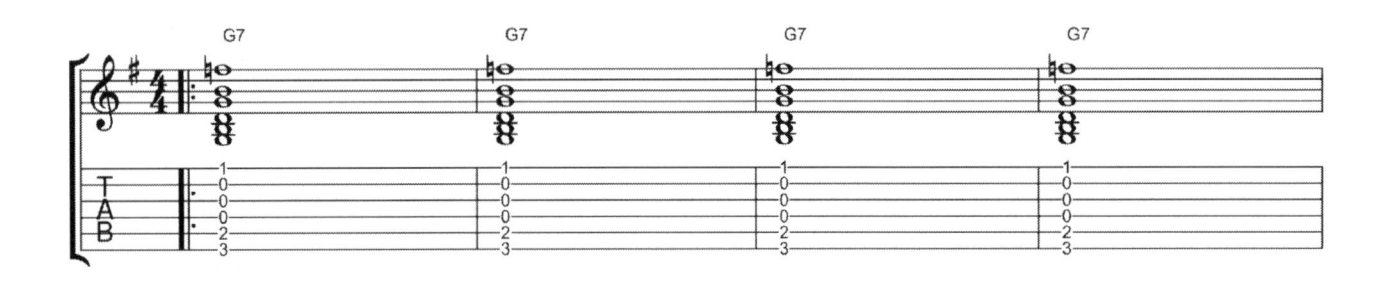

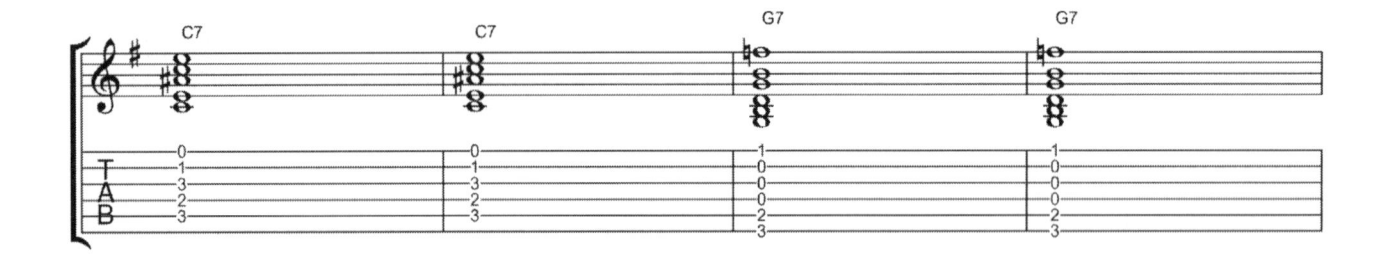

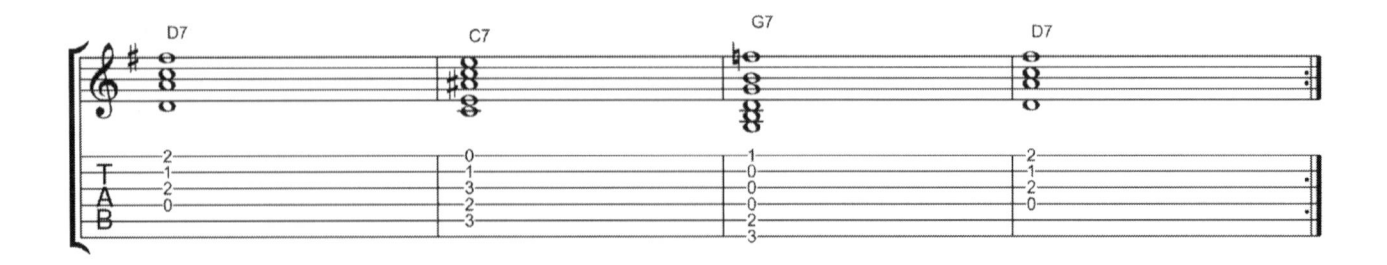

Syncopated strumming works well with a twelve-bar blues, as shown here.

Example 3g

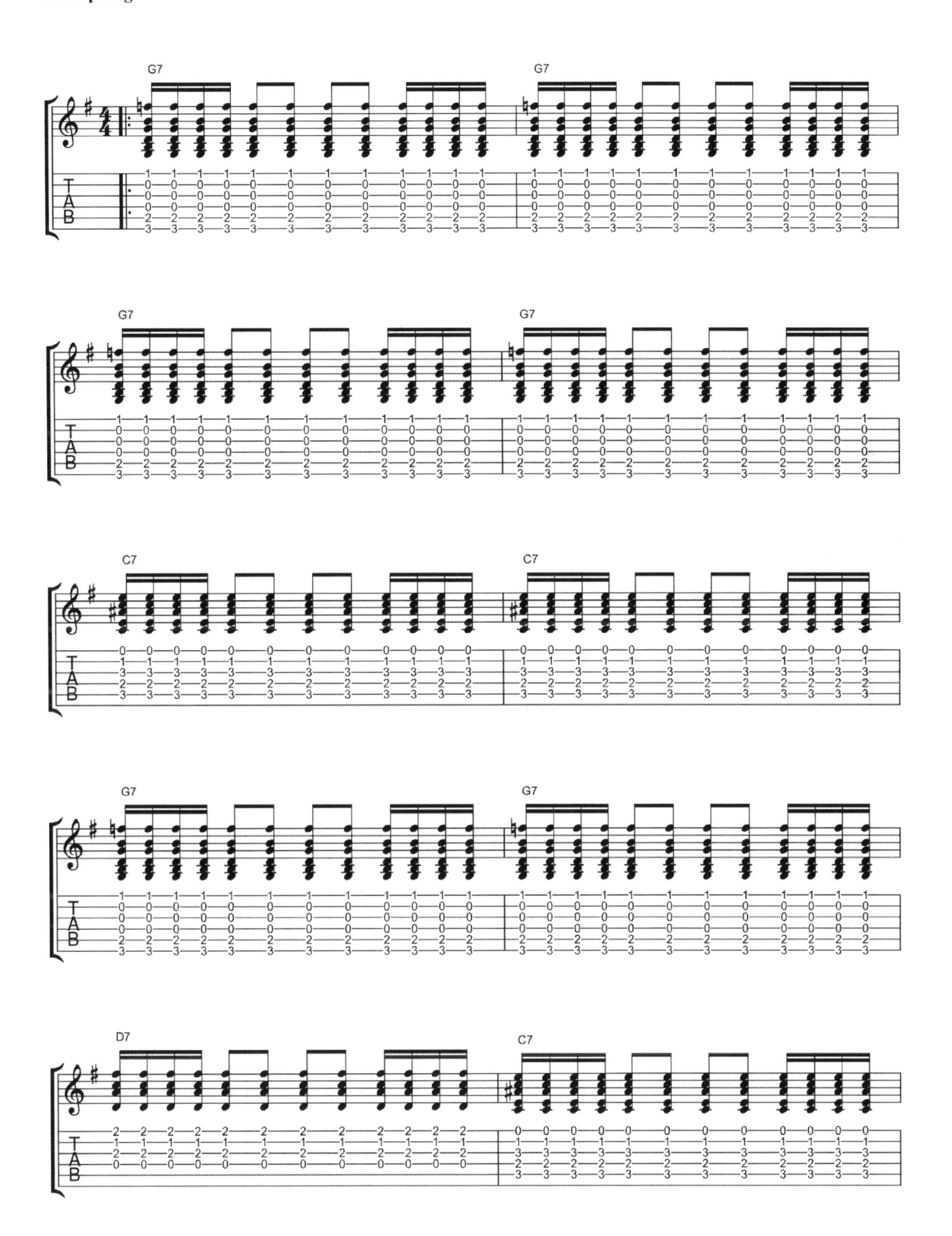

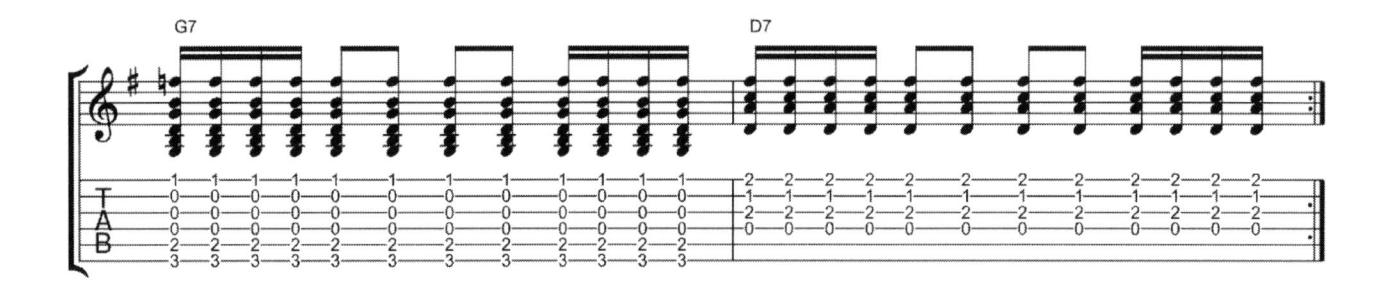

Pop Patterns

Now you have mastered some twelve-bar blues patterns that use dominant 7th chords, it is useful to learn some standard pop patterns that use them too.

Pick through each chord in the sequence paying careful attention to the E7 and G chords where the A string is missed out in the arpeggio pattern.

Example 3h

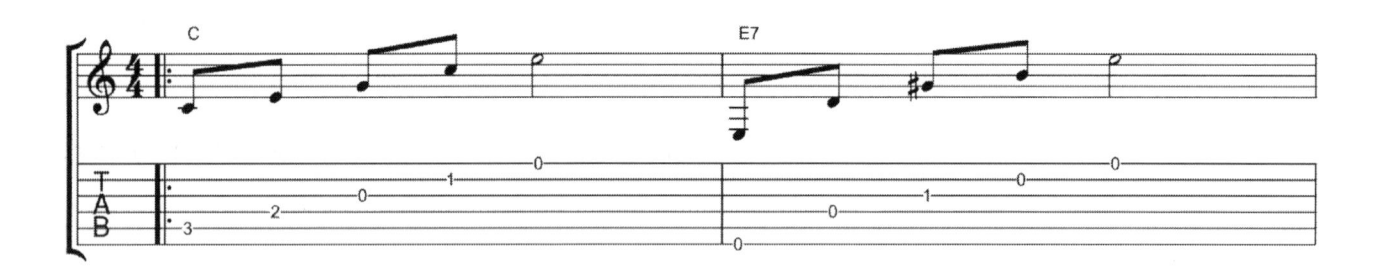

Adding little fills between each chord adds excitement to the rhythmic patterns. I recommend practicing the fills on their own before including them in the full chord sequence.

Example 3i

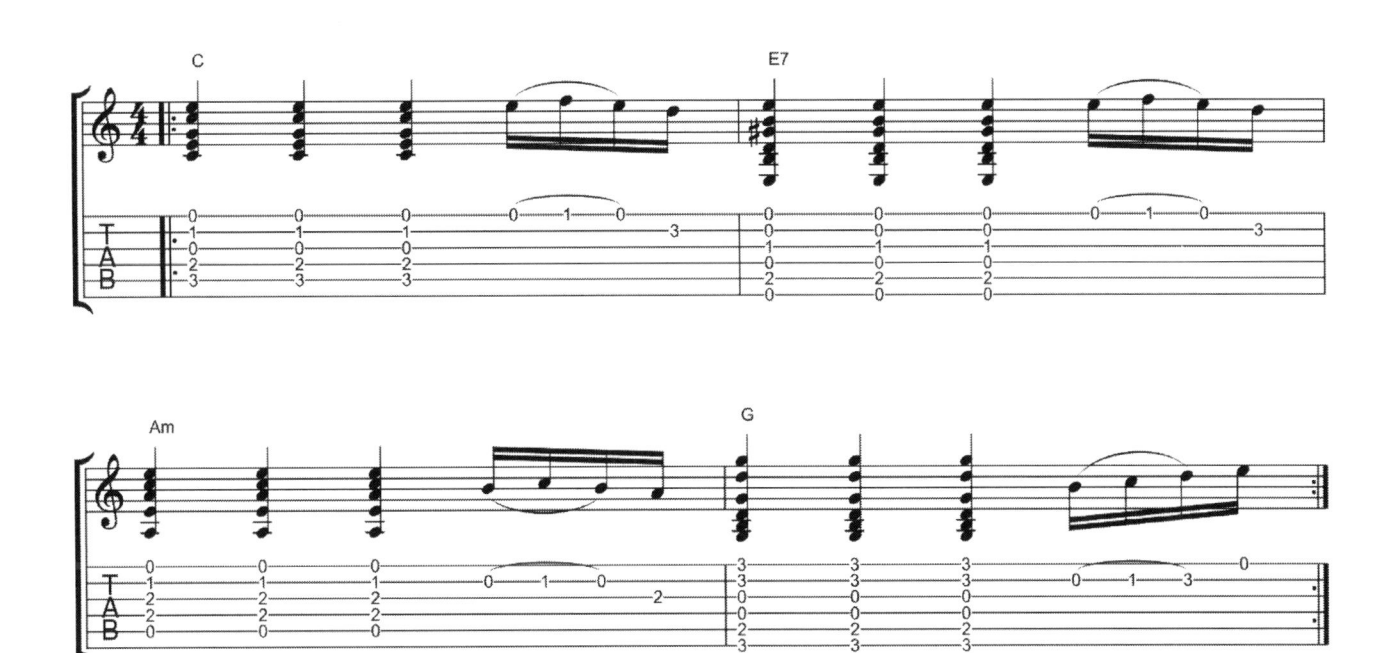

Now move the same progression into the key of G. This chord progression can be found in the Bruno Mars track The Lazy Song.

Example 3j

Remember that it is not always necessary to play every note in the chord at once. This example shows a useful arpeggio pattern that focuses around the G, B, and E strings.

Example 3k

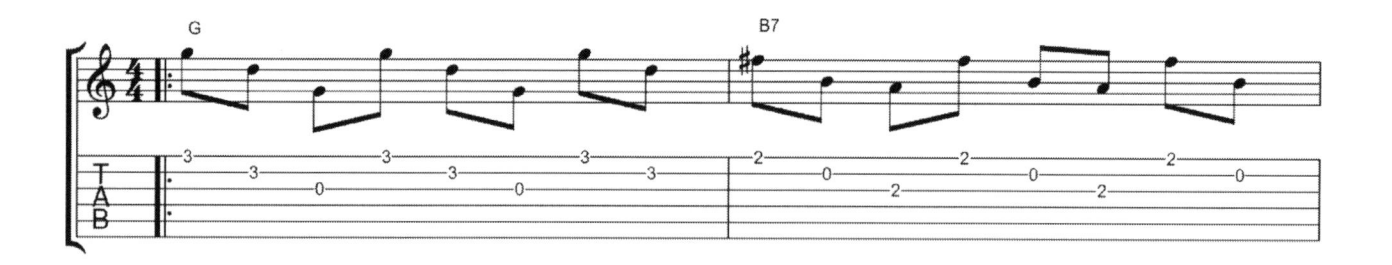

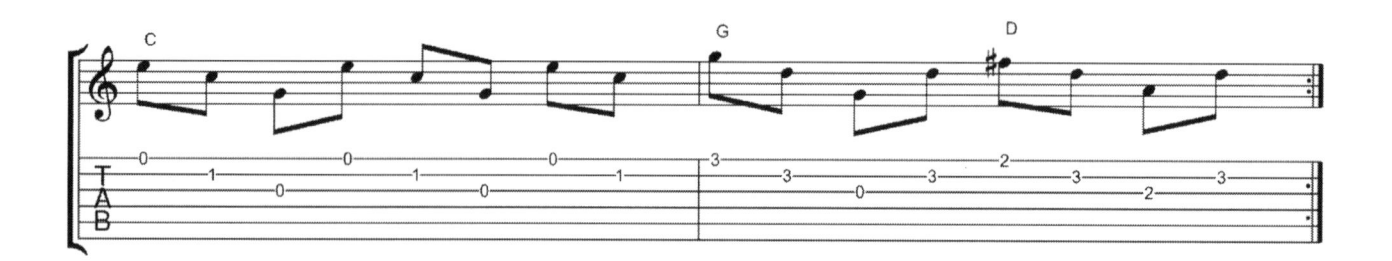

Test Yourself

- What chord is in bar five of a twelve-bar blues in E?
- What chord is in bar 11 of a twelve-bar blues in G?

Answers on the final Page!

Chapter Four – Barre Chords

This chapter focuses on using barre chords to create movable chord progressions. The advantage of these barre chords is that they don't contain any open strings, so you can easily move a chord progression into any key. When working through this chapter, make sure you play the chords in as many different keys as possible.

If you are unfamiliar with how barre chords are constructed or are struggling with how to fret then you can refer to Joseph Alexander's book The First Hundred Chords for Guitar.

Major Barre Chord Progressions

Example 4a uses E Major and A Major shape barre chords to create a common pop chord progression.

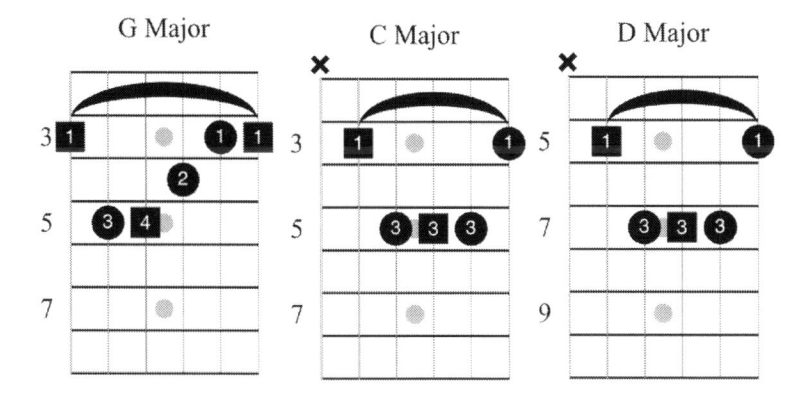

Example 4a

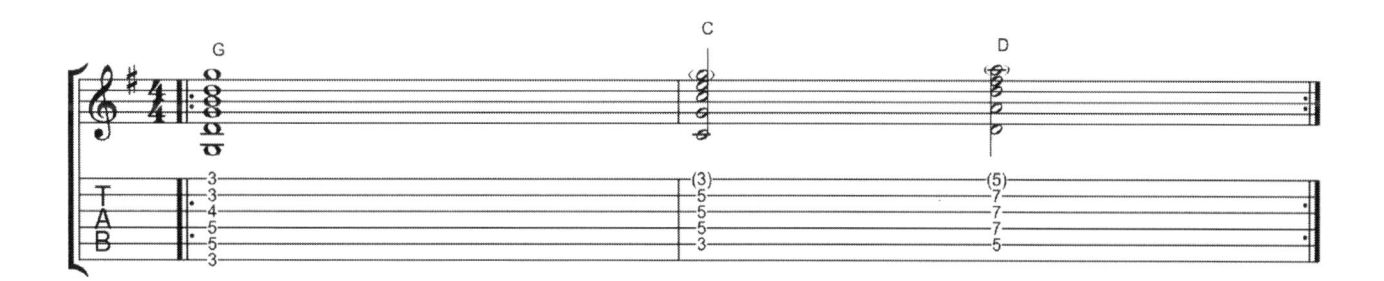

To demonstrate the flexibility of barre chords, this time I have played a G Major on the fifth string, and the C and D Major chords on the sixth string.

Example 4b

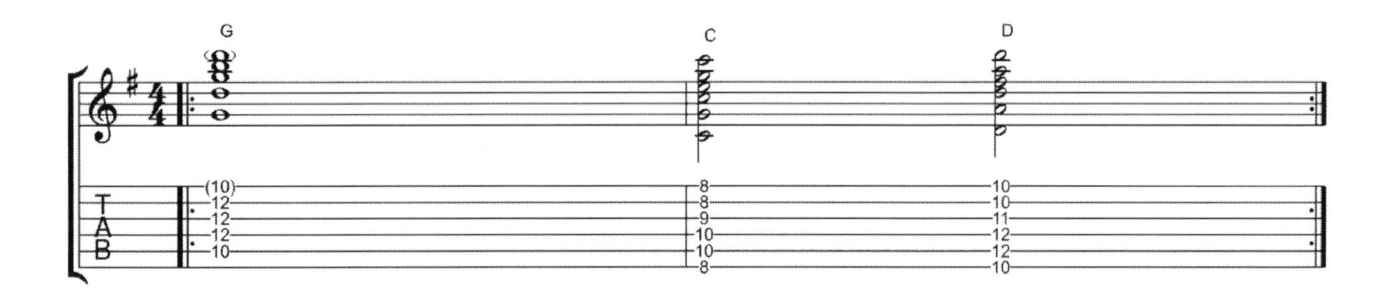

Next, add in an E Minor chord to the G, C, and D Major chords learnt in the previous examples.

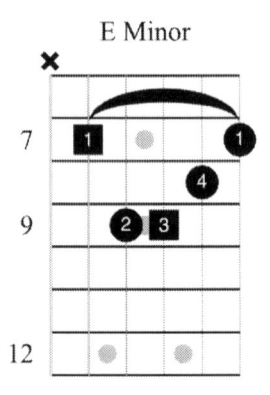

Example 4c

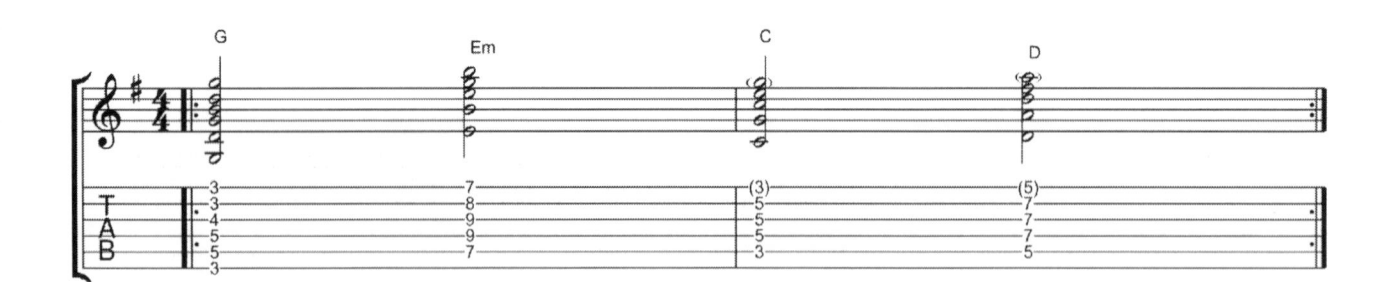

120

Now play the same chord sequence but alternate where the barre chords are played on the neck.

Example 4d

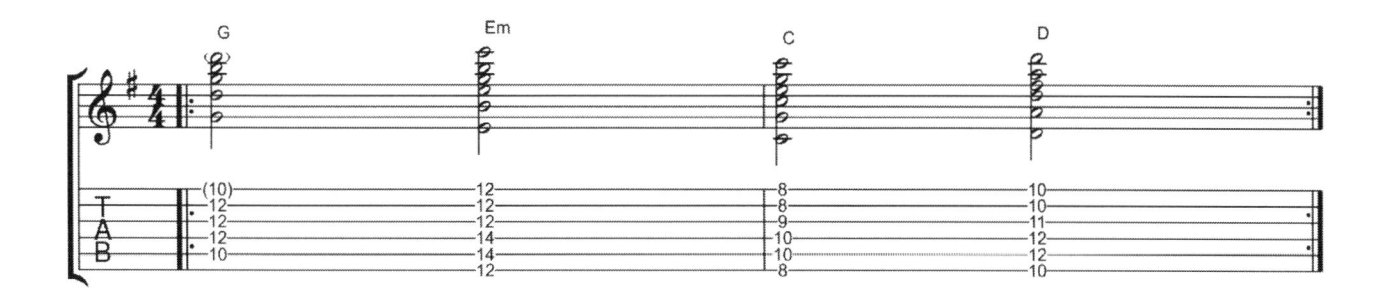

```
        G           Em          C           D
(10)               12          8          10
 12                12          8          10
 12                12          9          11
 12                14         10          12
 10                14         10          12
                   12          8          10
```

Example 4e shows another pop sequence, this time replacing the C Major chord with an A Minor.

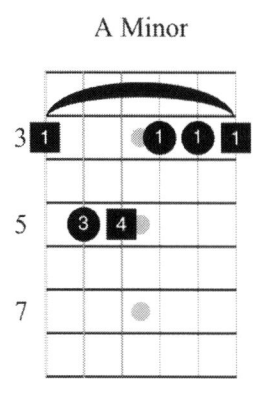

A Minor

Example 4e

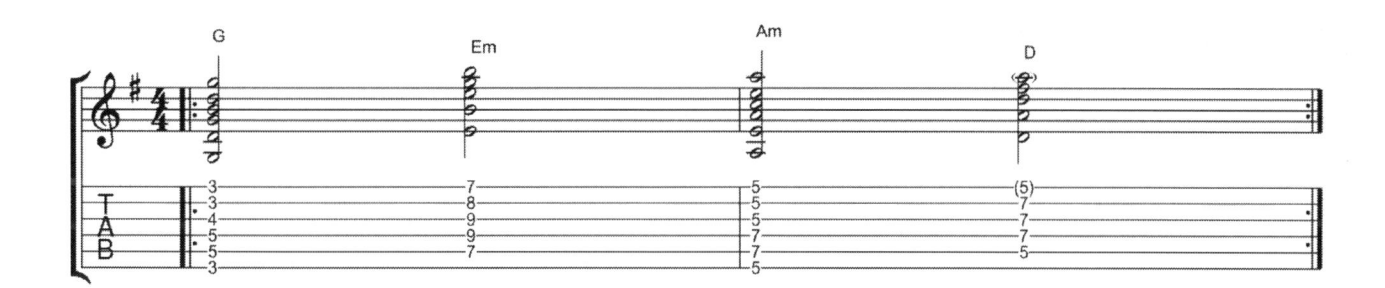

```
        G           Em          Am          D
 3                  7           5          (5)
 3                  8           5           7
 4                  9           5           7
 5                  9           7           7
 5                  7           7           5
 3                              5
```

I don't often advise playing barre chords above the 12th fret as they can interfere with a vocalist's range in a band situation. That said, I have seen examples of them being used in modern indie bands where they sound fantastic. Experiment to see if the sound works for you.

121

Example 4f

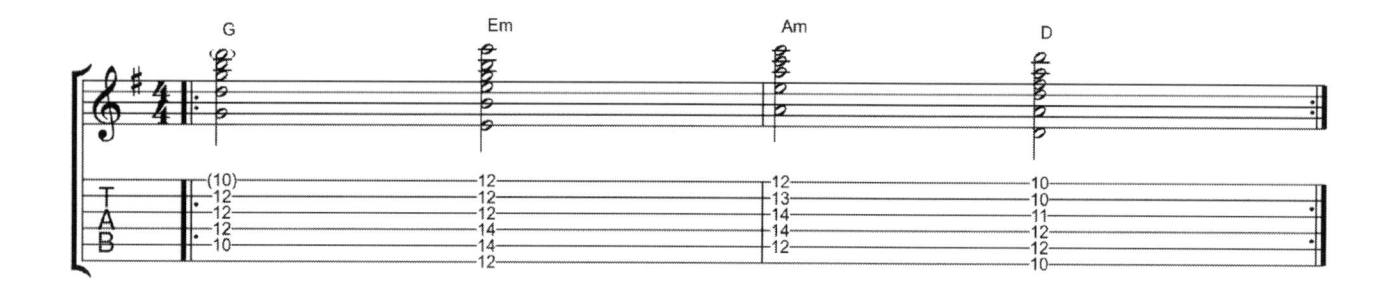

Next, we see the common chord progression of G, D, E Minor, and C played with two different barre chord varieties.

Example 4g

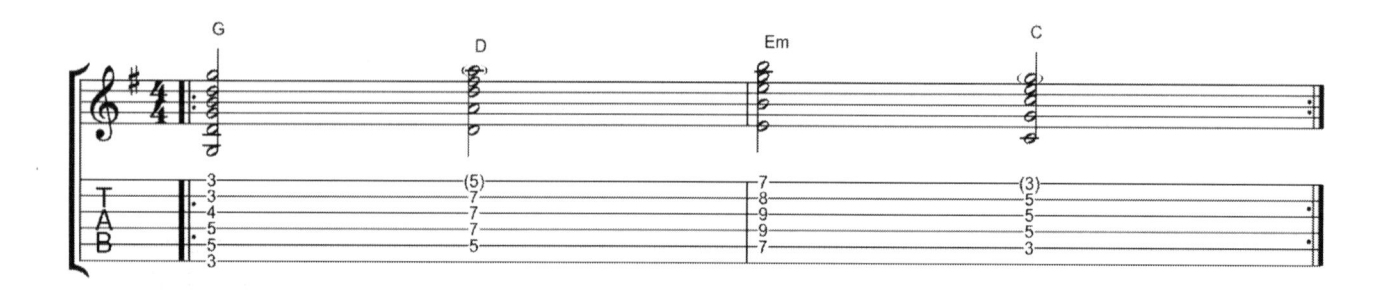

Example 4h

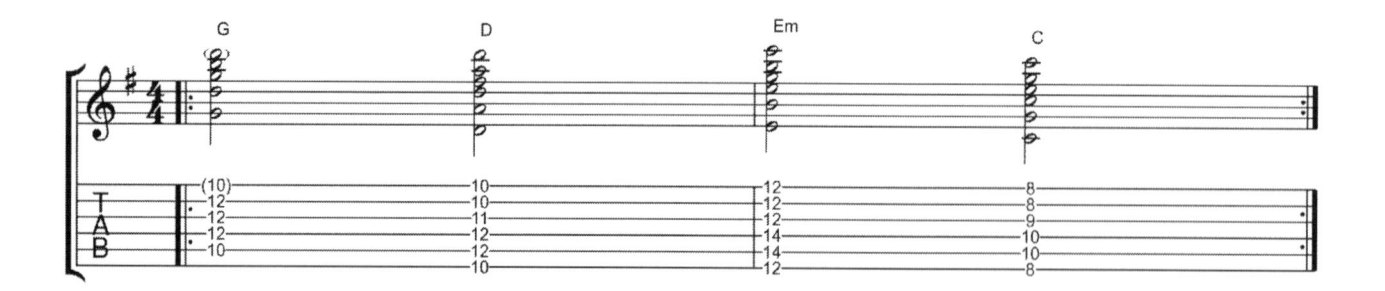

Minor Barre Chord Progressions

Now that you feel comfortable with the major barre chord progressions, here are some common minor patterns.

Used in rock, blues, and funk, example 4i is a must know minor barre chord progression. Once you have learnt it in A Minor, move it into different keys around the neck.

Example 4i

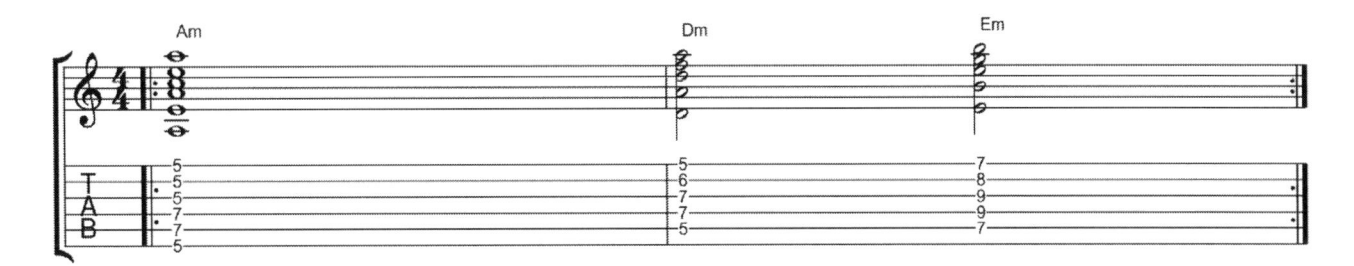

```
   Am              Dm              Em
|--5--|---------|--5--|---------|--7--|
|--5--|---------|--6--|---------|--8--|
|--5--|---------|--7--|---------|--9--|
|--7--|---------|--7--|---------|--9--|
|--7--|---------|--5--|---------|--7--|
|--5--|---------|-----|---------|-----|
```

Now learn the progression with alternate barre chord shapes.

Example 4j

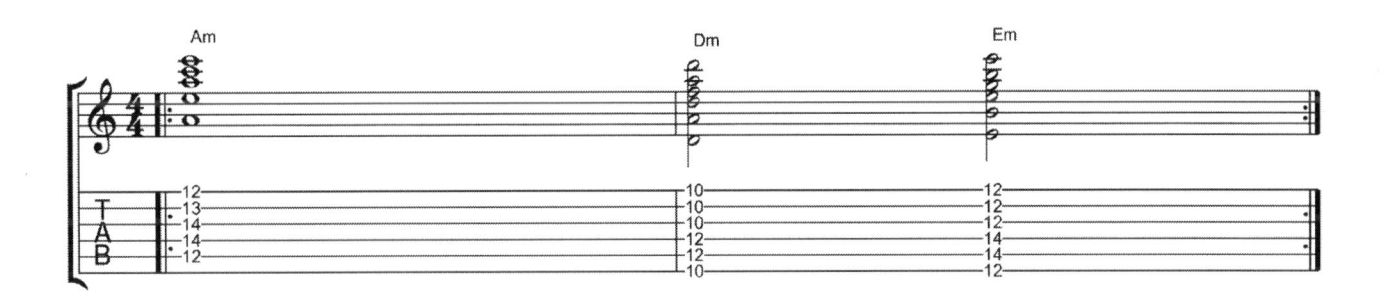

```
   Am              Dm              Em
|--12--|--------|--10--|--------|--12--|
|--13--|--------|--10--|--------|--12--|
|--14--|--------|--10--|--------|--12--|
|--14--|--------|--12--|--------|--14--|
|--12--|--------|--12--|--------|--14--|
|------|--------|--10--|--------|--12--|
```

Example 4k shows the progression heard in the solo section in Stairway to Heaven by Led Zeppelin.

Example 4k

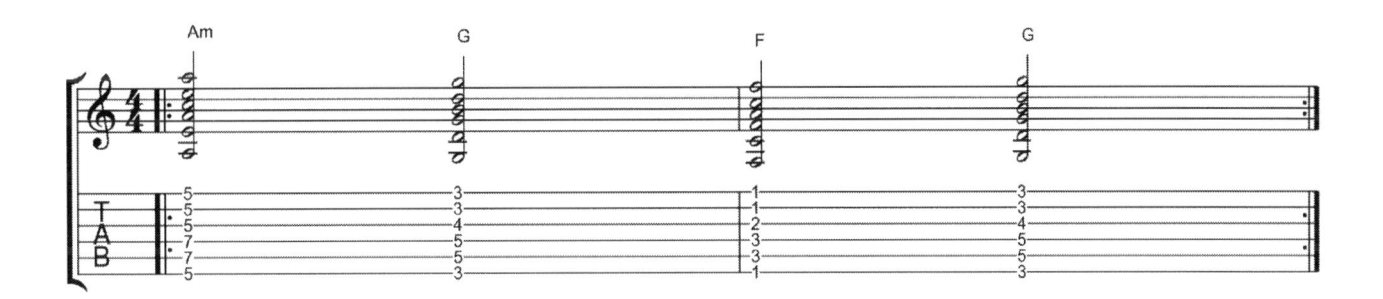

```
   Am        G         F         G
|--5--|---|--3--|---|--1--|---|--3--|
|--5--|---|--3--|---|--1--|---|--3--|
|--5--|---|--4--|---|--2--|---|--4--|
|--7--|---|--5--|---|--3--|---|--5--|
|--7--|---|--5--|---|--3--|---|--5--|
|--5--|---|--3--|---|--1--|---|--3--|
```

Example 4l shows the same progression as the previous example, but this time all the barre chords are located on the A string. This chord progression is one of my favourite patterns to practice soloing over.

Although out of the scope of this book, try using the A Minor Pentatonic scale to solo over this chord progression.

Example 4l

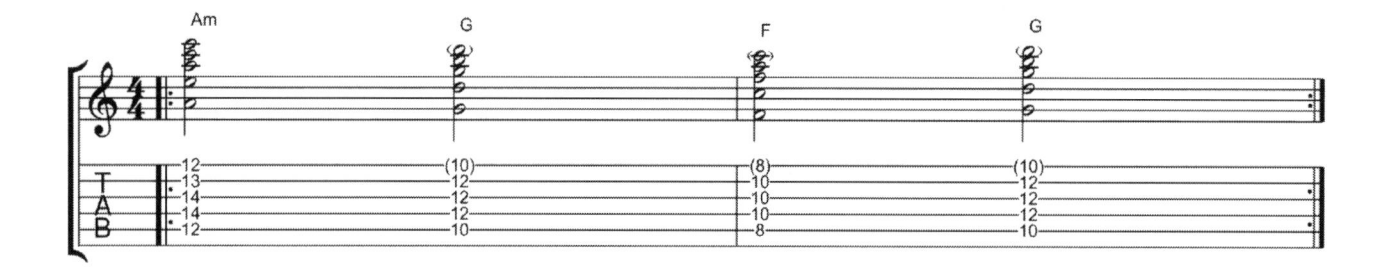

Countless pop and rock tunes are built on the chord sequence featured in examples 4m and 4n, making it a must-know pattern for all rhythm guitarists.

Example 4m

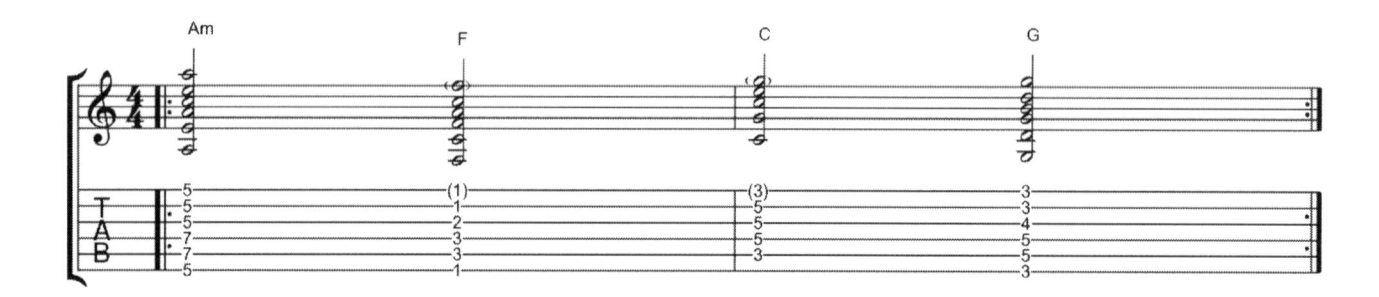

Example 4n

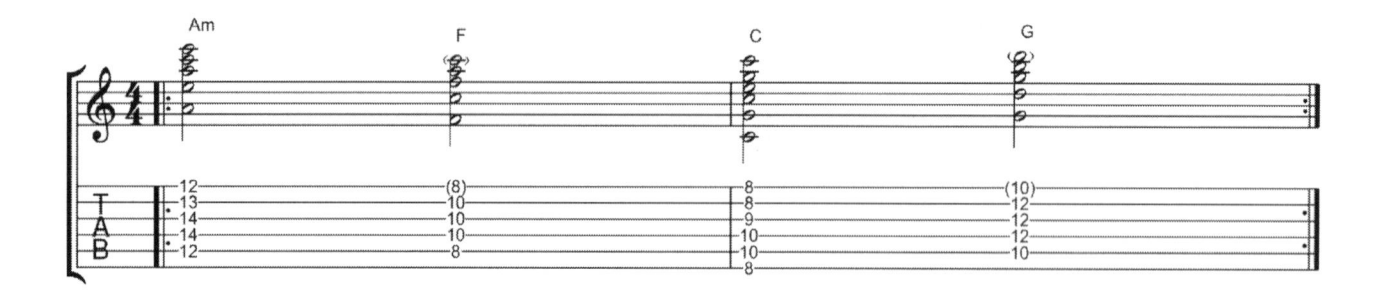

Example 4o is the chord progression used in the Lenny Kravtiz song Fly Away. Although Lenny plays it using power chords, it works equally as well with the barre chords shown.

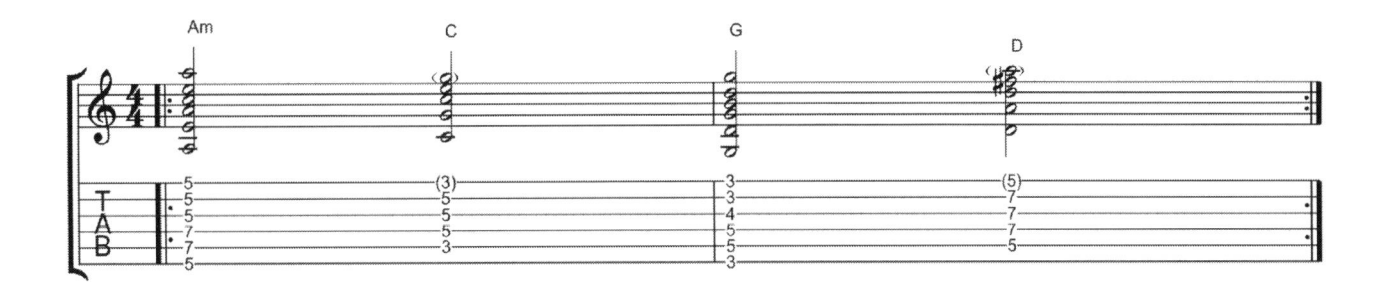

Example 4o

Now play the Fly Away chord progression higher up the neck.

Example 4p

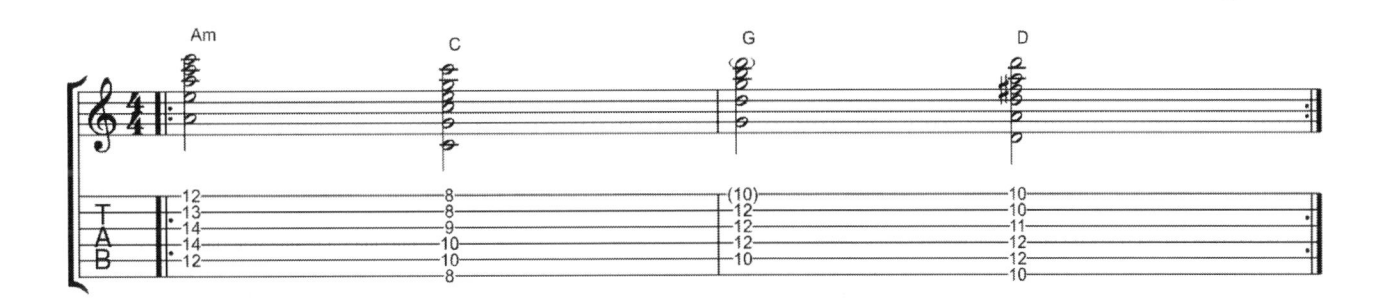

Try adding the rhythm patterns you learnt earlier to the chord progressions in this chapter.

Barre Chord Songs to Learn

When you have learnt the examples featured in this chapter, learn the songs listed below to cement your barre chord knowledge.

- Radiohead – Creep
- The Eagles - Hotel California
- Jack Johnson – Better Together / Flake
- Eric Clapton – Layla (acoustic version from the Unplugged album)
- Jimi Hendrix – All Along the Watchtower
- Red Hot Chili Peppers – Dani California
- Plain White Tees – Hey There Delilah
- Jason Mraz – I'm Yours
- Daniel Merriweather – Red
- Donavan Frankenreiter – It Don't Matter
- Oasis – Don't Look Back in Anger
- Damien Rice – The Blowers Daughter
- Led Zeppelin – Stairway to Heaven (Solo section)

Chapter Five – Extended Barre Chords

This chapter will examine dominant 7th barre chord shapes so you can play new progressions that use them in any key. Learn the two shapes shown below before continuing.

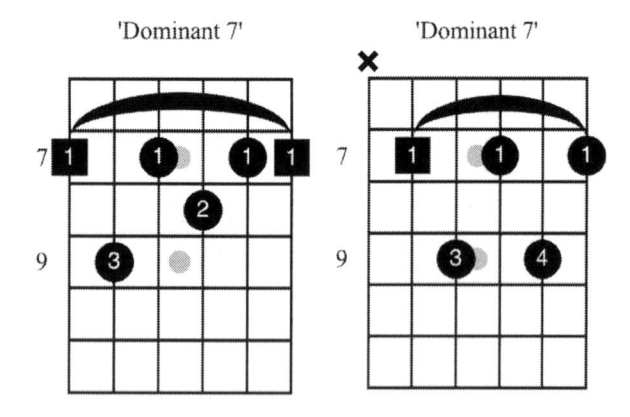

Pop Quiz

- Which chord is shown in the first neck diagram above?
- Which chord is shown in the second neck diagram above?

Answers on the final page!

Twelve Bar Blues Form Using Barre Chords

B♭ is a very popular key to play a twelve-bar blues in, as it fits very well with instruments like saxophones and trumpets.

Example 5a shows a new way to play a twelve-bar blues in B♭ using dominant 7th barre chords. Although B♭ is a top pick in jam sessions, remember that with barre chord shapes you are not restricted to one key. Move this progression around the neck and be comfortable playing it in any key, that way, if someone says "let's play it in C tonight" you won't feel out of your depth.

Example 5a

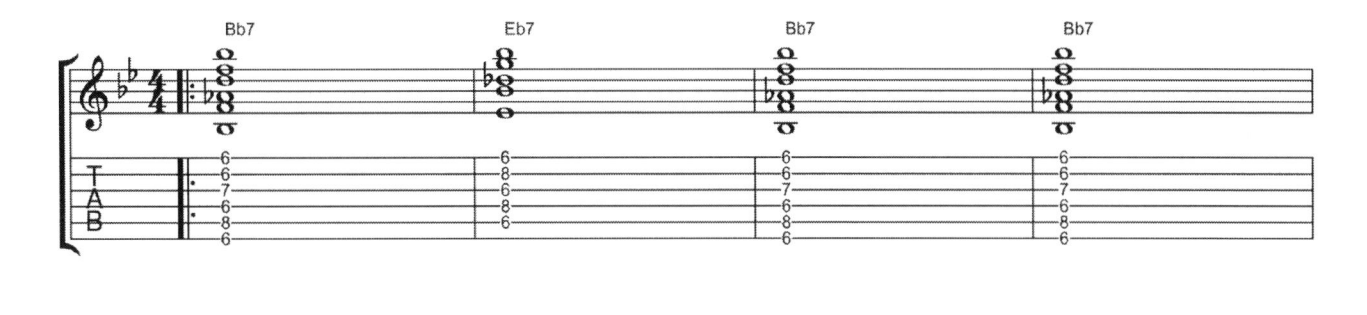

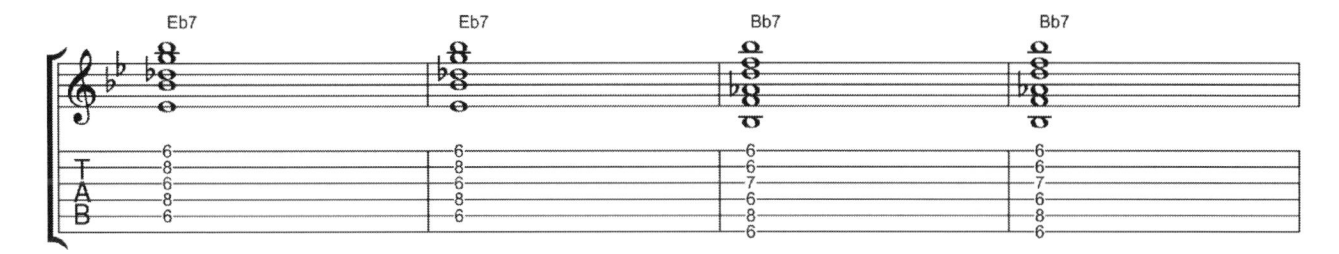

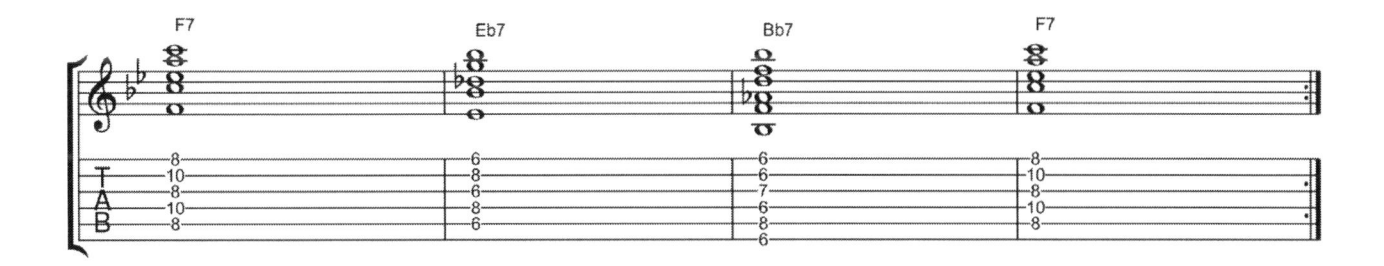

Adding a note chromatically a semi-tone (one-fret) below or above the chord you are approaching creates melodic interest in your rhythm guitar parts.

To test you, I have left out the chord names in this example. As you play recite the chords from memory.

Example 5b

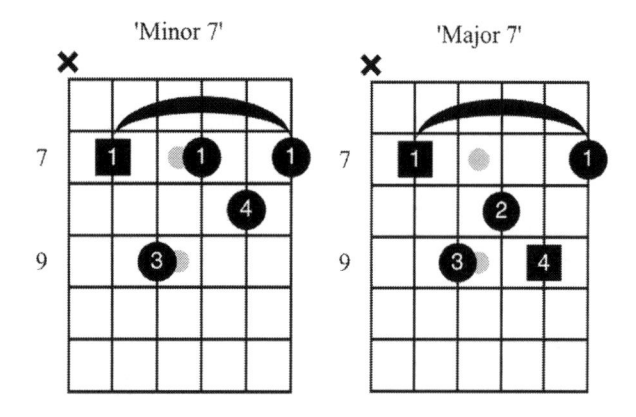

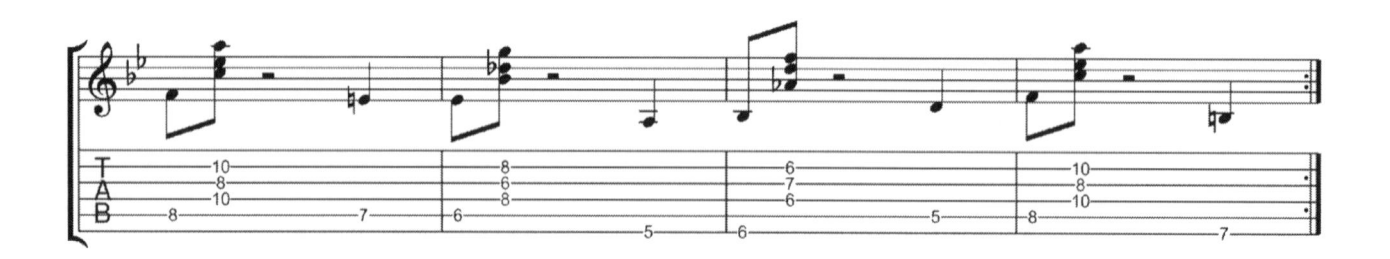

128

The II V I Progression

In jazz, an essential progression to learn is the II V I. It is built from the 2nd, 5th, and 1st chord in any key.

In example 5c I have demonstrated how to play a II V I progression in the key of C Major.

Example 5c

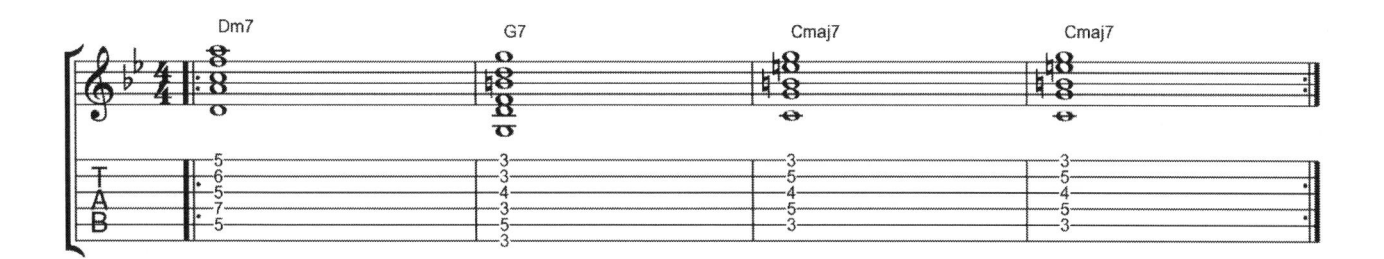

Dm7 | G7 | Cmaj7 | Cmaj7

Example 5d uses the II V I progression example, but plays it through all 12 keys. This is an excellent exercise to get to know your guitar neck!

Example 5d

'Minor 7'

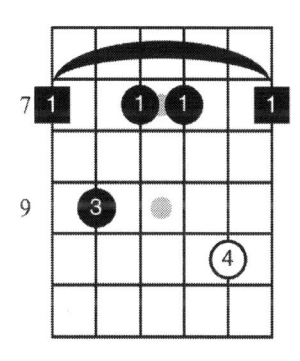

Dm7
G7
Cmaj7
Cmaj7
Gm7
C7
Fmaj7
Fmaj7
Cm7
F7
Bbmaj7
Bbmaj7
Fm7
Bb7
Ebmaj7
Ebmaj7
Bbm7
Eb7
Abmaj7
Abmaj7

Ebm7
Ab7
Dbmaj7
Dbmaj7
Abm7
Db7
Gbmaj7
Gbmaj7
C#m7
F#7
Bmaj7
Bmaj7
F#m7
B7
Emaj7
Emaj7
Bm7
Emaj7
Amaj7
Amaj7

132

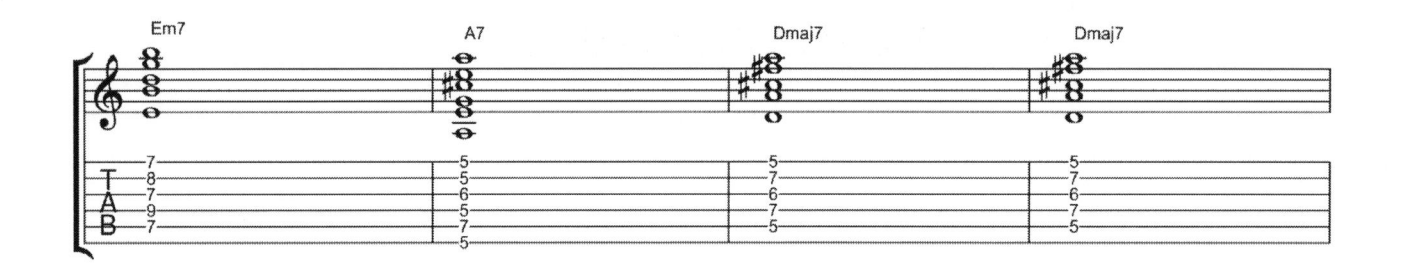

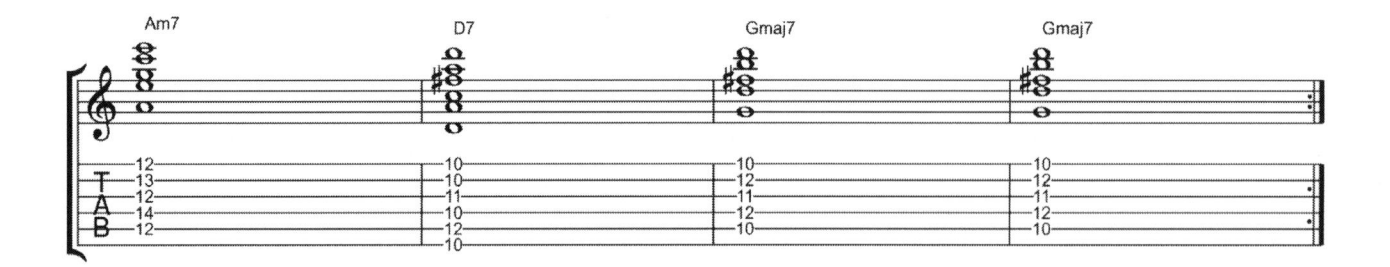

Two Funk Progressions

Let's start with a minor 7 chord sequence in the style of one of my guitar heroes, Nile Rodgers.

Example 5e

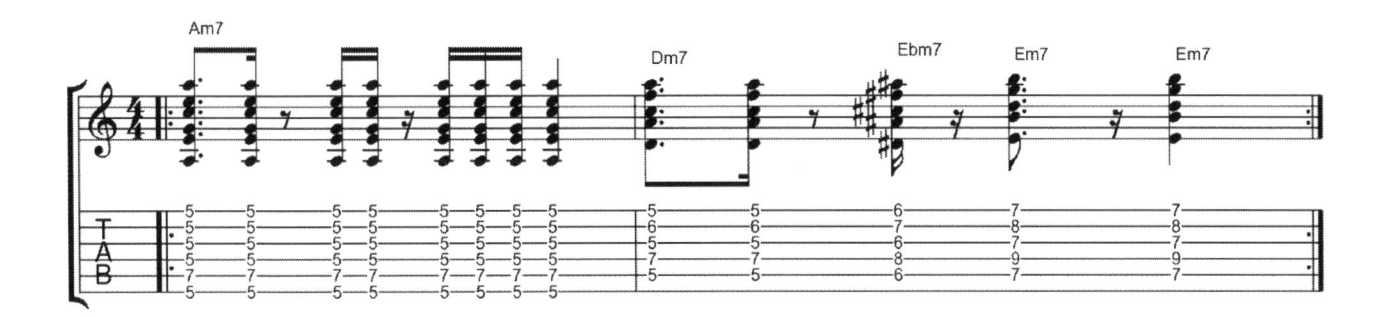

The chord progression in example 5f is similar to the sequence used in George Benson's smash instrumental hit Breezin'.

Example 5f

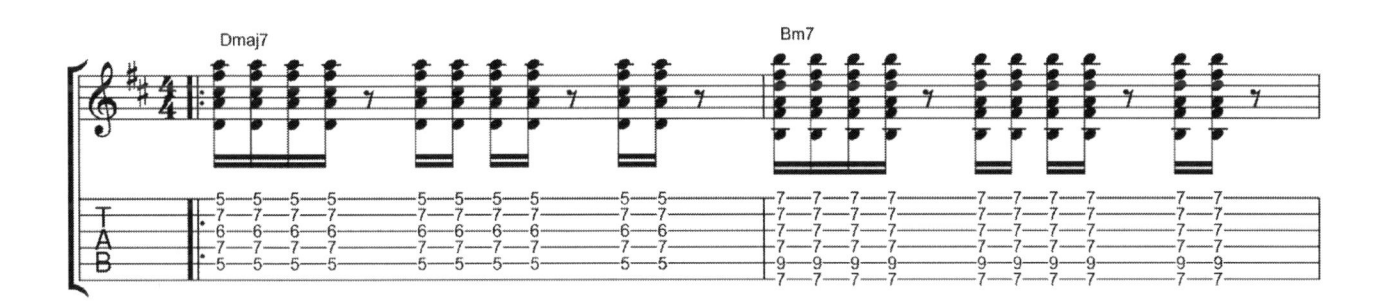

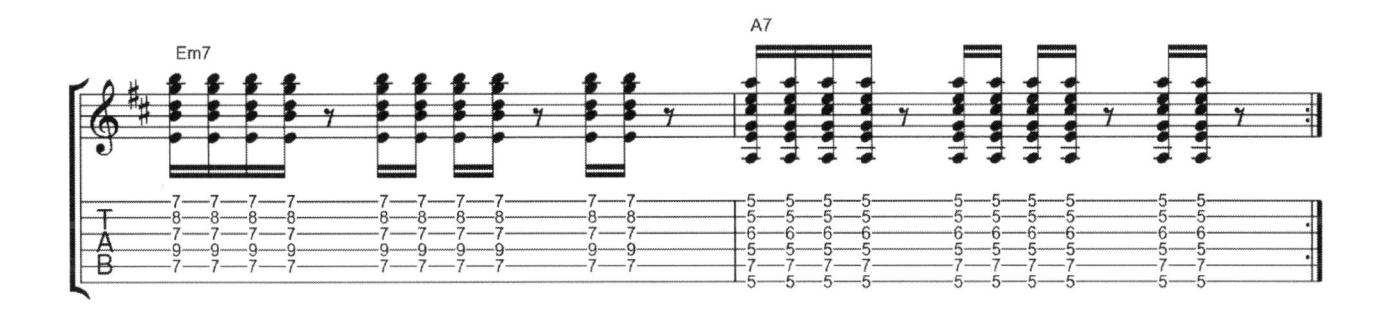

Other Common Jazz Progressions

Now that you have mastered the twelve-bar blues, the major II V I progression, and two funk examples in the styles of Nile Rodgers and George Benson, it's time to look at a few more jazz progressions.

Example 5g is a typical jazz chord sequence that is often looped or used to finish a piece of music.

Example 5g

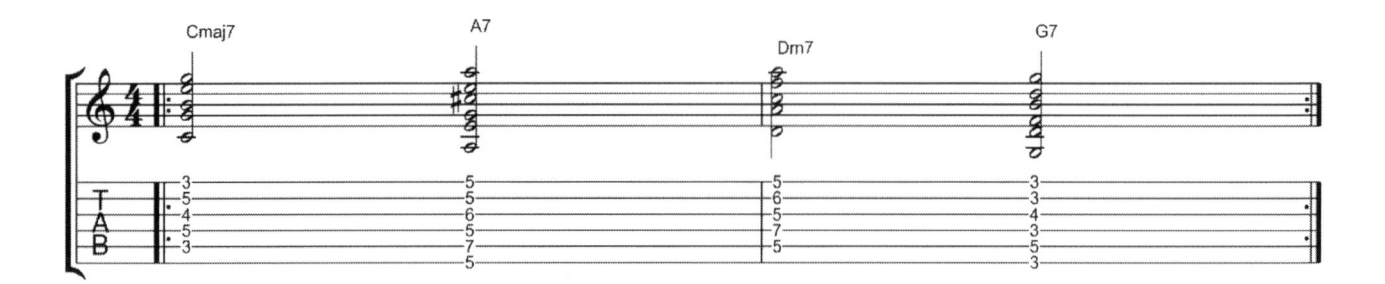

Playing on beats 2 and 4 of the bar is common in jazz rhythm guitar. Remember, often the silent notes are as important as the played notes.

Example 5h

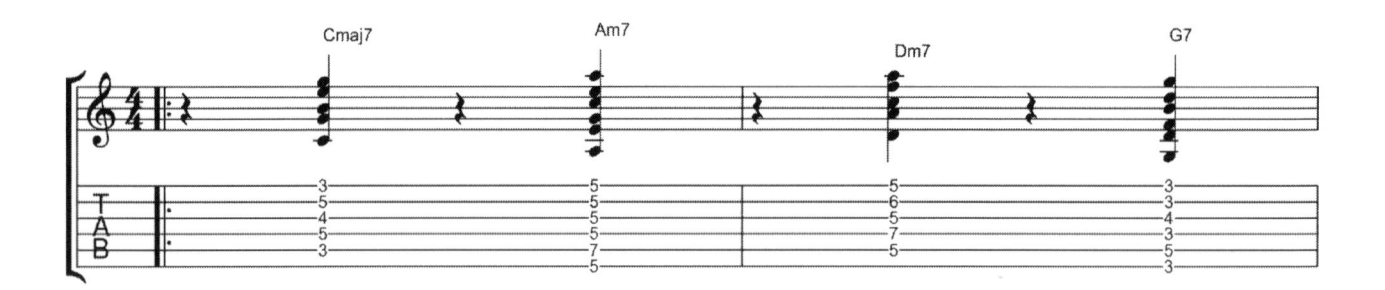

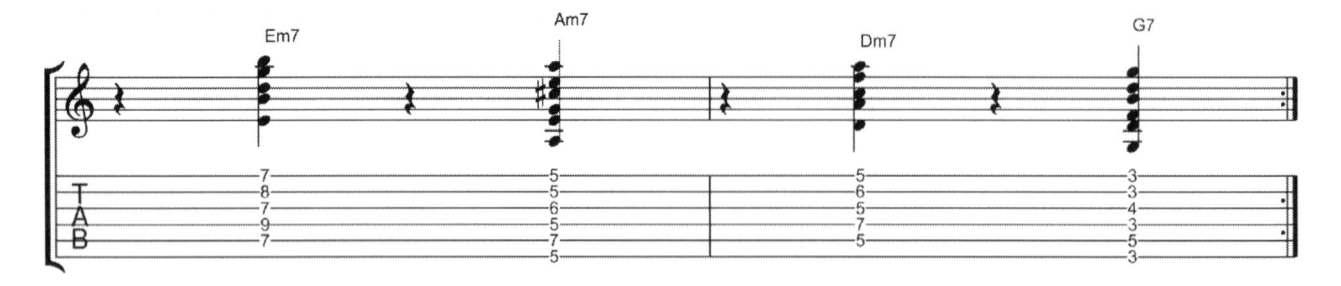

The final example shows a major 7 chord in C Major followed by a II V I progression into the chord of B♭ Major 7. This pattern is used a lot to move between different key centres and the more you get into jazz, the more often you will see it.

'Major 7'

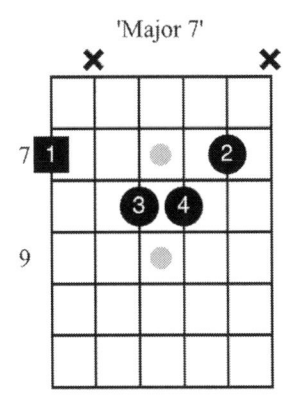

Example 5i

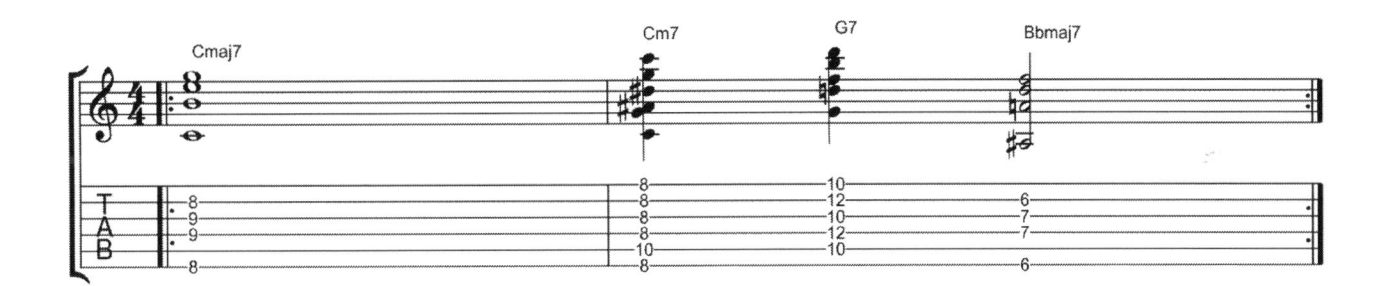

Jazzy Chord Songs to Learn

- Sixpence None the Richer – Kiss Me
- George Benson – Breezin'
- Diana Ross – I'm Coming Out
- Doobie Brothers – Long Train Runnin'
- Jack Johnson – Banana Pancakes
- Chic – I Want Your Love
- B.B King – The Thrill Is Gone
- Any jazz standard such as Summertime, Autumn Leaves, Blue Bossa, Take the A Train, Tune Up, Blue Seven, Milestones.

Chapter Six – Lush Open Chords

From The Edge to Slash, Taylor Swift to Ed Sheeran, lush open chords rule the world when creating exciting rhythm guitar progressions. Although the traditional open chord voicings shown in Chapter Two are your 'bread and butter', the lush open chord voicings shown in this chapter will open your eyes and ears to the beautiful sounds they can create.

I created a video lesson on how to apply these techniques. Check it out here:

www.fundamental-changes.com/open-string-chords

A *suspended* or 'sus' chord is one that replaces the 3rd with either the 2nd or the 4th.

Instead of 1 3 5, the formula is 1 2 5, or 1 4 5.

Instead of C E G, the notes are C D G, or C F G.

When the 3rd is replaced with the 2nd, the chord is named 'sus2'. When the 3rd is replaced with the 4th, then the chord is named 'sus4'.

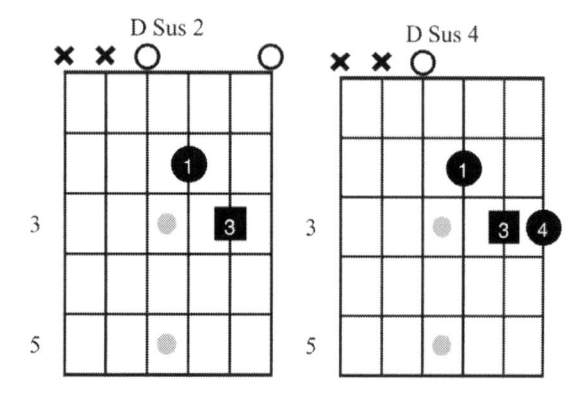

I love playing open chords! They have a ringing quality which is hard to match with barre chords. I find them especially useful when it is just a vocalist and myself.

Example 6a demonstrates the two new chord voicings of Dsus2 and Dsus4. A suspended chord has an airy quality to it and can be used to replace either a major or a minor chord shape. U2's guitarist The Edge is synonymous with playing these chord voicings with lots of reverb and delays.

Example 6a

Strumming these chords with a syncopated rhythm that includes rests works equally well.

Example 6b

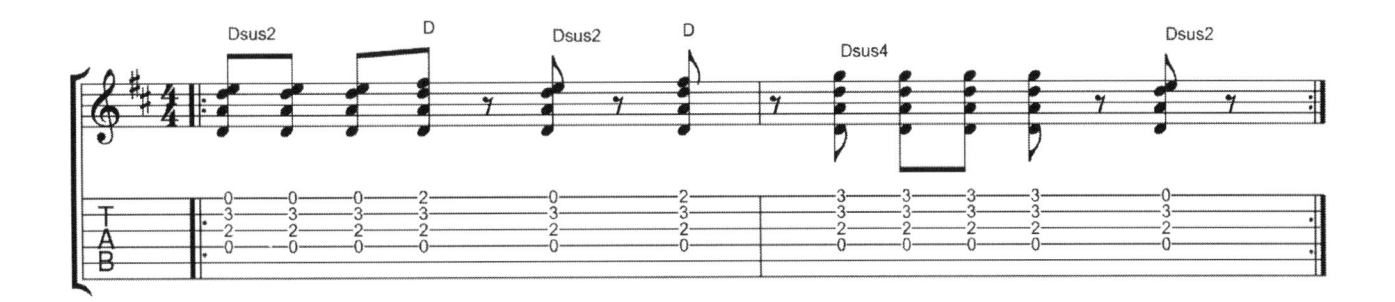

Another common place to play open suspended chord voicings is in the key of 'A'. Example 6c shows the Asus2 and Asus4 chord shapes.

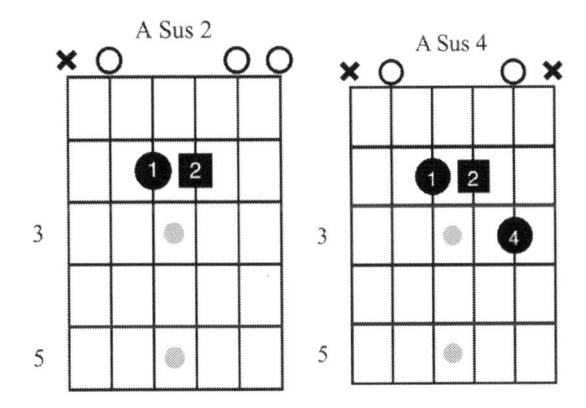

Check out James Taylor's masterpiece Fire and Rain for an example of this chord in action (you'll need a capo to play along in the original key.)

Example 6c

137

Another useful suspended chord voicing is the open Esus4 shape.

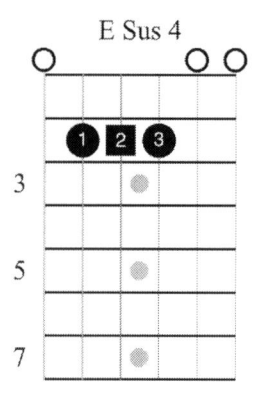

Example 6d

Instead of playing a traditional open A, D, and E chord progression, example 6e includes the new suspended chord voicings learnt in the previous examples.

Example 6e

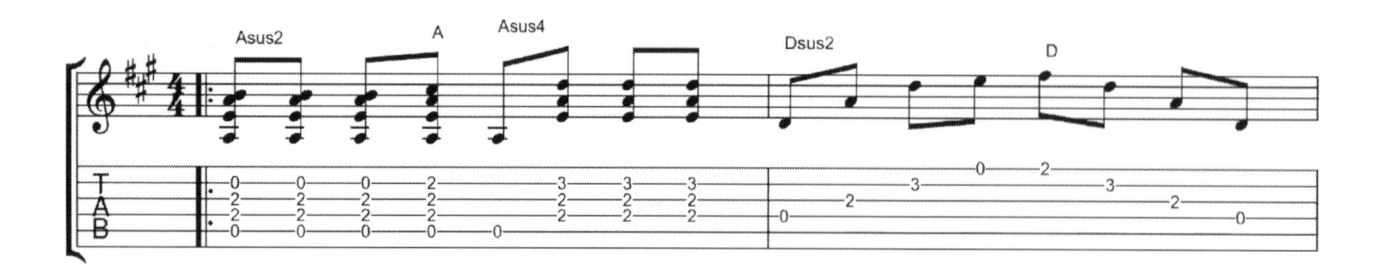

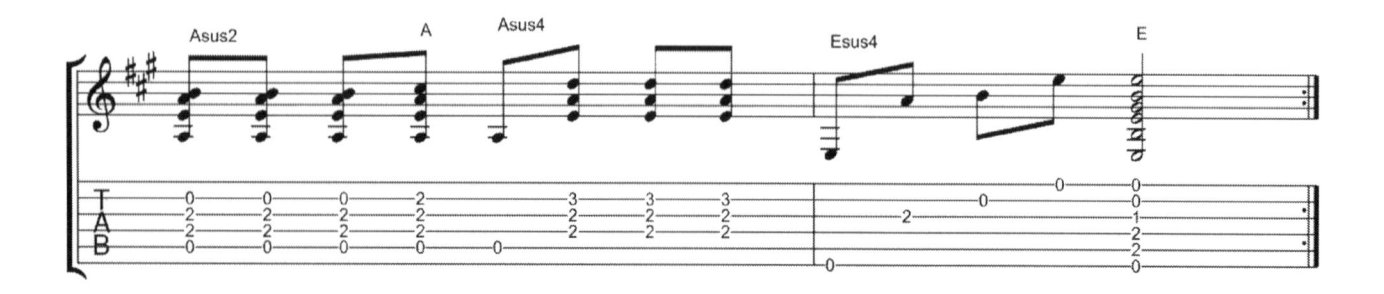

Imagine if the song Kiss Me by Sixpence None the Richer was played by The Beatles. The C Major 7 voicing featured here can make a useful replacement for a standard C shape.

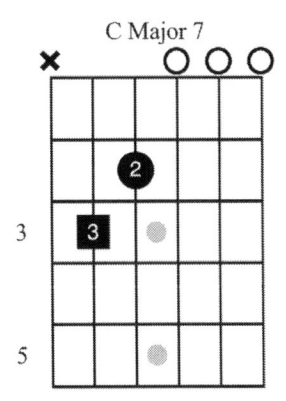

Example 6f

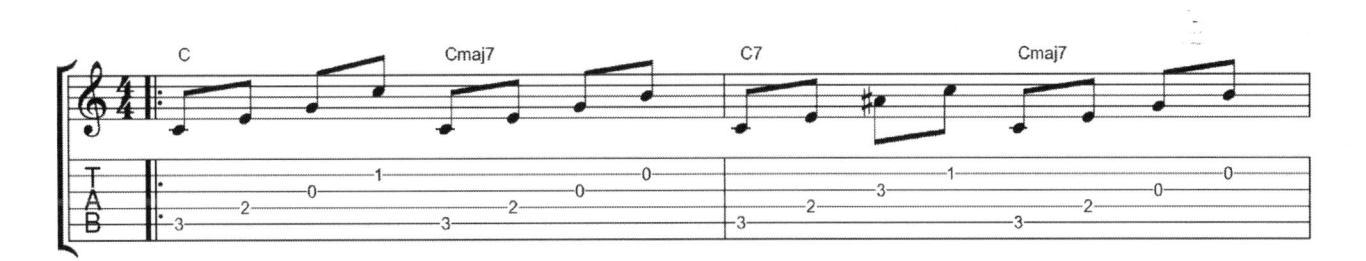

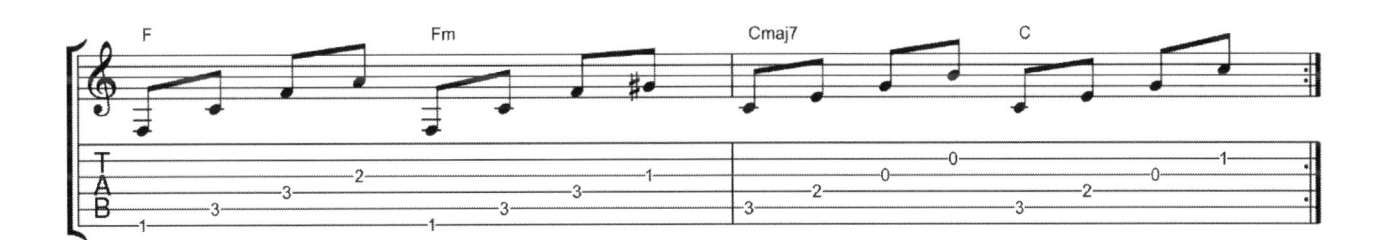

Another lovely voicing to learn is the D Major 7 chord. Once you have mastered the shape, play it in the progression featured in example 6g.

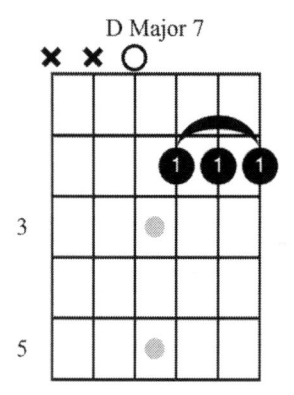

Example 6g

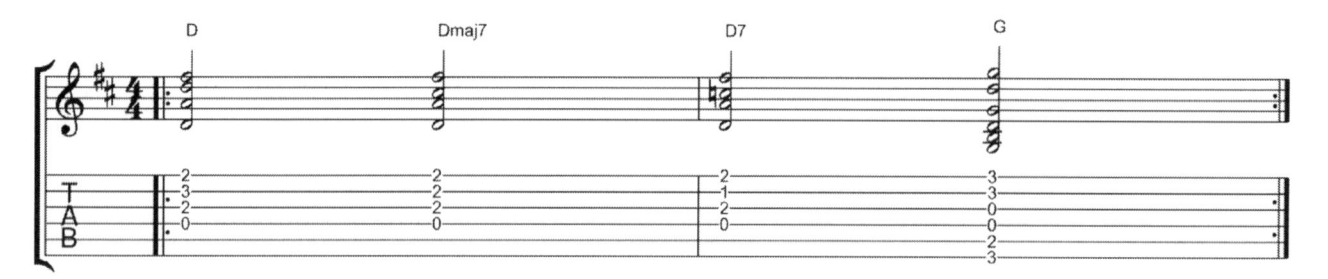

Now learn the A Major 7 voicing shown in the neck diagram, and play it in the sequence shown in this example.

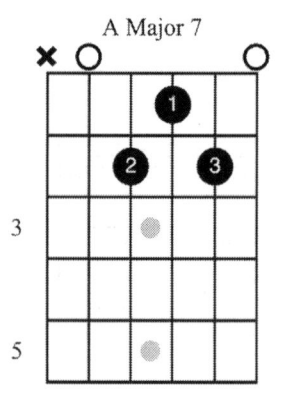

Example 6h

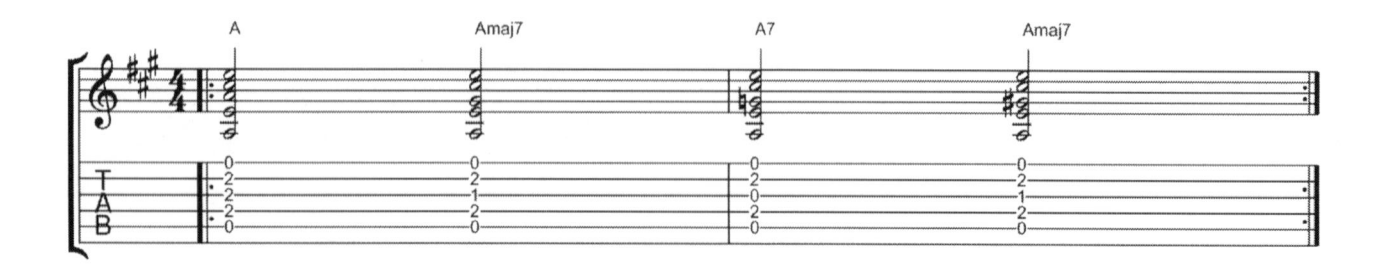

Although technically this B Minor 7 voicing is not an open chord, it is a useful replacement for a B Minor barre.

B Minor 7

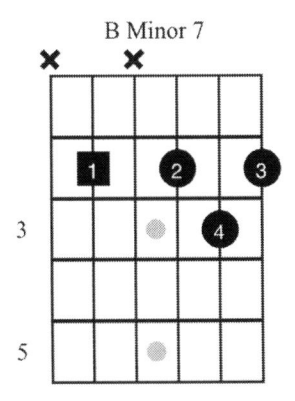

Sometimes, instead of learning a load of new chord voicings, you can simply change a bass note to create a new chord progression. In example 6i I have made a bass note pattern that goes B, A, F#, G while retaining the upper part of the B Minor 7 chord.

When we add in a note other than the root note, we create what is called a 'slash' chord.

This is not named after the famous Guns N' Roses guitarist, but after the way the it is written. Bm7/A means play a B Minor 7 chord, but play the note of A as the bass note instead of B.

For more information on slash chords, check out my video lesson here.

www.fundamental-changes.com/major-slash-chords-video-guitar-lesson

Example 6i

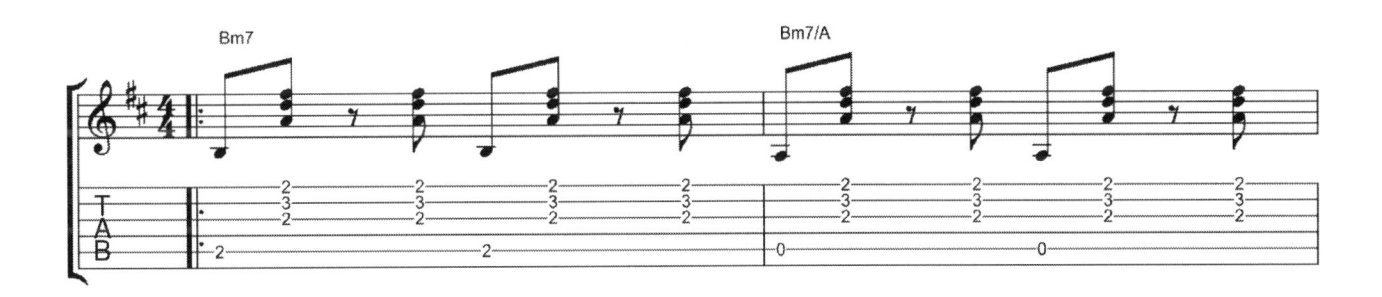

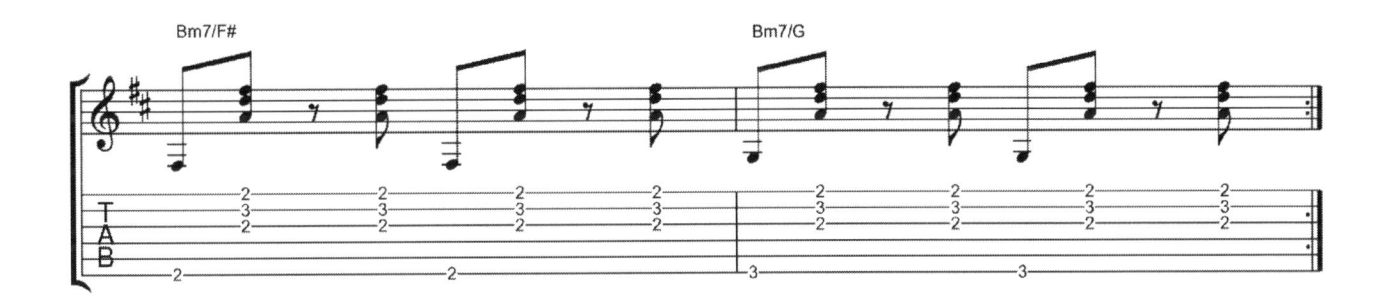

Open Minor 7 chord voicings sound just as good as their major counterparts. This progression is in the style of the Gary Moore song Parisienne Walkways. Notice the Dm7/G slash chord. It has a D Minor 7 as the main part of the chord and G as the bass note.

D Minor 7   A Minor 7

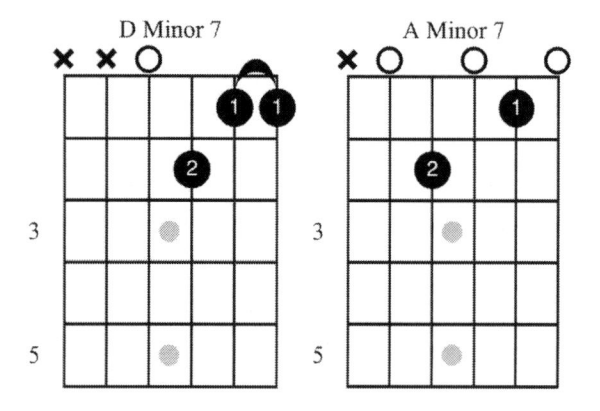

Example 6j

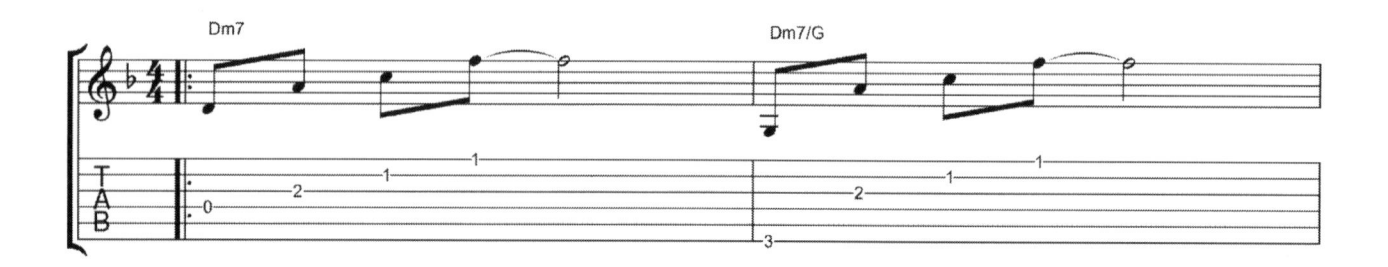

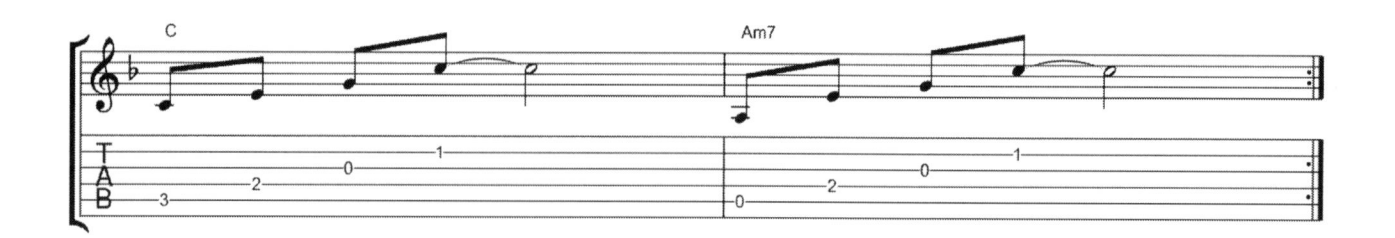

Two more useful open chord shapes are E Minor 7 and F Major 7.

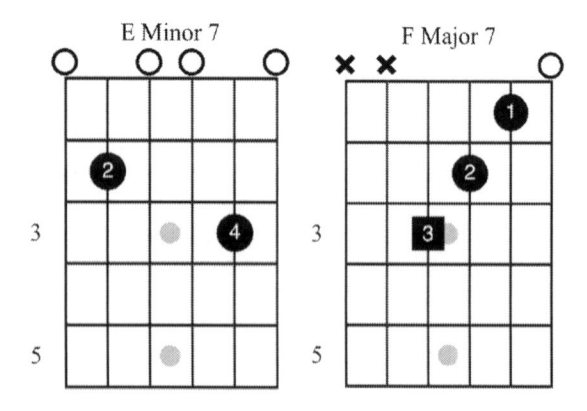

E Minor 7   F Major 7

Example 6k

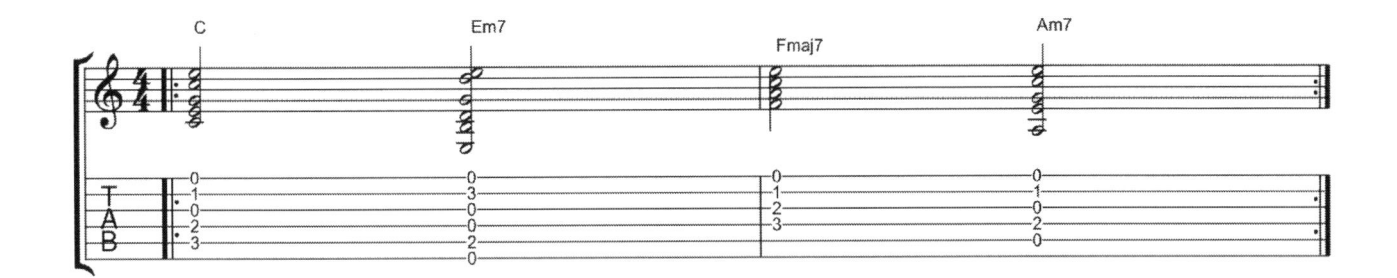

Sometimes all you want to do is sit and play a twelve-bar blues! Example 6l shows you how to do that using open chord shapes of A6, D6, and E6.

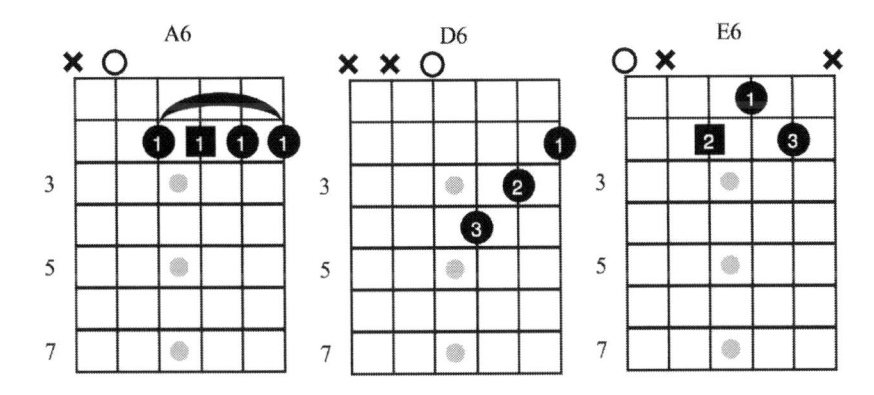

Example 61

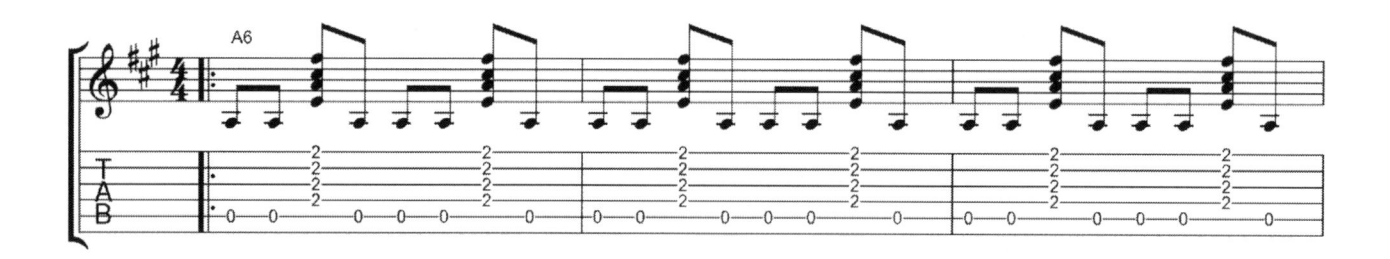

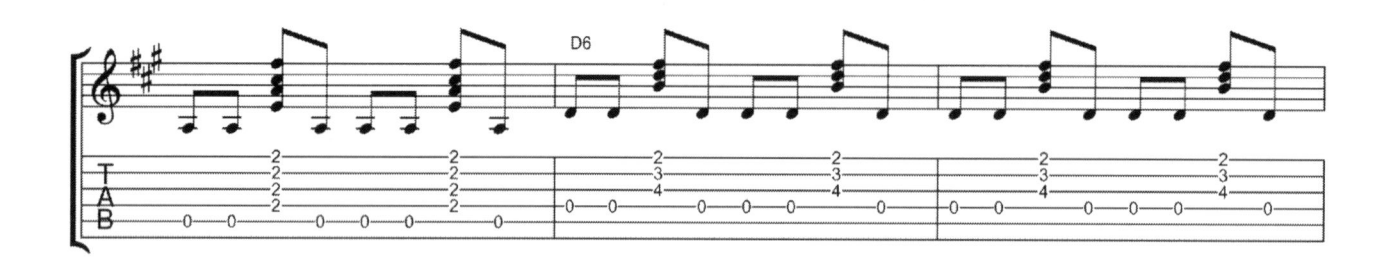

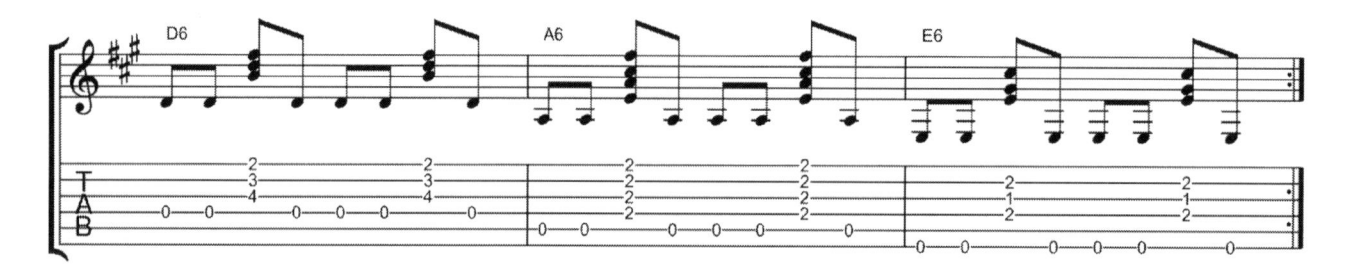

In this chapter, I have introduced you to lush ringing open chords and slash chords. There are, of course, hundreds of open chord shapes and slash chords for you to study, some of them featured in the songs listed below.

Be sure to record and document any new chord voicings and progressions that you learn. I recommend making a video diary of your playing, even if it is just a few minutes a day. That way you will be able to see a date and what level your playing was at, as well as hear what you were working on. By doing this you can gauge your progress.

Don't worry about having a super high-quality recording, the cameras available on smartphones and tablets will suffice.

For extra credit, why not start an Instagram account and tag @fundamentalchanges in your videos when you are learning something from our books.

Songs That Include Lush Open Chords or Slash Chords

- James Taylor – Fire and Rain
- Ed Sheeran – Thinking Out Loud
- Tom Petty /John Mayer – Free Fallin'
- Joe Satriani – Starry Night
- Jimi Hendrix – The Wind Cries Mary
- Pink Floyd – Wish You Were Here
- Pearl Jam – Better Man

Some of these songs may require a capo to play them in their original key.

Chapter Seven – Extended Barre Chords

Now that you have mastered a wide range of open and barre chord progressions, here are a few patterns that are great fun to jam with, but will require a little more work to perfect. Listen to the audio examples at least three times before you play them and start off extremely slowly.

The dominant 9th chord is synonymous with funk music and in particular with James Brown, so much so that it is often referred to as the 'James Brown' chord. The full barre chord shape is below, but if you are struggling to finger the barre across the top strings, aim to play the chord with separate fingers and leave out the high E string.

When I was studying at the Guitar Institute, we had to do multiple live performances every week. It was week three and the song was Tina Nina Nu. I remember spending countless hours honing the dominant 9th barre chord. Getting on stage that week was one of the most fun band experiences I have ever had, and also the moment that my love of all things funky began.

For a less common version of this track, check out Stevie Ray Vaughan's rendition.

This book is all about giving you chord progressions that are immediately useful. I can guarantee that the funky chord sequences shown throughout the following examples will be a favourite among both your band mates and your audience.

James Brown Style 9th Chords

You can also play this Dominant 9 chord using your third finger to barre the G, B, and E strings if you prefer.

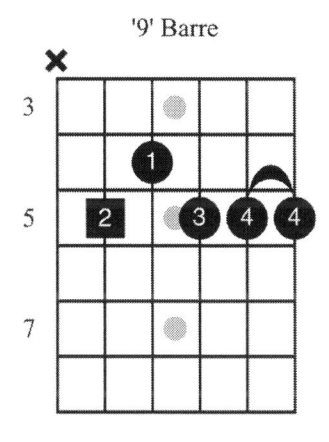

Example 7a shows a fundamental funk pattern using the E9 chord. Listen to songs like Sex Machine and Papa's Got a Brand New Bag by James Brown to hear this chord in action.

Example 7a

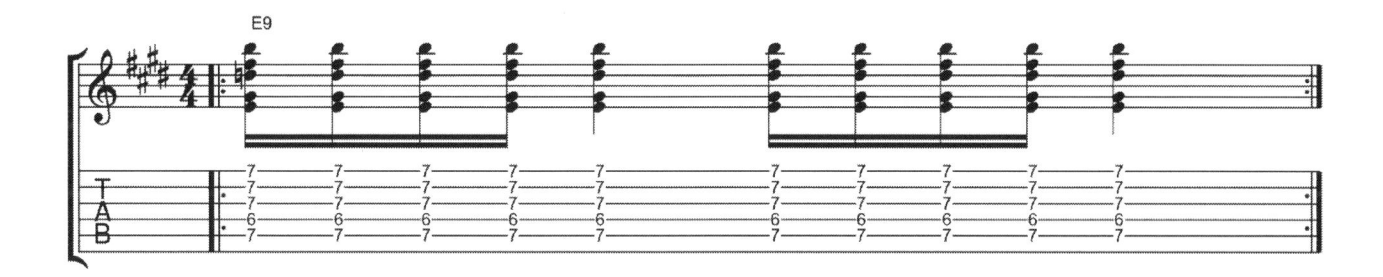

By adding your fourth finger to the 9th fret on the high E string, you can create the E13 chord heard in Sex Machine by James Brown.

Example 7b

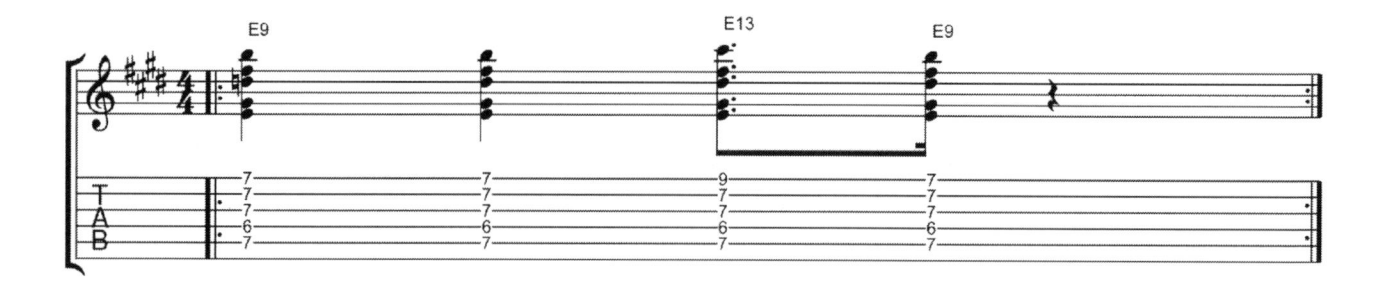

Sliding a barre chord is tricky but well worth the effort. Practice the slide between an E♭9 to E9 on its own before adding the root notes as well. Push firmly into the guitar when doing this slide. If you are struggling with the barre element of the chord, fret it with individual fingers as shown below.

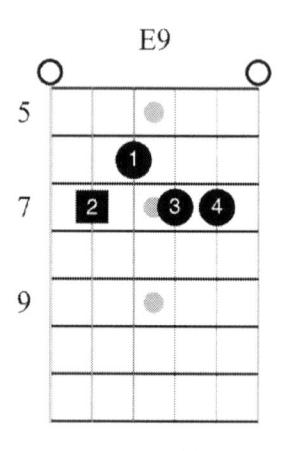

Example 7c

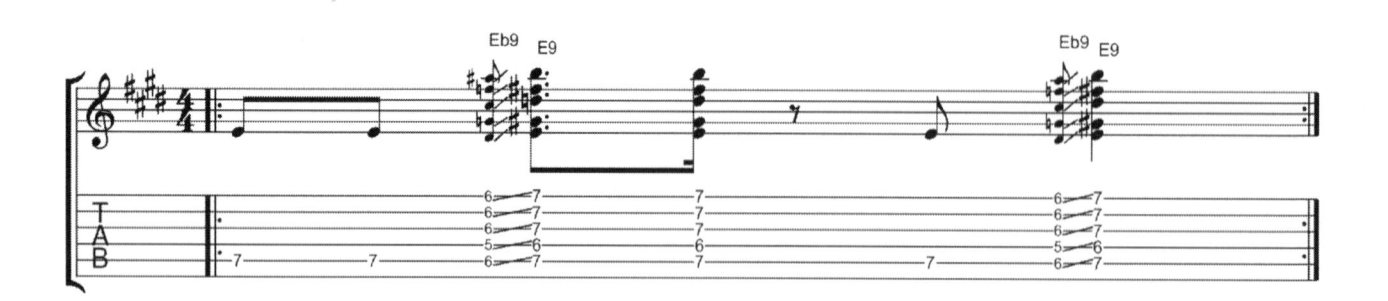

Example 7d is a small homage to the song Tina Nina Nu. It is a twelve-bar blues in the key of E that uses the Dominant 9 chords of E9, A9, and B9.

Example 7d

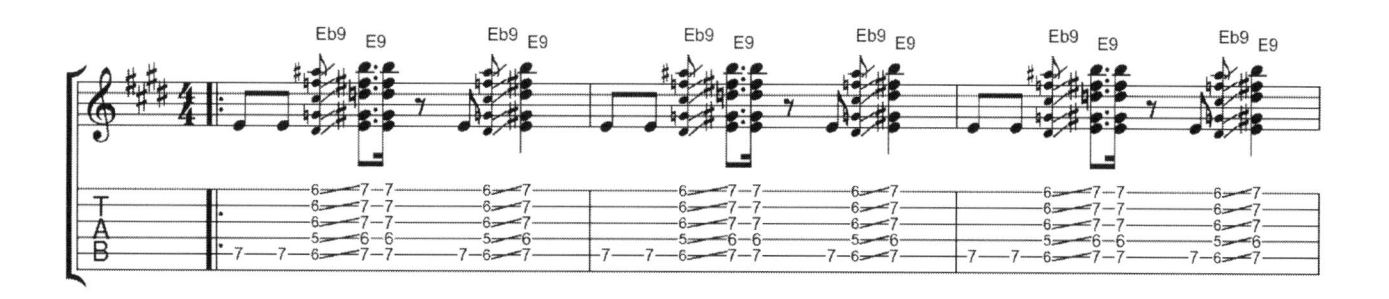

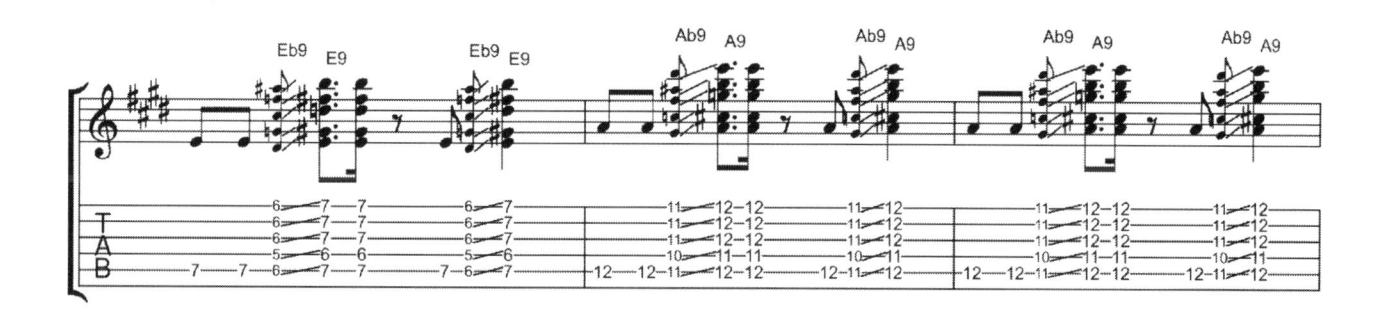

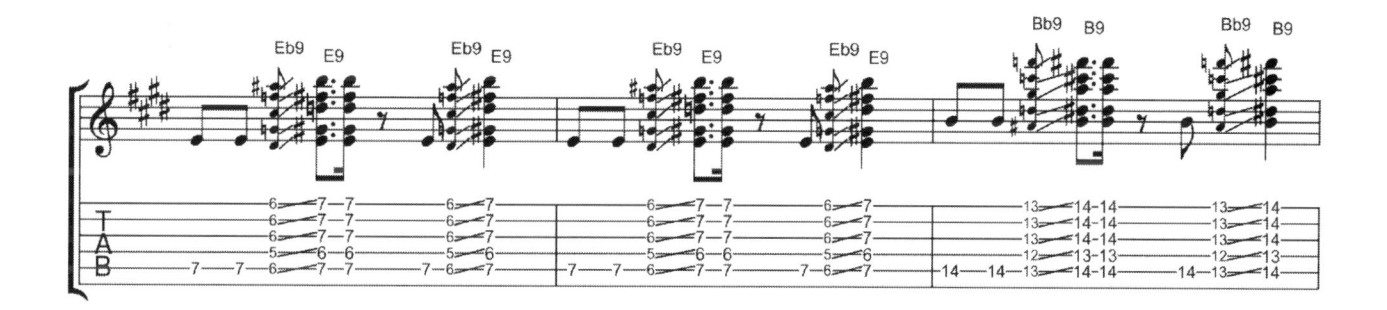

Twelve-Bar Blues Using 6th Chords

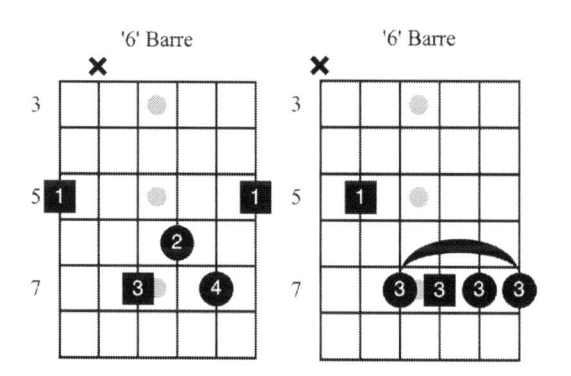

Example 7e uses the 6th chord shape in the key of A, D, and E to create a nice, movable twelve-bar chord progression.

Suspended Chords

Suspended chords can be used to replace either a minor or a major chord and come in two varieties, a Sus2 and a Sus4 chord. Although I have shown you some useful open suspended chord voicings, I've included barre chords so you can move them into any key.

Example 7f is in the style of the Michael Jackson song, Black or White.

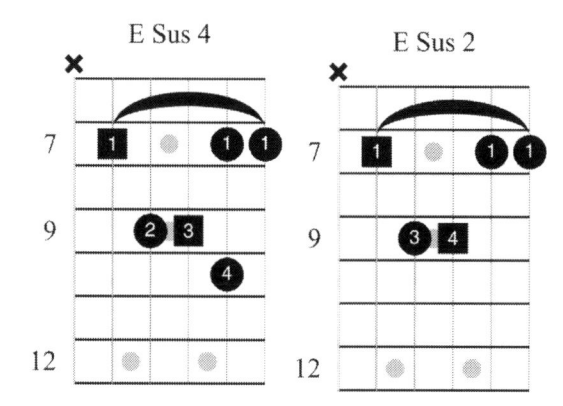

Example 7f

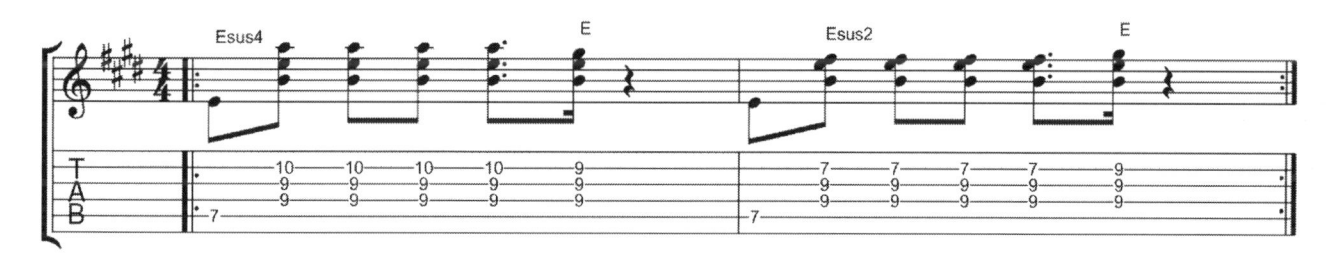

I fell in love in love with suspended chords when I heard the song Don't Dream It's Over by Crowded House. The most important element of example 7g is to let the notes ring into each other as you play through the barre chord shapes. Listen to how I achieve this in the audio example.

149

Example 7g

Minor II V I's

The final chord progression is the minor II V I sequence. Used commonly in jazz, it has a darker, sadder sound than its major II V I equivalent.

These examples will also introduce some commonly used altered chords. To understand what an altered chord is, and how it is built, refer to Joseph Alexander's book The First 100 Chords for Guitar.

Example 7h shows the foundational minor II V I voicings in the key of A Minor. Do not move on from this example until you have perfected it and can play it at 90 bpm. Make sure you mute the A and E strings.

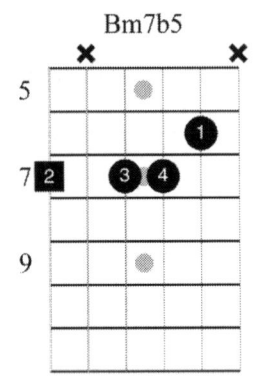

Example 7h

Next, replace the 'standard' E7 chord with an E7#9 chord. The 7#9 chord is often referred to as the 'Hendrix' chord as he used it frequently in his music, most famously in songs like Purple Haze, and Foxy Lady.

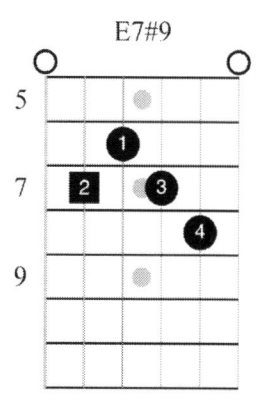

Example 7i

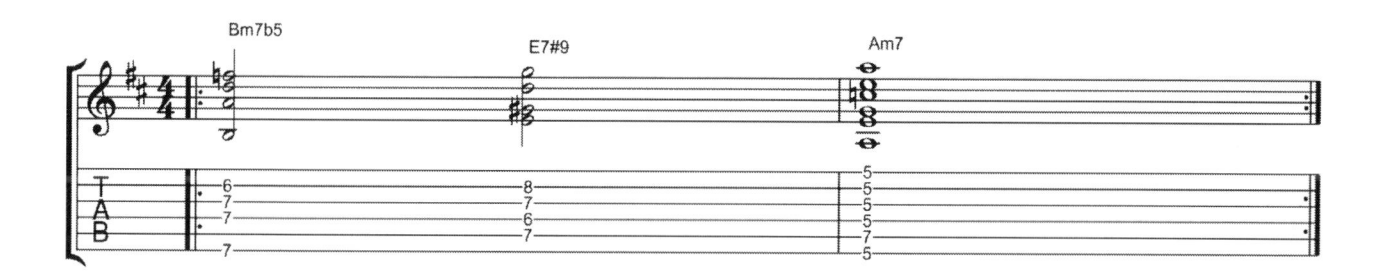

Another common minor II V I progression uses a 7b9 chord. Shown here in the key of E.

One song that combines both the E7#9 and E7b9 chord is Ain't No Sunshine by Bill Withers. You can play that chord sequence by playing Am7| E7#9, E7b9| Am7.

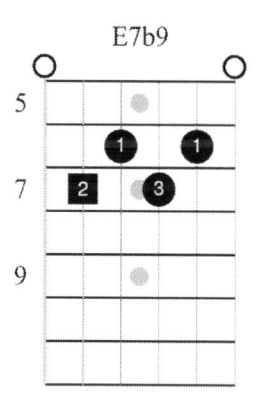

Example 7j

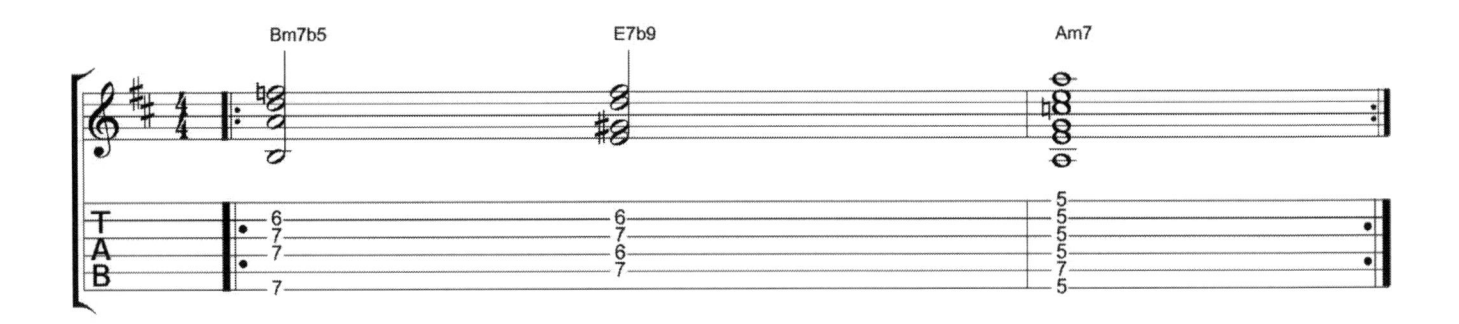

To make things even jazzier, example 7k demonstrates an E7#9#5 chord. Don't be put off by these names. It is far more important to learn how to play the shapes and how they sound, than to know how they are constructed.

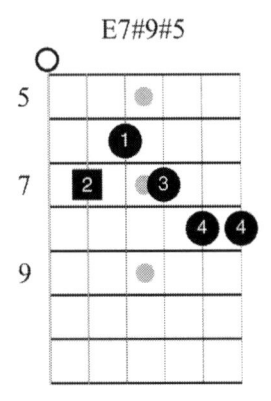

Example 7k

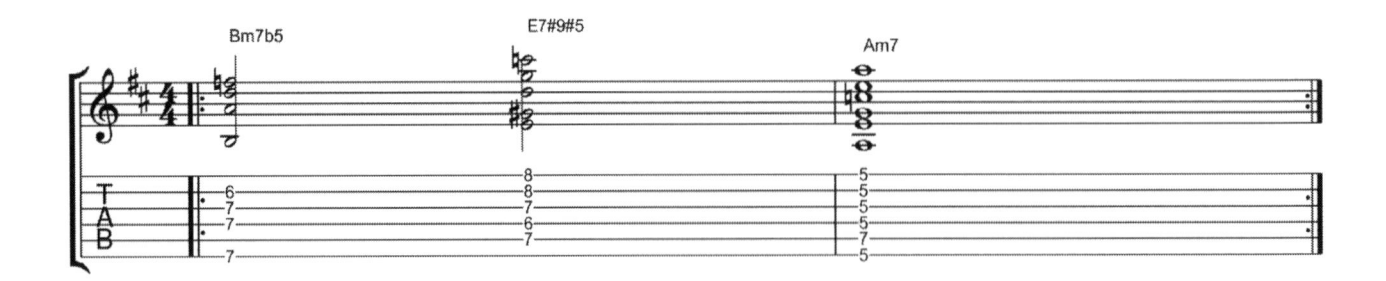

Next, learn this E7b9b5 voicing and use it in the minor II V I in A Minor.

Example 7l

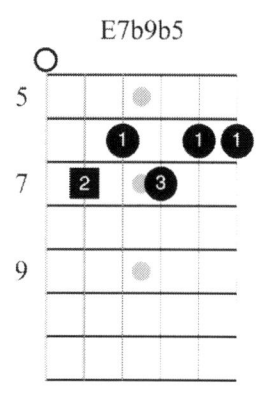

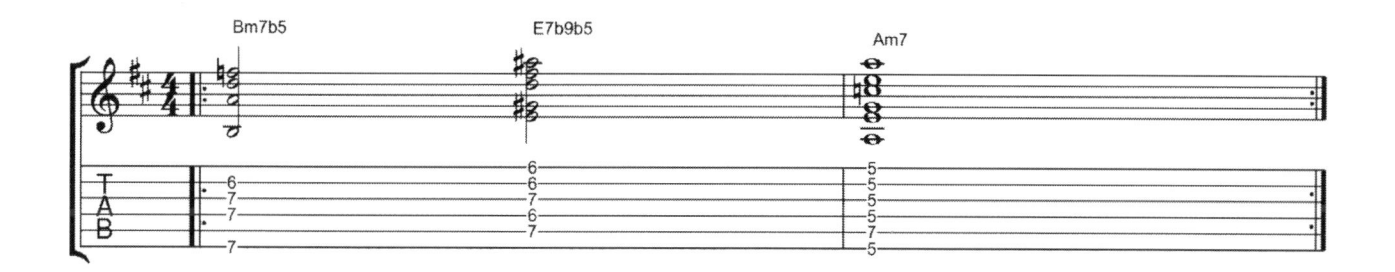

Example 7m includes a lovely E7#5 voicing high up the neck.

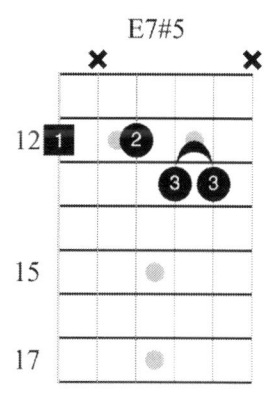

Example 7m

153

When learning chord progressions on the guitar, it is important to play them in more than one position on the neck. The final example features the same minor II V I progression in A Minor, but higher up the fretboard.

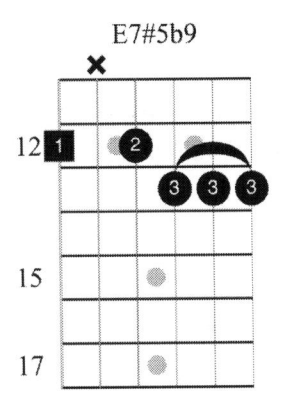

Example 7n

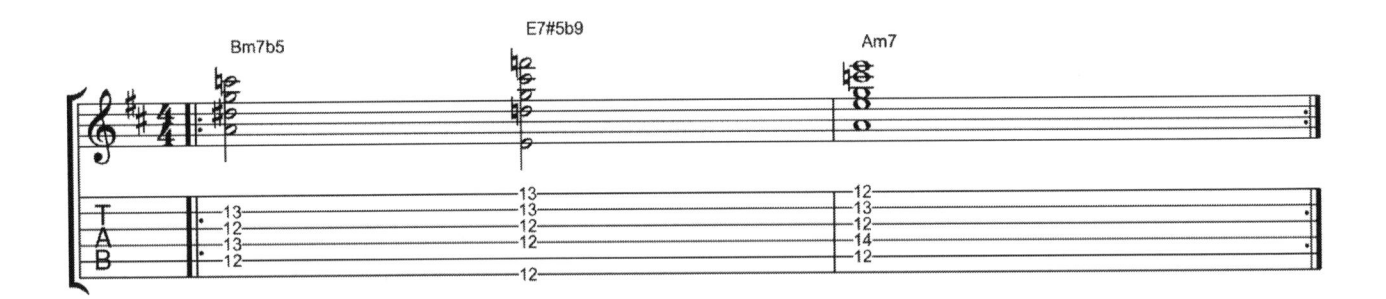

Songs that Include Chords from this Chapter

- James Brown – Sex Machine / Papa's Got a Brand New Bag.
- Slim Harpo (others) - Tina Nina Nu.
- Jimi Hendrix – Purple Haze.
- Michael Jackson – Black or White.
- Crowded House – Don't Dream It's Over.
- Jazz standards including Blue Bossa, Autumn Leaves, Days of Wine and Roses, and My Funny Valentine.

Test Yourself

Now you have worked through this book, test yourself and see how much you have memorised. Remember, it is far better to learn five progressions and be able to use them confidently, than to have played every example in this book and not memorised any at all.

If you struggle with any of the following questions, go back to the relevant chapter and recap what is required. There is absolutely no rush when learning to play the guitar, everyone progresses at different speeds and the main thing is to have a passion for playing!

Play an open E Minor chord – how many strumming patterns can you play from memory?

Play an open E Minor chord – how many arpeggio patterns can you play from memory?

Play an open E Minor chord – how many mixed patterns of strumming and arpeggios can you play from memory?

How many open chord progressions can you play from memory?

How many open twelve-bar blues progressions can you remember?

How many barre chord progressions can you play from memory?

Can you play a twelve-bar blues in B♭?

Can you play a Major II V I in all keys?

Can you describe what a slash chord is?

Can you play a James Brown style E9 funk groove?

Can you play lush open chords, including suspended 7th and 6th chords?

Can you play a variety of Minor II V I progressions?

Have you learnt the suggested songs throughout the book?

When you can put a tick next to all of these questions, move onto the next chapter to apply all that you have learnt in a practical context.

Chapter Eight – Creative Application

Imagine you are told you have four new songs to learn for a gig tomorrow.

In this chapter, I have arranged four chord charts and a wide range of backing tracks to replicate this scenario. Each of the chord charts has a drum track, a drum and bass track, and a full band track. The chord diagrams above each chart are only a suggestion, and you can use any voicing you wish to play along with the tracks. The challenge is to create a rhythm guitar part that fits the style and mood of each of these tracks. Each of the backing tracks is played at 90 bpm.

What I recommend is that you listen to at least a minute of the backing track through headphones before even touching the guitar. This discipline gets you used to listening to the band instead of 'noodling' endlessly.

When playing over these chord charts, play a rhythm guitar progression over the drum track first, then over the drums and bass track, and finally over the full backing track.

1. (Backing Tracks 1 – 3)

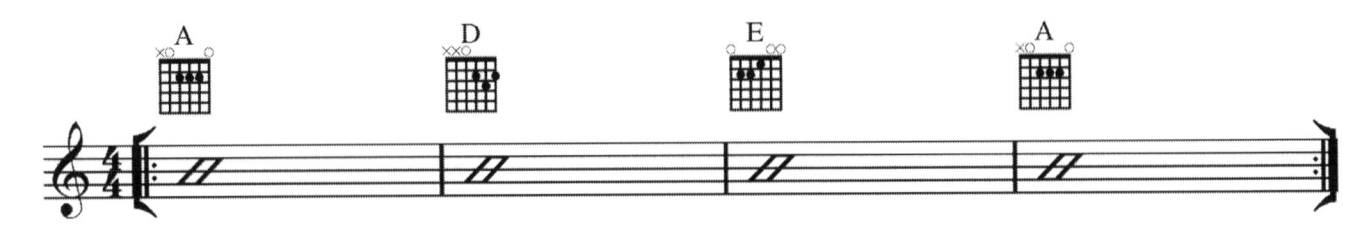

| A | D | E | A |

2. (Backing Tracks 4 – 6)

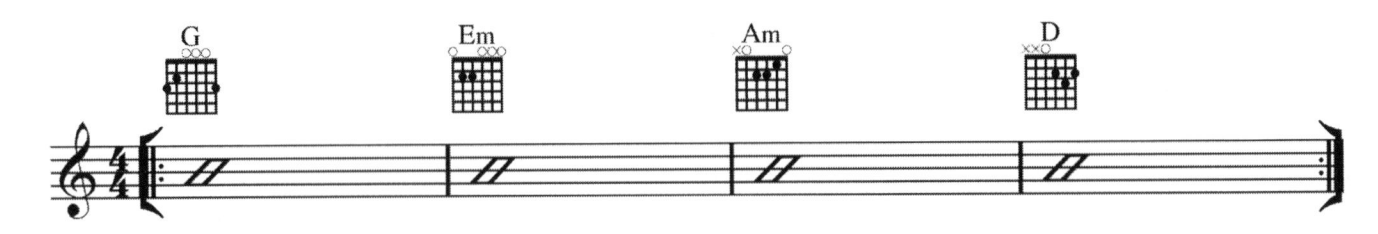

| G | Em | Am | D |

3. (Backing Tracks 7 – 9)

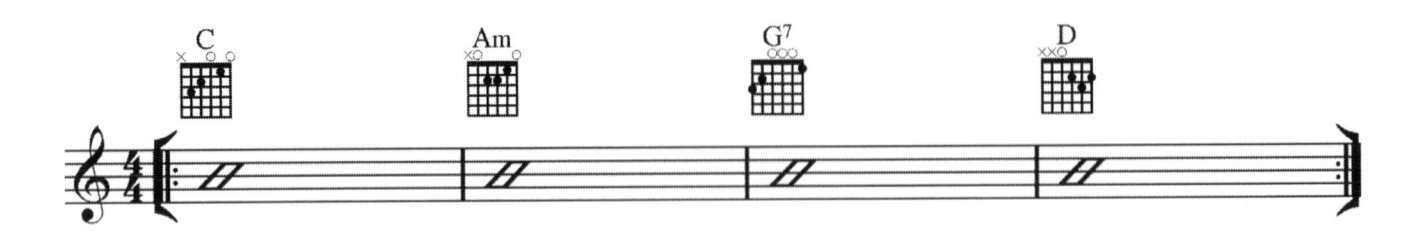

| C | Am | G7 | D |

4. (Backing Tracks 10 – 12)

| DMaj7 | GMaj7 | Bm7 | A7 |

Once you are familiar with all four backing tracks, create a different rhythm part over each. Refer to Chapter One if you need a refresher on some common rhythm patterns for chord progressions.

Another thing to try is to fingerpick through the chords progressions featured here. Finger picking works particularly well on an acoustic guitar and with a capo. For an introduction to finger picking check out this lesson:

www.fundamental-changes.com/fingerpicking-patterns-for-guitar

Dissecting Chords

Now you have mastered a wide selection of chord progressions in a cross section of genres, I want to give you my best tips and tricks on how to bring them to life.

View every chord as a group of individual notes, not just as a chord shape. You can play any number of those notes at once, instead of strumming all the notes at the same time.

Let's dissect this a bit further.

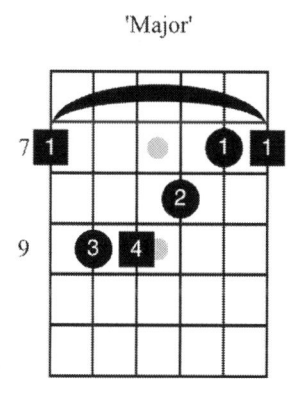

'Major'

Here we see a B Major barre chord. Within that shape are a huge variety of "mini chord shapes" that can be used instead of playing all six notes at a time.

One of the most useful shapes you can derive from this full barre chord shape is the two-note power chord shape.

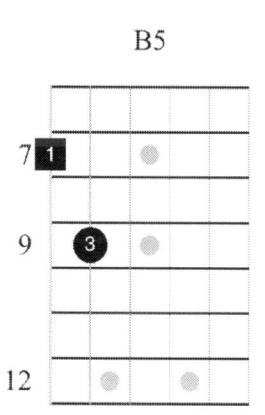

B5

157

Two-Note Shapes

After you have learnt the two-note power chord shape, you can then combine any two notes of the B Major barre chord to create new patterns. These strings do not have to be adjacent. Some of the most common two-note patterns are shown below.

Adjacent strings

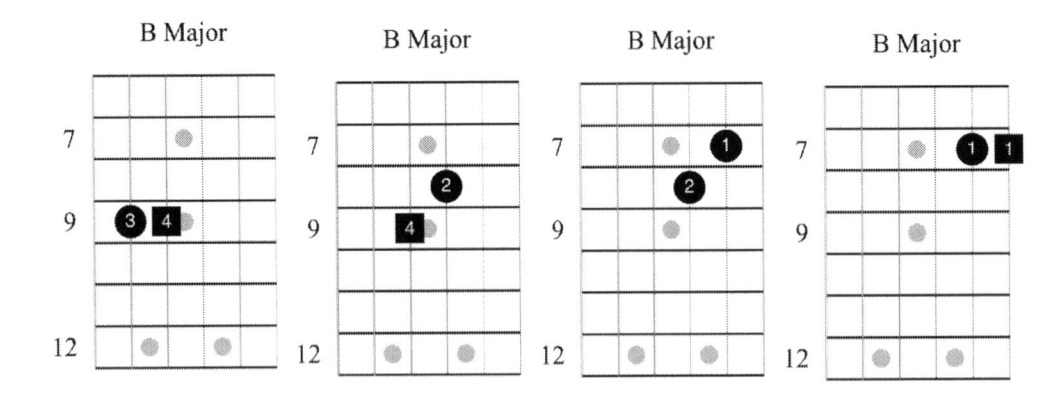

Non-Adjacent strings

158

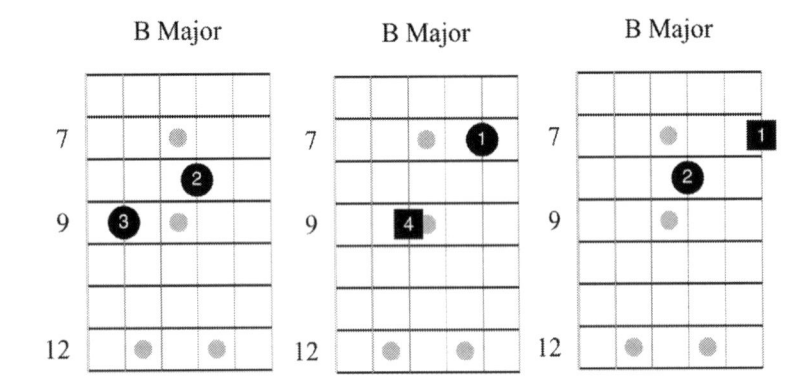

Three-Note Shapes

You can also create three-note chord shapes. Below are some common adjacent and non-adjacent voicings.

Adjacent strings

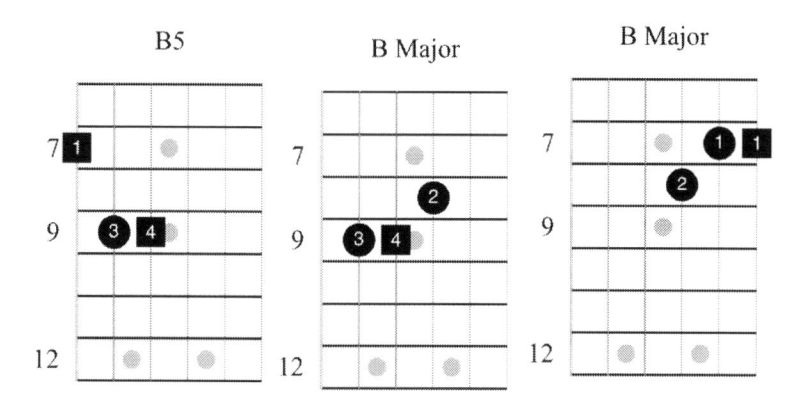

Non-Adjacent strings

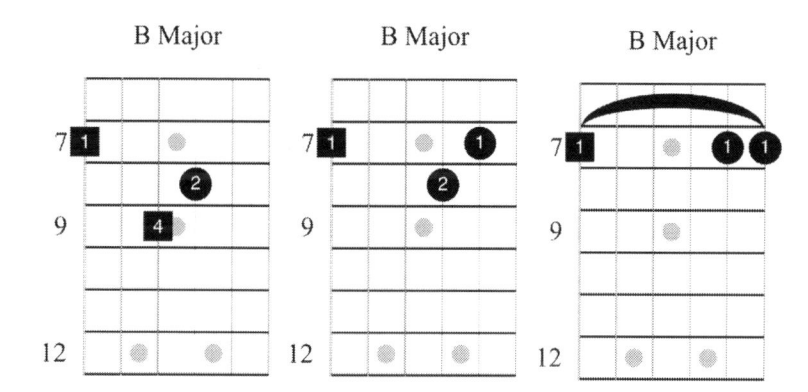

By splitting a chord into two-note and three-note chunks, it is possible to create a wide variety of voicings that will keep your rhythm playing sounding fresh. People often think they need to learn a huge range of chord voicings and progressions, when actually it can be more beneficial to dissect what you already know.

Exercise

Now you have dissected a B Major chord shape, pick four chords that you enjoy playing and apply this strategy to them. Once you have completed that, and got a whole new array of mini chord shapes, write a chord progression that uses them.

This is an exercise you can repeat forever and it will constantly push you forward as a guitarist.

Congratulations! You made it! I hope you have discovered a wealth of new chord progressions that you can keep coming back to for years. Like everything with guitar playing, these techniques require work but, as I always say, "The more time you devote to playing your guitar, the better friend it will be".

Chapter Nine – The Big List of Chord Progressions

In this section, I will break down all the chord sequences covered in this book into formulas so you can play them in any key.

To do this, I will introduce you to the Roman numeral system of chord notation. This is a shorthand that most musicians know and can easily use to communicate any chord sequence in any key. It is extremely useful.

The Roman Numeral System

The quickest way to describe a scale is with a formula. For example, any major scale (such as C Major C D E F G A B) is given the formula: 1 2 3 4 5 6 7. However, when we talk about *chords* instead of scale *notes*, we tend to use the Roman numeral system.

Instead of labelling the notes 1, 2, 3, 4, 5, etc, the chords are given a Roman numeral equivalent.

1 = i or I, 2 = ii or II, 3 = iii or III, 4 = iv or IV, 5 = v or V, 6 = vi or VI, 7 = vii or VII.

This is to avoid confusion when we're talking about interval distances, for example, when combining ideas like interval distances (3rds, 4ths and 5ths), and chords: (iii, IV or V).

You will notice that both upper and lower-case letters are used. Musicians use capital letters to describe major chords, and lower-case letters to describe minor chords.

Later, you'll see how we can use this Roman numeral system to change keys, but for now let's look at how to play the chords of the C Major scale.

When you harmonise (build chords on) the notes of the C Major scale, you create the following sequence of chords.

Notice that some are major and some are minor.

The Harmonised C Major Scale

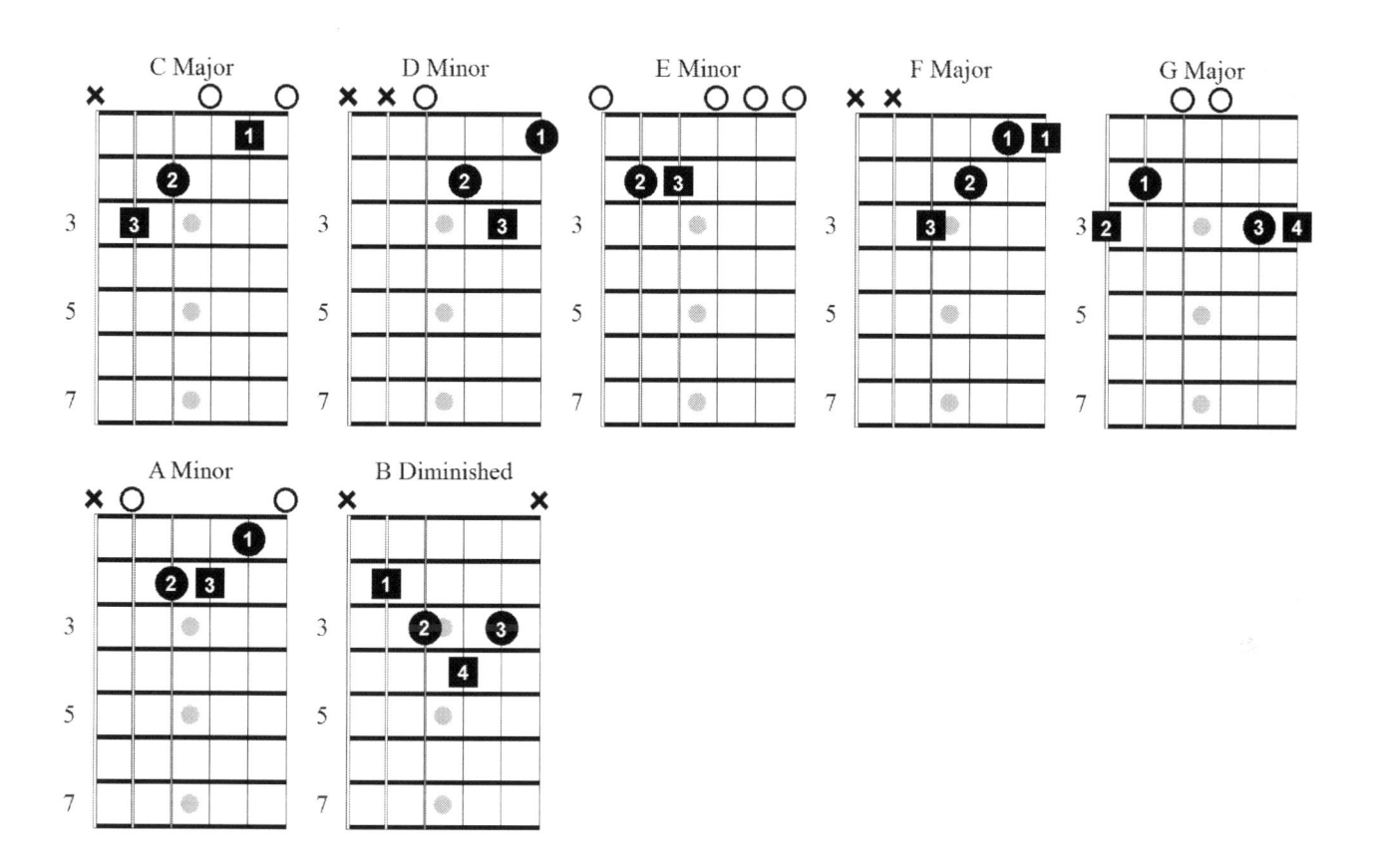

In the Roman numeral system, Major chords have upper-case letters and minor chords have lower-case letters. The chord of the C Major scale above can be described as follows:

Chord 1 (I)	C Major
Chord 2 (ii)	D Minor
Chord 3 (iii)	E Minor
Chord 4 (IV)	F Major
Chord 5 (V)	G Major
Chord 6 (vi)	A Minor
Chord 7 (vii)	B Minor ($b5$) or B *Diminished*

Common Chord Progressions from the Major Scale

Now you know how the basic chords of the major scale are notated with Roman numerals, it is important to play them and get to know how they function in modern music. There is no right or wrong in composition, just whether you like how your music sounds. That said though, there are some great starting points to learn before you start to break the rules.

In this section, I will give you a list of the common chord progressions in modern music.

Each example is given as both a chord chart and a formula which you can use to transpose the chord progression into other keys. Every example has been taught in earlier chapters, so the patterns should feel familiar.

I IV V (1 4 5)

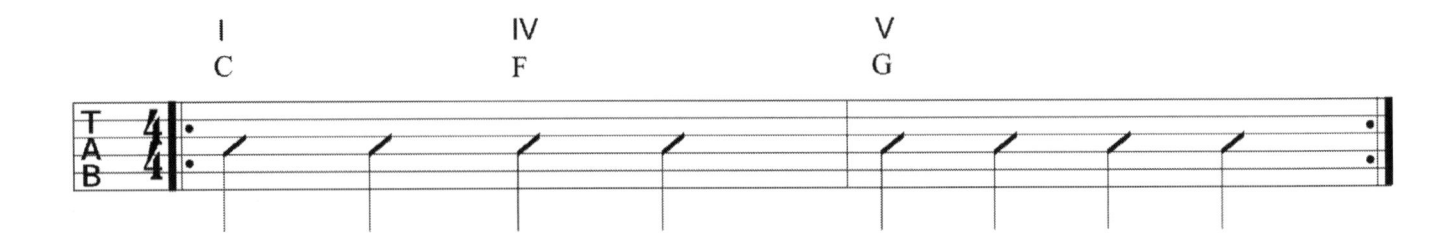

I - C   IV - F   V - G

I IV I V (1 4 1 5)

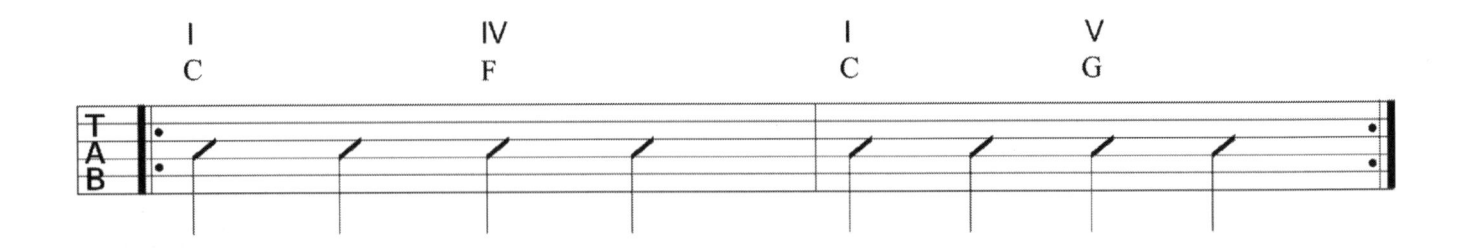

I - C   IV - F   I - C   V - G

I VI II V (1 6 2 5)

I - C   VI - Am   II - Dm   V - G

I V VI IV (1 5 6 4)

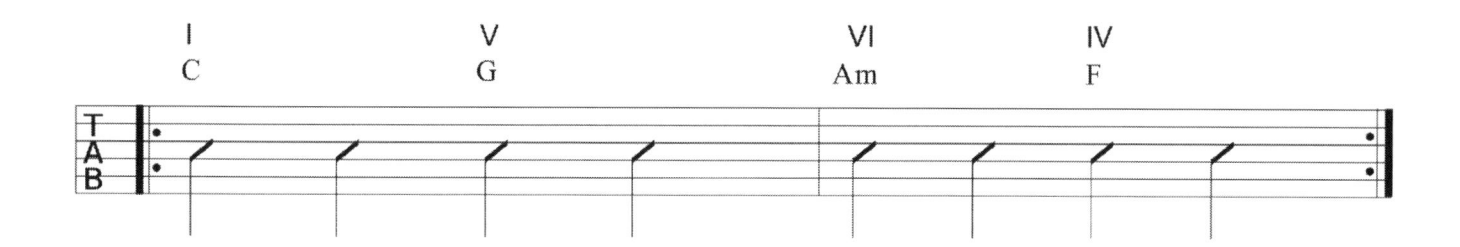

I	V	VI	IV
C	G	Am	F

I VI IV V (1 6 4 5)

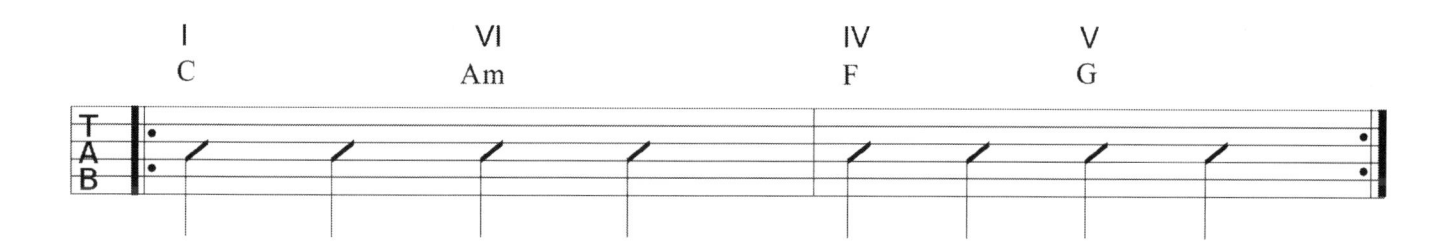

I	VI	IV	V
C	Am	F	G

VI IV I V (6 4 1 5)

VI	IV	I	V
Am	F	C	G

I7 IV7 V7

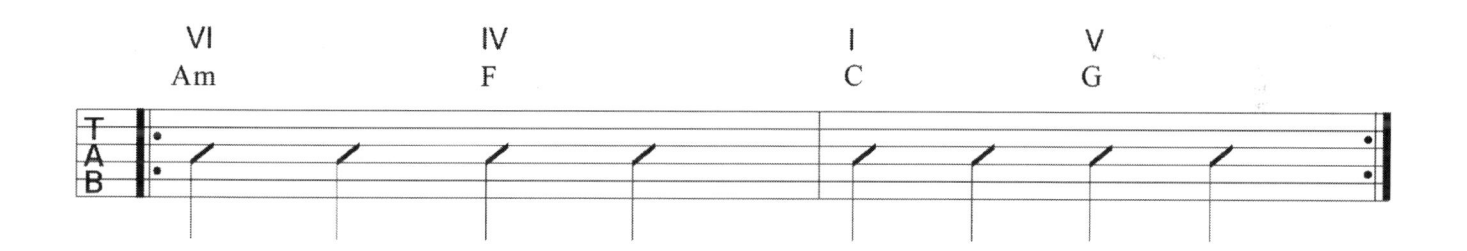

I7	IV7	V7
C7	F7	G7

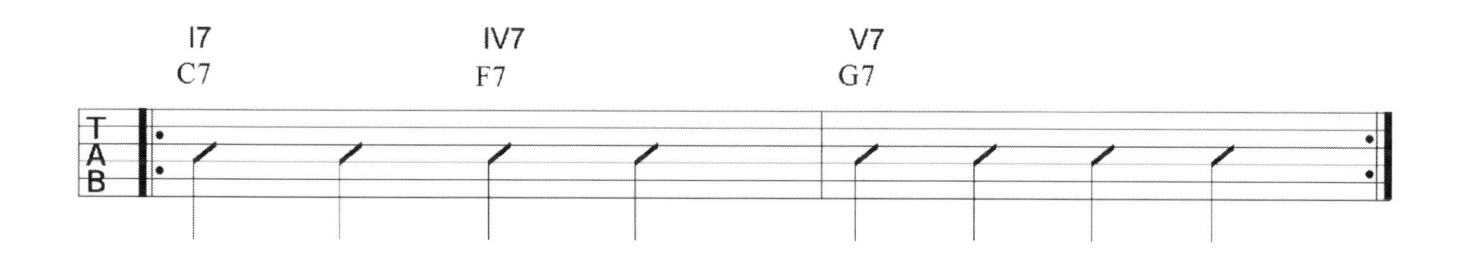

Twelve-bar blues structure 1

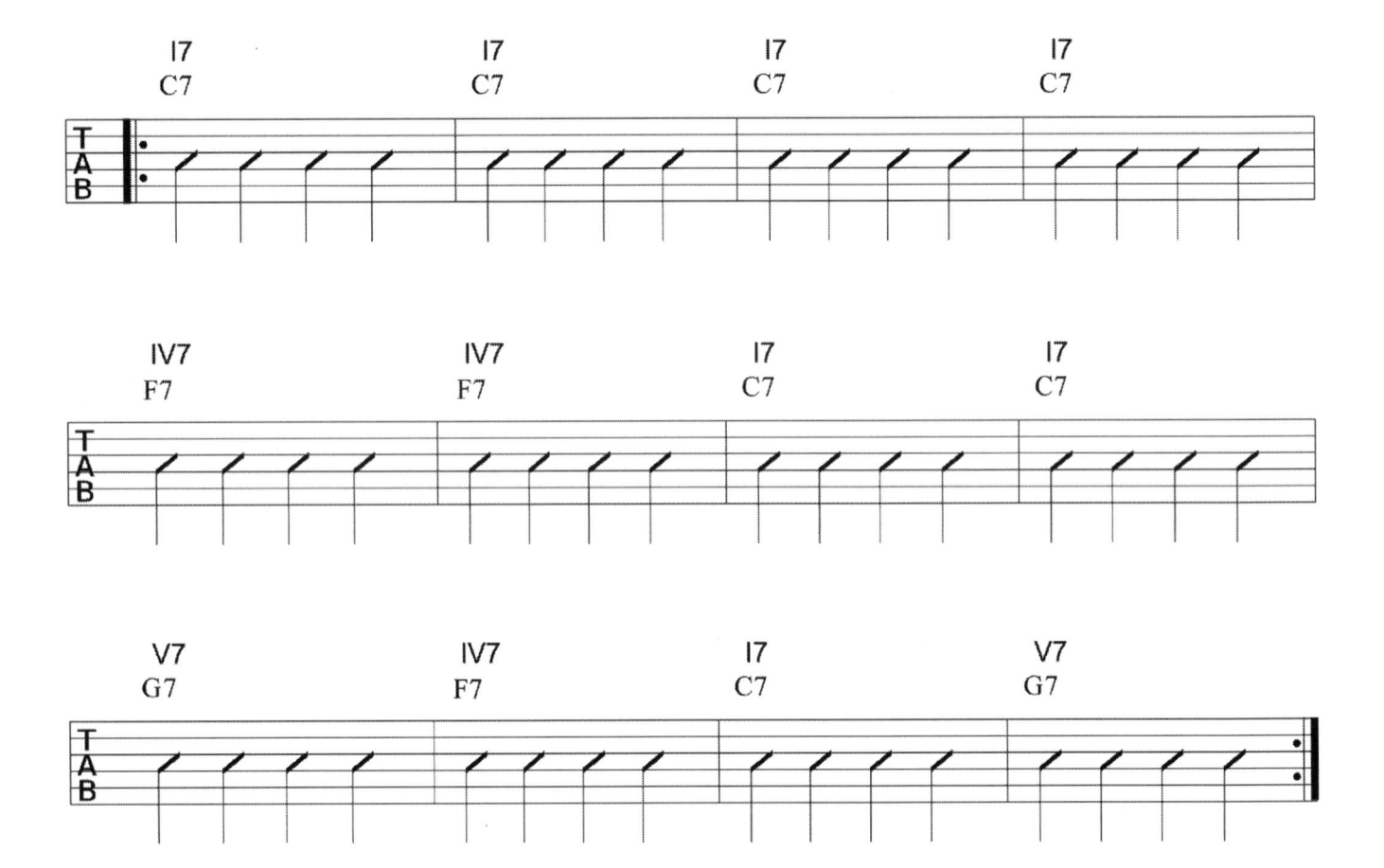

Twelve-bar blues structure 2

I III7 VI V (1 3 6 5)

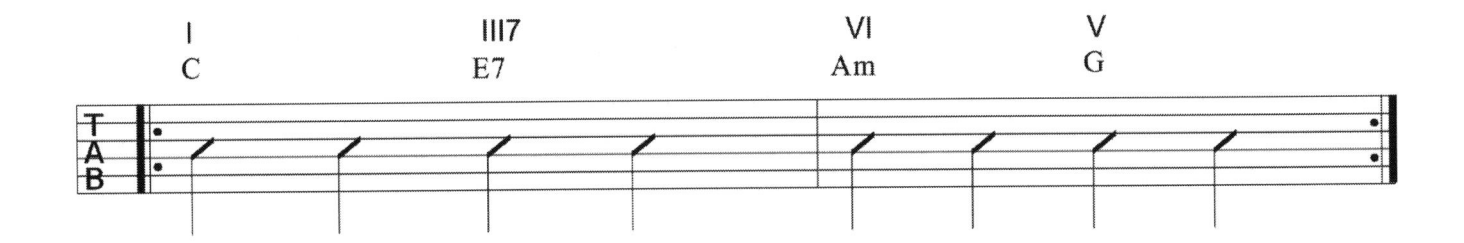

I	III7	VI	V
C	E7	Am	G

Im IVm Vm (1 4 5 minor)

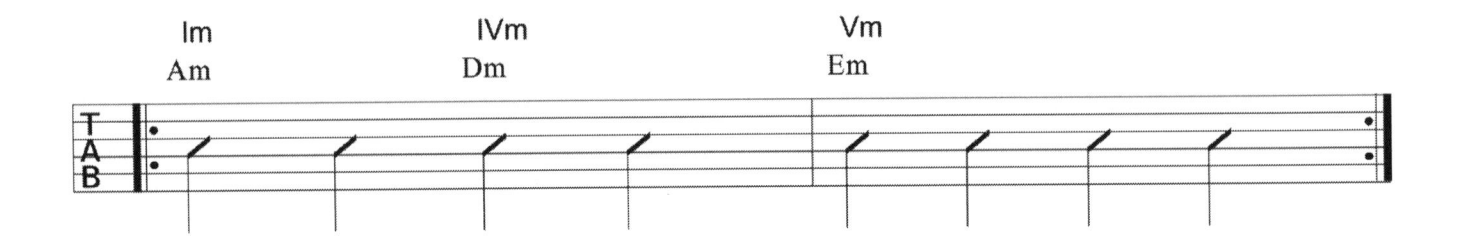

Im	IVm	Vm
Am	Dm	Em

VI V IV V (6 5 4 5)

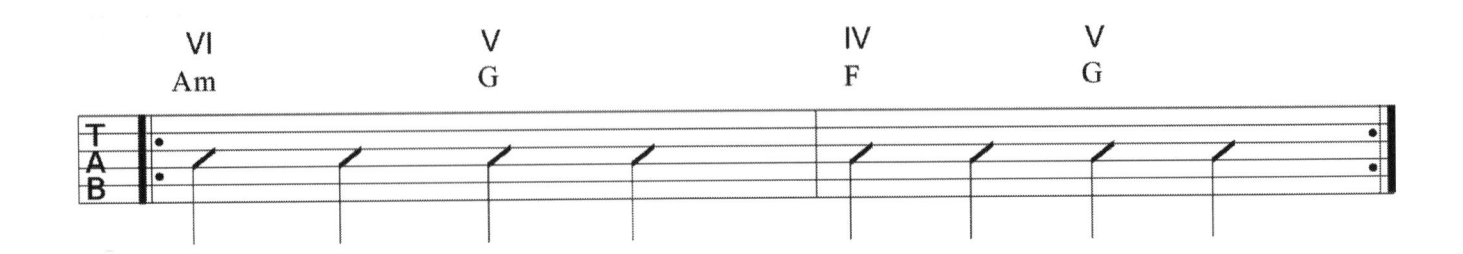

VI	V	IV	V
Am	G	F	G

VI IV I V (6 4 1 5)

VI	IV	I	V
Am	F	C	G

II V I (2 5 1) Mini

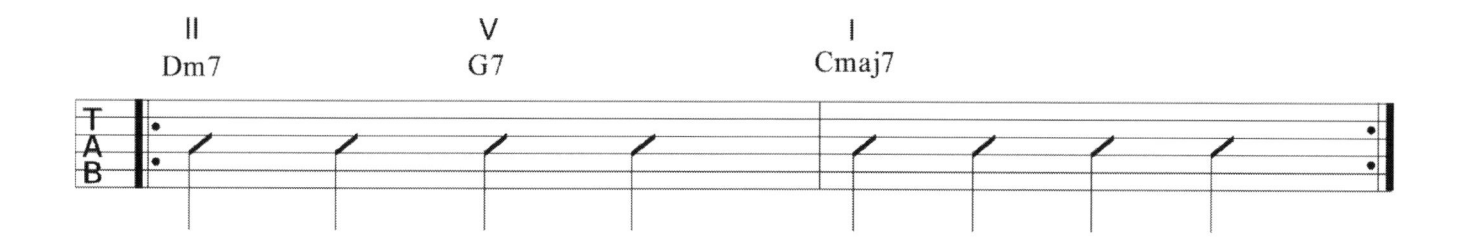

II Dm7　　**V** G7　　**I** Cmaj7

II V I (2 5 1) Longer

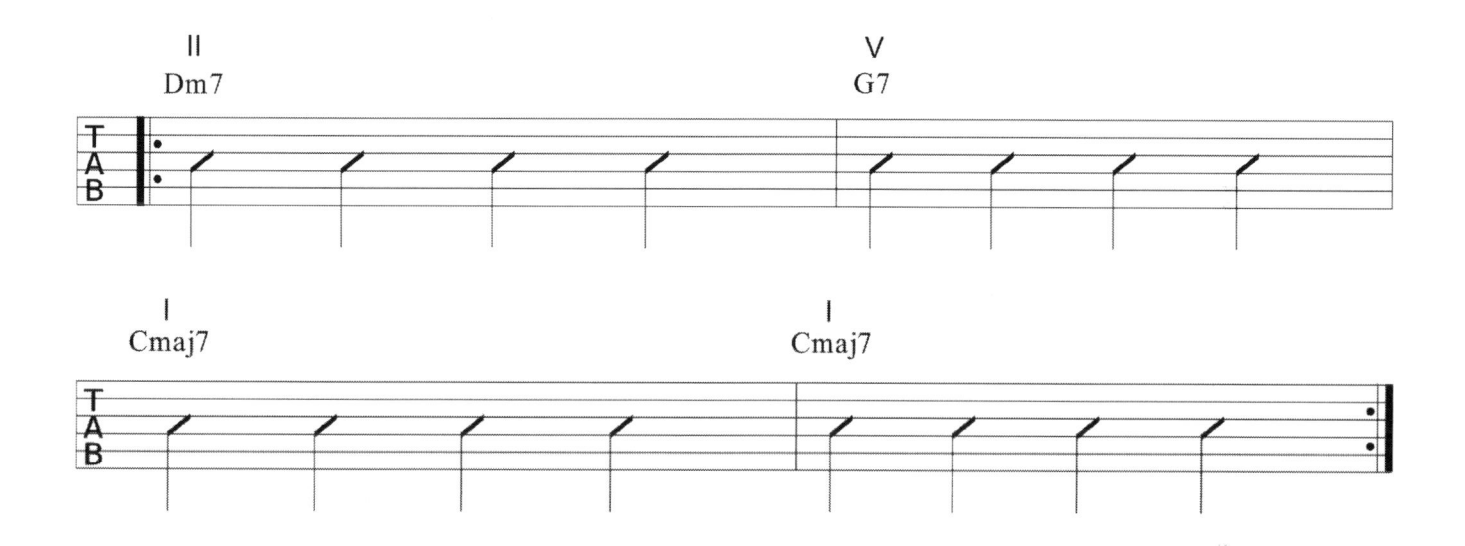

II Dm7　　**V** G7

I Cmaj7　　**I** Cmaj7

I VI II V (1 6 2 5) With 7th Chords

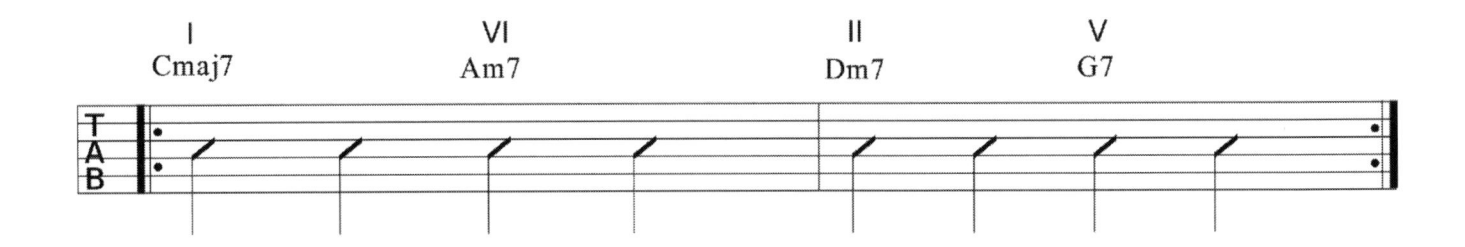

I	VI	II	V
Cmaj7	Am7	Dm7	G7

I VI II V (1 6 2 5) Variation

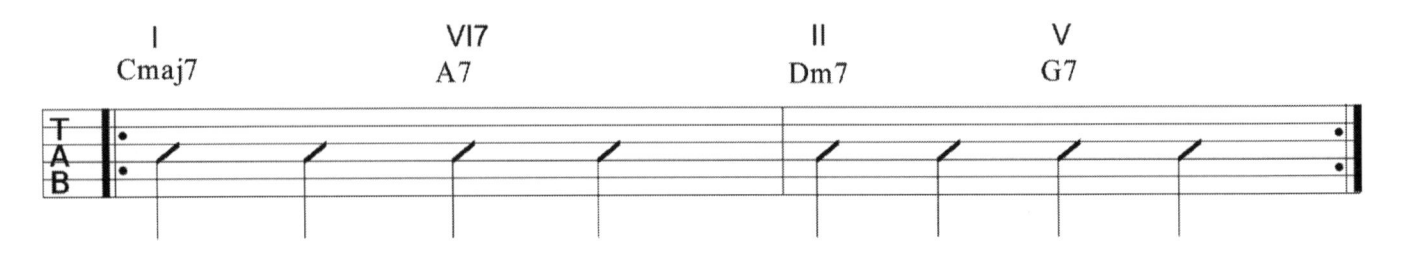

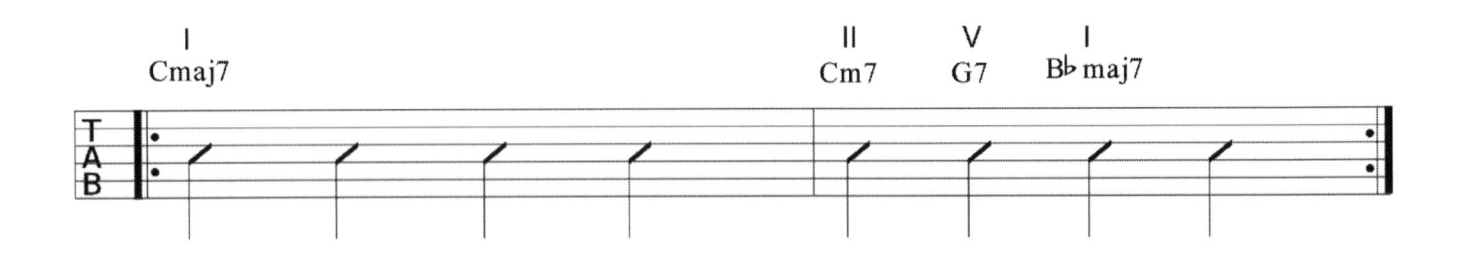

I	VI7	II	V
Cmaj7	A7	Dm7	G7

I – II V I (1 – 2 5 1)

I		II	V	I
Cmaj7		Cm7	G7	B♭maj7

C9 vamp

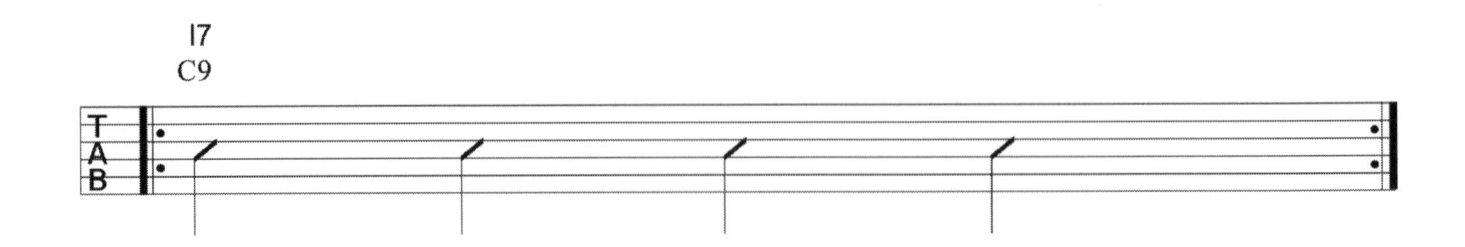

I7
C9

168

Minor II V 1 (2 5 1)

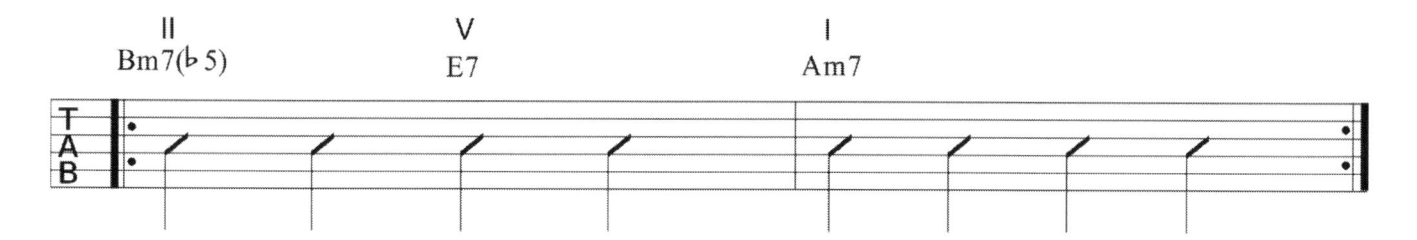

II	V	I
Bm7(♭5)	E7	Am7

Minor II V 1 (2 5 1) with altered chord

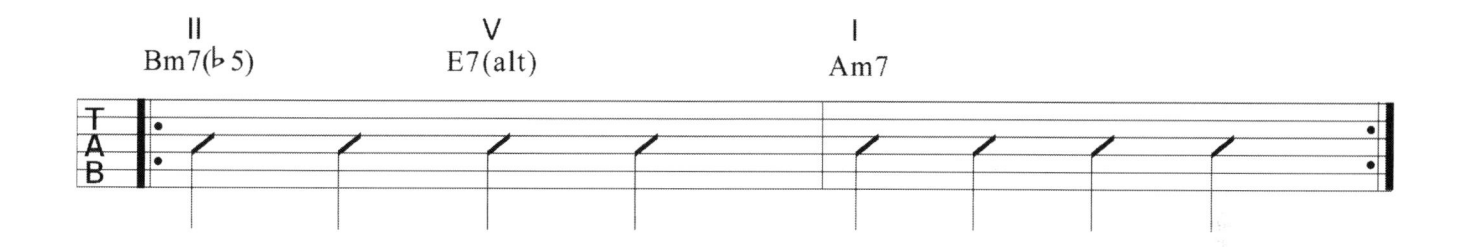

II	V	I
Bm7(♭5)	E7(alt)	Am7

Now that you have mastered these chord progressions in the key of C, you can look at how to move them into other keys.

Transposing Chord Progressions into Other Keys

As we have seen, common chord progressions often follow set formulas. Because of this, it is easy to transpose a chord sequence into another key once we have worked out how each chord fits into the Roman numeral system.

For example, take the following chord progression in the key of C Major:

Example 8a:

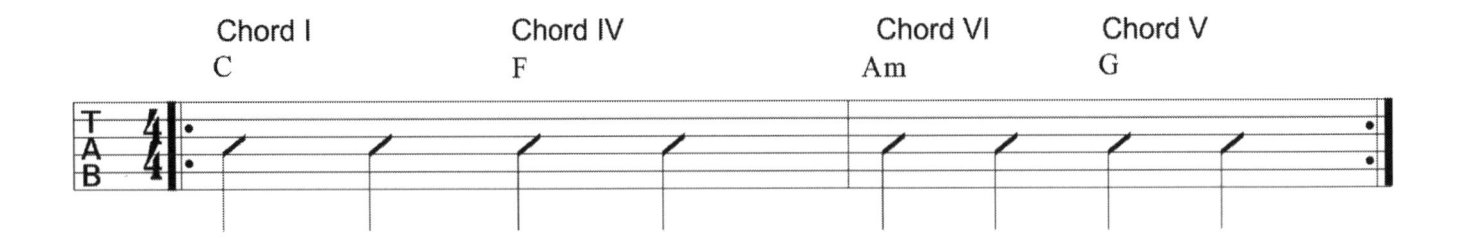

Chord I	Chord IV	Chord VI	Chord V
C	F	Am	G

Analysing it with Roman numerals shows us that in the key of C (C D E F G A B C) we are playing

Chord I, Chord IV, Chord VI, and Chord V.

We can now shift this progression into any other key by simply transferring the same chord pattern into a new major scale. For example, let's move it to the key of A Major (A B C# D E F# G#).

Note	A	B	C#	D	E	F#	G#
Scale step	1 (I)	2 (ii)	3 (iii)	4 (IV)	5 (V)	6 (vi)	7 (vii)

Chord I is A Major

Chord IV is D Major

Chord VI is F# Minor

Chord V is E Major.

The transposed progression becomes:

Example 8b:

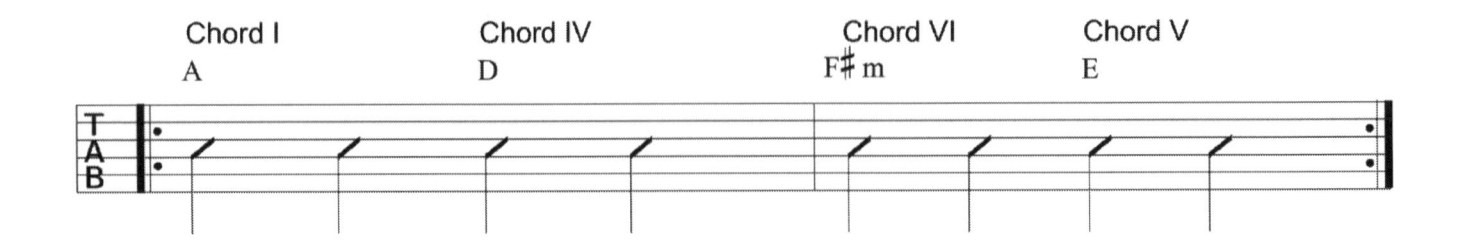

Chord I	Chord IV	Chord VI	Chord V
A	D	F#m	E

In the key of E (E F# G# A B C# D#) it becomes:

Example 8c:

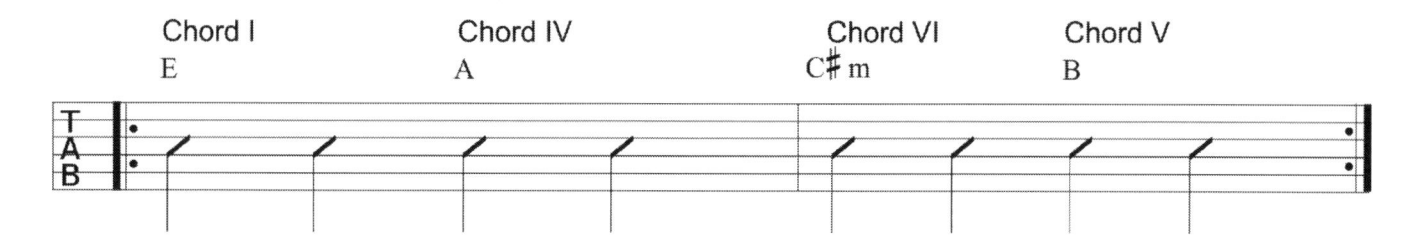

Chord I	Chord IV	Chord VI	Chord V
E	A	C#m	B

Notice how the musical effect of the previous three progressions is the same as each chord has the same relationship, despite being in a new key.

Try writing out the following two chord progressions in two different keys.

a) I vi ii V

b) IV V I vi

Work out the Roman numerals for the following two chord progressions in G Major and then transpose them into the key of E Major.

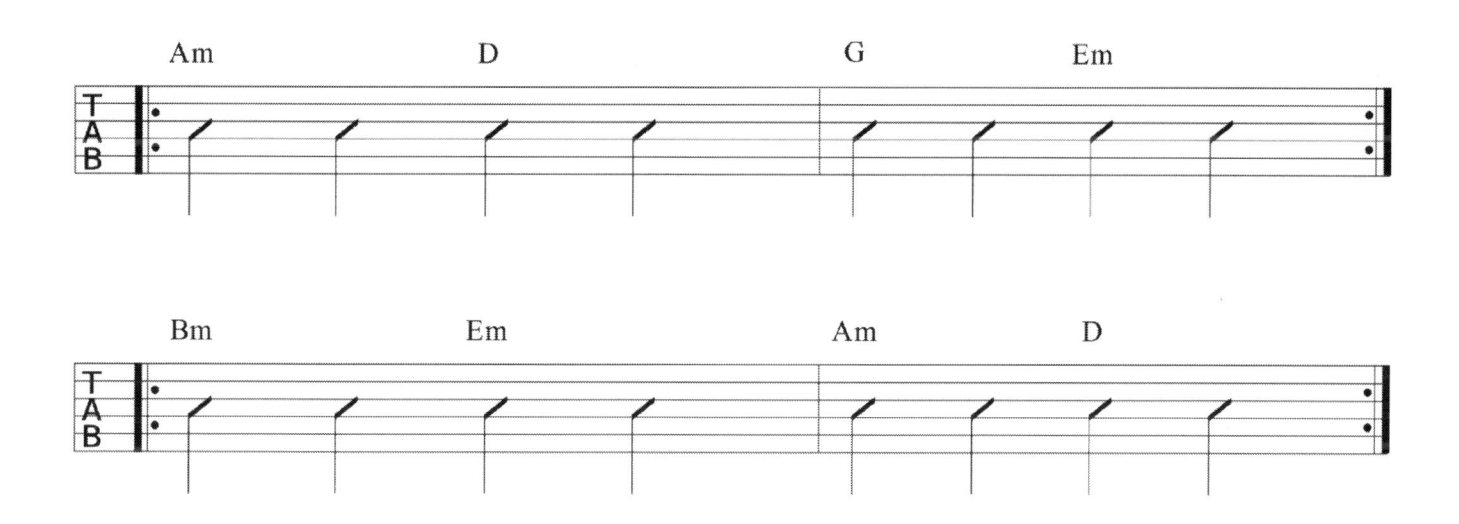

Am   D   G   Em

Bm   Em   Am   D

It is easy to practice transposition by analysing a song you are already familiar with, writing it out in Roman numerals and then moving those numerals into another key.

Chords from Outside the Key

Study the following chord progression:

Example 8d:

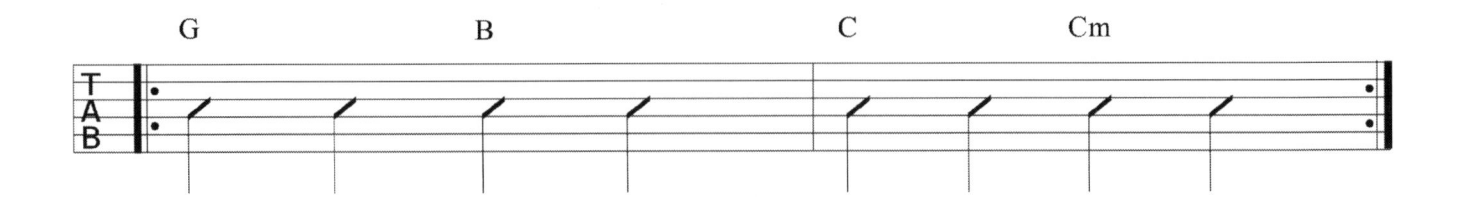

| G | B | C | Cm |

This progression is based on a song by Radiohead and is in the key of G, however when you analyse it, you will come across some chords that are not formed from the harmonised G Major scale. The second chord in the song is B Major. The note B is the third note in the key of G and when you harmonise the third degree of a major scale, you always form a minor chord.

It is clear that the diatonic B Minor chord has been replaced with a B Major chord. This is perfectly fine to do, and happens often. It makes the chord progression more interesting and is clearly what the composer intended to write. The only question is, how do we write this in Roman numerals?

The chord is still functioning as chord iii, but as it has been altered to become a major chord instead of a minor one, we simply write, 'III Major'. Notice the capital I's? Lower-case is for minor, upper-case is for major.

The C Major in bar three is correct to the key (it is chord IV major), but in bar four, the C Major becomes a C Minor chord. This would be written as 'iv minor'. Again, lower-case numerals indicate that this is a minor chord.

The full progression, therefore would be written as: I, III(major), IV, iv(minor).

A minor blues like example 8e could be written i(minor), iv(minor), v(minor), i (minor).

Example 8e:

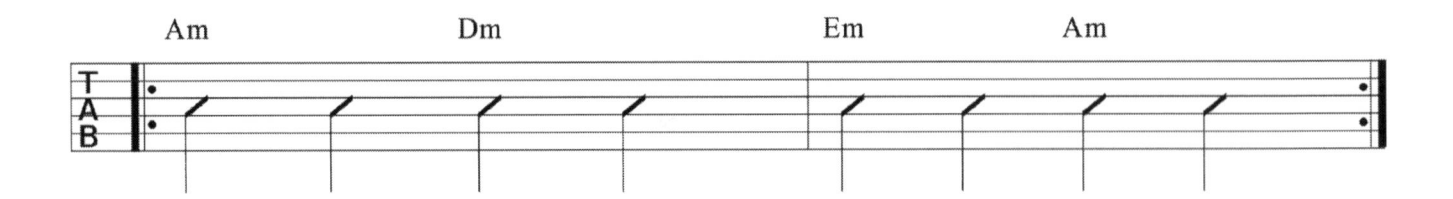

| Am | Dm | Em | Am |

Sometimes, however, a chord may not even exist inside the scale of the parent key. The following chord progression comes from the middle section of Sitting on the Dock of the Bay, by Otis Redding. It is in the key of G.

All the chords are derived from the key of G Major, except for the F in bar 3. The scale of G Major (G A B C D E F#) does not contain the note F, (it should be F#). If we were to analyse the progression with Roman numerals, we would deal with the F Major by writing *b*VII (major) as the 7th degree of the G Major scale (F#) has been 'flattened' to become the note F, and it is being played as a major chord.

The whole progression is written as I, V, IV, I, *b*VII (major), V.

Example 8f:

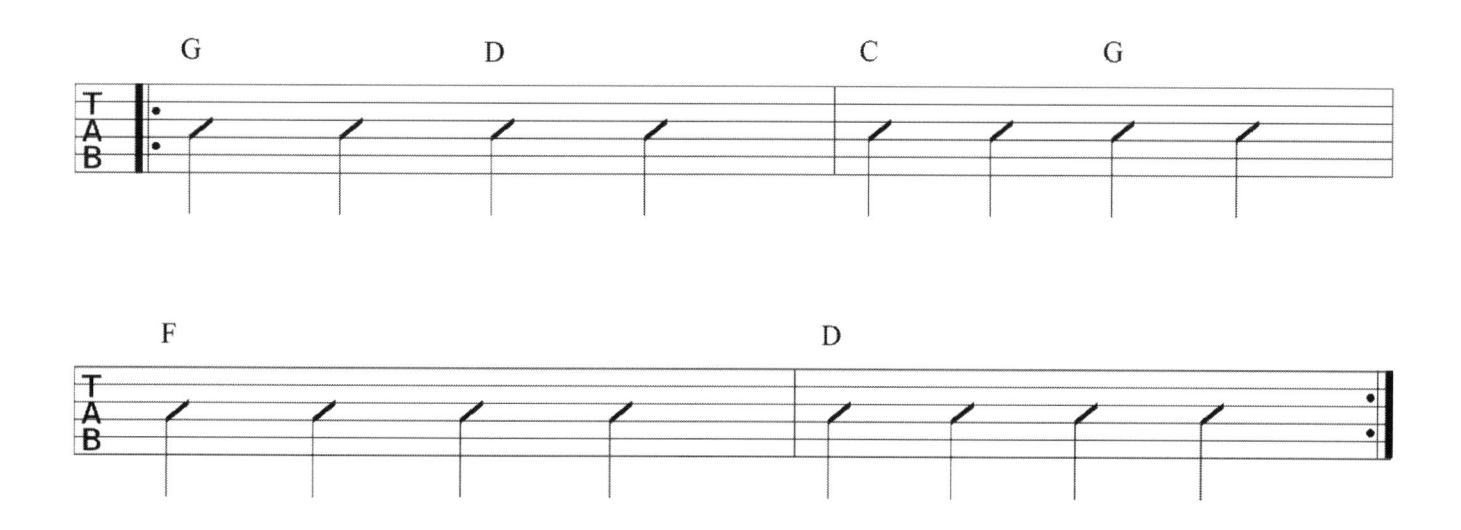

G	D	C	G

F		D	

Another great use of the *b*VII (major) is in the Blues Brothers' Everybody Needs Somebody. This progression is I, IV, *b*VII(Major), IV

Example 8g:

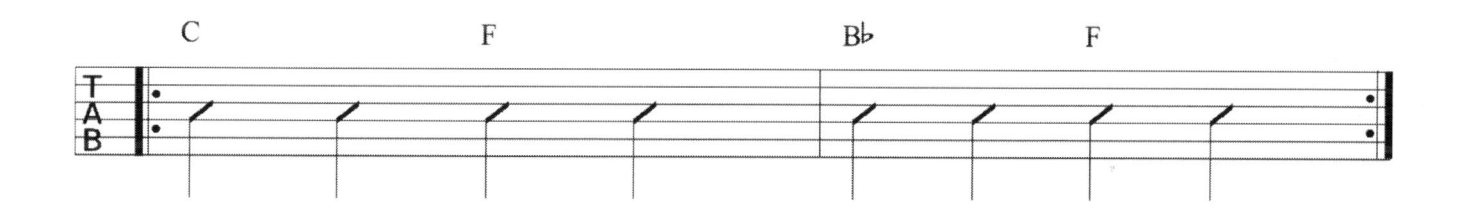

C	F	B♭	F

173

Another common non-diatonic chord is *b*III(major), used here in the key of A. This progression is I, V, *b*III(major), IV, I.

Example 8h:

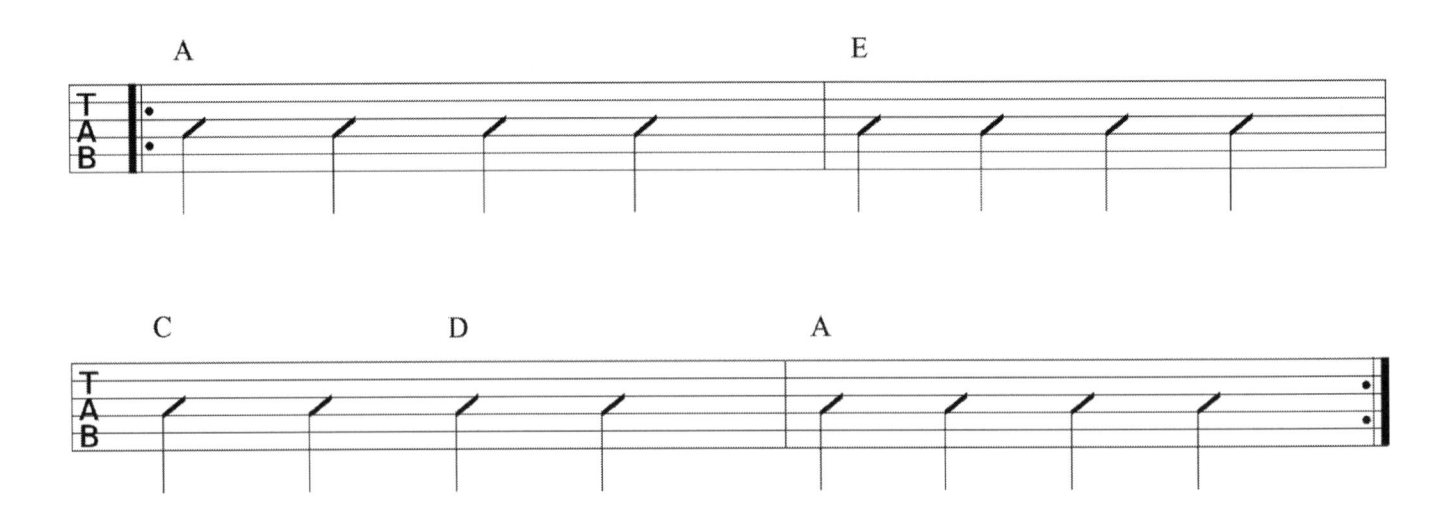

[Tab notation: A | E | C | D | A]

One chord The Beatles used to good effect was *b*VI(major). Here it is in the key of C. The progression is I, IV, *b*VI(major), I.

Example 8i

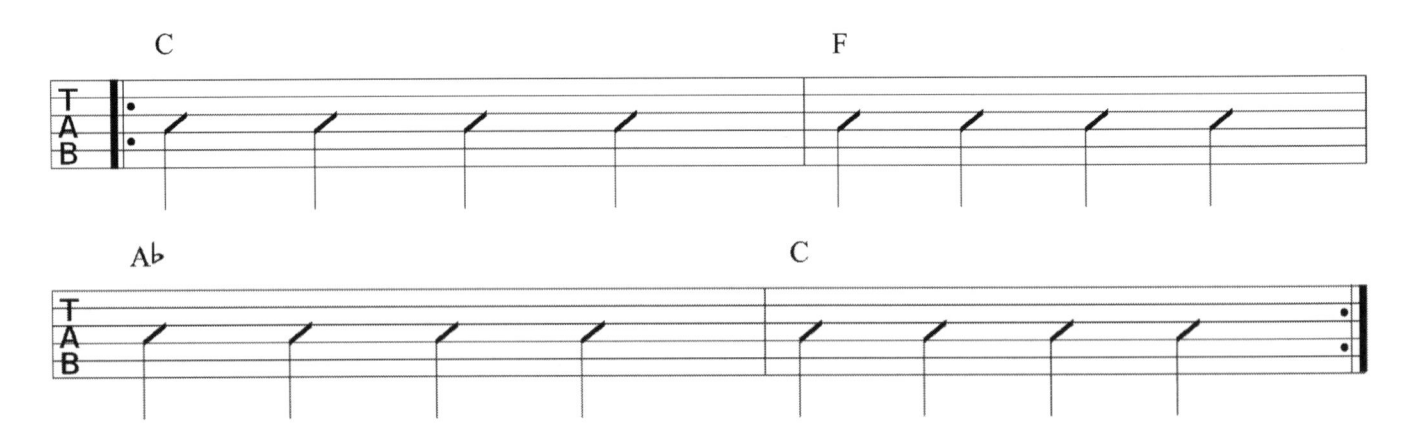

[Tab notation: C | F | Ab | C]

Try writing these examples in other keys. More importantly, make sure you can play them and recognise them.

Chord Extensions

Once you are confident playing common chord progressions in a variety of keys, you can experiment with adding in chord extensions. A chord extension is anything other than a straight Minor, Major, or Dominant 7th chord. Examples of this featured throughout this book would be Minor 7th chords, Major 7th chords and Dominant 9th chords.

Often just by changing a major chord for a major 7th, or a minor chord for a minor 7th, you can create a much more sophisticated chord sequence.

For more information on how a chord extension is built, refer to Joseph Alexander's book **The Practical Guide to Modern Music Theory.**

Chapter Ten – Practice Workouts

The perfect practice workout is one that fits around your individual needs, interests and ability. I have created 10, 15, 30, and 60-minute workout suggestions for you below. These workouts are a guide, and can be customised any way you wish.

Use a metronome and a timer for each workout!

10 Minute Workout

Example Number	Metronome Speed	Total Time
1c	60bpm (Increase Daily)	1 Minute
1e	60bpm (Increase Daily)	1 Minute
1p	60bpm (Increase Daily)	1 Minute
2c	60bpm (Increase Daily)	1 Minute
2w	60bpm (Increase Daily)	1 Minute
3c	60bpm (Increase Daily)	1 Minute
4d	60bpm (Increase Daily)	1 Minute
4n	60bpm (Increase Daily)	1 Minute
5b	60bpm (Increase Daily)	1 Minutes
7d	60bpm (Increase Daily)	1 Minutes
		10 Minutes

15 Minute Workout

Example Number	Metronome Speed	Total Time
1h	60bpm (Increase Daily)	1 Minute
2c	60bpm (Increase Daily)	1 Minute
2w	60bpm (Increase Daily)	1 Minute
3e	60bpm (Increase Daily)	1 Minute
3j	60bpm (Increase Daily)	1 Minute
4e	60bpm (Increase Daily)	1 Minute
4p	60bpm (Increase Daily)	1 Minute
5c	60bpm (Increase Daily)	1 Minute
5f	60bpm (Increase Daily)	1 Minute
7i	60bpm (Increase Daily)	1 Minute
Creative Application	Backing Tracks	5 Minutes
		15 Minutes

30 Minute Workout

You should now be spending longer on each example, giving you more time to practice any patterns or sequences you find challenging.

Example Number	Metronome Speed	Total Time
1j	60bpm (Increase Daily)	2 Minutes
2l	60bpm (Increase Daily)	2 Minutes
2m	60bpm (Increase Daily)	2 Minutes
3k	60bpm (Increase Daily)	2 Minutes
4h	60bpm (Increase Daily)	2 Minutes
4p	60bpm (Increase Daily)	2 Minutes
5b	60bpm (Increase Daily)	2 Minutes
6g	60bpm (Increase Daily)	2 Minutes
7b	60bpm (Increase Daily)	2 Minutes
7n	60bpm (Increase Daily)	2 Minutes
Dissecting chords	N/A	2 Minutes
Creative Application	Backing Tracks	8 Minutes
		30 Minutes

60 Minute Workout

Example Number	Metronome Speed	Total Time
1n	60bpm (Increase Daily)	3 Minutes
2f	60bpm (Increase Daily)	3 Minutes
2k	60bpm (Increase Daily)	3 Minutes
3j	60bpm (Increase Daily)	3 Minutes
4b	60bpm (Increase Daily)	3 Minutes
4g	60bpm (Increase Daily)	3 Minutes
5a	60bpm (Increase Daily)	3 Minutes
5c	60bpm (Increase Daily)	3 Minutes
5i	60bpm (Increase Daily)	3 Minutes
6b	60bpm (Increase Daily)	3 Minutes
6l	60bpm (Increase Daily)	3 Minutes
7d	60bpm (Increase Daily)	3 Minutes
7h	60bpm (Increase Daily)	3 Minutes
7n	60bpm (Increase Daily)	3 Minutes
Dissecting chords	N/A	3 Minutes
Creative Application	Backing Tracks	15 Minutes
		60 Minutes

Conclusion

Whether you are just beginning your journey or you are an experienced soloist, your playing will benefit by making melody your priority. Use the examples in this book as a starting point for creating musical lines, phrases and songs. Try to let your ears guide you, and don't rely on the finger patterns and scale shapes that you know to be the 'safe' notes. Remember the saying "If it sounds good it is, if it sounds bad….it probably is too".

Practice what you don't know, not what you do! - This is quite simply the best advice I can give any musician. Use a metronome to help you master each example and use backing tracks to create a more musical approach to practicing.

A great way to build confidence in your playing is to go busking. Although it may sound daunting at first, it can be really thrilling and you can play as little or as much as you like. Make sure you are aware of your local authority's rules and regulations.

An important musical goal should be to play with other people, so while you are developing your skills in this book find time to jam with other musicians. Playing with other instrumentalists is the best way to improve your musicianship.

If you want to apply melodic rock soloing ideas to different pentatonic scales, then check out my book **Exotic Pentatonic Soloing for Guitar**, which is also available through www.Fundamental-Changes.com

My passion in life is teaching people to play and express themselves through the guitar. If you have any questions, please get in touch and I will do my best to respond as quickly as possible.

You can contact me on simeypratt@gmail.com or via the **Fundamental Changes YouTube channel**.

Answers to Questions

- Example 2t: C and G.
- The chord that is in bar five of a twelve-bar blues in E is A7.
- The chord that is in bar 11 or a twelve-bar blues in G is G7.
- The chord shown in the first neck diagram is a B7 chord.
- The chord shown in the second neck diagram is an E7 chord.

The Beginner Lead Guitar Method

Introduction

Have you ever wondered why people play air guitar solos at a party or guitar hero on their gaming console? The answer is simple; It's because playing the guitar is awesome and everyone wants to do it!

When friends mimic guitar parts it is likely they are pretending to play a lead guitar solo. In this book, I will give you the tools to play your first *real* guitar solos so you can wow the people around you with your new found skills.

This book teaches you essential scale shapes, technical exercises, drills, rhythm, licks, and full solos. If you are new to playing lead guitar, I recommend working your way through the book from start to finish. That way you will learn and develop techniques and skills in a logical fashion. If you can already play some lead guitar and are just looking for new ideas, then feel free to dive into any chapter you wish.

The most important thing you can do when starting to play lead guitar is to listen! Before you start any of the material in this book, I want you to listen to ten classic guitar solos. The songs presented here are in a blues/rock genre as that will be the primary focus of this book. Make sure you check out the discography at the back of this book for a larger list of great guitar solos.

- Led Zeppelin – Stairway to Heaven (Jimmy Page)
- The Eagles – Hotel California (Don Felder and Joe Walsh)
- Michael Jackson – Beat It (Eddie Van Halen)
- Pink Floyd – Comfortably Numb (David Gilmour)
- Jimi Hendrix – All Along the Watchtower
- Guns N Roses – Sweet Child O Mine (Slash)
- Chuck Berry – Johnny B Goode
- Queen – Bohemian Rhapsody (Brian May)
- Stevie Ray Vaughan and Double Trouble – Texas Flood
- Derek and The Dominos – Layla (Eric Clapton)

When you are listening to these songs, put headphones on and get rid of any other distractions around you, such as your phone or the TV. Shut your eyes and think about what makes these solos so popular. Start a guitar journal with the title 'listening', and write down everything you like about each of the different solos. You can continually add to this listening list throughout your lead playing career. The more you listen, the better! You can, of course, add your favourite solos from any genre of music, not just from rock and blues, but this is a great starting point.

Once you have listened to the tracks mentioned above and started your guitar listening journal, read the tips mentioned on the next page before diving into the exciting world of guitar soloing.

At the end of the book I have provided sample 'workouts' to help you create a balanced practice regime that combines elements from each chapter. These workouts are divided into 15-minute, 20-minute, 30-minute and 60-minute sessions.

The audio for this book is available from **http://www.fundamental-changes.com/download-audio** so you can hear how I play and *phrase* each example.

Happy Playing!

Simon

Tips

Before you dive into the hundreds of musical examples featured throughout this book, take note of these tips featured here.

Relax

Aim to keep as relaxed as possible in all muscles in your hands and arms. If you feel any tension, make a conscious effort to relax or stop playing take a break and come back to what you were working on later.

Breathing

Keep your breathing regular when you play. Sometimes when people concentrate hard on new material they forget to breathe normally.

Don't Get Discouraged

It takes time to learn to play lead guitar solos so maintain a regular practice regime for optimal results.

Short Fingernails

Keep your fingernails short. This will stop any complications from a nail getting in the way of fretting a note.

Sitting Down

At first, I highly recommend sitting down to practice all the material featured in this book. Once you feel comfortable playing the examples you can experiment by standing up. If you are rehearsing for a gig or a live performance make sure you practice the pieces you are working on standing up as well as sitting down. This may sound basic advice, but it can feel strange to play standing up, especially if the first time you stand up while playing guitar is on stage!

Alternate Pick

In general, stick to using alternate picking throughout the examples in this book. Whenever you play a note with a down-pick, the next note should be picked using an up-pick, and vice versa.

Metronome

When you are learning the examples in this book, always use a metronome.

Begin playing each example very slowly with the metronome set at 50bpm and make sure that every note is clean and audible.

Watch your picking hand and notice if you are applying the strict 'down, up' alternate picking pattern required. When you can play an example perfectly three times in a row at 50bpm, raise the metronome up to 53bpm. Continue to increase the metronome speed in increments of 3 beats-per-minute up to your target speed of 80bpm and beyond.

This form of structured practice means that you will only increase your speed once the example is played accurately.

I use the *Tempo* app (by *Frozen Ape*) on my phone as I know I will always have my phone with me, so I never have an excuse to practice without a metronome.

Pain

Stop if you feel any pain. When it comes to guitar playing, 'no pain no gain' is never the way forward. Stretch thoroughly before you play the examples in this chapter and stop if you feel any strain.

Have fun

The most important tip I can give you when playing music is to have fun. Play with other musicians, backing tracks, drum tracks, YouTube videos and enjoy every minute of playing this incredible instrument.

If there is any notation you don't understand, listen to the included audio examples and try to play along with the recorded versions.

Chapter One – The A Minor Pentatonic Scale

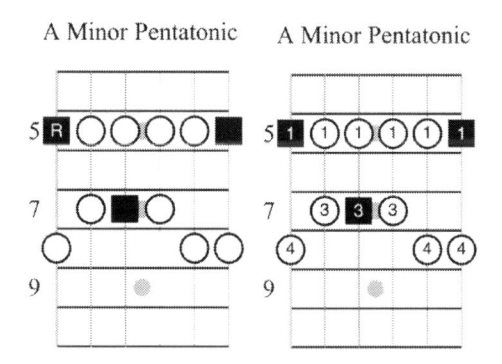

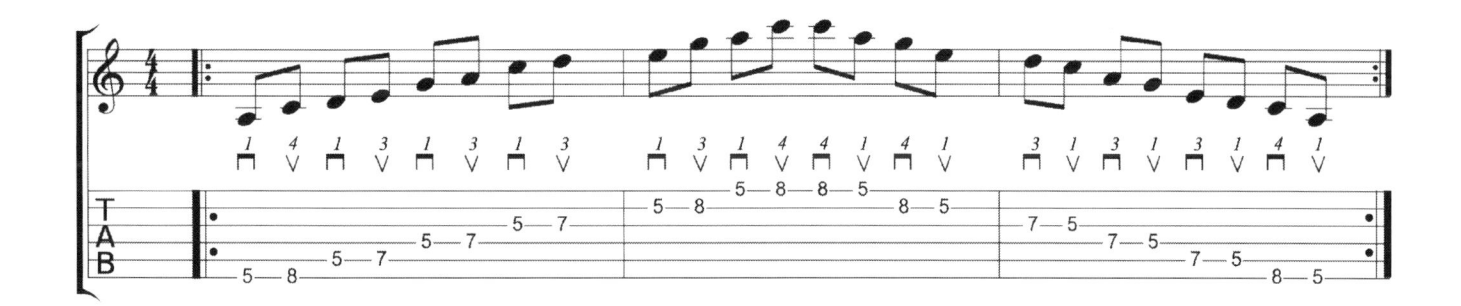

Backing Tracks: One-Four

Pentatonic scales contain five notes, and they are your ticket to creative, expressive soloing. In this book, you will look at how to use different types of pentatonic scales in blues, rock, jazz, pop and funk music.

The starting point is the Minor Pentatonic scale as it is the 'bread and butter' approach for most modern guitarists. The guitar allows complete freedom of expression and these pentatonic scales form a palette of colours to enhance your art.

The Minor Pentatonic scale is, without a doubt, the most commonly used scale by guitarists. From the playing of Jimi Hendrix to Eric Clapton, and Larry Carlton to Carlos Santana, many of the greatest guitar solos are based around minor pentatonic ideas.

This scale shape is popular because it is accessible, easy to play, and also sounds fantastic! The Minor Pentatonic is at the root of all blues music and therefore is the basis of every genre of modern music that grew from the blues, such as rock, jazz and funk.

The word 'pentatonic' describes the *construction* of the scale. '*Pent*' means five and '*tonic*' means tones. All the scales in this book, therefore, contain five separate tones.

The A Minor Pentatonic scale contains the notes **A C D E** and **G**.

The examples in this chapter are all in the key of A minor, and each one fits perfectly over an A minor chord or a backing track in A minor such as Backing Track One.

In this chapter, I am going to show you how to get the most out of practising a scale shape. I call the following exercises 'ultimate lick builders'. By learning the examples shown in this chapter you will gain dexterity as well as fretboard fluency within the A Minor Pentatonic scale.

The Minor Pentatonic scale shape is an important starting point when learning to play lead guitar. It will act as a basis for almost all the content you will see in rock guitar, so take your time to digest this scale shape.

Example 1a – A Minor Pentatonic scale

Play the 5th fret of the thickest string (E), with your first finger, then play the 8th fret on that same string with your fourth finger. The next three strings (A, D and G) play frets 5 to 7 using your first and third fingers. On the top strings (B and E) play the 5th and 8th frets with your first and fourth fingers.

Make sure to play this scale shape both ascending and descending using alternate picking (down-pick on the first note and up-pick on the second note of each string.)

Example 1b is identical to the previous example except you pick every note of the A Minor Pentatonic scale twice.

Example 1b –

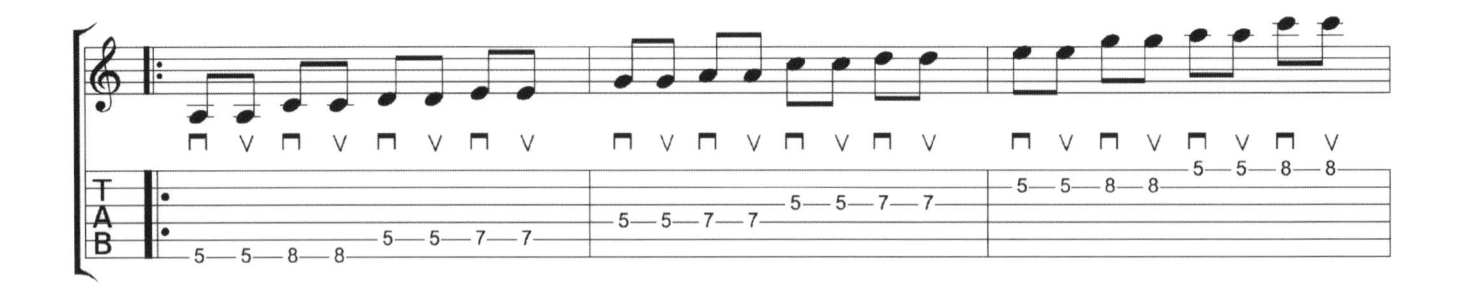

Next, pick every note of the A Minor Pentatonic scale three times. The rhythm used in this example is called a triplet. Listen to the audio to hear how I play this example.

Example 1c –

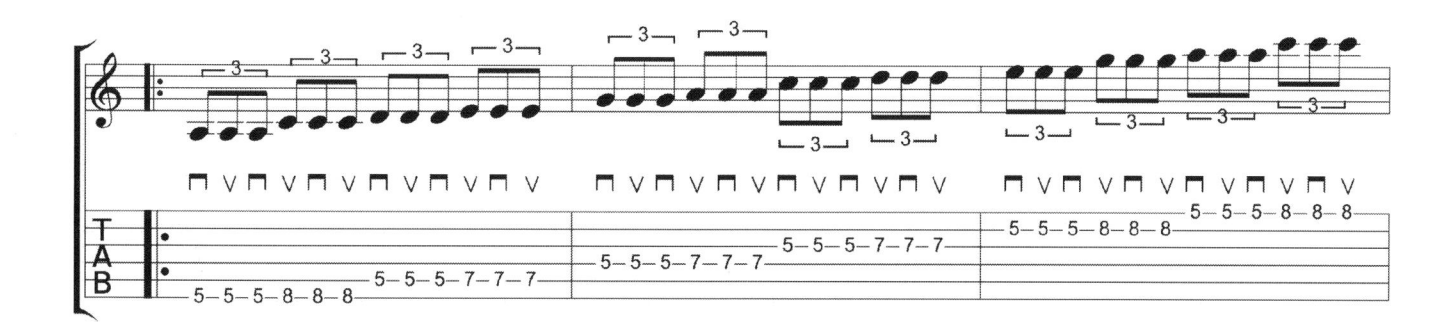

This example shows the A Minor Pentatonic scale with every note being picked four times.

Example 1d –

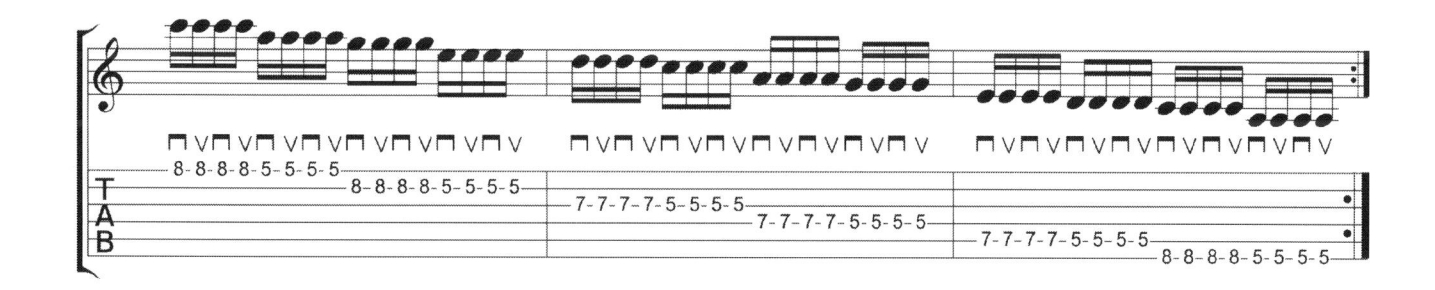

Play through the A Minor Pentatonic scale starting on the highest fret on each string.

Example 1e –

Now work your way back through the A Minor Pentatonic scale shape but start from the lower note on each string.

Example 1f –

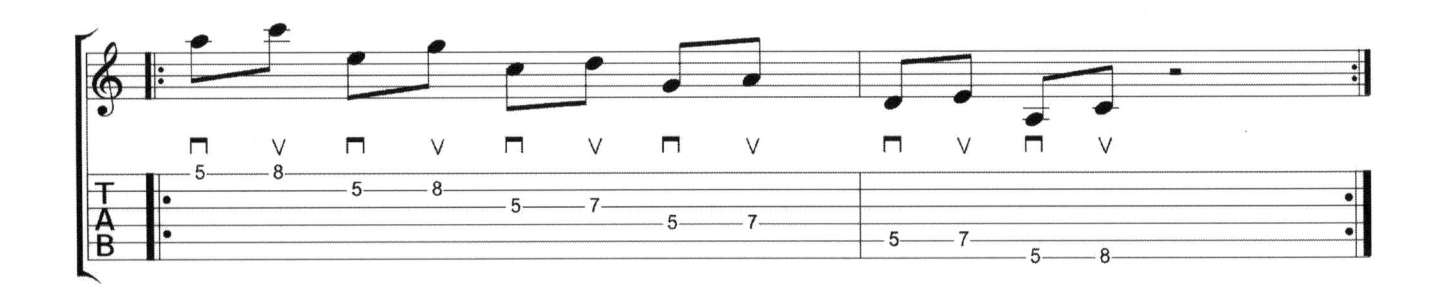

The next two examples introduce a string skip. By avoiding playing on adjacent strings, you can add exciting musical jumps into your practice regime.

Example 1g –

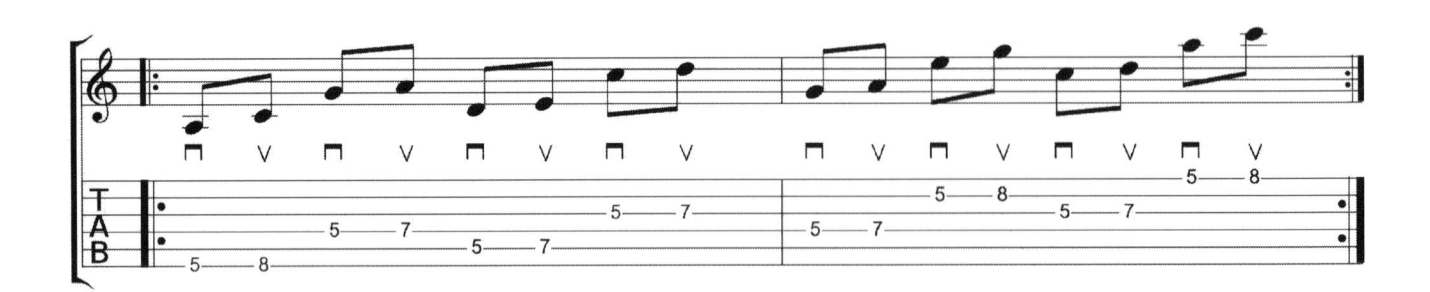

Example 1h –

Another way to practice scales is to group them into patterns of three notes. Play the first three notes of the A Minor Pentatonic scale, then start on the second note of the scale and play three ascending notes. Continue this pattern throughout the whole scale shape.

Example 1i –

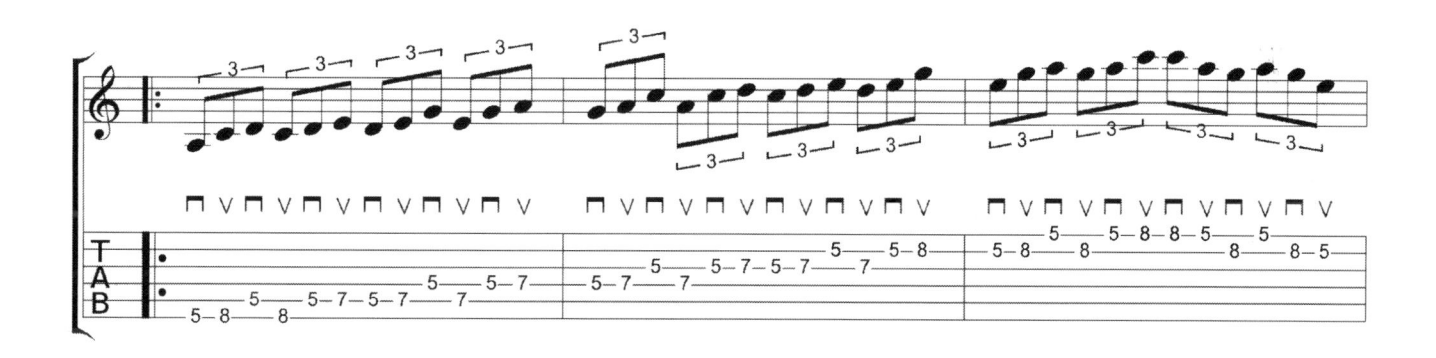

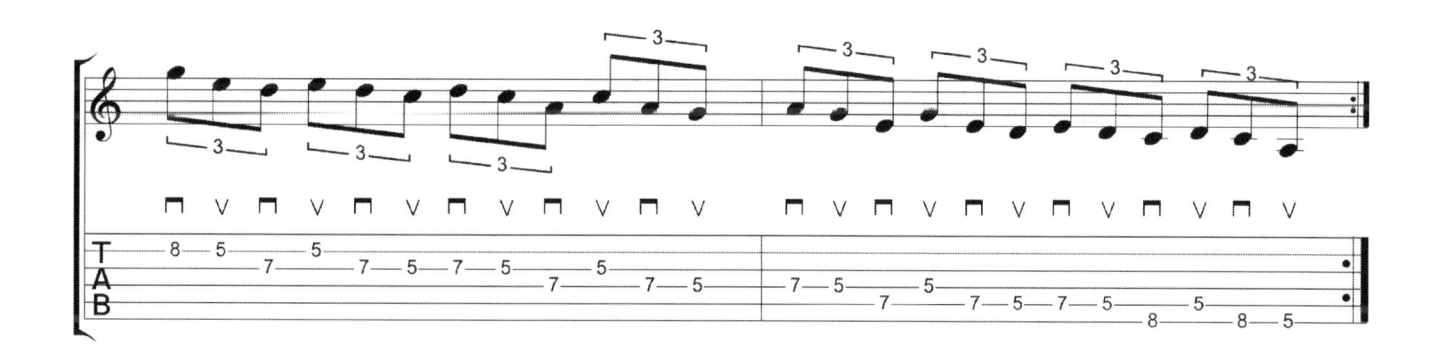

Example 1j –

Now group the A Minor Pentatonic scale into a pattern of four notes.

Example 1k demonstrates playing the scale using a grouping of six notes. This is a common rock guitar pattern used by guitarists like Zakk Wylde.

Example 1k –

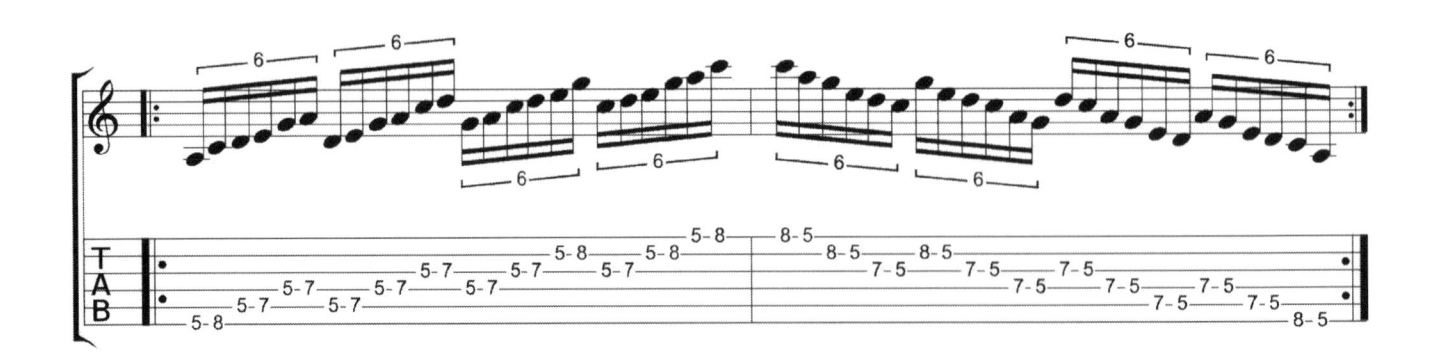

You can create an exciting technical exercise by adding musical jumps. This helps break away from predictable scale runs.

Example 11 –

The exercises in this chapter will make all the following musical ideas easier. Training your fingers to learn a scale shape off by heart does require some work, but you will reap the benefits when you no longer have to think about the scale shape you are playing when soloing.

Practice these scale exercises with a metronome very slowly (around 50 beats per minute) and only raise the tempo when you can play an example perfectly three times in a row.

Chapter Two – Building Melodies

Backing Tracks One to Four.

This chapter shows you how to build your own solos from short fragments of melody. All examples in this section are created using the A Minor Pentatonic scale. These melodic building blocks can act as the stepping stone to creating longer licks and eventually solos. Make sure you play these examples along with backing tracks one to four.

Example 2a uses the notes A and G with a simple rhythmic pattern to create a bite-sized A Minor Pentatonic phrase.

Example 2a –

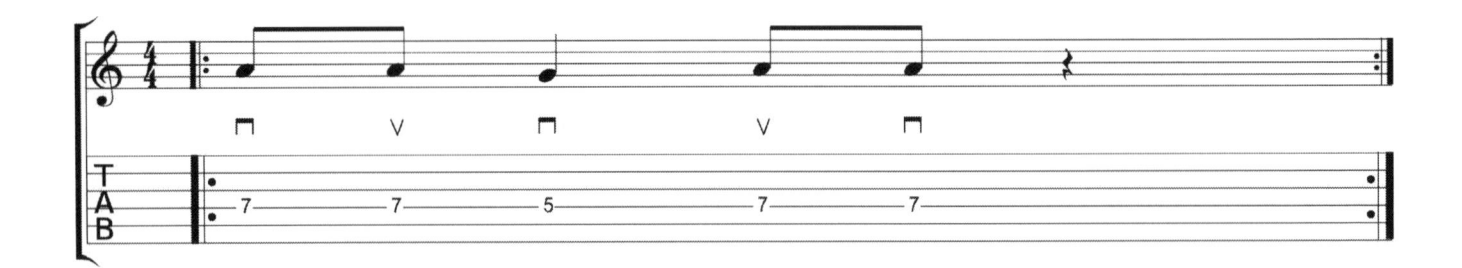

Example 2b uses the same rhythmic pattern but uses the frets on the A string.

Example 2b –

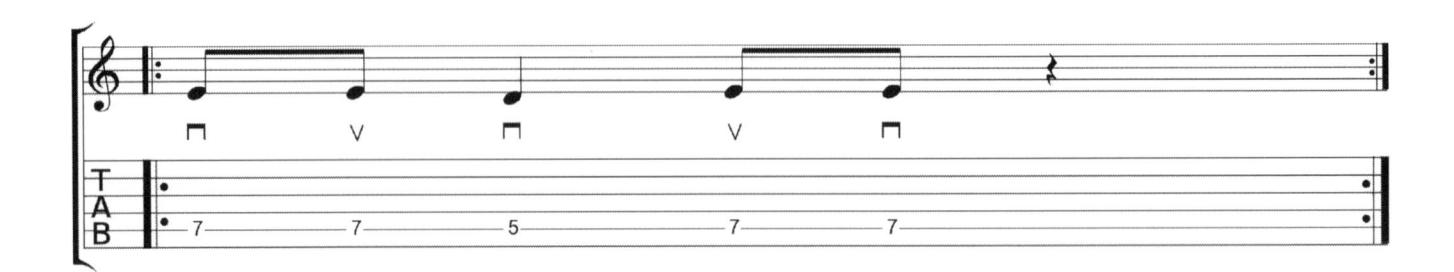

Now combine the previous two examples to create this two-bar motif.

Example 2c –

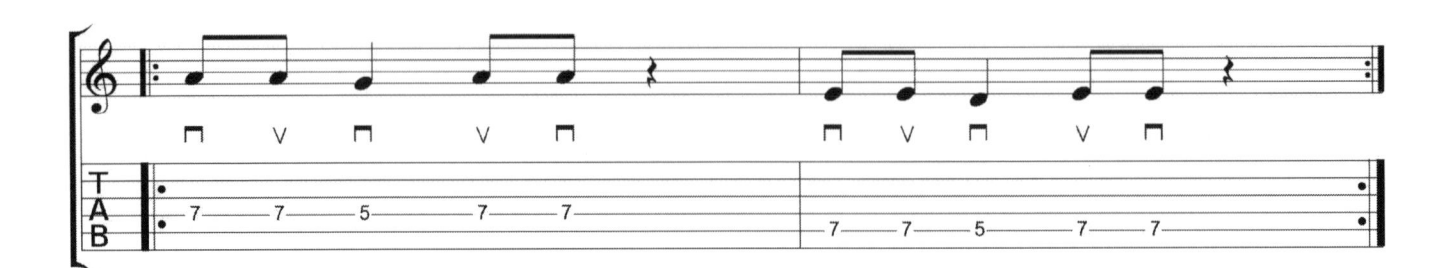

Example 2d is a typical Minor Pentatonic pattern that occurs a lot in blues and rock guitar playing. Make sure you listen to the attached audio files to see how I phrase every example.

Example 2d –

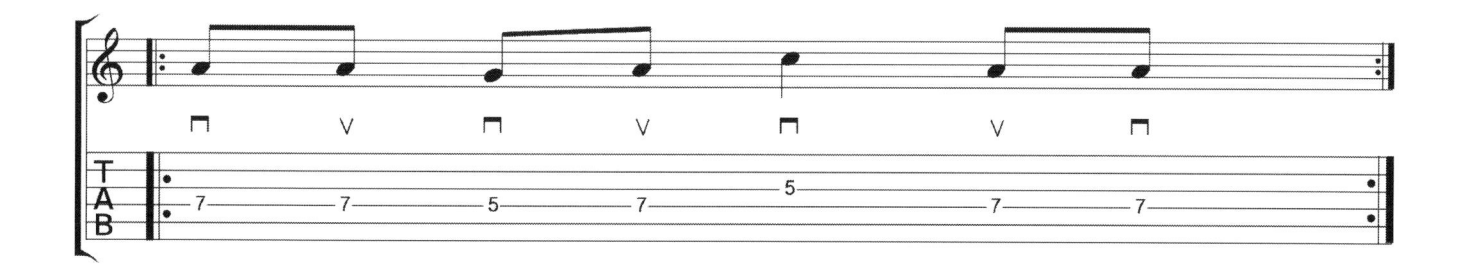

Next, repeat the pattern in the previous example but now start the pattern from the A string.

Example 2e –

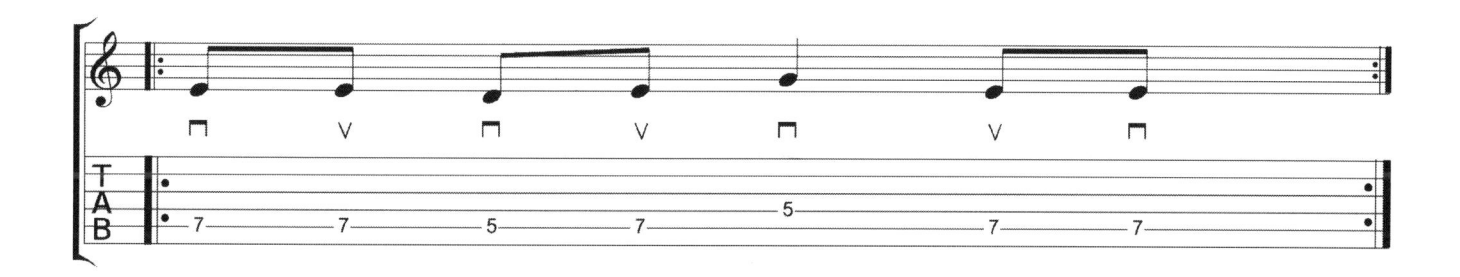

By combining example 2d and 2e, you can create a two-bar phrase.

Example 2f –

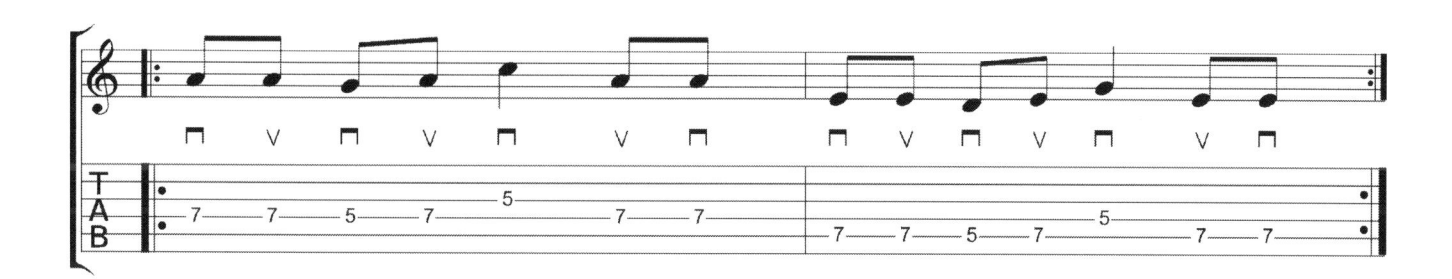

Example 2g demonstrates a simple melodic line using the higher pitched notes of the A Minor Pentatonic scale.

Example 2g –

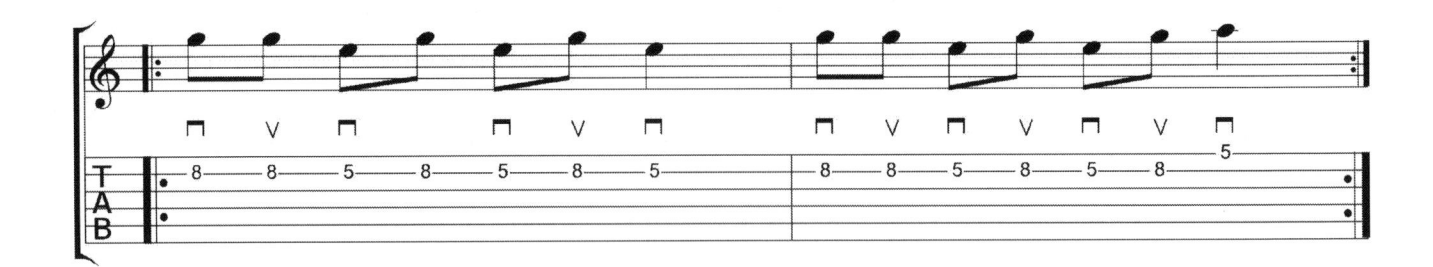

Before playing each example make sure you listen to the accompanying audio tracks available to download from **www.fundamental-changes.com**

Example 2h –

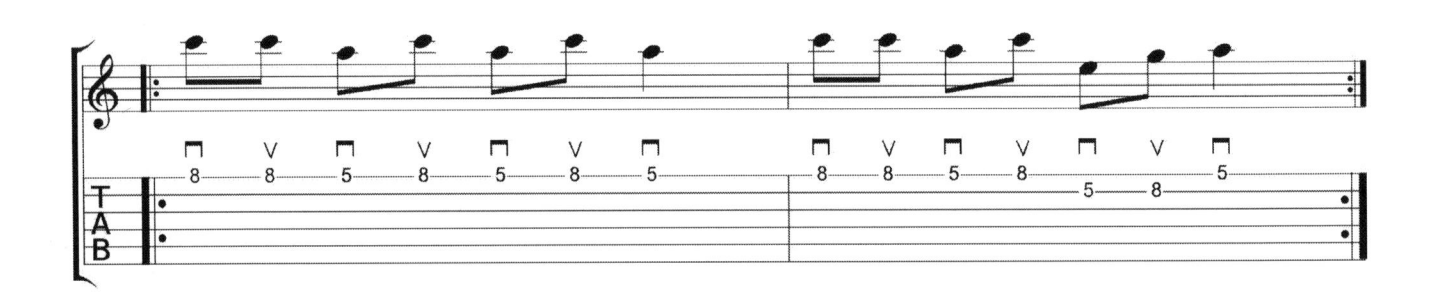

Melodic phrases can be easily combined to create longer licks and solos. Example 2i shows this by combining the previous examples to create a four-bar Minor Pentatonic phrase. This example is a fun one to play over backing track one.

Example 2i –

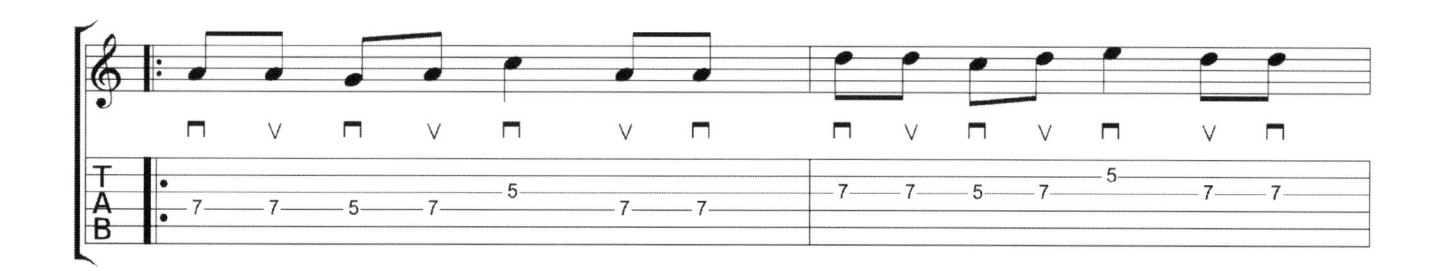

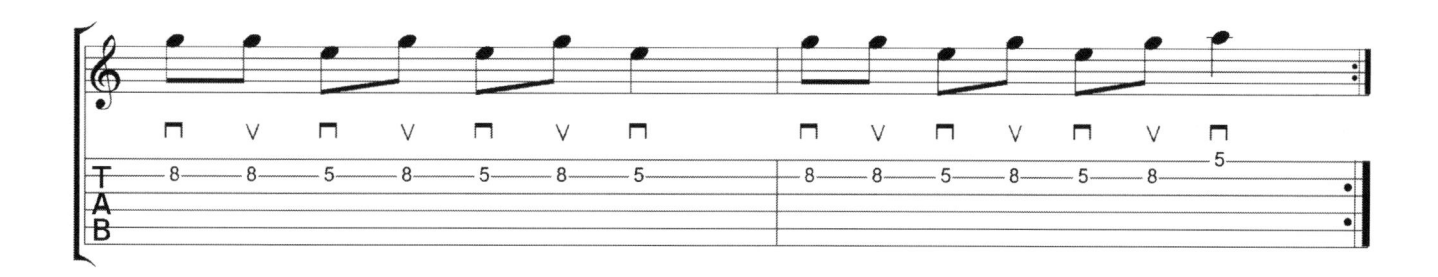

Mini Solos

The next examples are written to compliment different A Minor backing tracks. These examples introduce the concept that you do not have to play on every beat of the bar, in fact, leaving space is one of the most important things in music. As Mozart once said, "The music is not in the notes, but in the silence between". Listen to how I phrase every example then practice each one along with the backing tracks or metronome.

Examples 2j and 2k should be played over Backing Track One.

Example 2j –

Example 2k –

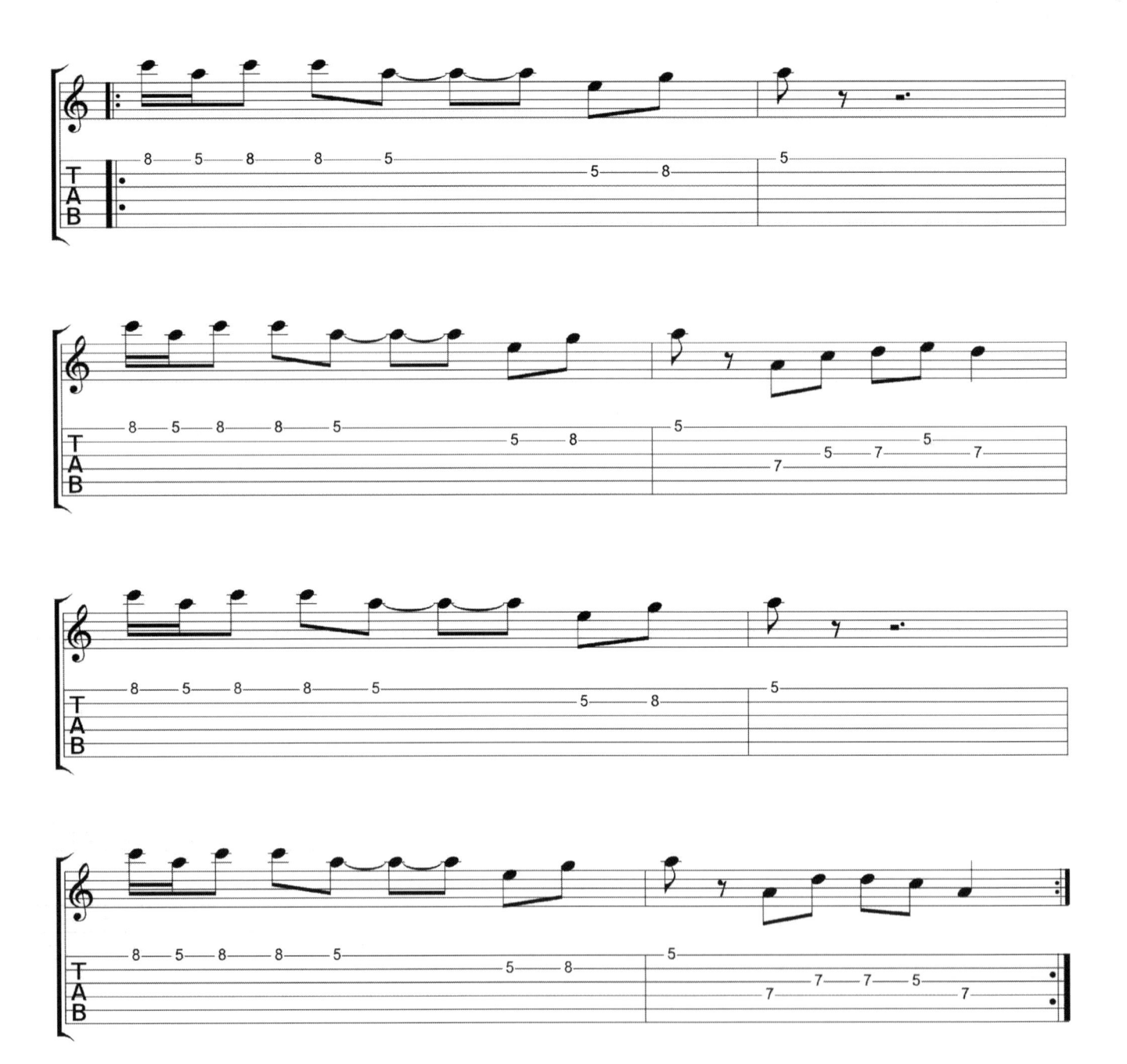

Use Backing Track Two for example 2l.

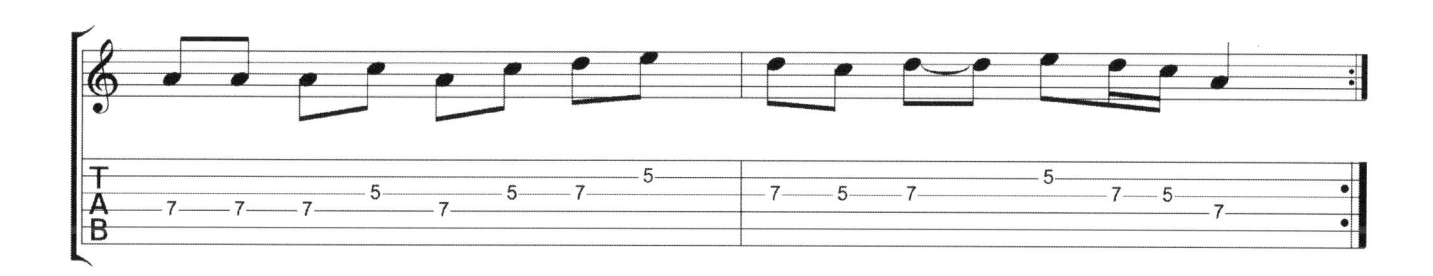

Example 2l -

Example 2m shows that sometimes you can leave a large amount of silence at the start of a solo before creating a big impact later in bar one. Play this example with Backing Track One.

Example 2m –

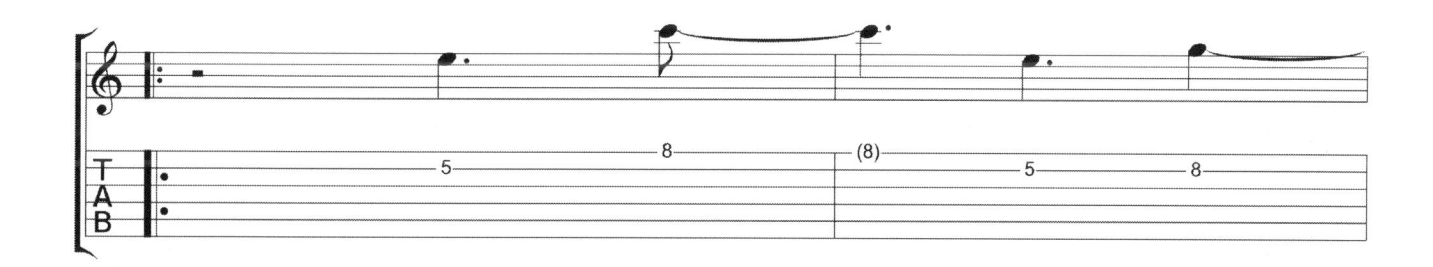

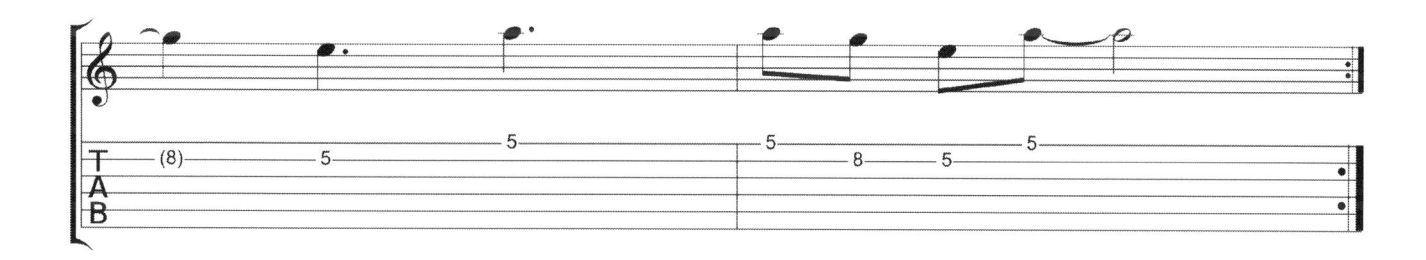

Here is the same melody line is written in a lower octave. Once again use Backing Track One for this example.

Example 2n –

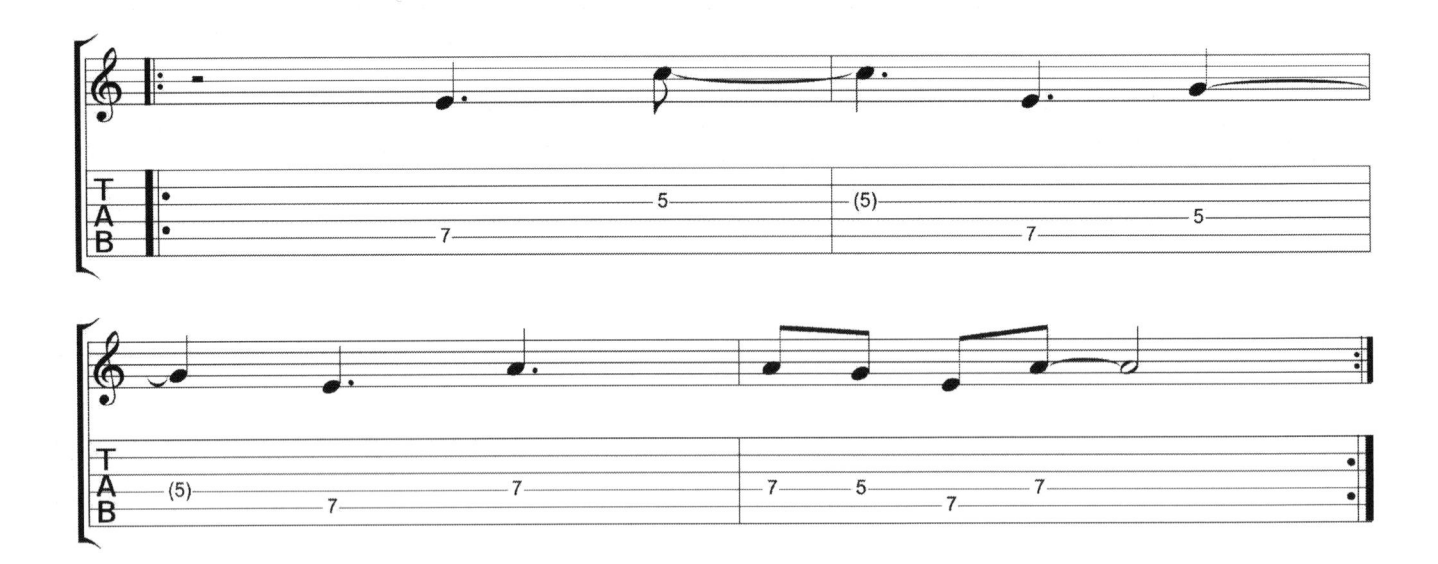

By combining the previous two examples, an eight-bar solo fragment can be created.

Example 2o –

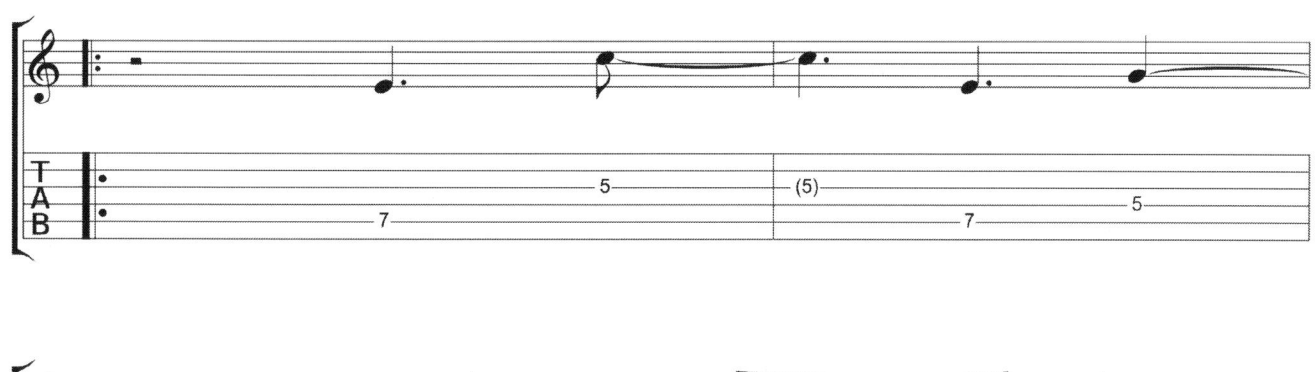

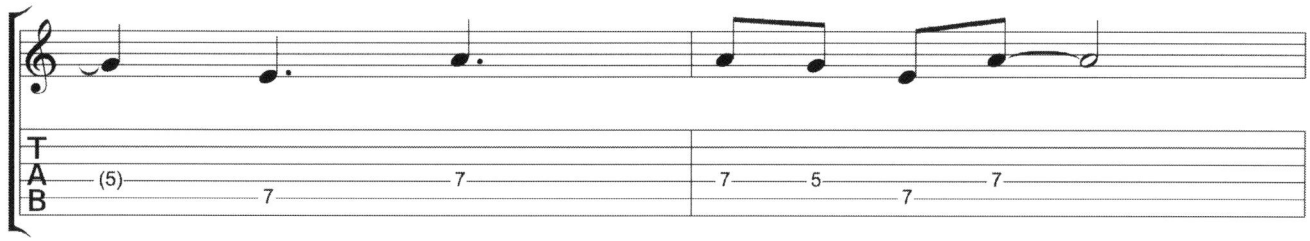

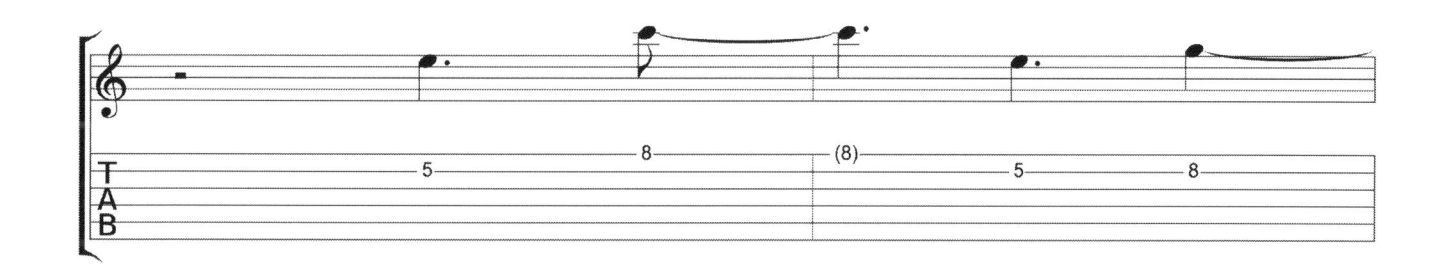

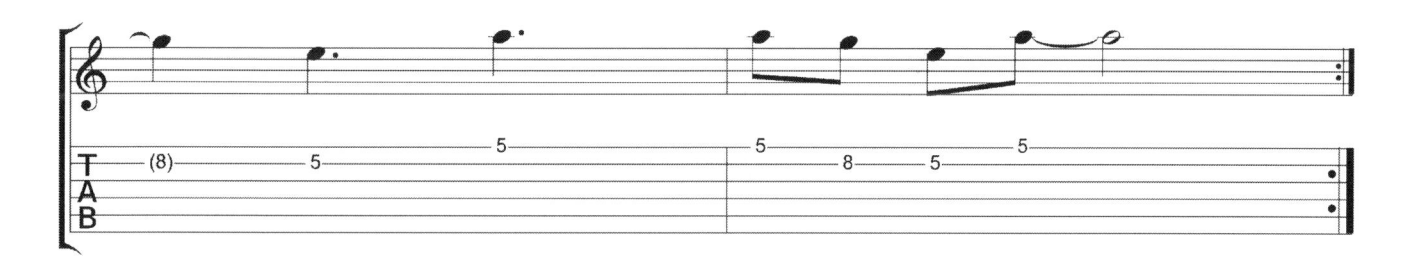

Pop Quiz

What are the notes in the A Minor Pentatonic Scale?

What is the point of learning melodic building blocks?

How many of the examples featured in this chapter can you play without reading them?

Answers on the final page!

Chapter Three – Slides

The concept of a slide is simple: Fret a note on any string, pick it, and then slide your finger to another note on the same string without re-picking. There are only two types of slides, an upward slide (from a lower pitch to a higher one), and a downward slide (from a higher pitch to a lower one).

Slides are particularly common in blues and rock guitar playing but can be found in almost any genre including country, jazz and funk.

The following examples use the A Minor Pentatonic scale.

The aim when learning to slide is to feel comfortable sliding on any finger. However, at first, just use your first finger when you learn these examples. After you have completed each exercise on your first finger, move onto your second, third and fourth fingers.

Upward Slide

Example 3a –

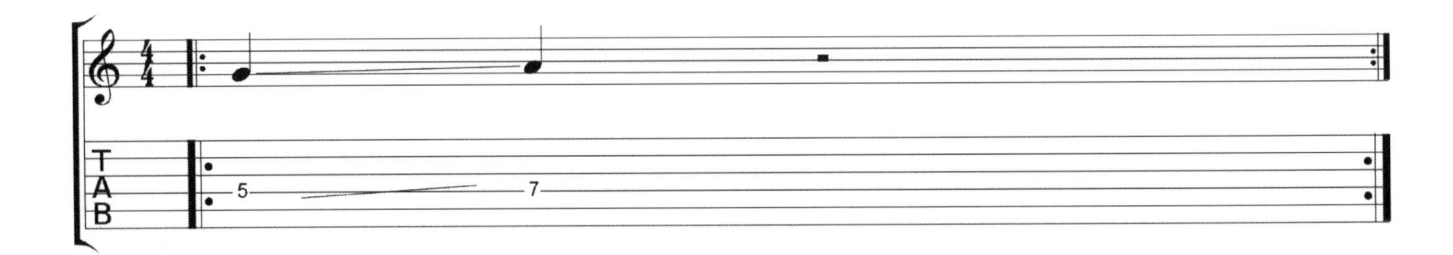

You may have found that after you picked the first pitch that the note 'died' as you tried to slide it up to the 7th fret. The crucial thing when sliding is to apply continuous pressure to the string to keep the note ringing.

Repeat example 3a but apply consistent pressure to the note as you slide it upwards.

In example 3b, play four slides in one bar, back to back. If you want an extra challenge, alternate which finger plays each slide.

Example 3b –

Downward Slide

Example 3c demonstrates the downward slide. Start on the 7th fret and slide down to the 5th fret. Once again apply continuous pressure throughout the slide.

Example 3c –

Now play four downward slides within one bar.

Example 3d –

Double Slides

Example 3e introduces a *double slide*. This time slide from the 5th fret to the 7th fret and back to the 5th fret again, all with one pick stroke. It is crucial to keep the pressure on the string while sliding. Aim to slide into the middle of the fret to avoid unwanted buzzes and muting.

Example 3e –

All of the slide examples featured in this chapter are as building blocks for future Minor Pentatonic licks.

Example 3f –

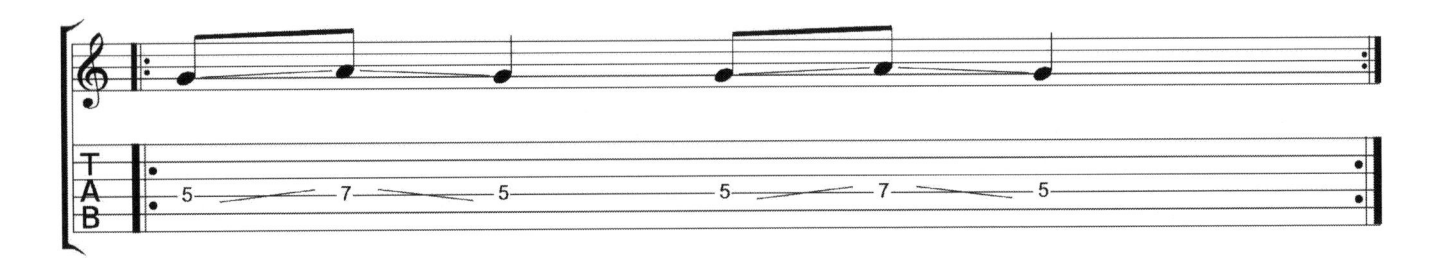

Changing String

Next, move onto the B string and slide from the 5th fret to the 8th fret.

Example 3g –

Now slide the 5th fret to the 8th fret four times in one bar.

Example 3h –

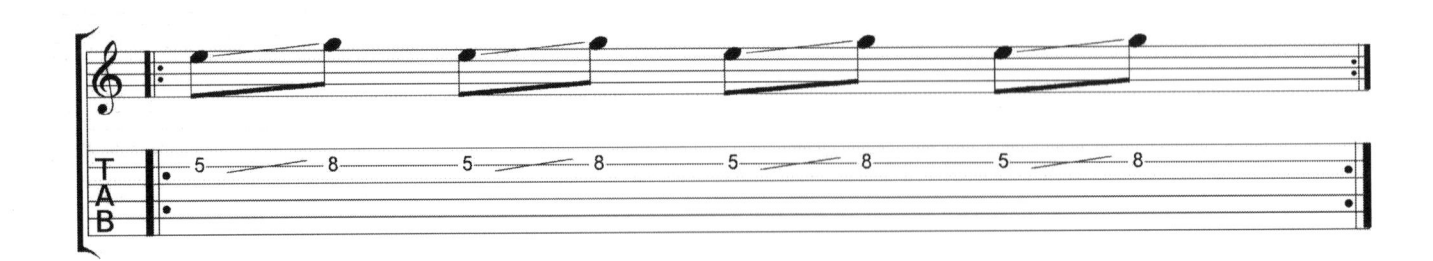

Play a downward slide from the 8th fret to the 5th fret to complete example 3i.

Example 3i –

Don't forget to play along to any of the A Minor backing tracks with the examples featured here.

Example 3j –

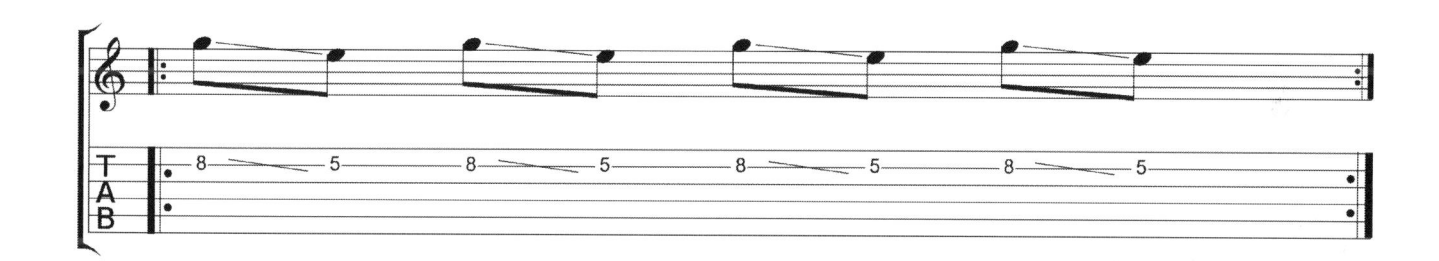

Now apply a double slide (up and down) on the B string between the 5th and 8th frets.

Example 3k –

Example 3l demonstrates two double slides within one bar.

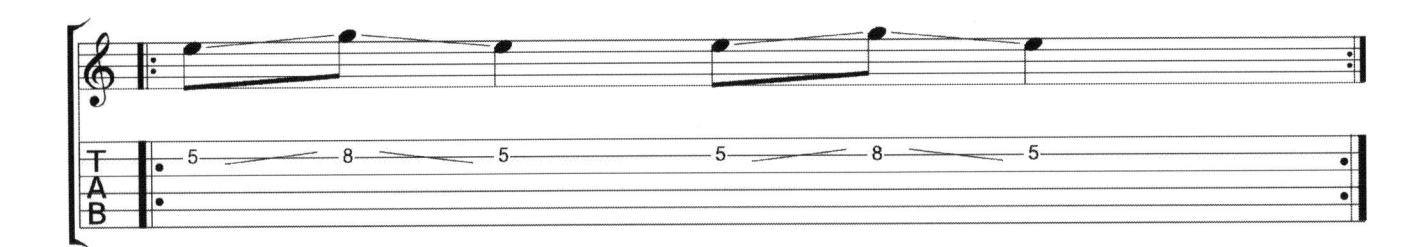

Example 3l –

Fundamental Slide Licks

Now that you have got the idea of slides is and how they are created, it is time to put them into a practical soloing context by creating licks with the A Minor Pentatonic scale.

Start the first example with your third finger and slide between the 5th and 7th frets of the A string. That way you will have fingers in the right place to play the rest of this blues lick.

Example 3m –

Once again, start with your third finger to complete the 5th to the 7th fret slide on the D string. You can also play the final double slide on your third finger too. If it feels uncomfortable to slide on your third finger, go back to the start of this chapter and complete the earlier examples on all fingers before attempting these slide licks.

Example 3n –

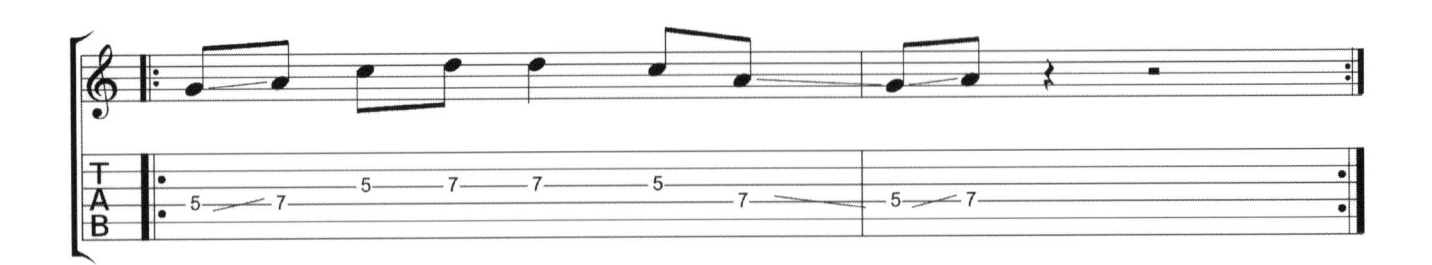

You can complete example 3o by playing all the slides with your first finger, but experiment by playing the slides on different fingers to see which combination feels most comfortable to you.

Example 3o –

Pop Quiz

How many types of slide are there?

What is an upward slide?

What is a double slide?

What genres of guitar playing might you hear slides being played?

Answers on the final page!

203

Chapter Four – Bends

Bending is the technique of raising the pitch of a note by increasing the tension on the string. String bending produces a smooth, expressive sound and gives a 'vocal' quality to your solos. By bending a string, you can create one, or several new pitches without picking any other notes. Many famous rock guitarists including David Gilmour, Jimi Hendrix and Carlos Santana are all instantly recognisable by their unique approach to string bending.

The idea of a bend is normally to raise the pitch of a fretted note by a set amount. For example, you may wish to bend the string up by a tone (whole-step), or up by a semitone (half-step). Making sure the bend is accurate and in tune is the priority when learning to bend strings. Developing both the strength needed to bend the string and the aural skill to hear when the bent note is played in tune requires dedicated practice. The following examples will teach how to bend perfectly in tune.

Consider your string gauge before attempting the exercises in this chapter. It is more difficult to bend thicker (heavier) gauge strings, despite the improved tone they produce. The audio examples were recorded using Ernie Ball Super Slinkys (gauge 9-42).

The semitone (one-fret) bend is a common bend, especially in Blues and Rock guitar. In the example 4a, the 8th fret of the G string acts as the target pitch when bending up from the 7th fret.

Example 4a –

Now bend the 7th fret on the G string up a semitone without using the 8th fret as a target pitch.

Example 4b –

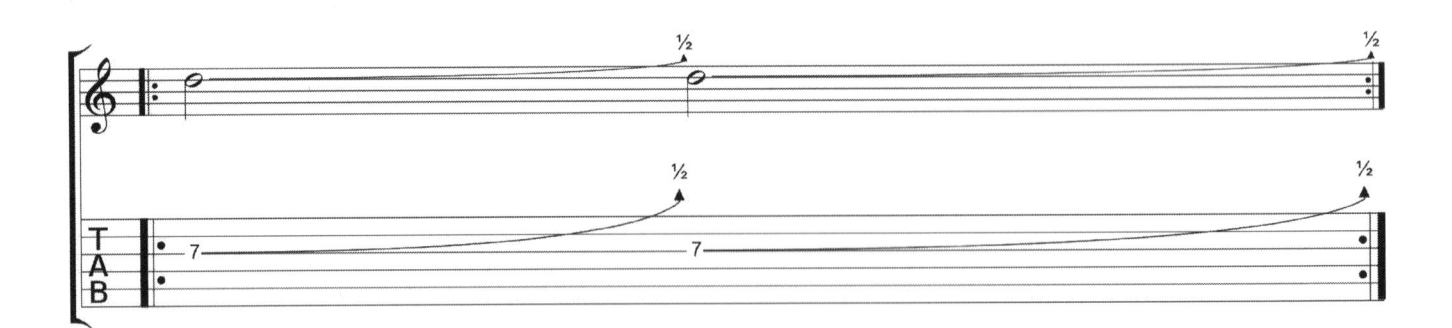

Example 4c demonstrates playing four semitone bends within one bar.

Example 4c –

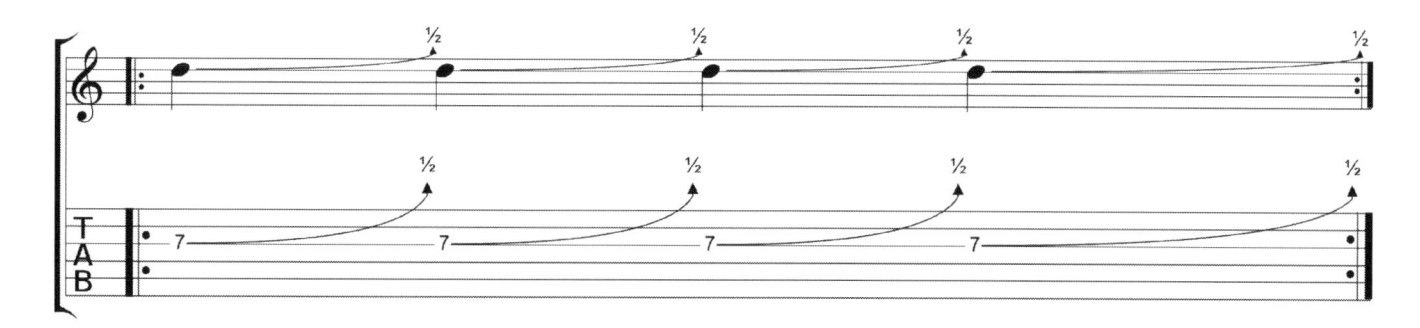

The whole-tone bend (two-frets) is the most common bend in modern electric guitar playing.

In example 4d, play the 9th fret of the G string as a reference or 'target' note before bending the 7th fret of the same string upwards until you have replicated the original 9th fret pitch.

Play the 7th fret note with your third finger and place fingers one and two on the same string (behind the fretting finger) to provide strength and support. Always support any bend with spare fingers whenever possible. This bend will require slightly more force than the previous examples.

Example 4d –

Next, bend the 7th fret a tone without using the 9th fret as your target pitch.

Example 4e –

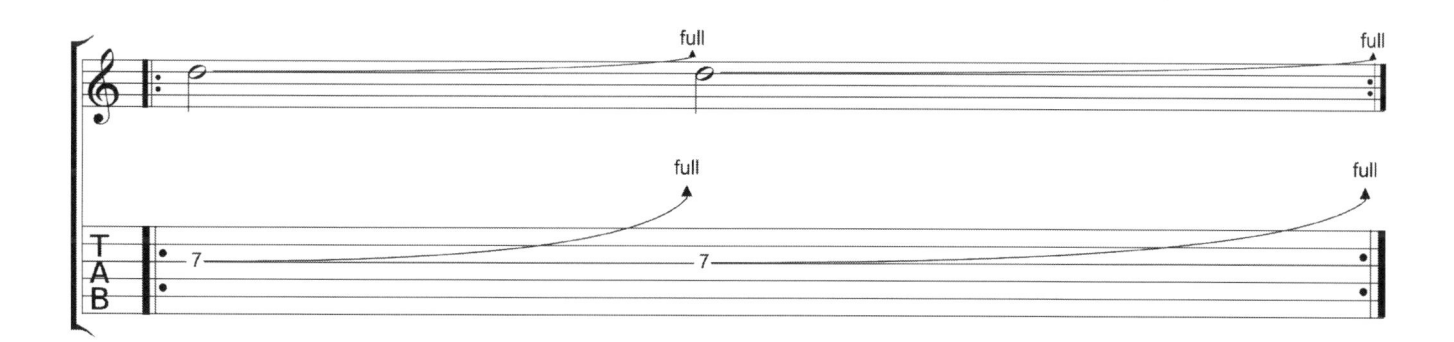

Play four, whole-tone bends in one bar in example 4f, one on each beat.

Example 4f –

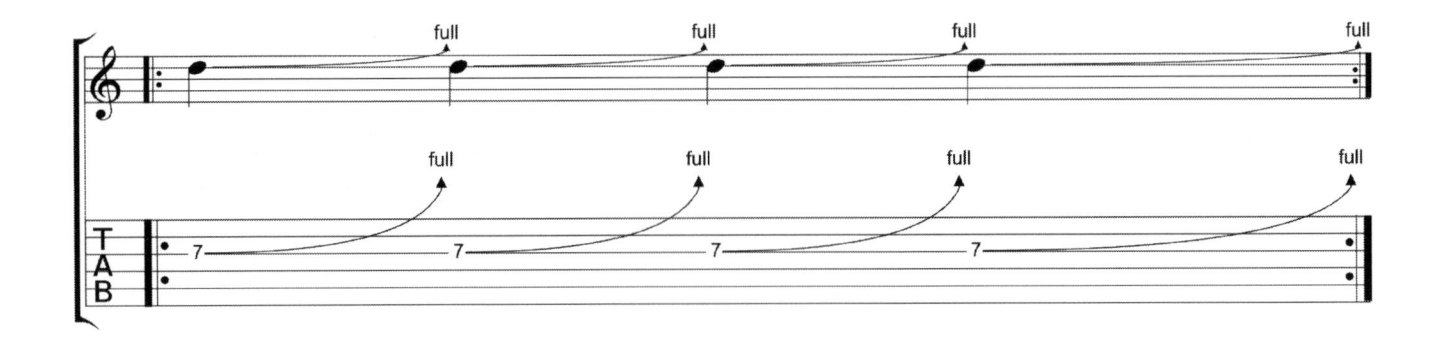

Now that you can play semitone and whole-tone bends on the G string, it is time to explore another common place to use a bend within the A Minor Pentatonic scale. Play the 10th fret of the B string as your target pitch and then bend the 8th fret until it matches that pitch exactly.

Example 4g –

Practice playing a whole-tone bend on the B string *without* using the 10th fret as a target pitch.

Example 4h –

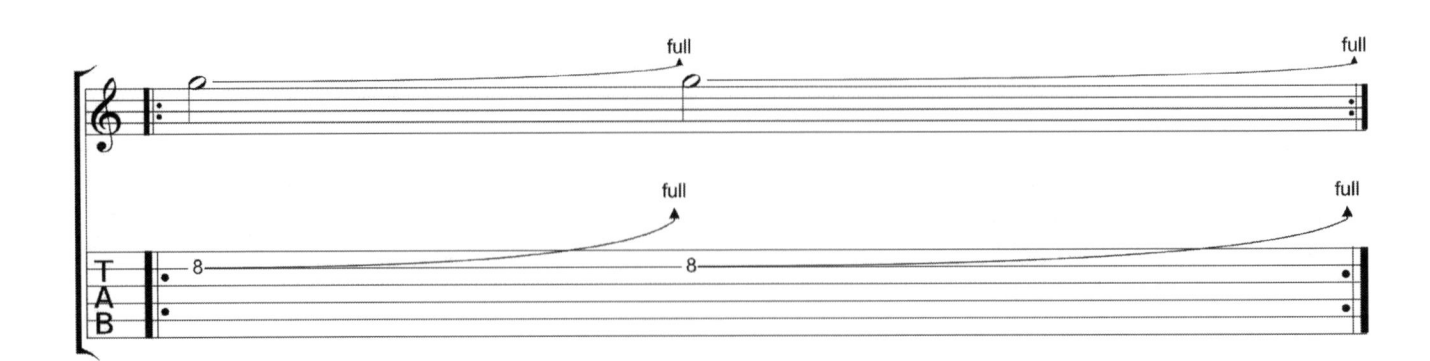

Play four, whole-tone bends on the B string, one on every beat of the bar.

Example 4i –

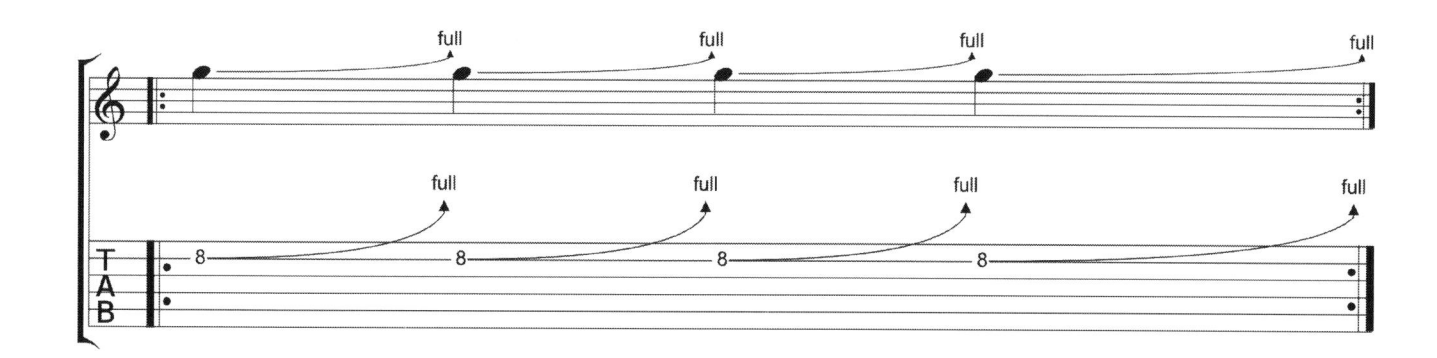

The final set of bends in this chapter use the high E string. Keeping to the A Minor Pentatonic scale, these bends are based around the 8th fret.

Example 4j uses the 10th fret as a target pitch before bending the 8th fret to match.

Example 4j –

Bend the 8th fret up a tone without playing a target pitch note first.

Example 4k –

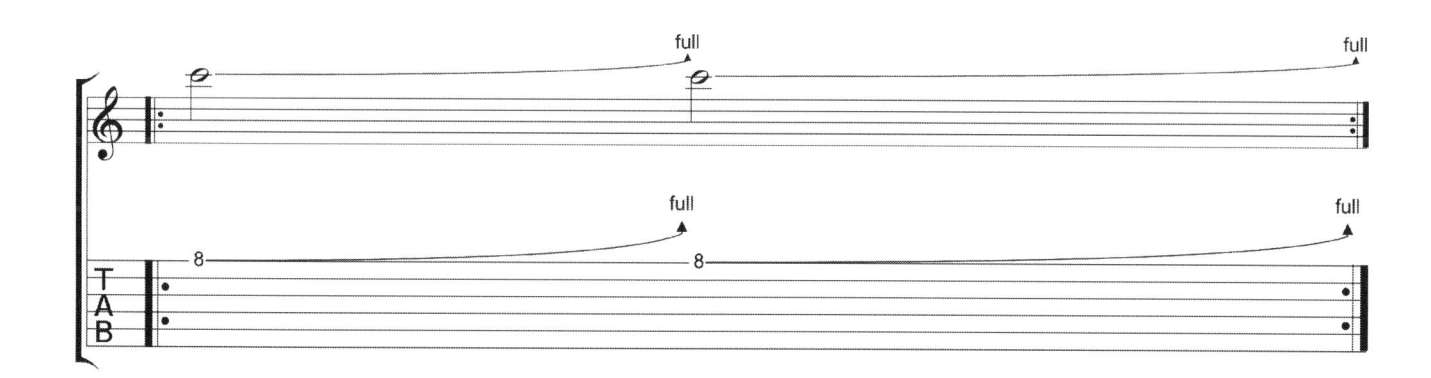

Four, whole-tone bends on the high E string make up example 4l. Make sure you download the audio for this book and listen to every example before playing it yourself.

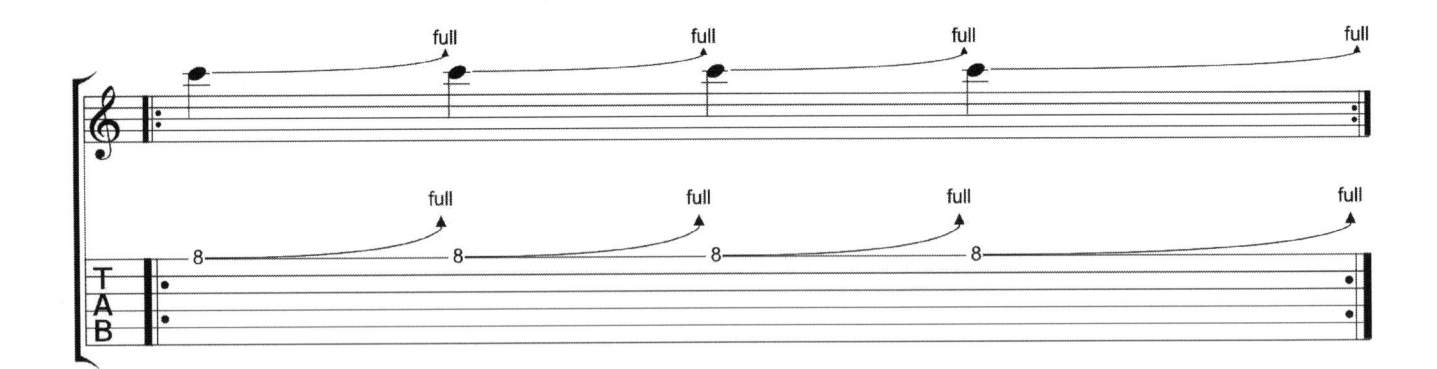

Example 4l –

Core Bending Licks

Once you have mastered how to play a semitone bend and a tone bend in multiple places you can move onto building blues-rock licks that use the A Minor Pentatonic scale. Play these along with Backing Tracks One – Four.

Bend the 7th fret of the G string and hold that bend for two beats before playing the 5th fret of the G string, then resolving to the 7th fret of the D string.

Bends Around the G String

Example 4m –

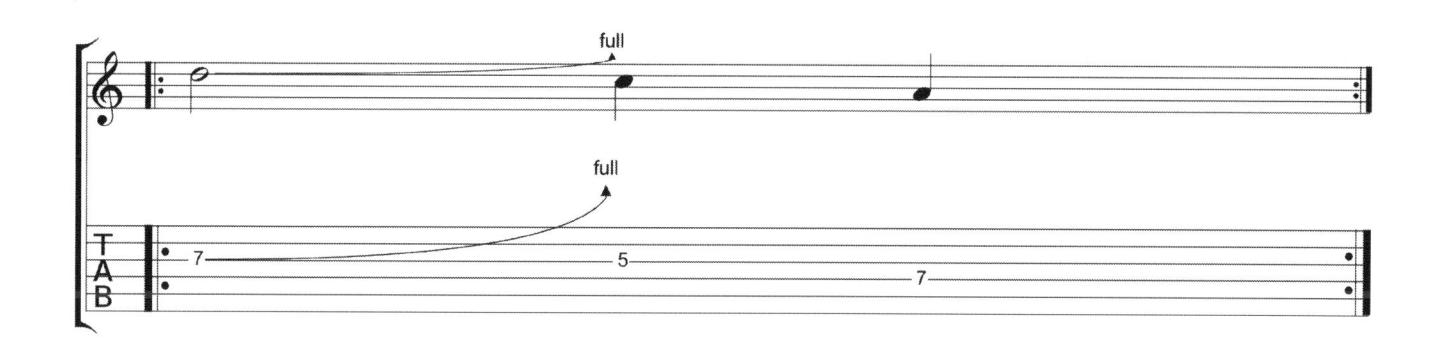

The tone bend is the most common bend in modern day guitar playing so if this still feels uncomfortable don't worry, just go back to practising it on its own before applying it to the licks written here.

Example 4n –

It is more important to internalise and remember these licks than it is to read them off the page. As you go through this chapter pick your favourites and spend extra time learning them.

Example 4o –

Example 4p –

As well as learning the above examples, I encourage you to experiment by creating your own ideas. Use these patterns as a basis, but change the order you play the notes. For example, you could play a phrase backwards by starting at the end of a bar.

Example 4p –

The last few examples have focussed around the tone bend on the 7th fret of the G string. The next examples focus around the tone bend at the 8th fret of the B string.

Bends Around the B String

Example 4q –

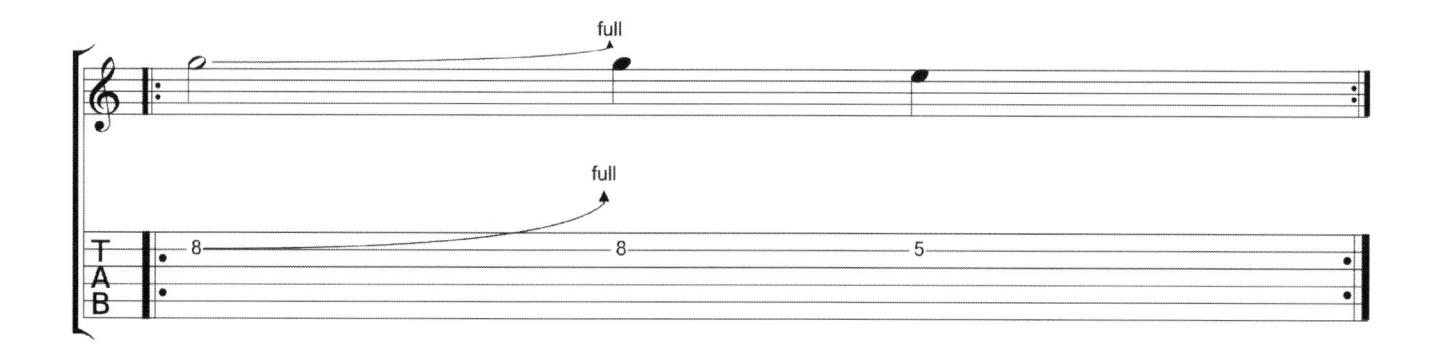

Example 4r –

Example 4s –

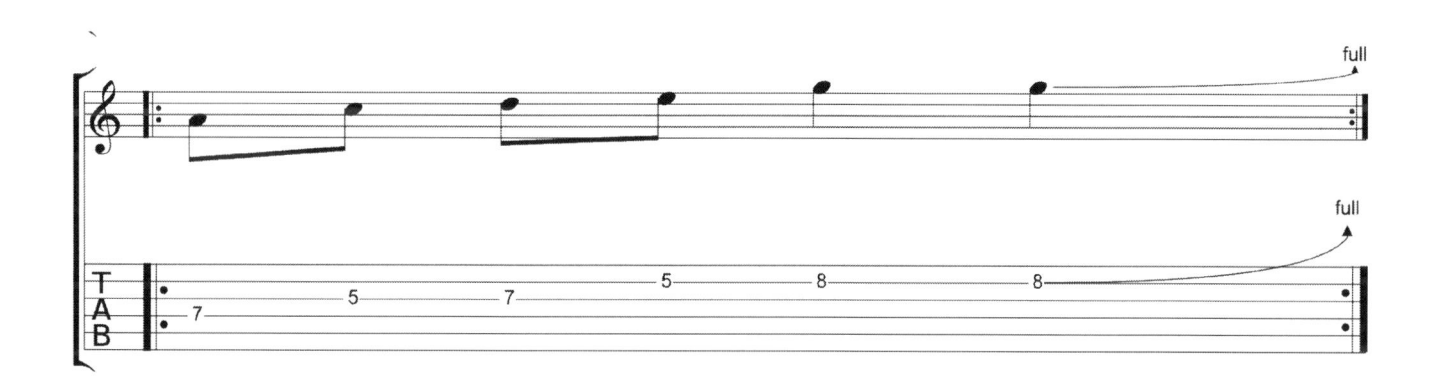

Now you can focus on building some core bending vocabulary around the tone bend on the 8th fret of the high E string.

Bends Around the E String

Example 4t –

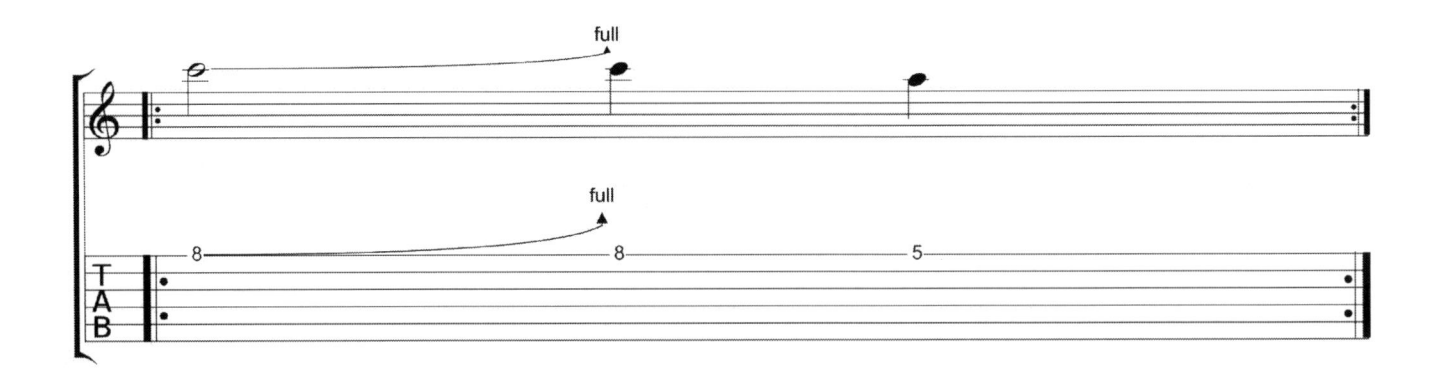

Example 4u –

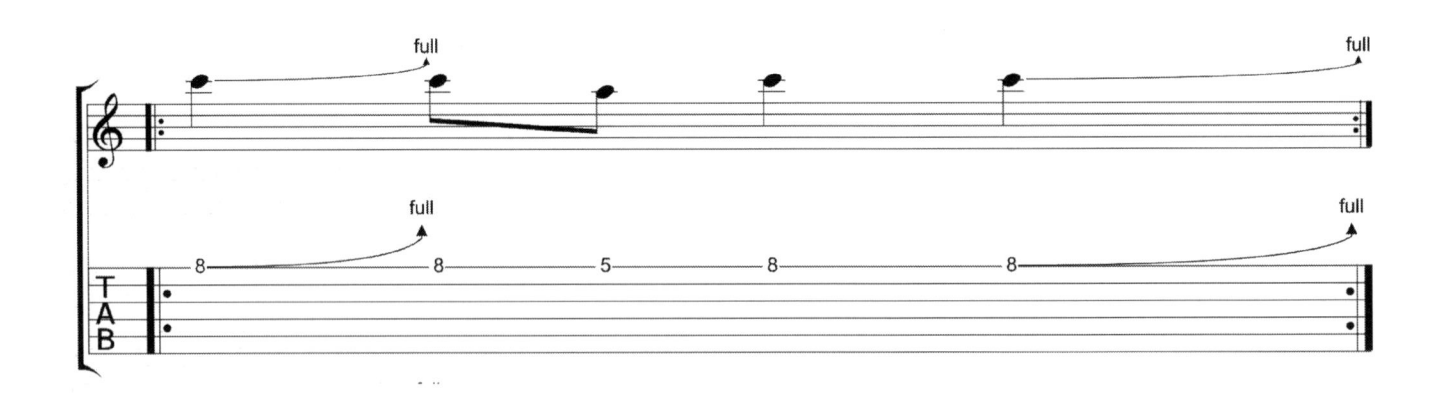

Example 4v –

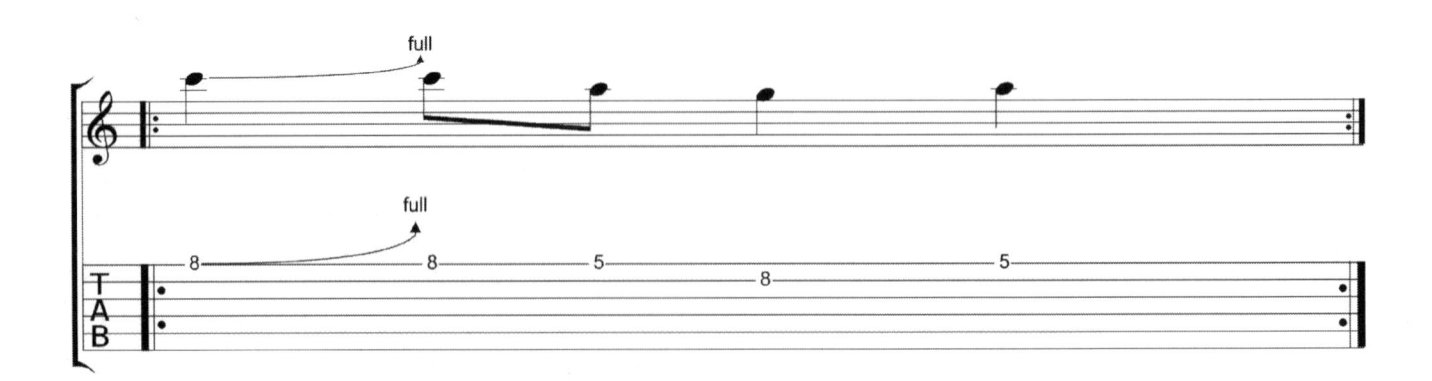

Licks with Multiple Bends

Using one bend in a lick is great, but for maximum impact you can use bends on different strings within one lick. The following examples show how you can build bending licks using the A Minor Pentatonic scale with bends on different strings.

Example 4w –

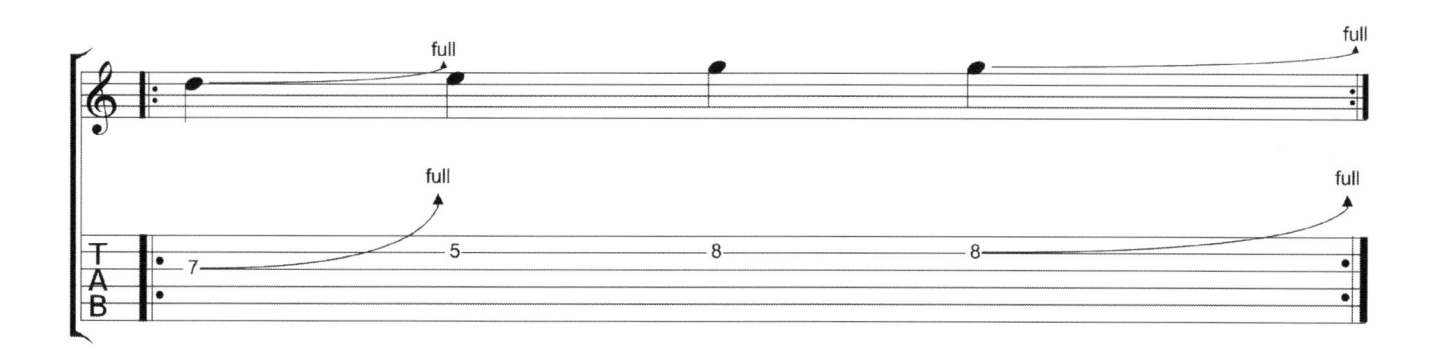

Example 4x –

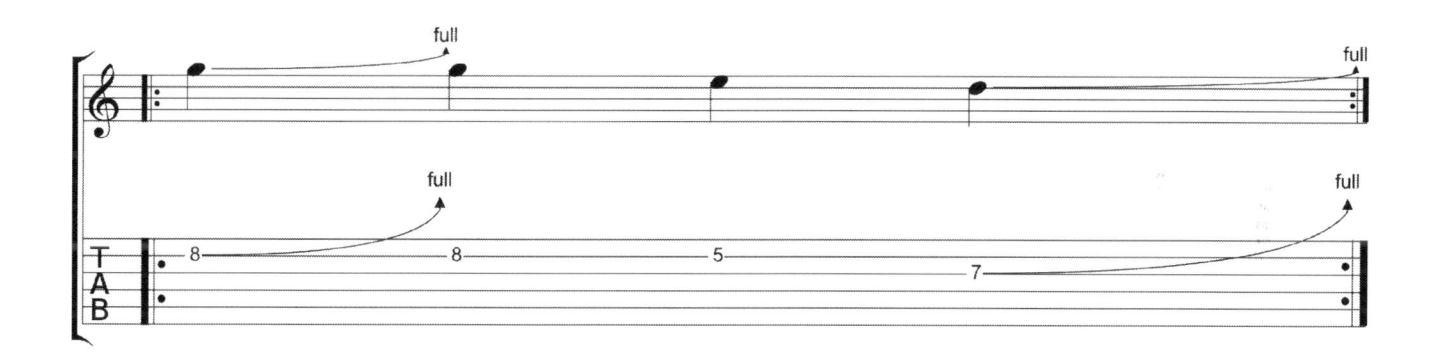

Example 4y –

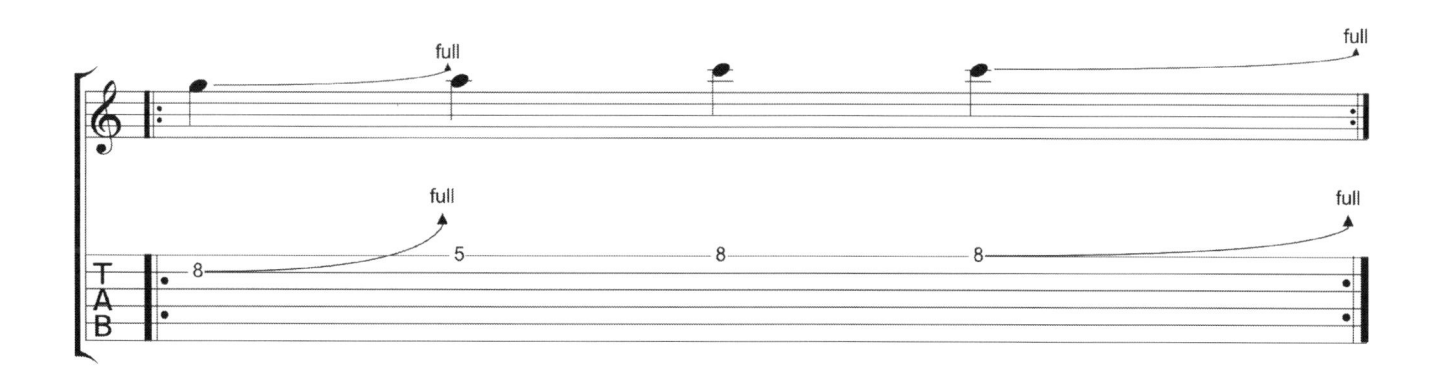

Example 4z –

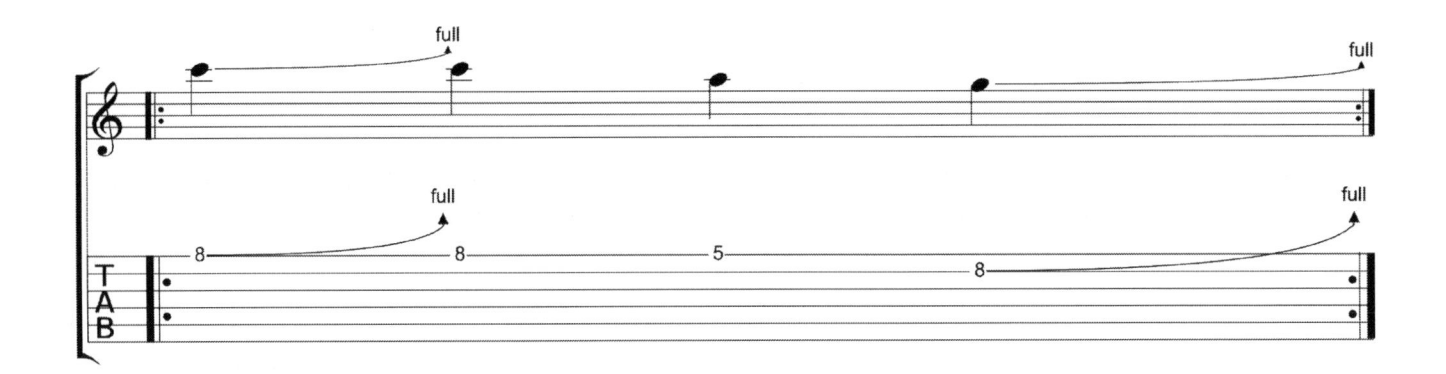

Pop Quiz

What is bending?

What is a semi-tone bend?

What is a tone bend?

What is the most common type of bend in modern electric guitar playing?

Name three guitarists who famously use bending in their playing.

Answers on the final page.

Chapter Five – Legato

In the late 1960s and early 1970s, rock guitarists like Jimmy Page and Brian May began to incorporate faster phrases into their solos. These quicker passages were often created by playing *hammer-ons* and *pull-offs*. Together, these two techniques are referred to as *legato* (Italian for 'smooth'). Some classic examples of legato playing are in Led Zeppelin's Stairway to Heaven solo, Queen's I Want It All solo, and the Red Hot Chili Peppers' track, Snow.

To create a hammer-on, play a note and then quickly 'hammer' a different finger onto a higher fret to create two notes from just one pick stroke. A pull-off is the reverse of a hammer-on. Begin by picking a fretted note and then pull your finger off the string (downwards towards the floor) to sound a fretted note *below* the first.

Legato guitar playing is all about smooth, flowing lines, and lends itself perfectly to melodic rock soloing. An important concern when playing legato is to *keep each note the same volume*. This means that the picked note and the legato notes that follow should all have very similar dynamics. Try recording yourself playing the following examples and pay attention to how smooth the transition is between the picked and legato notes.

There are many legato technique-building exercises, and, while useful for developing the fundamental principles, they are often not very musical. The following examples aim to keep each exercise musical while developing great technique. Listen to the audio examples first to hear how these examples should sound before trying them yourself.

Stick to the *one-finger-per-fret* rule when learning these examples unless otherwise stated. The idea behind the rule is that you allocate one finger to each fret that you play. For example, if you are playing notes between the 5th and 8th frets, use your first finger for the 5th fret's notes and your second finger for all 6th fret's notes, etc. This can be seen in the diagram below:

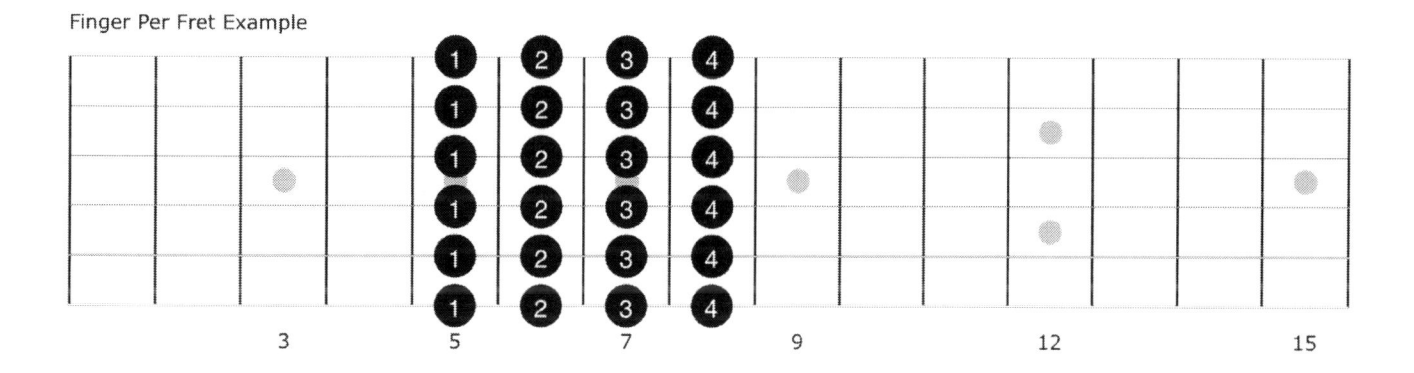

Finger Per Fret Example

Key points to consider:

1) Ensure there is space between the fingers of your fretting hand when playing legato. By learning to play legato with room between your fingers, you will develop strength in the correct tendons and muscles of the hand.

2) Keep your knuckles upright at all times.

3) Stop if you feel any pain. When it comes to guitar playing, 'no pain no gain' is *never* the way forward. Stretch and warm up thoroughly before you play difficult legato sequences and stop if you feel any strain.

The simplest legato technique is the semitone (one-fret) hammer-on which is demonstrated in the first example. Use your first and second fingers to play this exercise and keep some space between your fingers to help build strength and good technique.

One Fret Hammer-On

Example 5a –

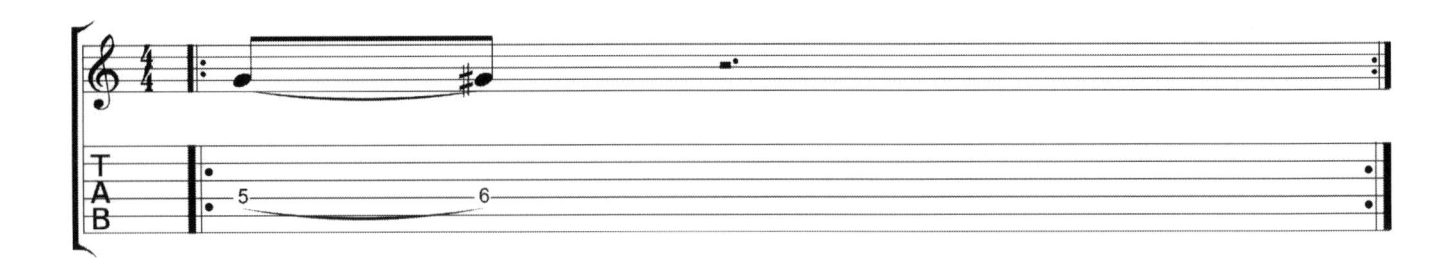

Now play two, one-fret hammer-ons within one bar.

Example 5b –

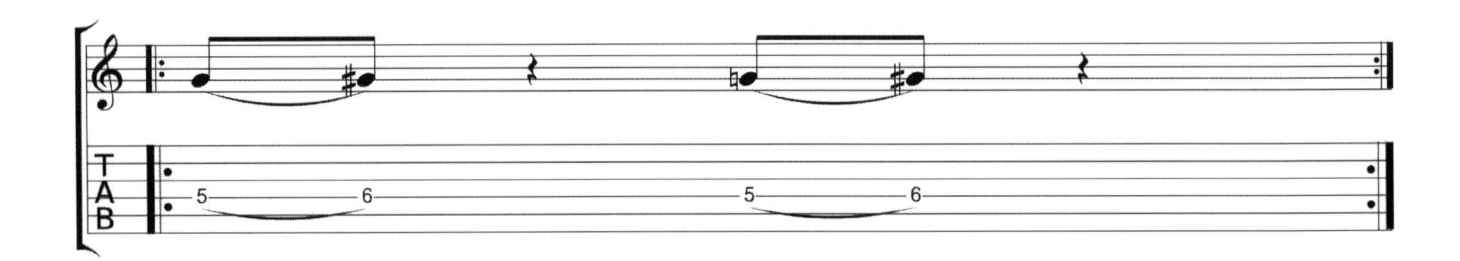

To build up your strength example 5c demonstrates playing four one-fret hammer-ons in one bar.

Example 5c –

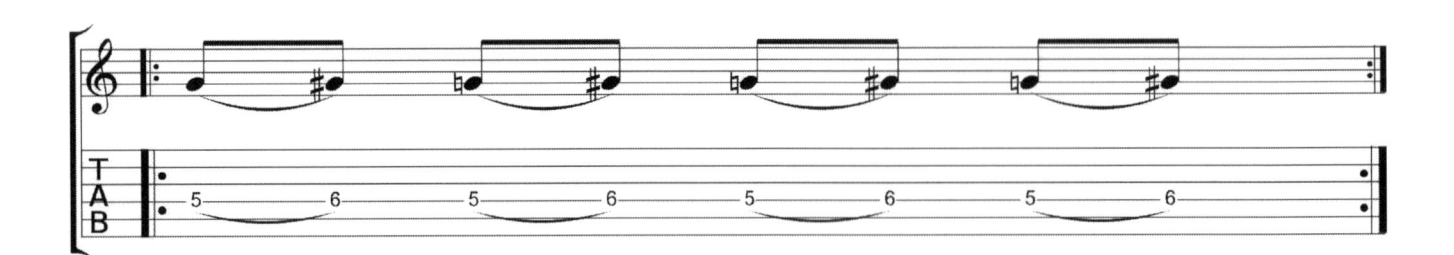

One Fret Pull-Off

Example 5d introduces a one-fret pull-off. Remember that you want to hear play notes using just one pick stroke. Place the 5th fret note on the fretboard with your first finger, then play the 6th fret with your second finger. To execute the pull-off, pull your second finger off the string (downwards towards the floor) to sound the 5th fret.

Example 5d –

Now play four, one-fret pull-offs within a bar.

Example 5e –

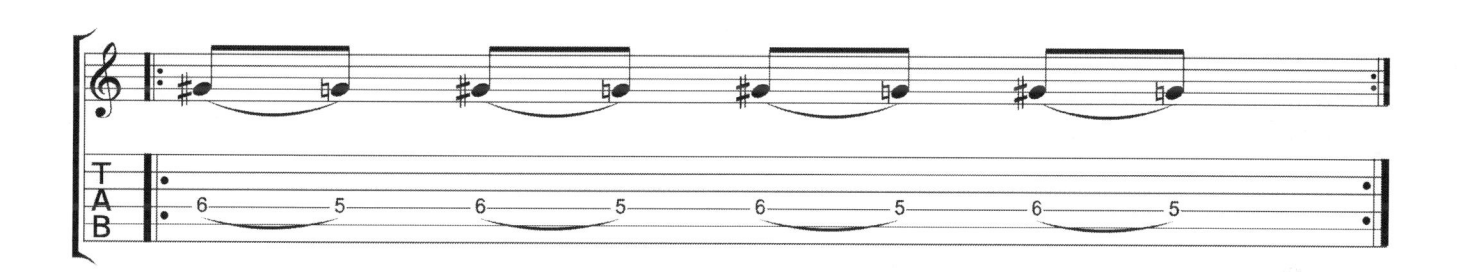

Although one-fret hammer-ons and pull-offs are useful, you will often find that two-fret, or even three-fret legato patterns are more common as they can be applied to many different scale shapes. All the following examples use legato patterns based around A Minor Pentatonic scale.

Example 5f uses a two-fret hammer-on on the D string. Use your first and third fingers to play this pattern.

Example 5f –

Now play two hammer-ons in one bar.

Example 5g –

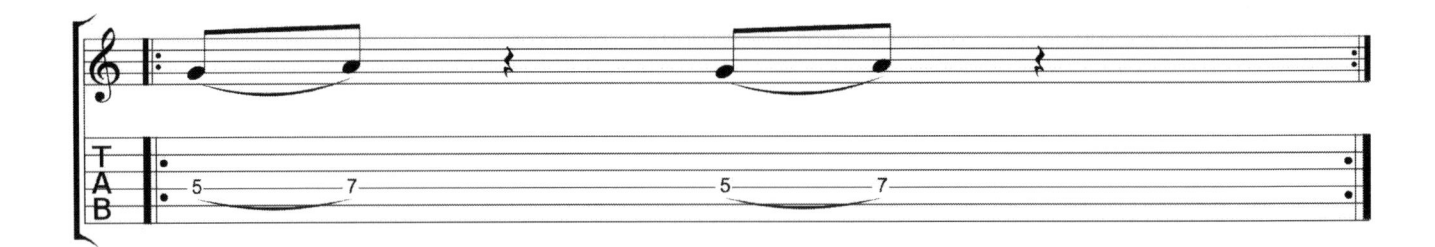

For a slightly tougher exercise, play the two-fret hammer-on from the 5th to the 7th frets four times within one bar. If you want to work on stamina and dexterity, be sure to check out my book Guitar Finger Gym.

Example 5h –

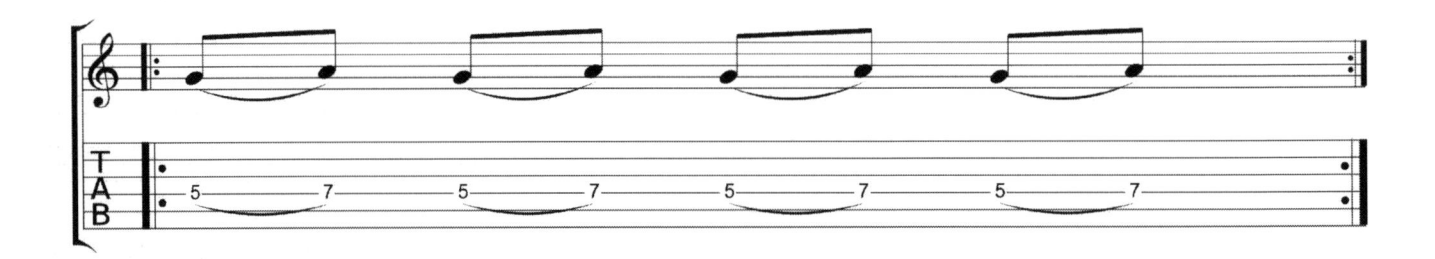

Next, play a 7th to 5th fret pull off on the D string.

Example 5i –

Now play two pull-offs within one bar.

Example 5j –

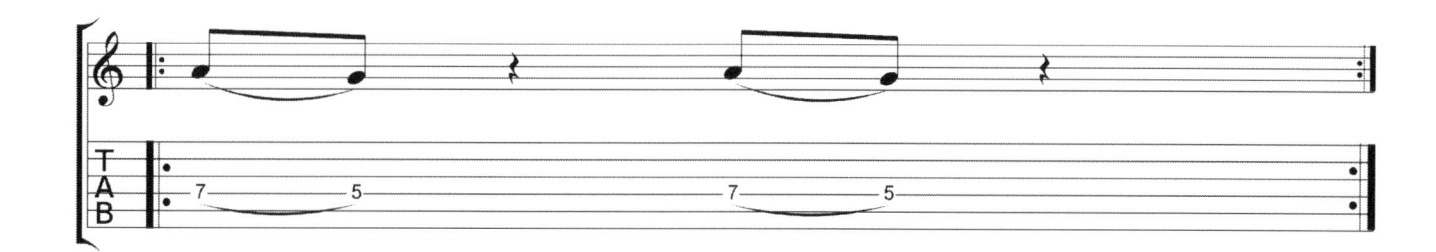

Build up your technique by playing four pull-offs within a one-bar phrase.

Example 5k –

Keeping to the A Minor Pentatonic scale, it is time to examine the three-fret hammer-on and pull-off on the B string. Complete these examples using your first and fourth fingers.

Example 5l –

Example 5m –

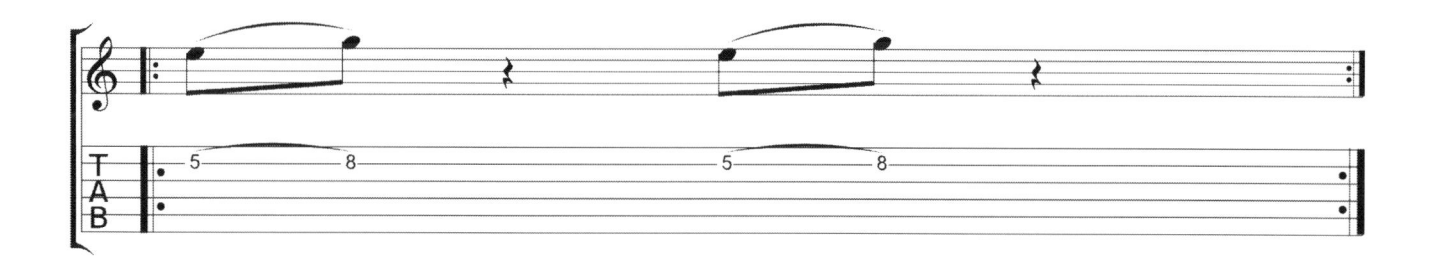

Example 5n –

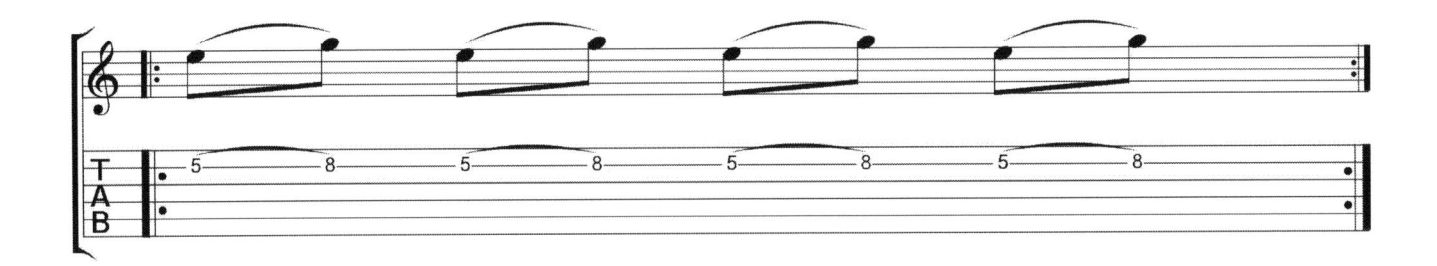

Now work on pulling-off three frets from your fourth finger to your first finger. Practice each example very slowly at around 50bpm before gradually speeding up the metronome when you can complete each example three times in a row.

Example 5o –

Example 5p –

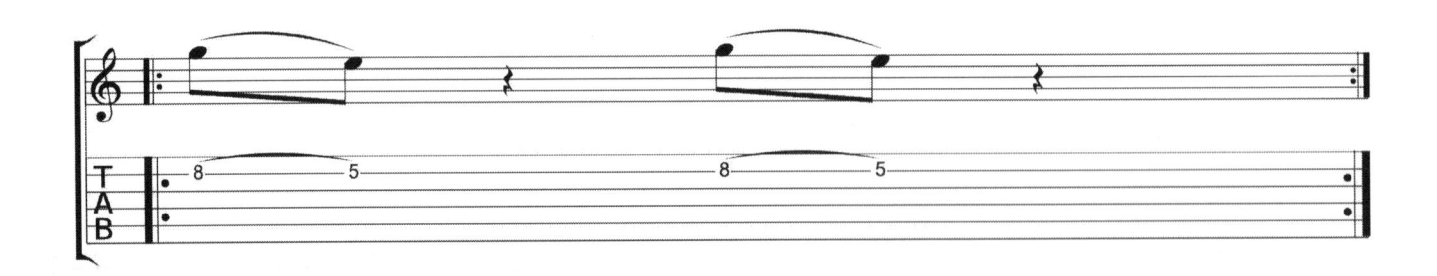

Example 5q –

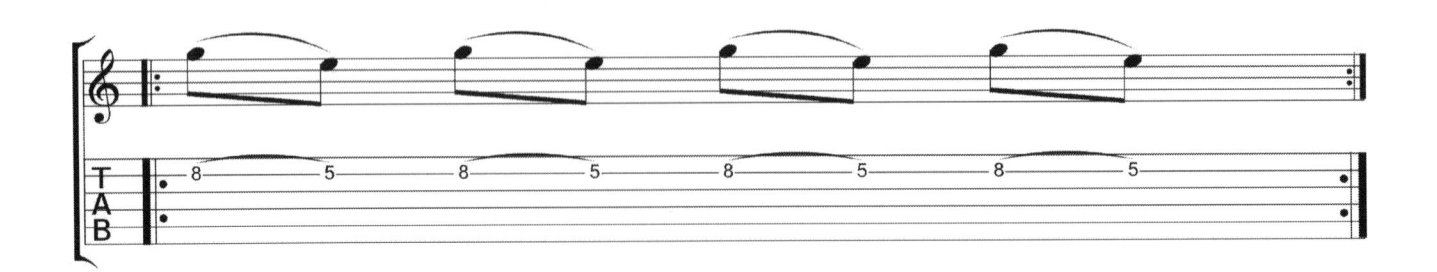

Core Legato Licks

By now it should be apparent that you can use bends and slides around the A Minor Pentatonic scale to create licks. You can also use legato (hammer-ons and pull-offs) to create licks and phrases. Play these licks with backing tracks one - four.

The next examples use hammer-ons to create core blues-rock vocabulary. Listen to the attached audio to see how I play and *phrase* each example.

Example 5r –

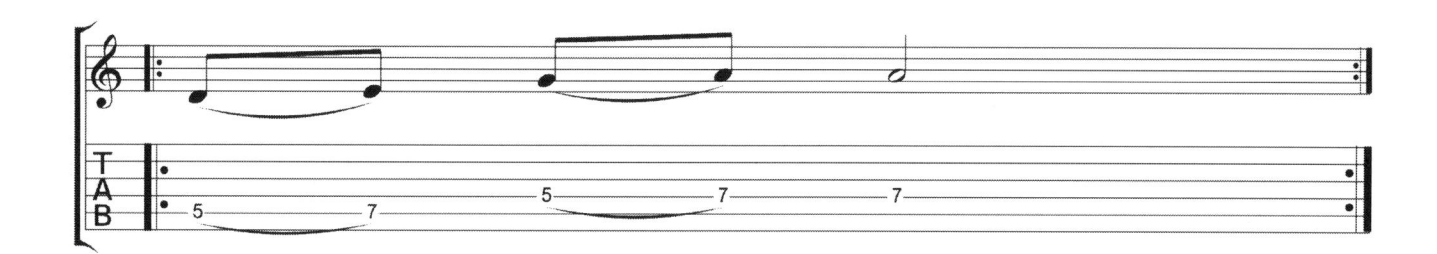

Example 5s –

Example 5t –

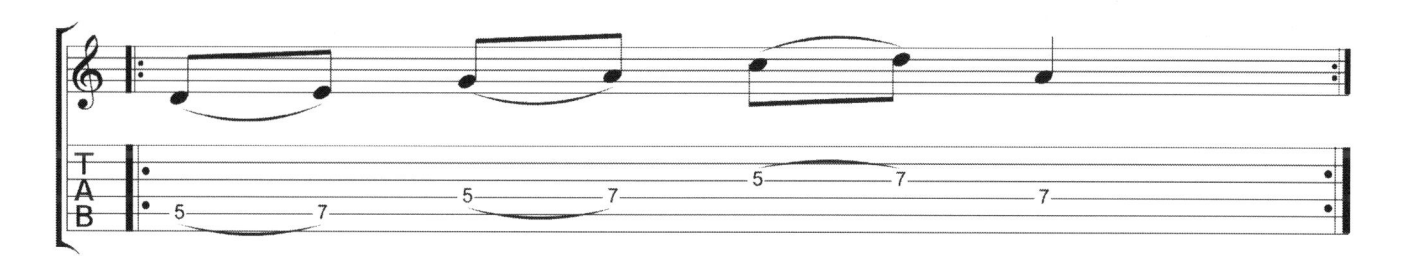

Now for some pull-off licks.

Example 5u –

Example 5v –

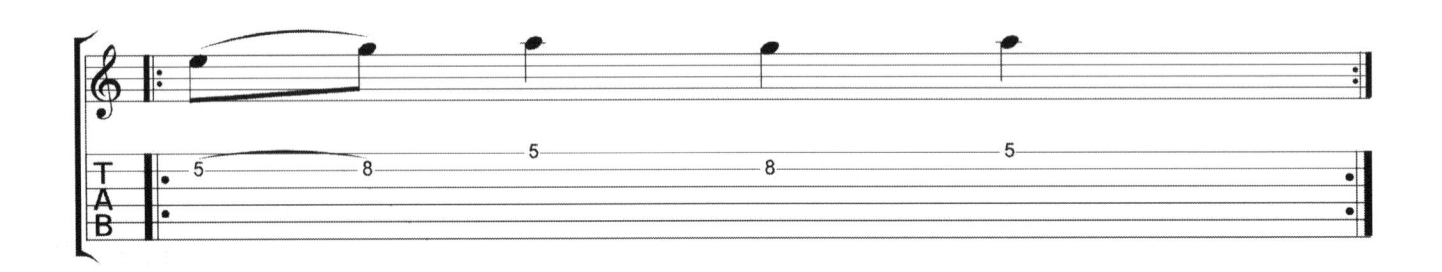

Example 5w –

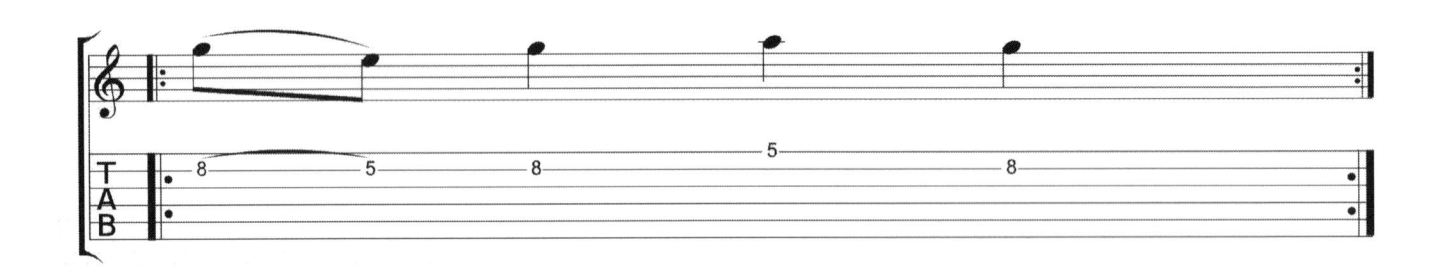

Example 5x –

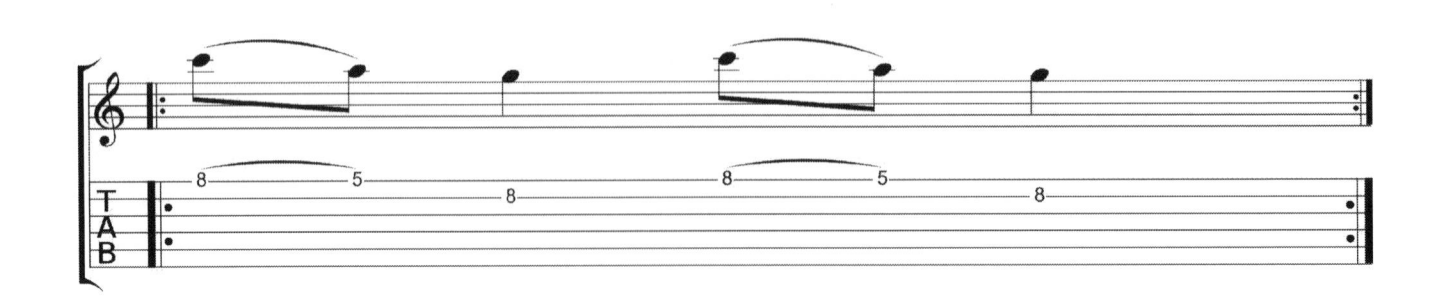

Example 5y –

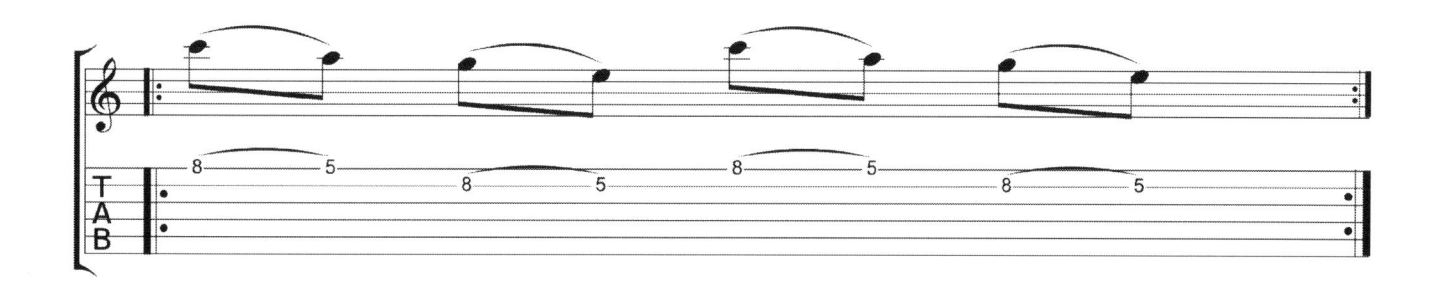

Once you are comfortable combining hammer-ons and pull-offs separately, you can create licks and phrases that combine both of them.

Go through each of these licks and highlight your favourites!

Example 5z –

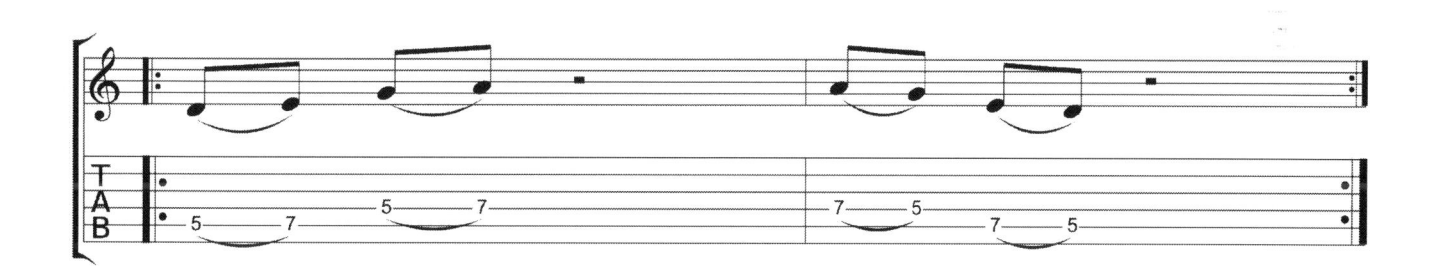

Example 5z1 –

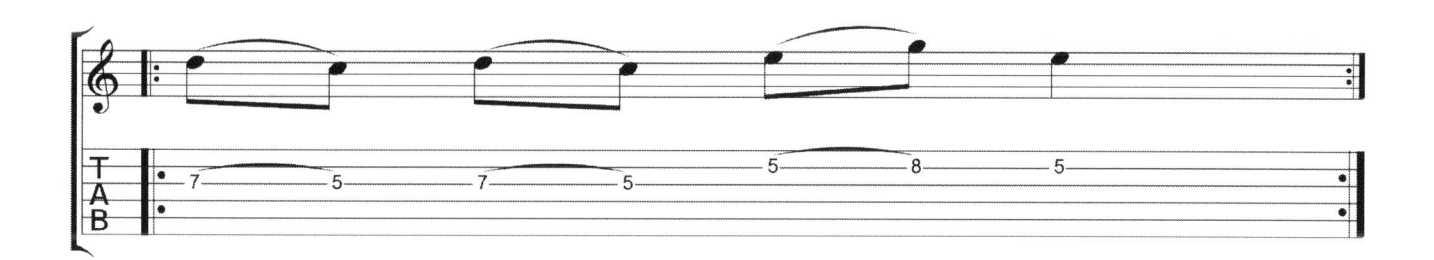

223

Example 5z2 –

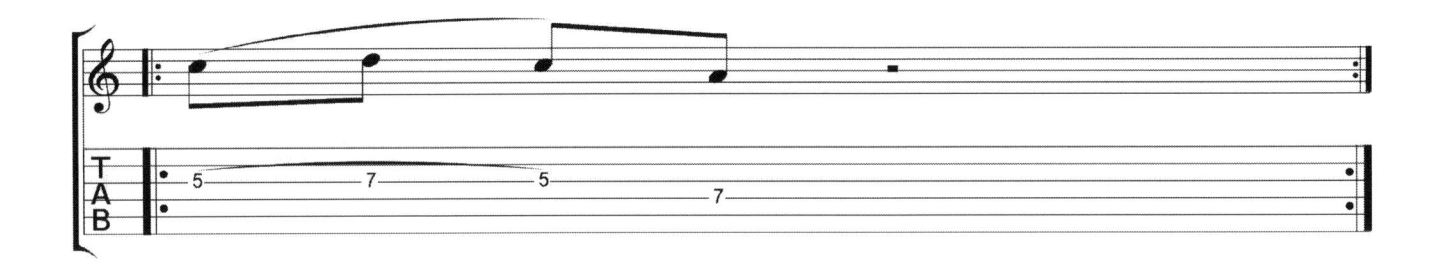

Example 5z3 –

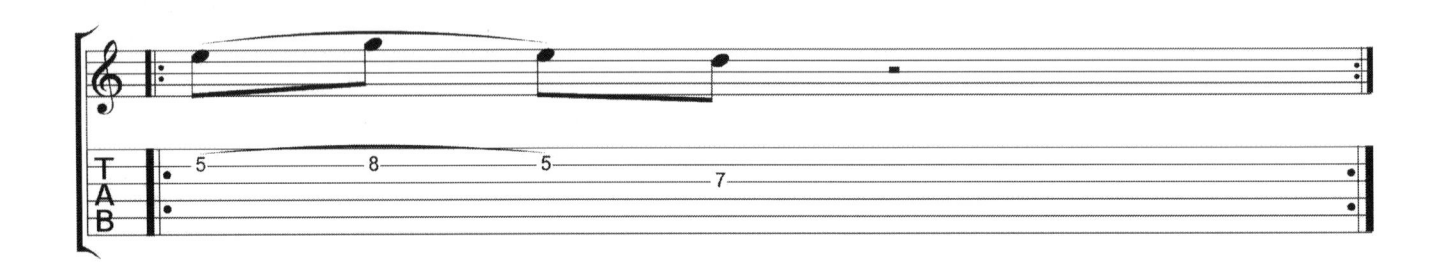

Example 5z4 –

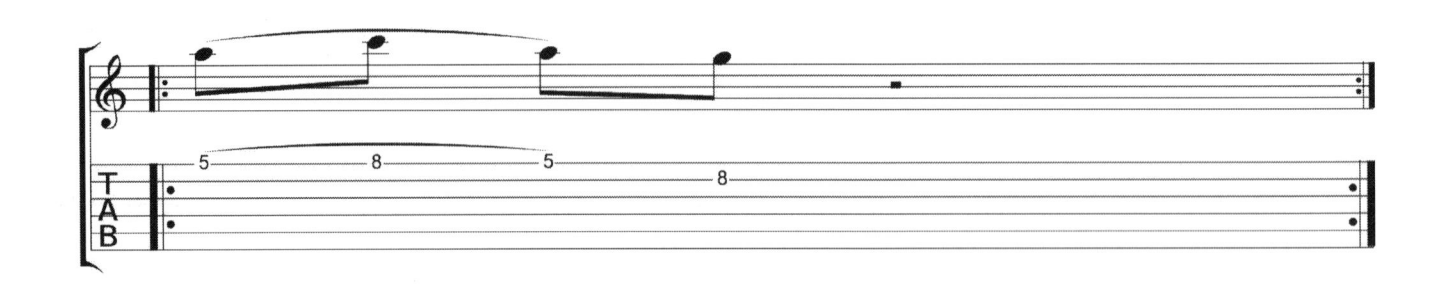

Example 5z5 –

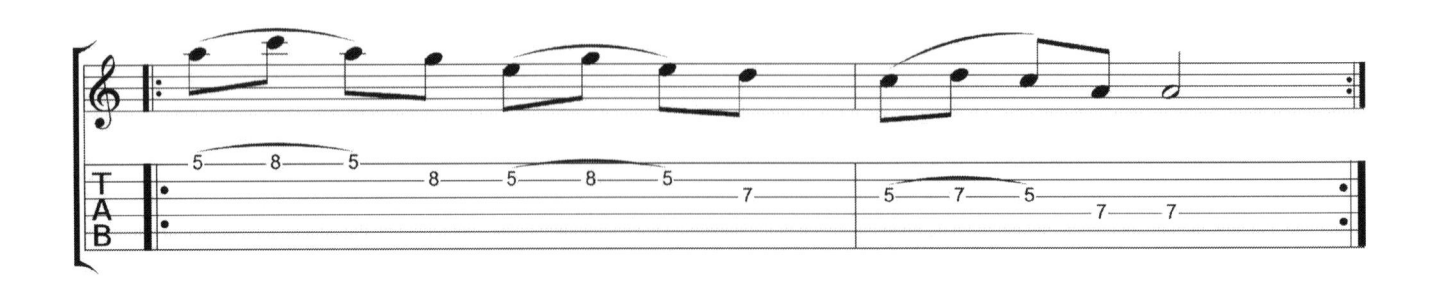

Modern Rock Vibrato

Vibrato adds expression and energy to a note by rapidly moving the pitch up and down. This allows a note to have a more vocal, human quality and gives passion and emotion to your guitar solos. Vibrato is personal and unique to each guitarist and can be added to any note by any finger. It is possible to alter its speed, duration, and the delay before it is added. The amount of vibrato used depends very much on the genre of music, with narrow subtle vibrato often used in the blues, and wide, obvious vibrato more commonly reserved for rock guitar.

Modern rock vibrato is applied by moving the string rapidly in the direction of the fret wire in a similar way to bending a string. This technique gives great control of the pitch variation of a note, and also allows us to add vibrato to a bend. Soft, gentle vibrato suits ballads and slower songs, while wide vibrato works well for harder rock tracks.

If you want a far more in-depth look at vibrato, check out my book **Melodic Rock Soloing for Guitar**.

Example 5z6 (Basic Modern Rock Vibrato Technique)

1. Pick and hold the 7th fret of the G string with your first finger.
2. Place your thumb as if you were going to bend the note.
3. Pull the string down towards the floor using your wrist as a pivot. The vibrato is created by the manipulation of the wrist, rather than the fingers. Release the wrist back to a normal position and let the note return to its original pitch.
4. Repeat this movement as many times as possible (although three times is usually enough in practice).
5. Repeat example 5z6 on each finger. (The fourth finger is used less often, but it is still good practice if you can manage it).

At first, the string might not move very far, but, just as with string bending, it becomes easier with practice.

When you are comfortable with this basic approach, experiment with the amount of vibrato you add and the speed of its manipulation.

The most crucial thing is to ensure that the note doesn't sound out of tune when the vibrato is applied. The more confident you become at using vibrato, the wider the vibrato you can add.

The full concept of how to apply vibrato is quite advanced and is out of the scope of this book but don't worry, if you want a far more in-depth look at vibrato check out my book **Melodic Rock Soloing for Guitar**.

There is a lot of content in this chapter so return here often so you can keep developing your technique.

Take your time and remember there is no rush to complete a chapter; it is not a race! What matters is that you progress consistently over the next few months and years, and that you continuously monitor your development.

Remember that this book, and your guitar playing, should be about enjoyment, so make having fun your priority, and any challenges will feel less significant in comparison.

Chapter Six – A Minor Pentatonic Licks

A guitar *lick* is a short series of notes (or *phrase*) that can be used as the basis for solos and lead guitar playing. Learning licks is like learning vocabulary in a new language. Always remember that music is a language!

In this chapter, I have created nine A Minor Pentatonic licks based on the techniques in the previous chapters. These licks include slides, bends and legato, so make sure you are confident with all these techniques before continuing.

At this point, I want to remind you again to listen to great lead guitar players and immerse yourself in as many different musical genres as possible. Refer to the introduction for ten essential solos, and to the discography at the end of the book for more vital listening.

Example 6a uses a *call and response* blues pattern: Bars one and three are identical and act as the 'call', and bar two and four vary slightly to create the 'response'. This is a fundamental of creating longer phrases by anchoring your solos around one memorable lick throughout.

Example 6a –

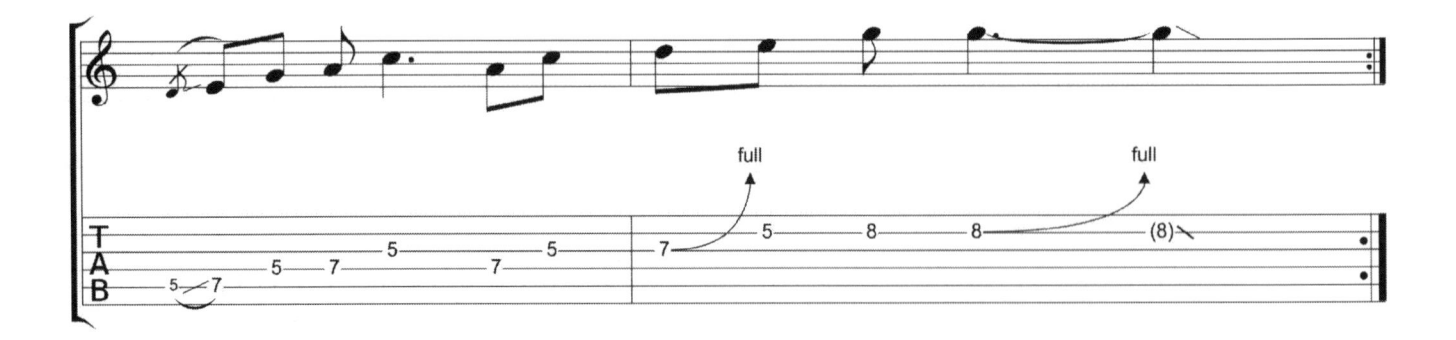

In example 6b, I again created a call and response pattern that alternates between a sliding lick in bar one and three and a hammer-on lick in bars two and four. Make sure you listen to the accompanying audio tracks before playing these licks.

Example 6b –

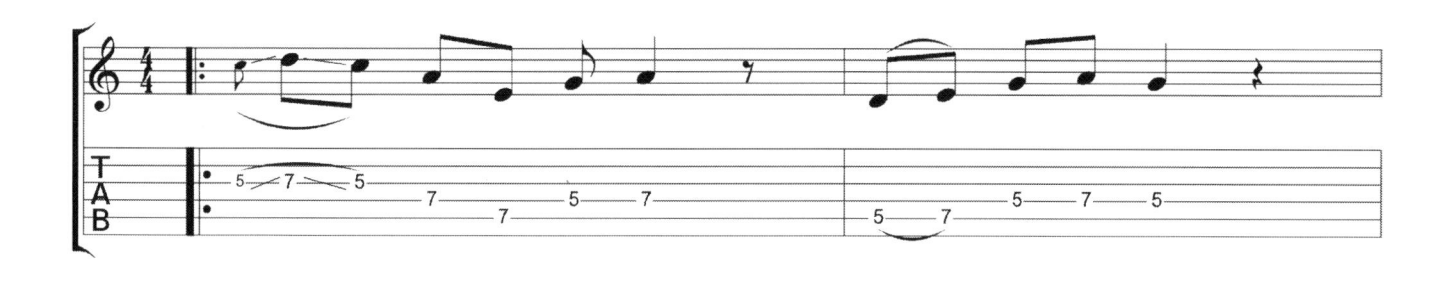

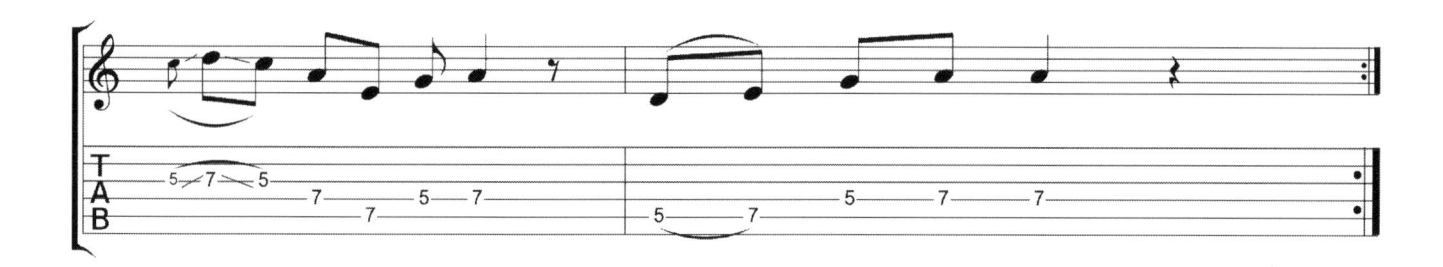

Until now, everything in this book has focussed on playing one note at a time. An excellent way to break up this habit is by using *double-stops* or 'playing two notes simultaneously'. Play the 5th fret notes with your first finger lying across the B and E strings. If you find it difficult to play both frets with just one finger, experiment by using separate fingers.

Chuck Berry uses double-stops a lot in his playing. Check out the classic guitar anthem Johnny B Goode.

Example 6c –

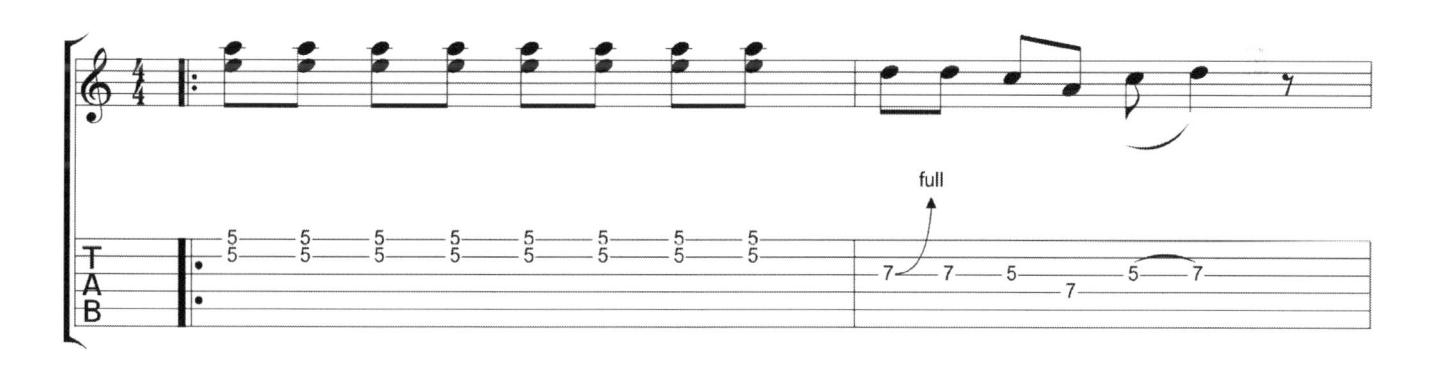

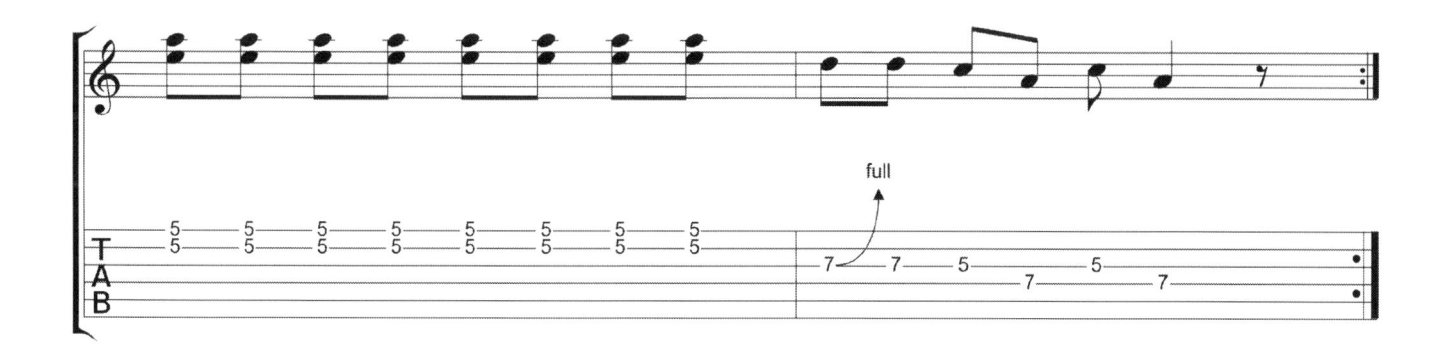

You don't have to play on every beat of the bar!

This tip stuck with me right from my early days of studying at the Guitar Institute. By having audible silence between the notes you play, your licks will sound well-constructed and thought-out.

Remember that 'the plectrum never runs out of breath.' Try singing your licks out loud. Where would the melody naturally pause? Where would you have to breathe? Try to copy this phrasing in your guitar playing.

Example 6d –

Slide from the 7th fret to the 5th, and back to the 7th fret on the A string using just one pick stroke. This double slide forms the basis of the next lick.

Example 6e –

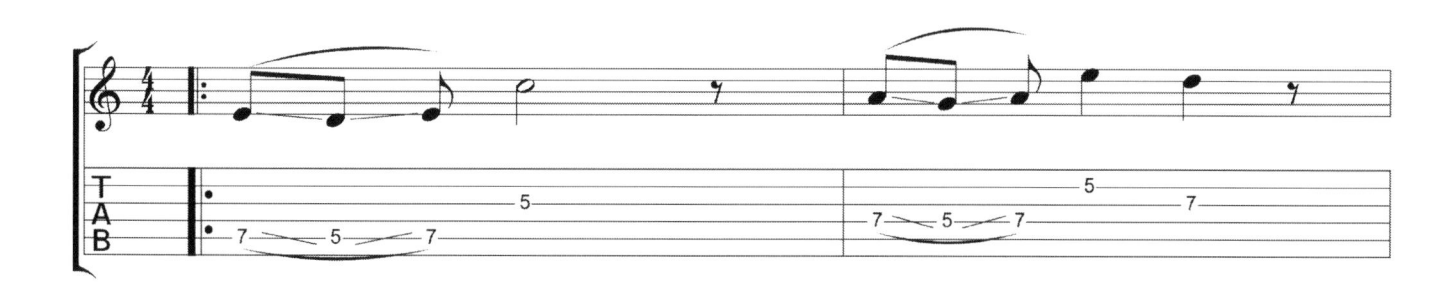

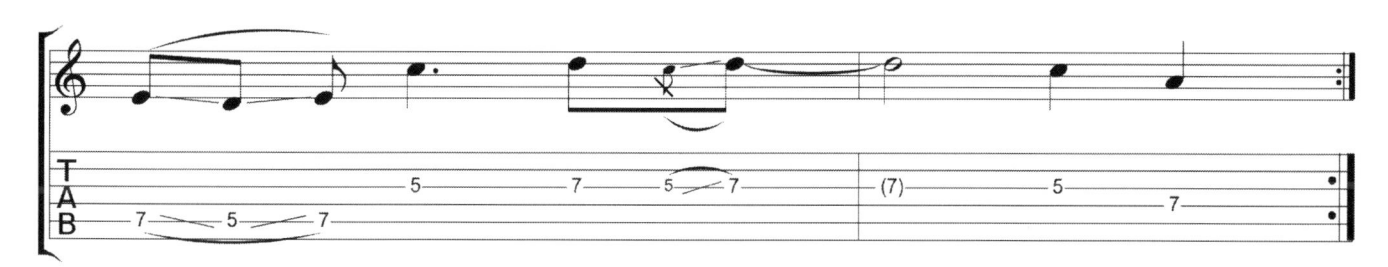

I have created four A Minor backing tracks for you to practice all these licks over. I believe that playing along to backing tracks is one of the most practical and fun ways for you to improve your lead guitar playing skills.

Example 6f –

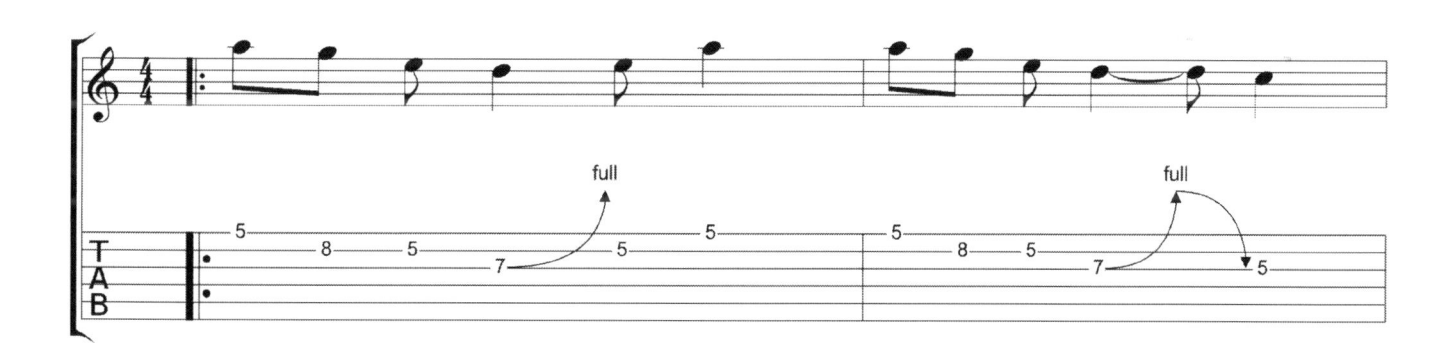

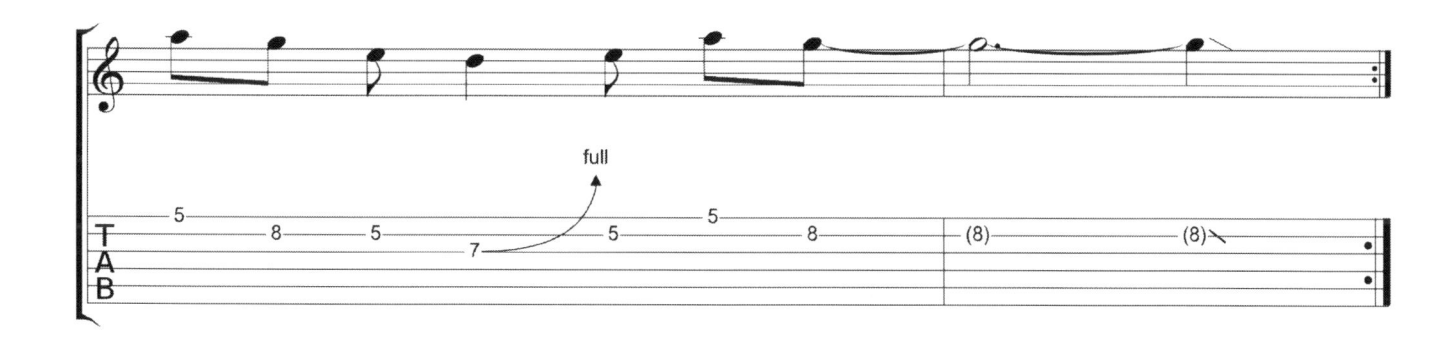

I often sing a melodic phrase first before playing that information on the guitar. This is how example 6g was created.

Example 6g –

Pull-off patterns are often seen in rock guitar solos. Check out the solo from the Dire Straits hit, Sultans of Swing for more ideas in this style.

Example 6h –

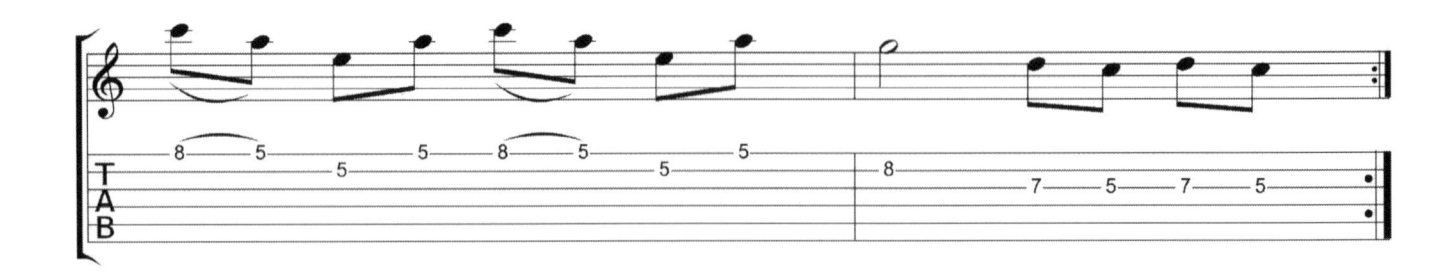

It is important to internalise these licks and not just read them off the page. Play them repeatedly with a backing track or a metronome until you can fret them without the need for the music.

Example 6i –

Now that you have learnt the nine licks, combine these licks in any way you would like. Remember you don't have to use a full lick every time, sometimes just using a few notes from one lick will suffice.

Example 6j –

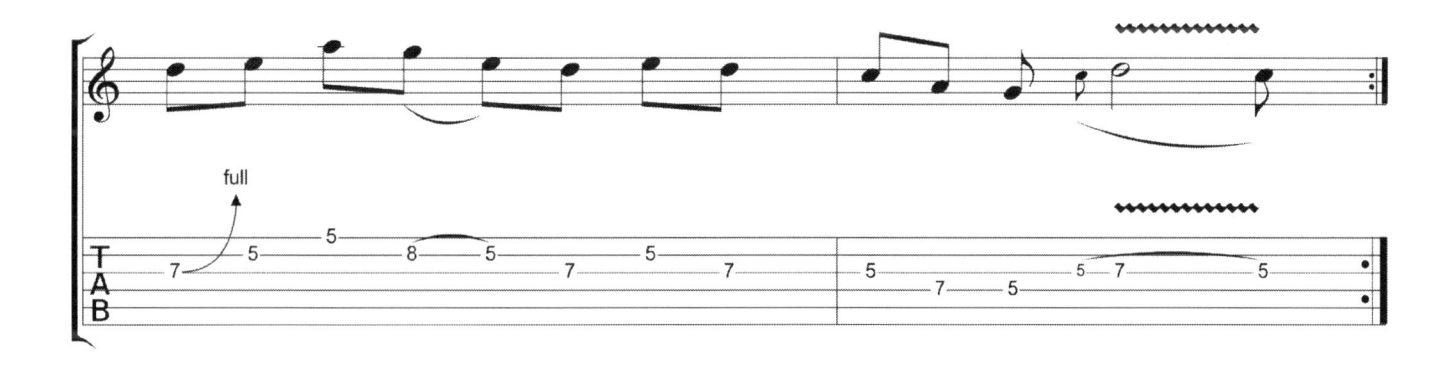

Chapter Seven – A Minor Pentatonic Full Solo

Backing Track One.

There is nothing quite like learning a guitar solo in its entirety to help you internalise and master new techniques. While learning licks and techniques are a solid base for progression on the guitar they won't ever provide the satisfaction that you get from playing along, note-for-note, with a piece of music.

The following solo combines all the techniques and ideas seen throughout this book into a fun, melodic solo. The solo is in the key of A minor and uses the A Minor Pentatonic Scale throughout.

Although, at first, this full solo may seem a little daunting, I have constructed it so that a lot of the licks repeat themselves. The licks featured in this solo are not identical to the licks in the previous chapter but often I have retained similar techniques and phrases so they won't feel completely alien to you.

As well as listening to my performance of this track, I have included a slowed down midi version so you can play along at a slower tempo.

By now you should be very familiar with the A Minor Pentatonic scale shape. One good idea is to learn the notes that the scale contains. In this diagram, you will see the notes of the A Minor Pentatonic scale written out on each string.

A Minor Pentatonic

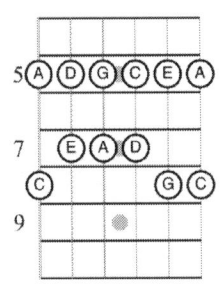

Make sure you have listened to example 7a multiple times in headphones to hear all the expressive phrasing and nuances, and aim to emulate all of them when you play it yourself.

Example 7a – A Minor Pentatonic Full Solo

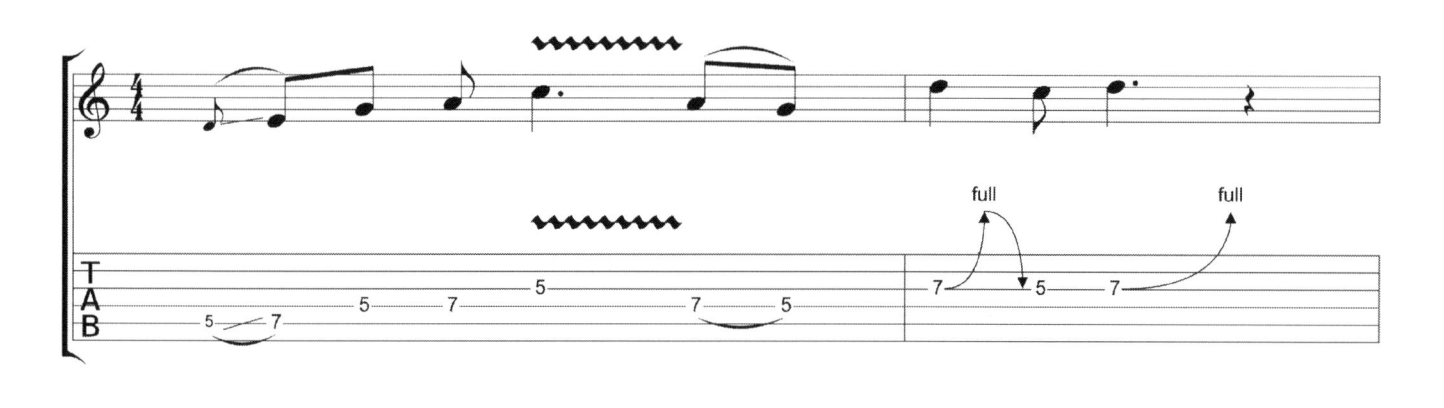

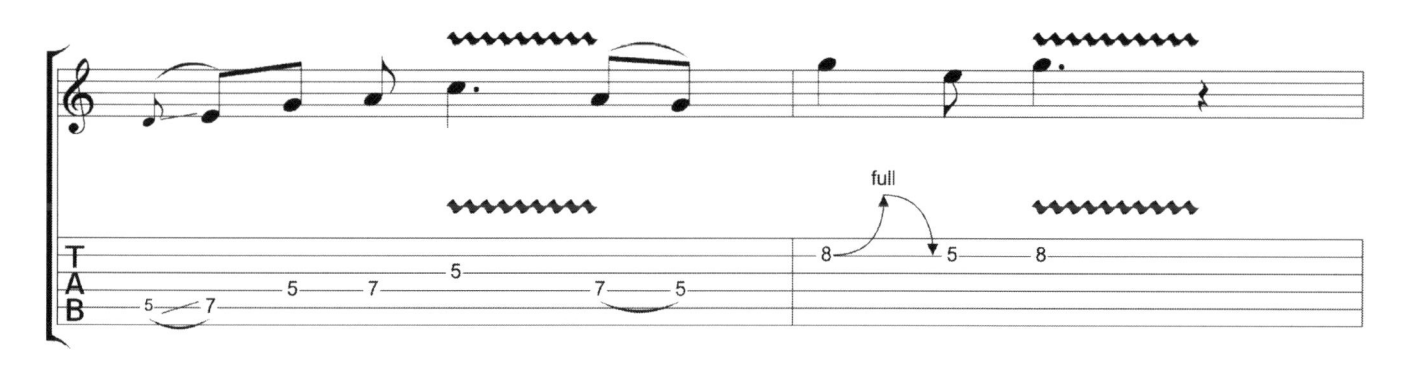

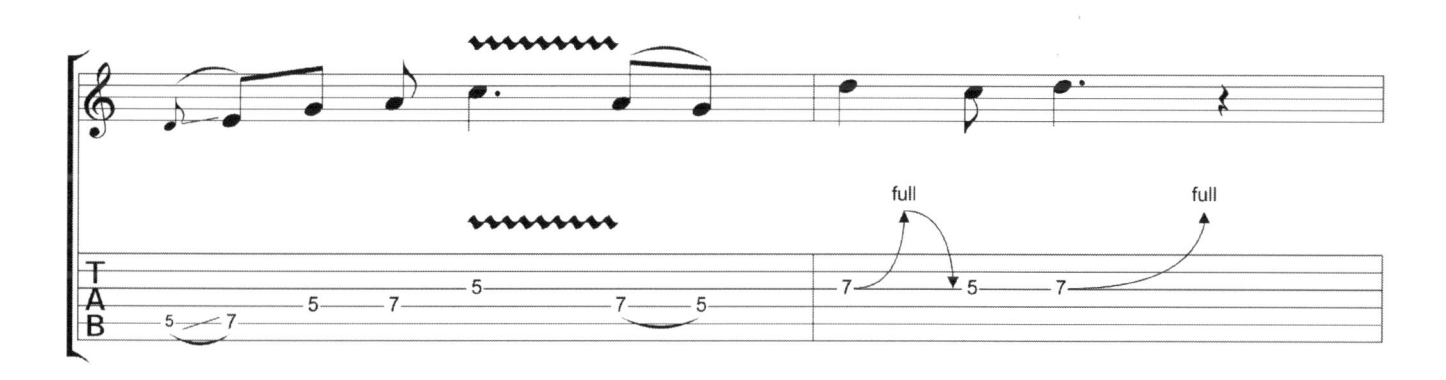

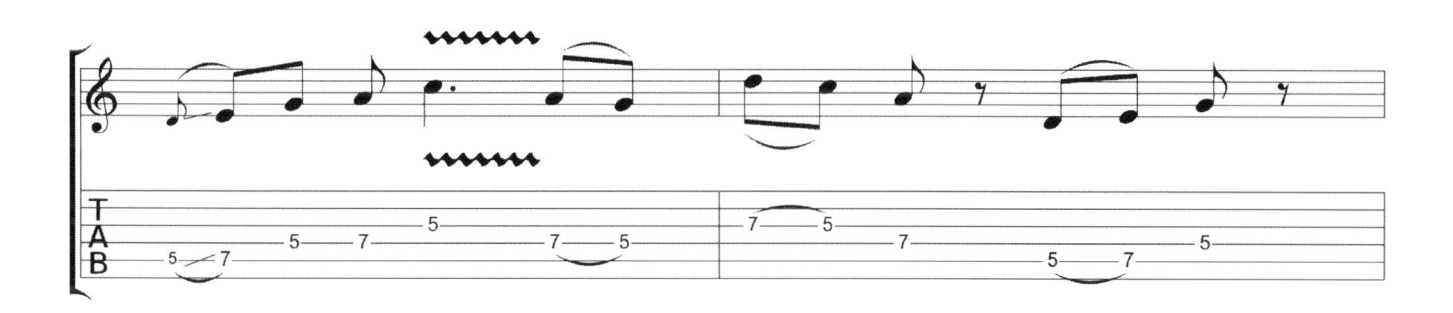

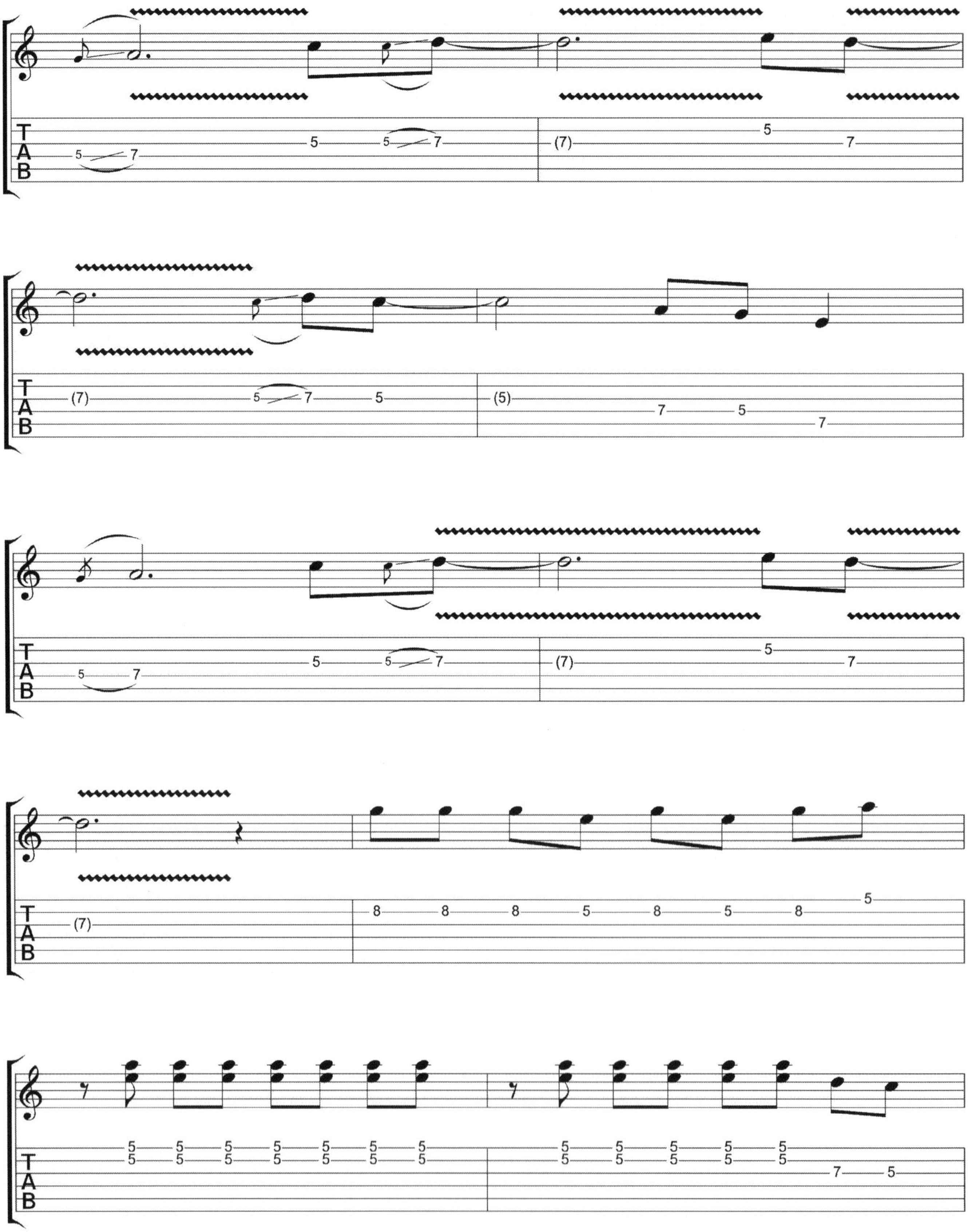

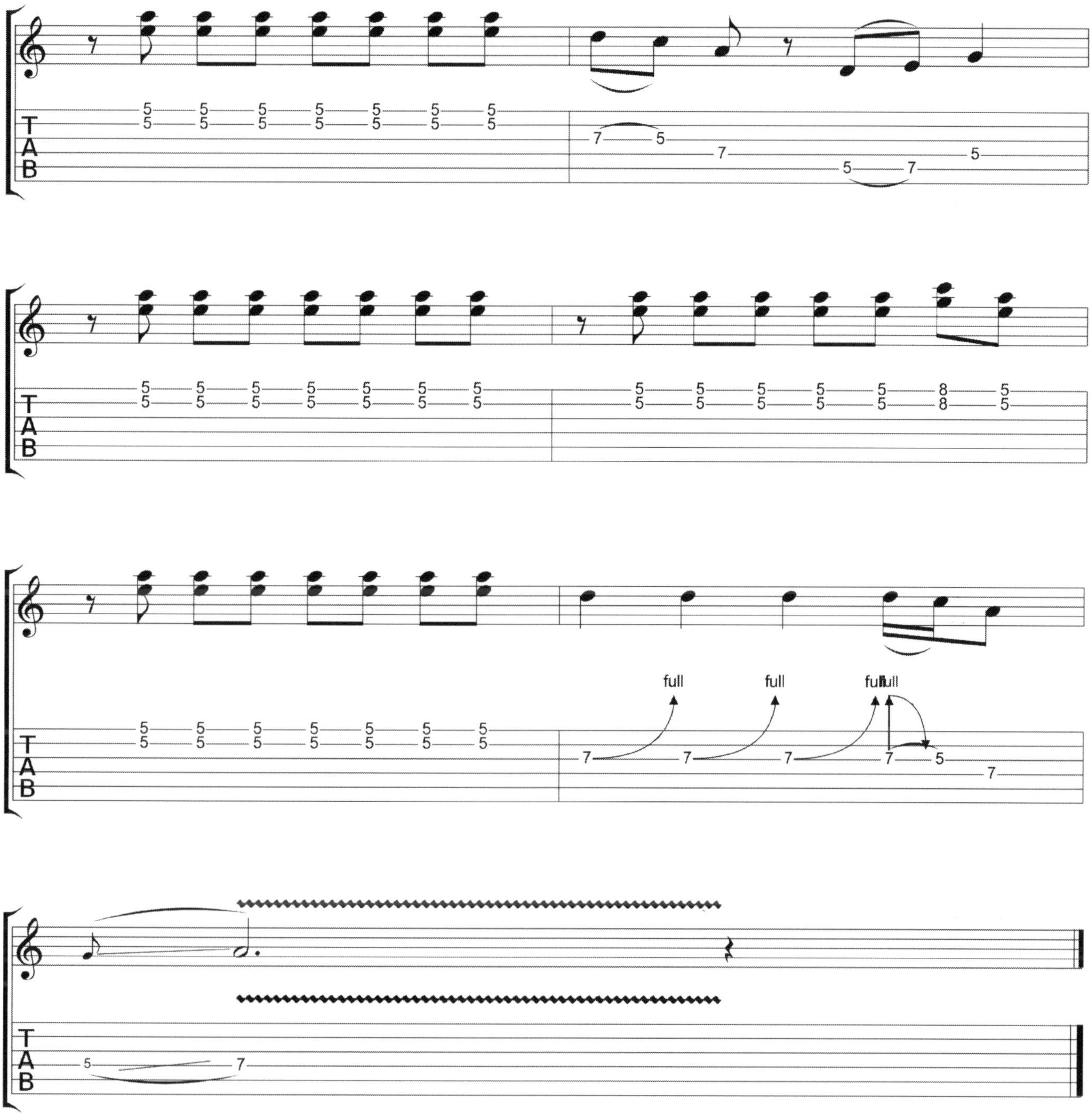
full
full
full
full

Chapter Eight – Moving to E Minor

Backing Track Five and Six

One of the best things about learning a scale shape on the guitar is that you can easily transfer it to another key by simply moving the scale shape to a different location. I am going to show you how you can move the nine A Minor Pentatonic licks you learnt in Chapter Six up the fretboard into the key of E minor.

Until now, you have learnt the A Minor Pentatonic scale starting from the 5th fret of the 6th string. Let's move that scale shape into the key of E minor by moving the whole shape up to the 12th fret of the 6th string.

Example 8a shows the E Minor Pentatonic scale (E G A B D) starting from the 12th fret of the low E string. Look at the second diagram below to see which finger should be placed in each fret.

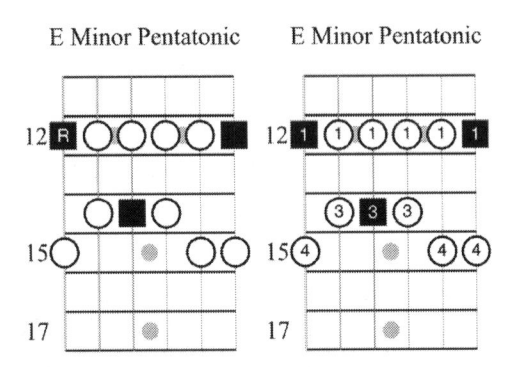

Example 8a –

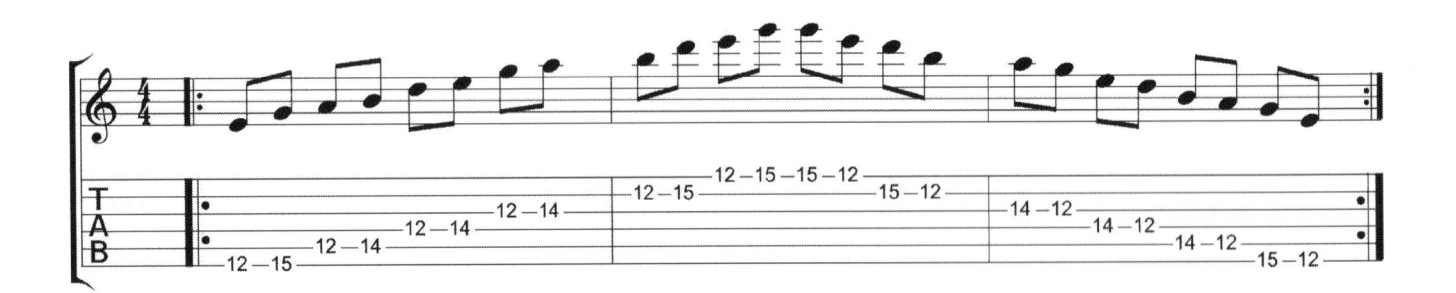

I am a long-term believer that everything you do on the guitar should be about maximising the information you already know. The nine licks I have created here are the same as in Chapter Six, but now they are moved up around the 12th fret shape of E Minor Pentatonic. These licks should feel comfortable quite quickly if you have spent time learning them earlier on. Having the ability to move licks into any key will mean you can play solos over a wide variety of tracks.

Example 8b demonstrates a four-bar, call and response blues pattern around the E Minor Pentatonic scale at the 12th fret.

Example 8b –

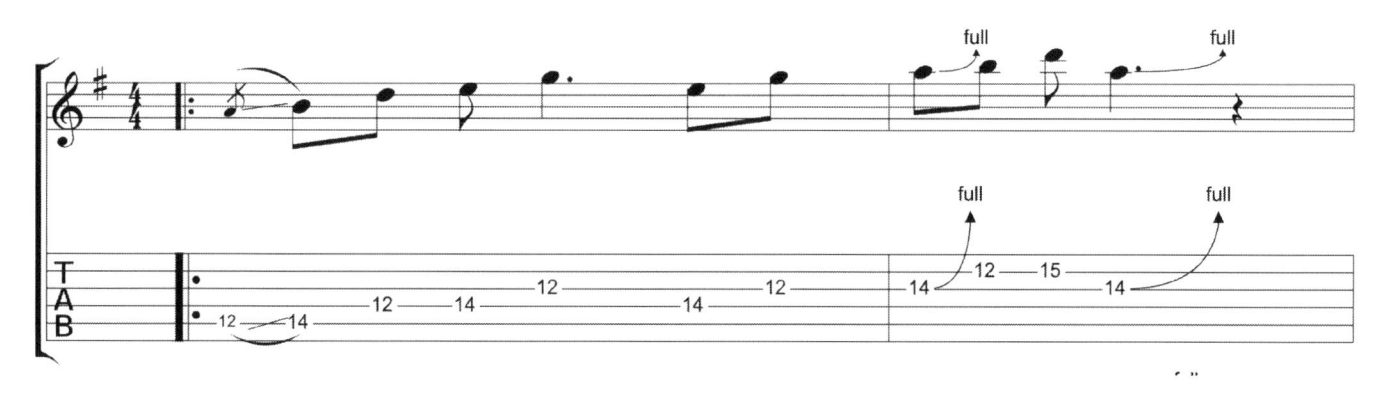

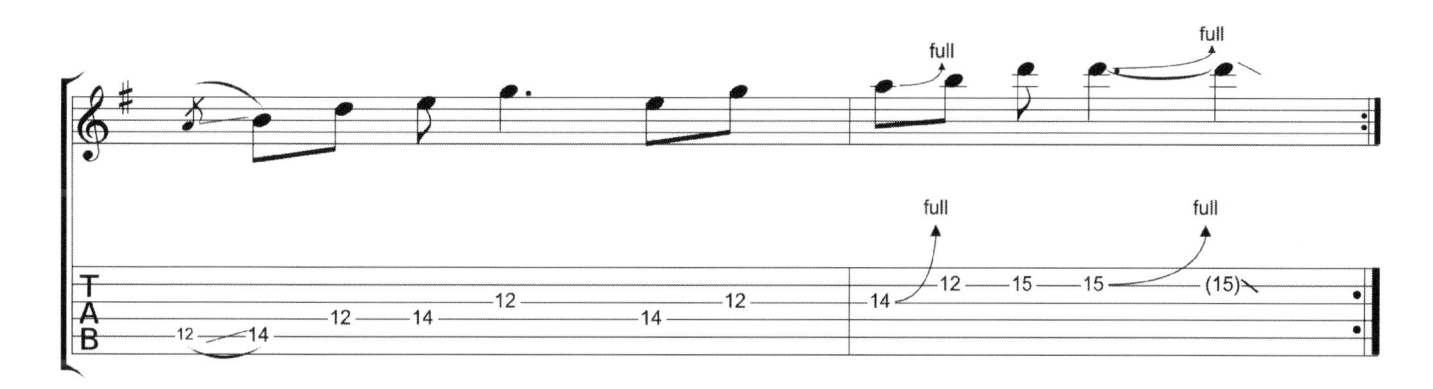

In example 8b I again created a call and response pattern using the E Minor Pentatonic scale. This alternates between a sliding lick in bar one and three, and a hammer-on lick in bars two and four.

Example 8c –

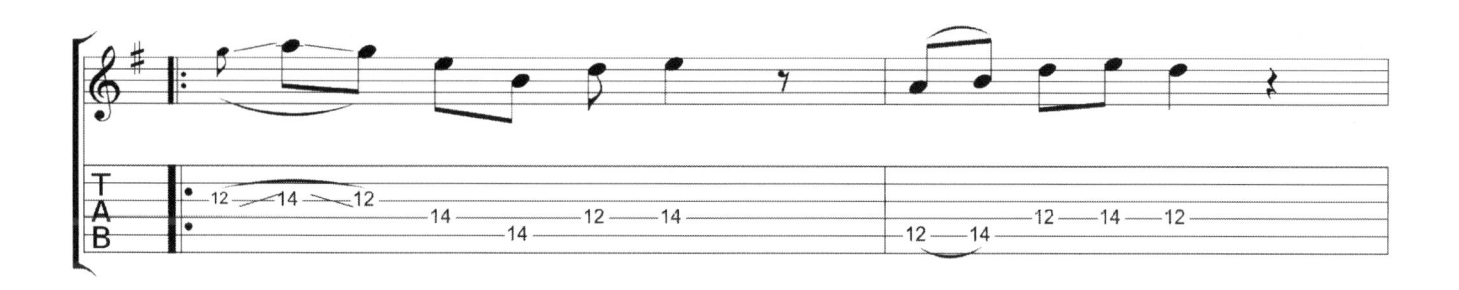

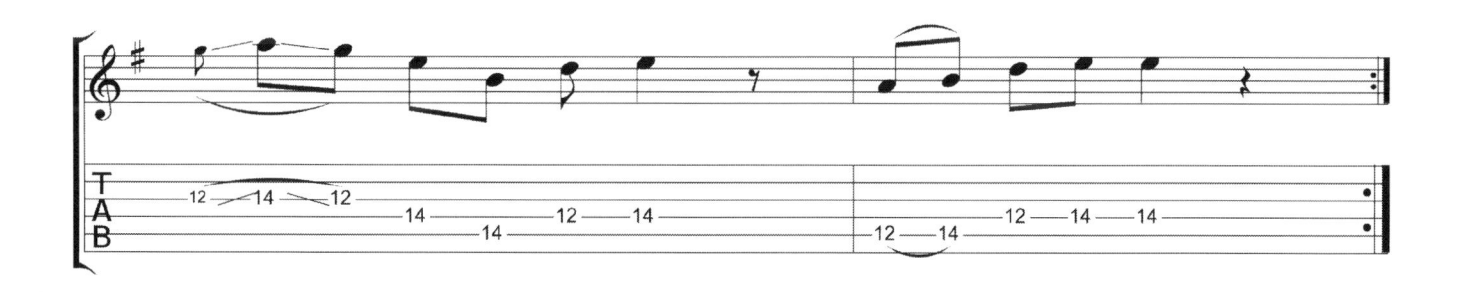

237

Now for a double-stop lick. Alternating between single-note and double-stop patterns adds a nice variation to your lead guitar sound.

Example 8d –

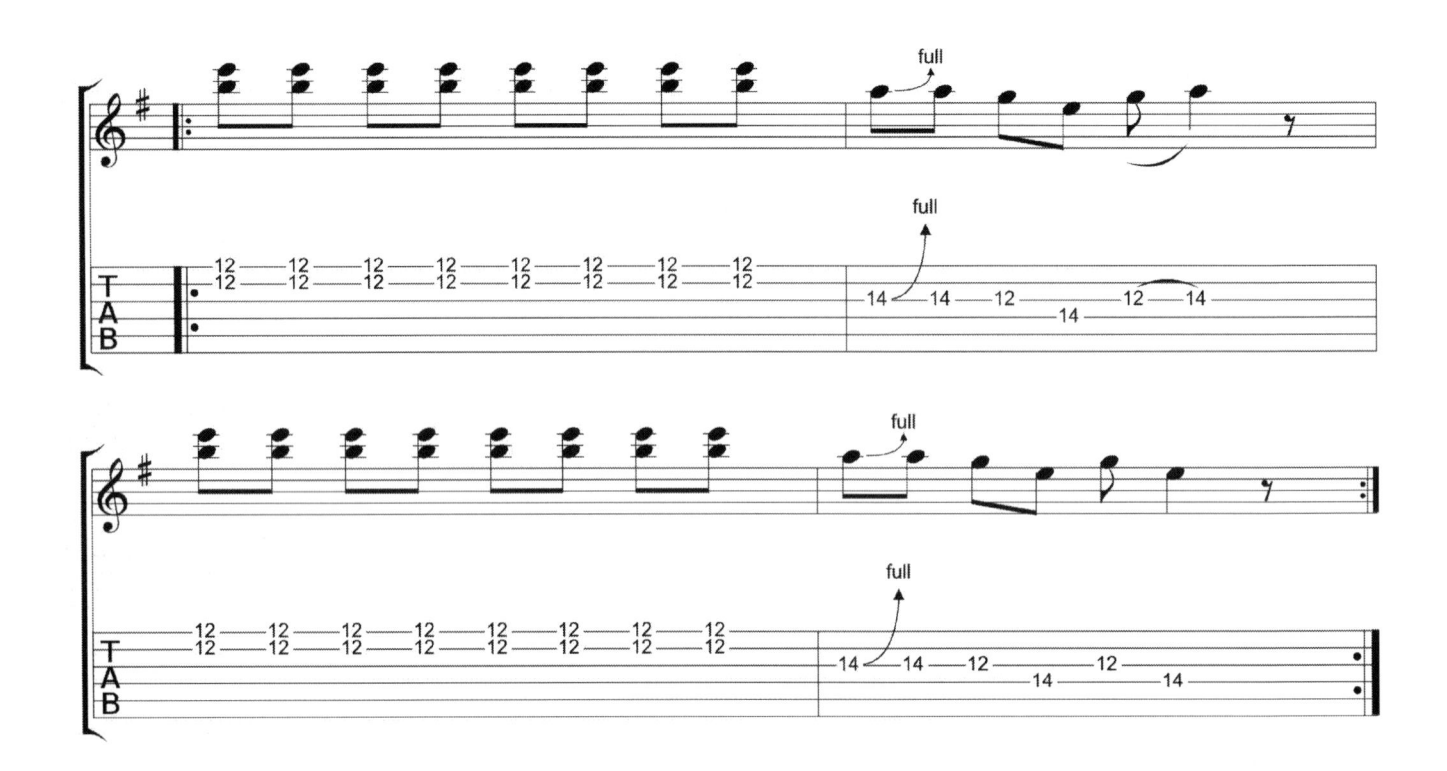

Adding in rests between notes adds a vocal quality to your licks.

Example 8e –

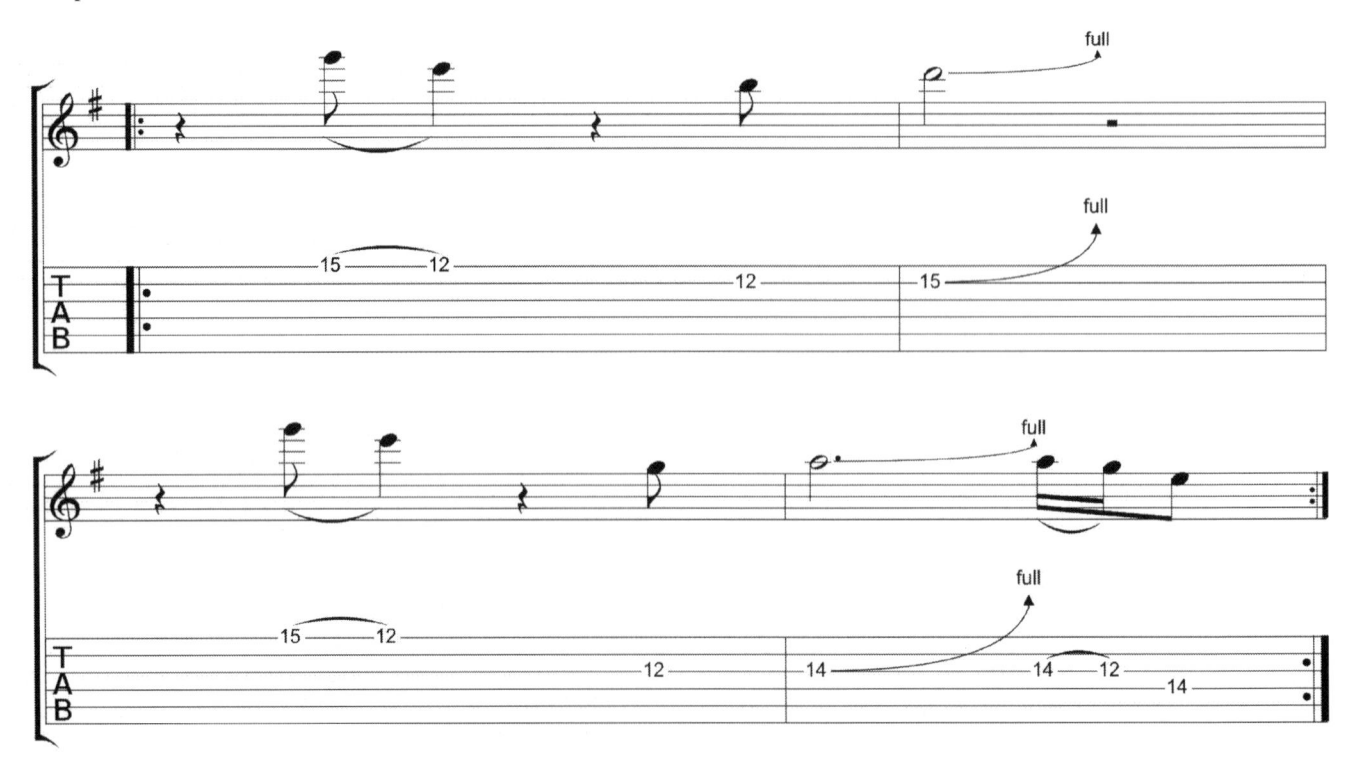

Check out the main melody of Steve Vai's masterpiece, For The Love Of God, for a great example of melodic slide vocabulary.

Example 8f –

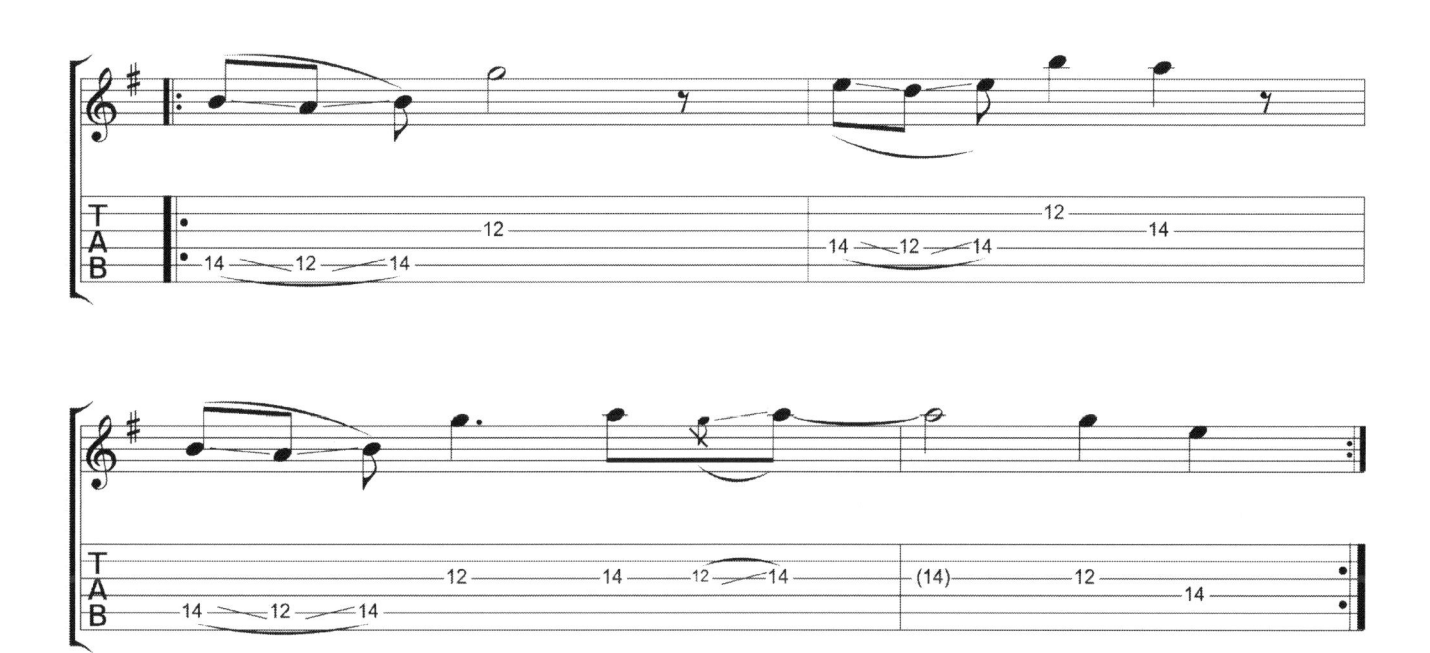

Example 8g is reminiscent of Jimi Hendrix as he often used the E Minor Pentatonic scale in his solos. Check out Hey Joe for an incredible example of this.

Example 8g–

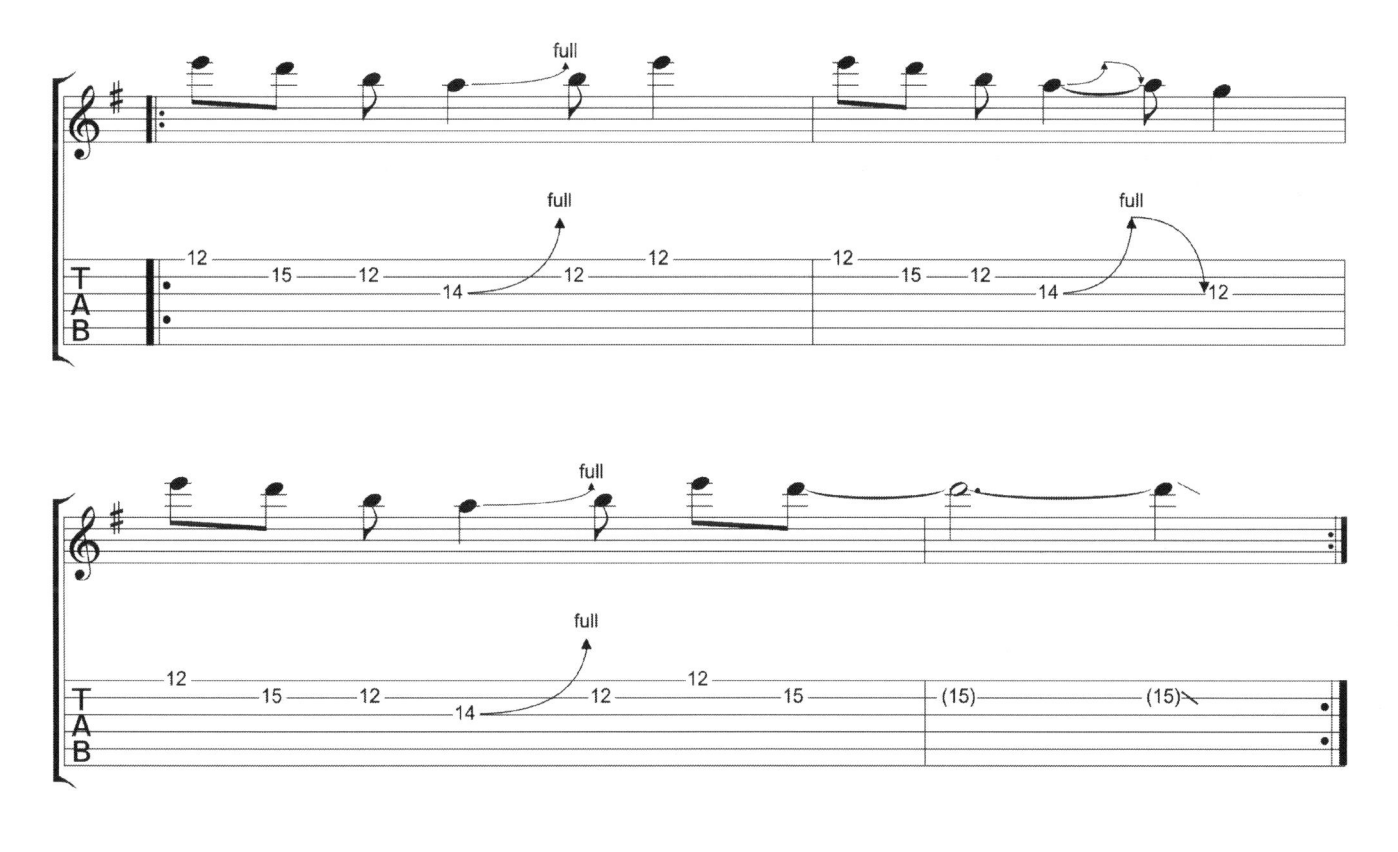

Listen closely to how I play each note with the accompanying audio tracks provided. In example 8h, I add subtle vibrato to each note to add an expressive vocal quality.

Example 8h –

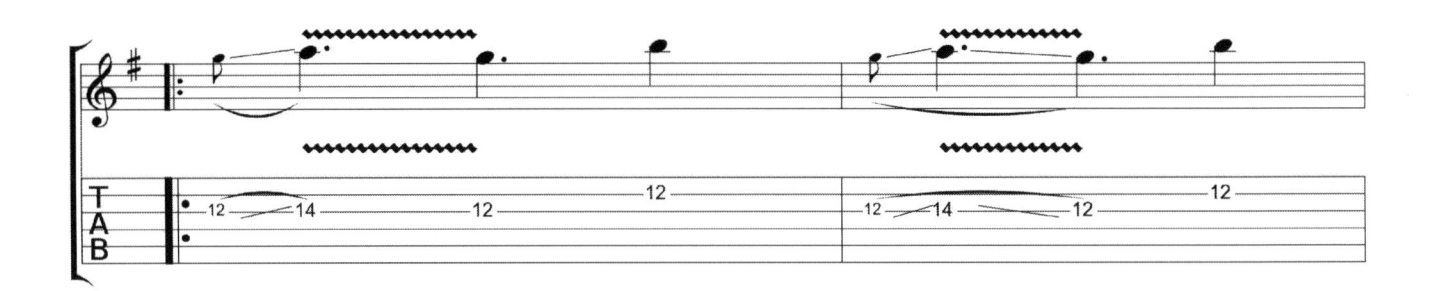

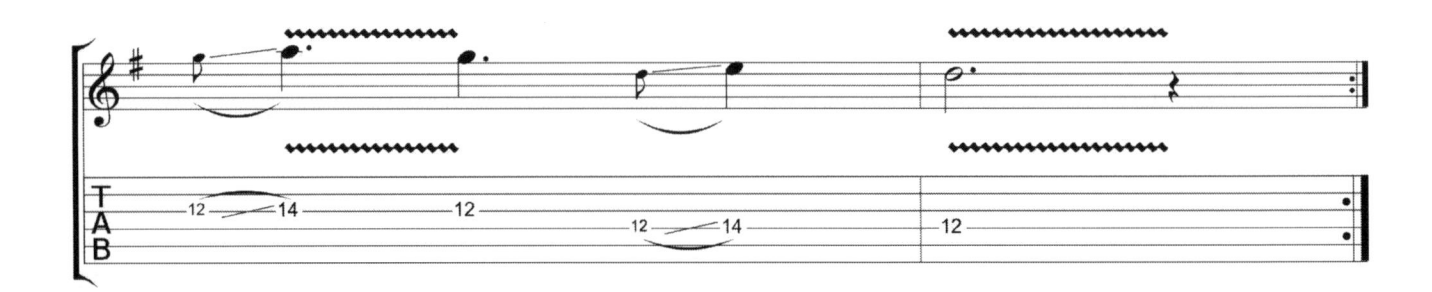

Aim to make your legato lines as fluid as possible by ensuring that the picked notes are the same volume as the hammer-ons/pull-offs.

Example 8i –

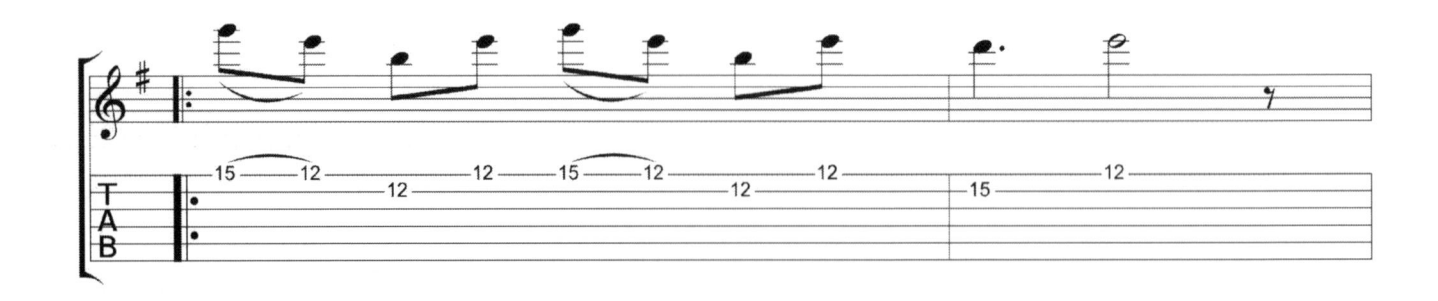

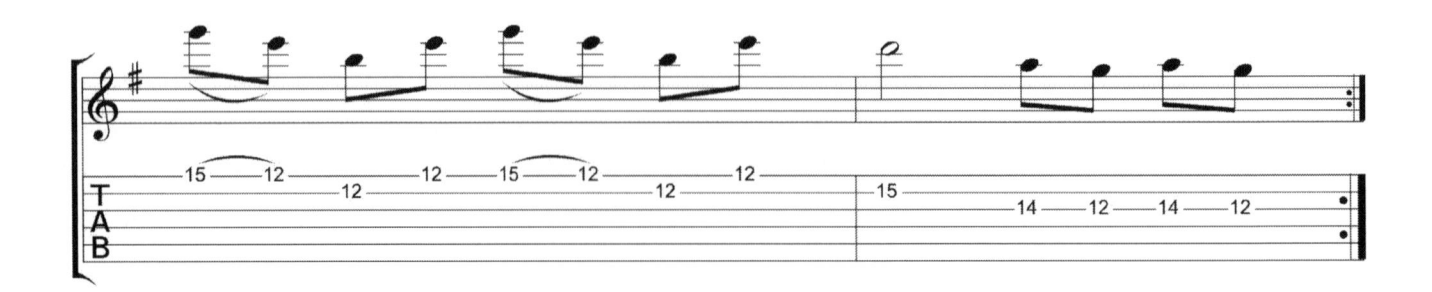

Although you can quite quickly build speed using legato techniques, it is more important that the notes are fretted correctly. Only build up speed when you can play a lick/phrase correctly three times in a row with a metronome.

Example 8j –

Practice your E Minor Pentatonic licks along to backing tracks five and six.

Example 8k –

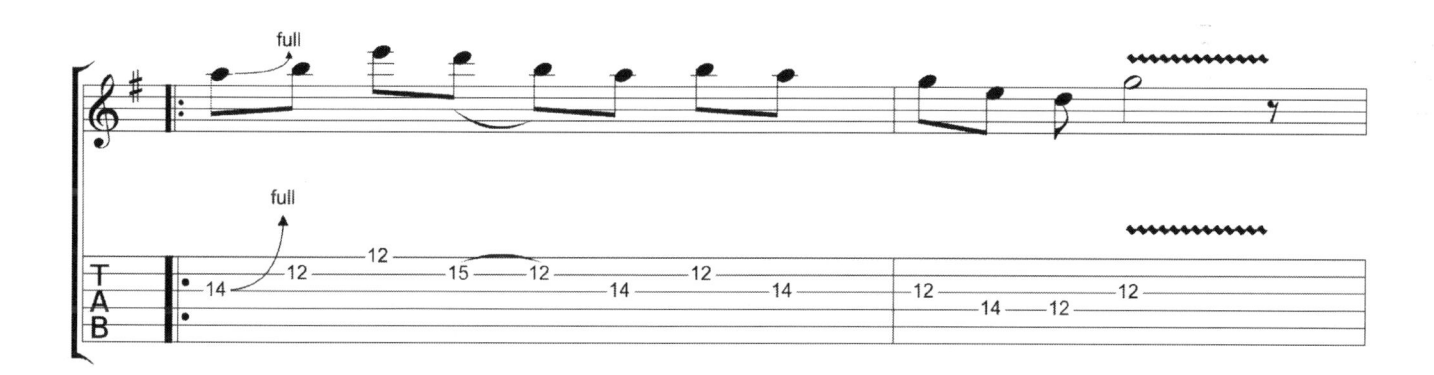

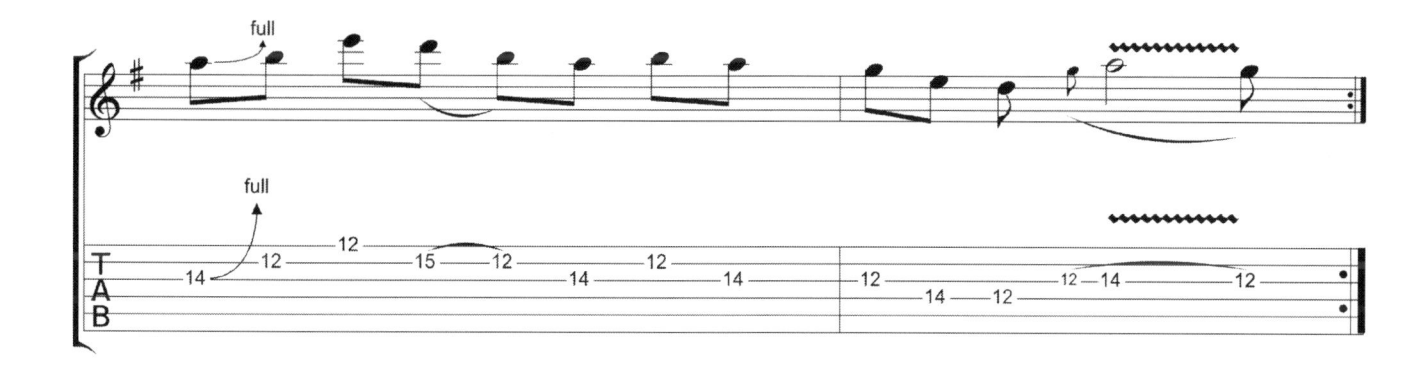

Now that you have learnt the E Minor Pentatonic scale shape and have been able to transfer licks from A Minor to E Minor, it is important to understand how you can move these licks into any key. The diagram below shows the notes on the 6th string. You can play the Minor Pentatonic scale starting from any of these notes on the 6th string. For example, if you start the Minor Pentatonic scale shape from the 7th fret you create B Minor pentatonic. Try moving all the licks from this chapter into a new key.

6th String Notes

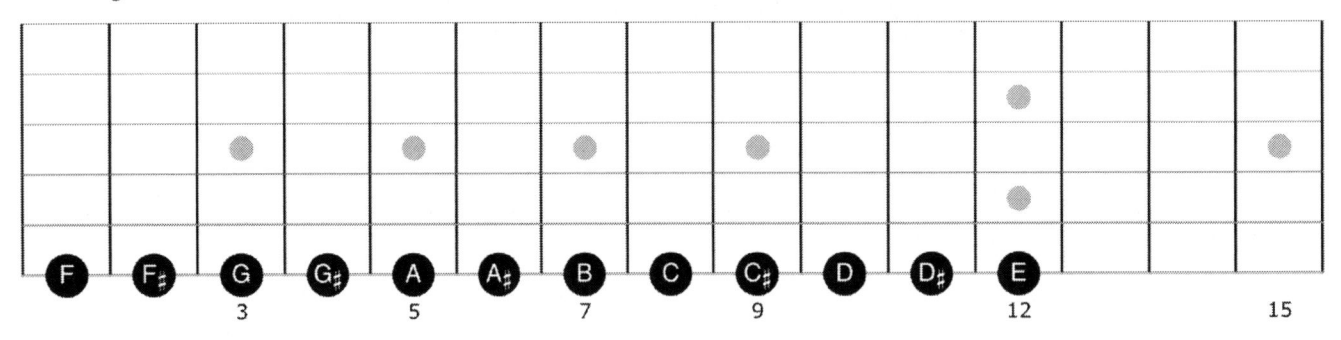

Chapter Nine – E Minor Solo

Backing Track Six.

Example 9a is a full solo that uses the E Minor Pentatonic scale that should be played over the top of Backing Track Six.

All the full solos in this book are constructed so that some of the licks repeat themselves. This helps to develop the theme of the solo and also prevents it from feeling too intimidating to attempt.

This solo uses both single-notes and double-stop patterns. In bar 9, use your first finger to cover both the D, and the G string; that way you will have your third finger free to complete the hammer-on. Remember that you should always aim to use the one-finger-per-fret rule, so if you have more than one note on one fret, use one finger to play both notes.

This solo presents a lot of material and is something you can both learn in full and steal individual licks from. Keep coming back to it over time, and you will find new fragments of lead playing vocabulary had not previously committed to memory.

Put headphones on and listen to example 9a at least three times before you attempt to play it. When your brain has a great idea of what something should sound like, it will help you zone in on the specific expressive techniques you need to play. This applies to learning any new melody, solo, or lead guitar phrase.

As well as my performance of this track, I have included a slowed down midi version so you can play along at a slower tempo.

Example 9a –

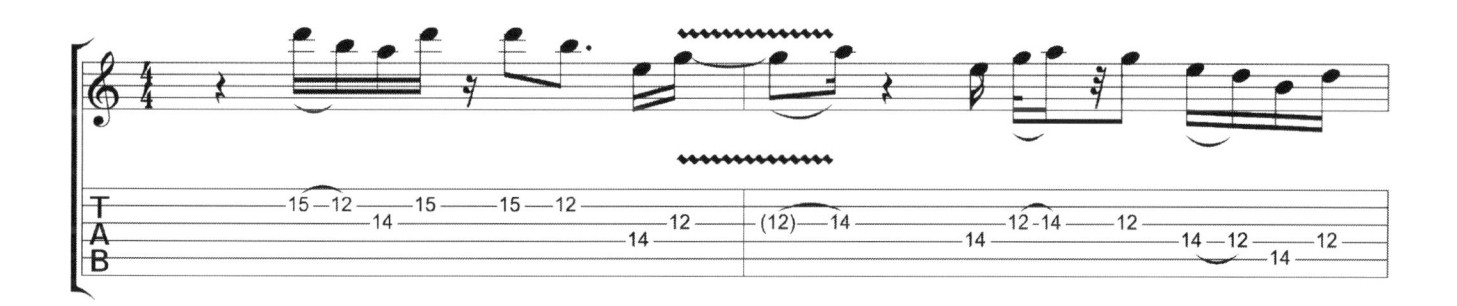

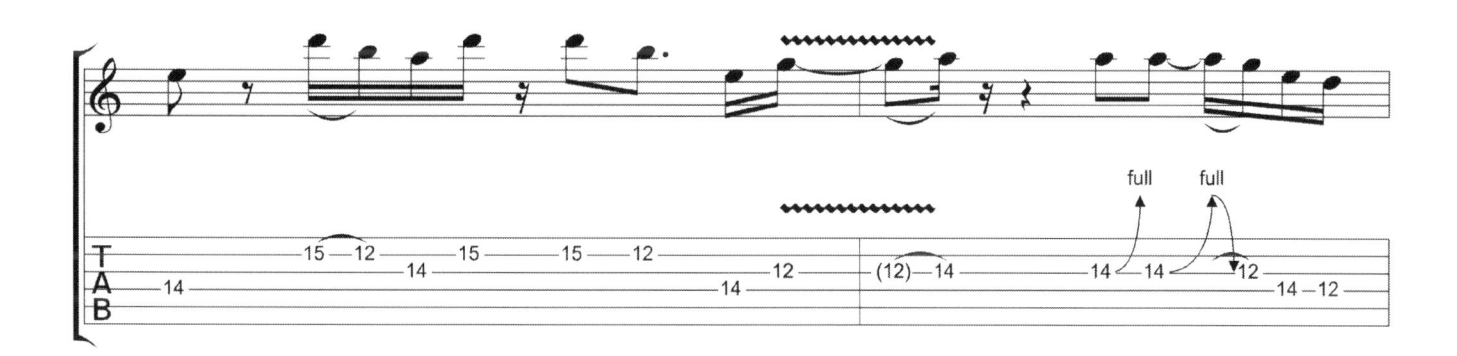

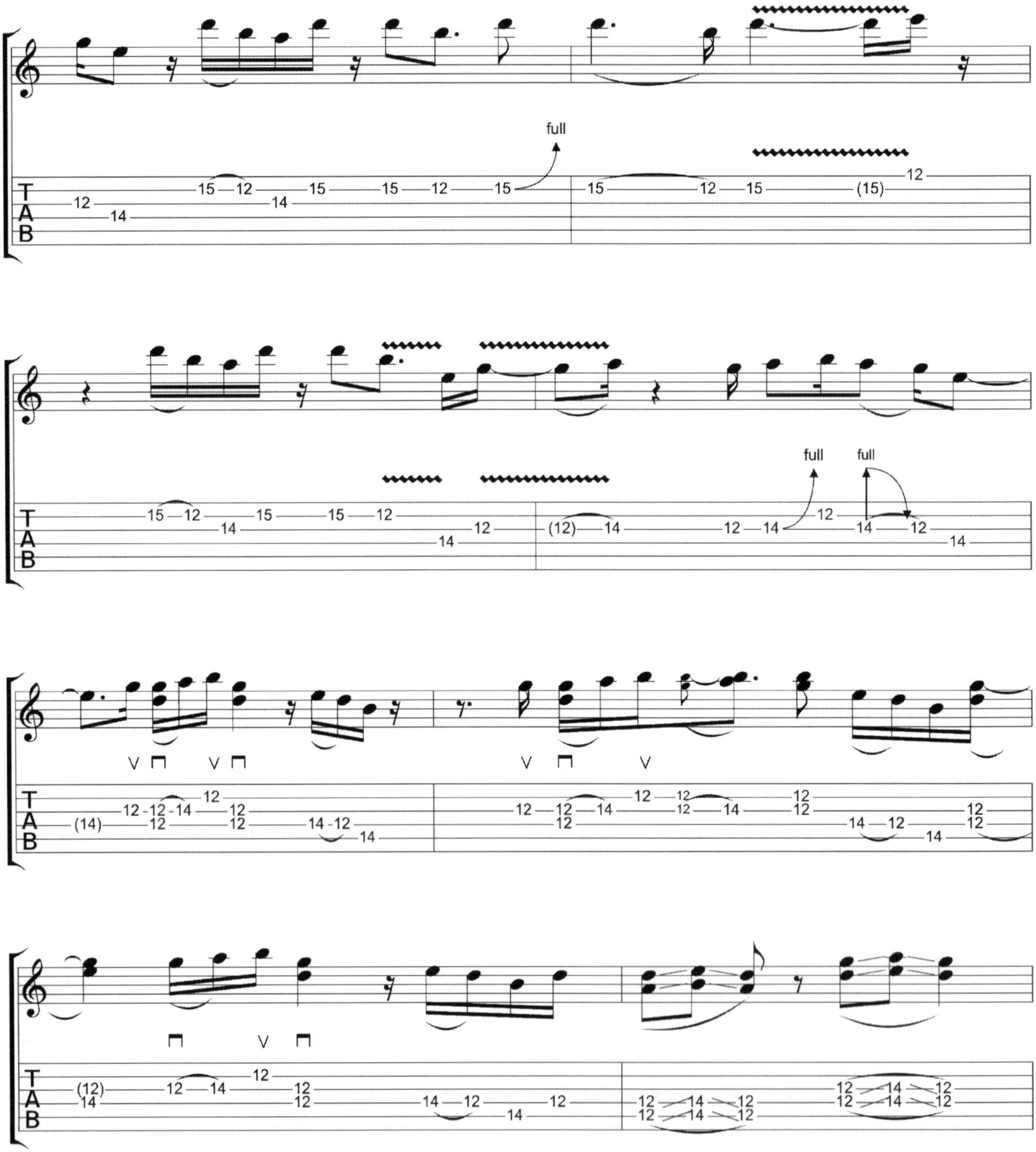
full
full
full
T
A
B

245

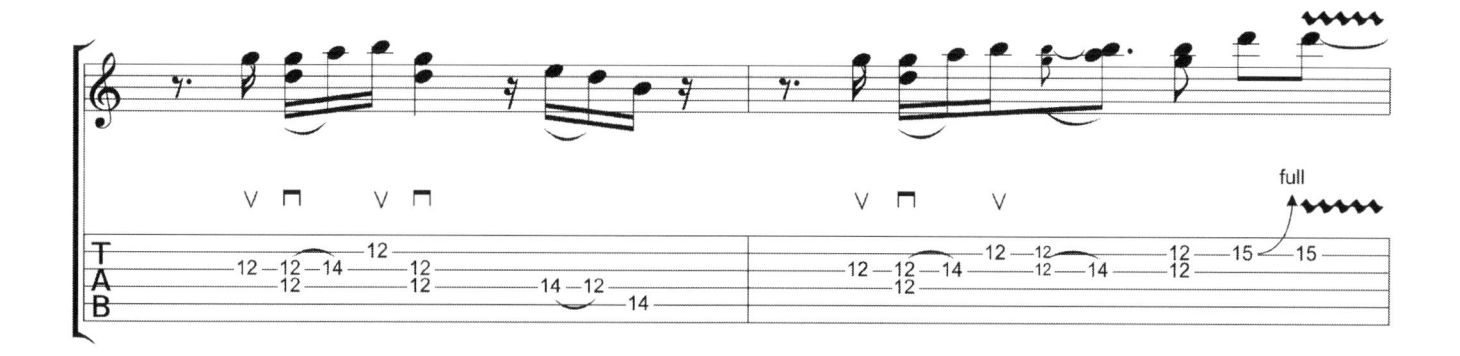

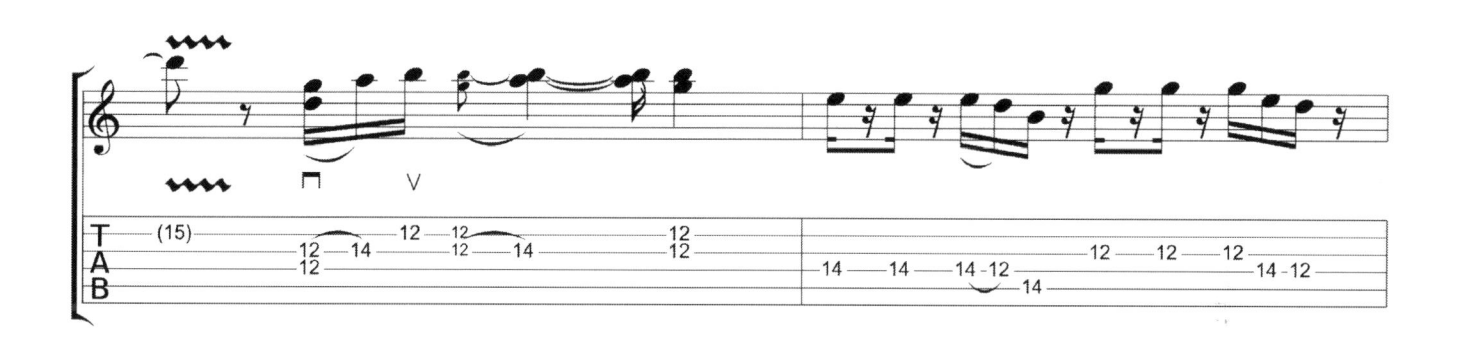

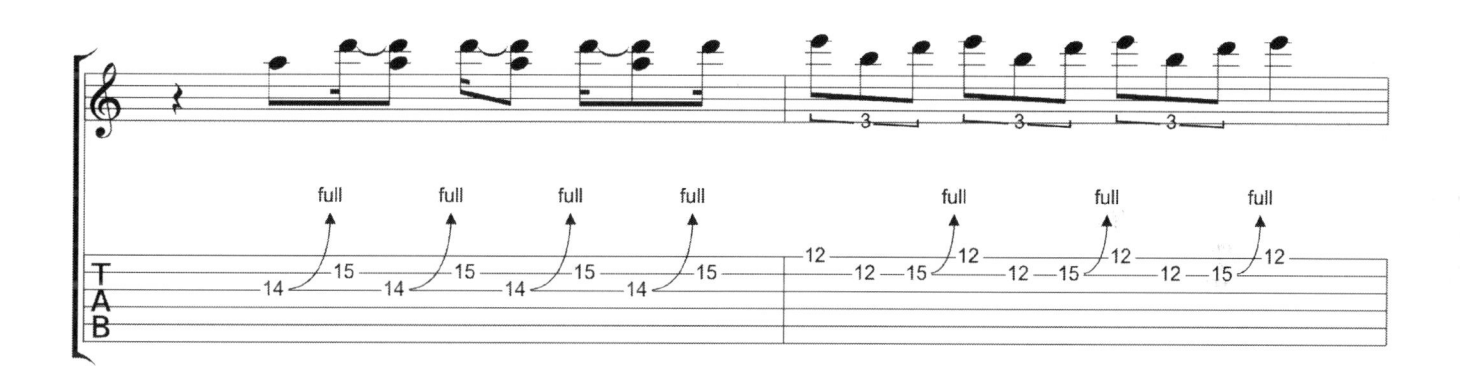

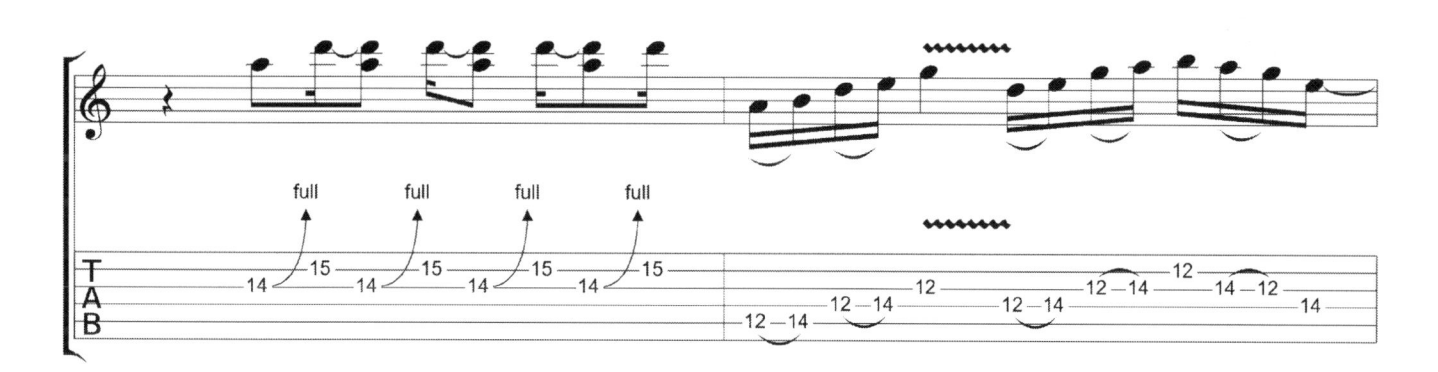

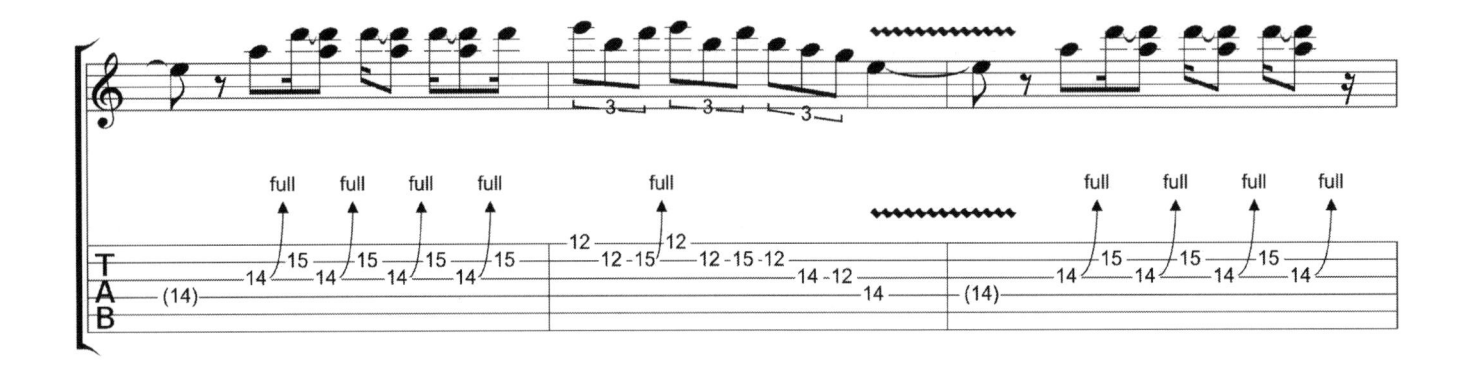

Pop Quiz

What notes are in the E Minor Pentatonic scale?

What is a double-stop?

How can you develop a theme in a solo?

How many times should you listen to a solo with headphones on before attempting to play it?

Answers at the end of the book!

Chapter Ten – The A Blues Scale

The A Blues scale is identical to the A Minor Pentatonic scale except that it contains one extra note, 'Eb'. The notes in the A Blues scale are **A C D Eb E G**.

The Blues scale is enormously popular among electric guitar players and is often used by guitarists like Angus Young and Joe Satriani.

The examples in this chapter are all in the key of A minor, and each lick fits perfectly over an A minor chord or a backing track in A minor such as Backing Track One.

By learning the examples shown in this chapter you will gain dexterity as well as fretboard fluency within the A Blues scale.

You can play The A Blues scale in the following way on the guitar:

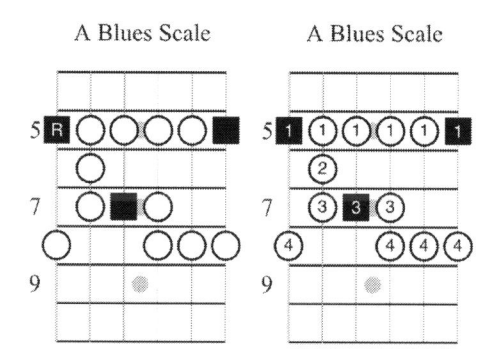

Ascend and descend the A Blues scale in example 10a. Stick to strict alternate picking (down, up) and use the finger-per-fret technique.

Example 10a –

Now double pick every note in the A Blues scale.

Example 10b –

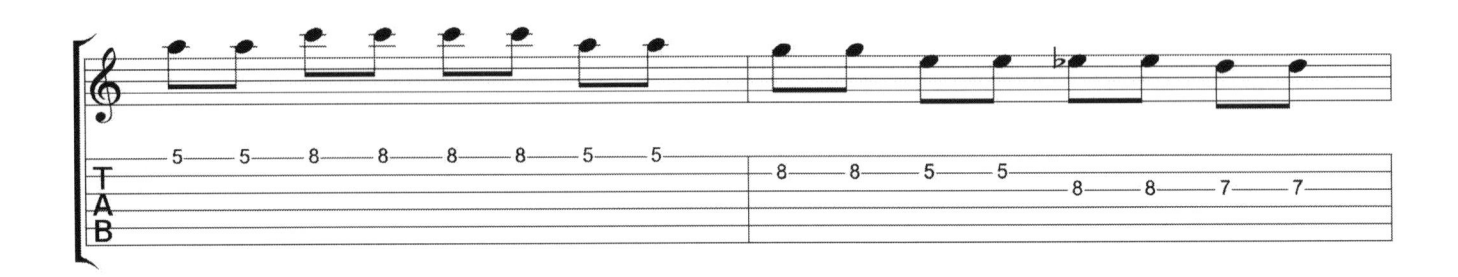

Triple pick each note of the A Blues scale using a triplet rhythm. Listen to the accompanying audio track to hear how to play this rhythm.

Example 10c –

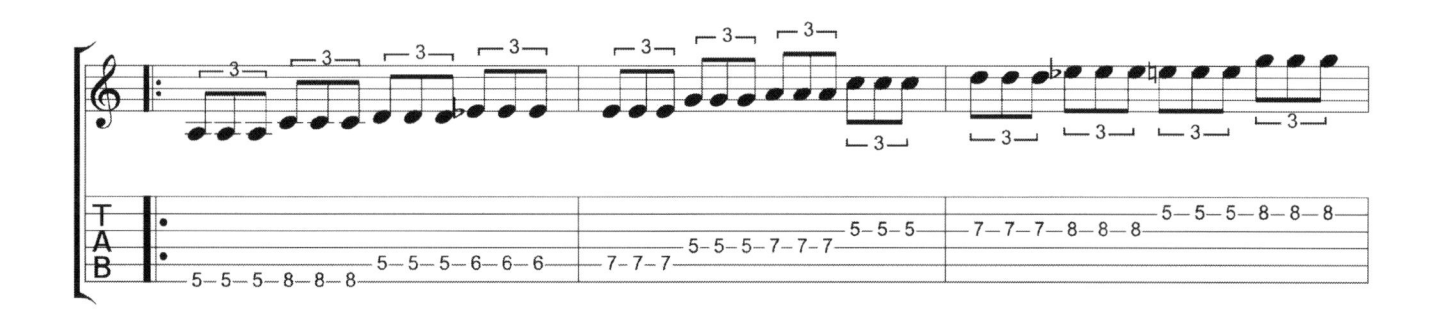

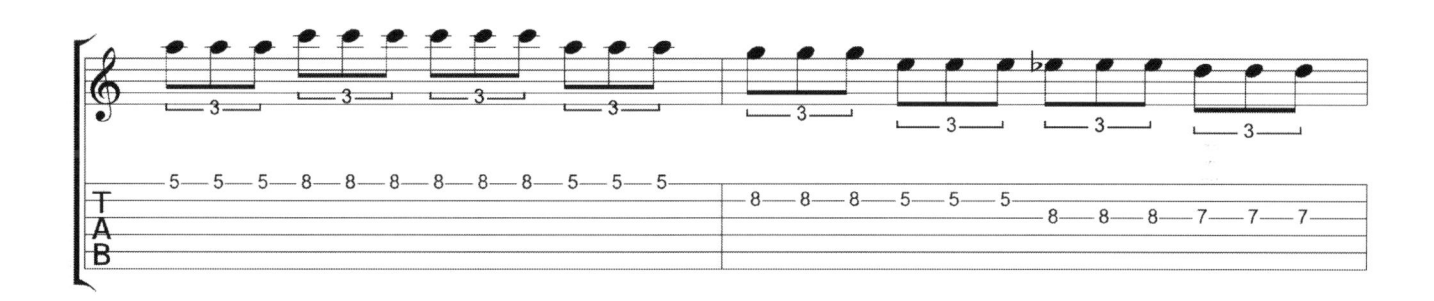

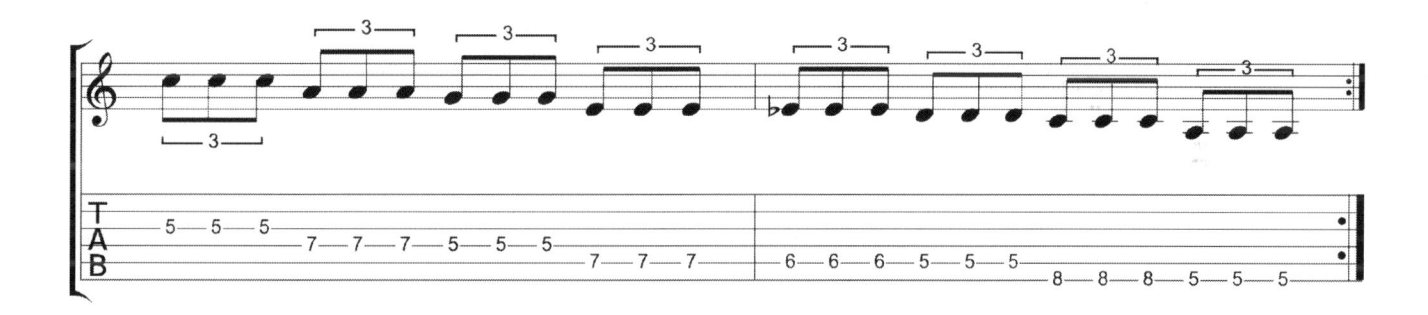

Play each of the notes of the A Blues scale four times in example 10d.

Example 10d –

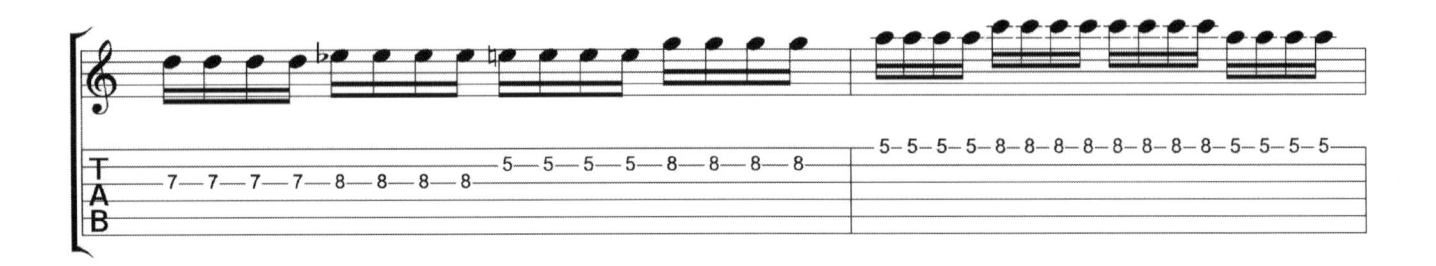

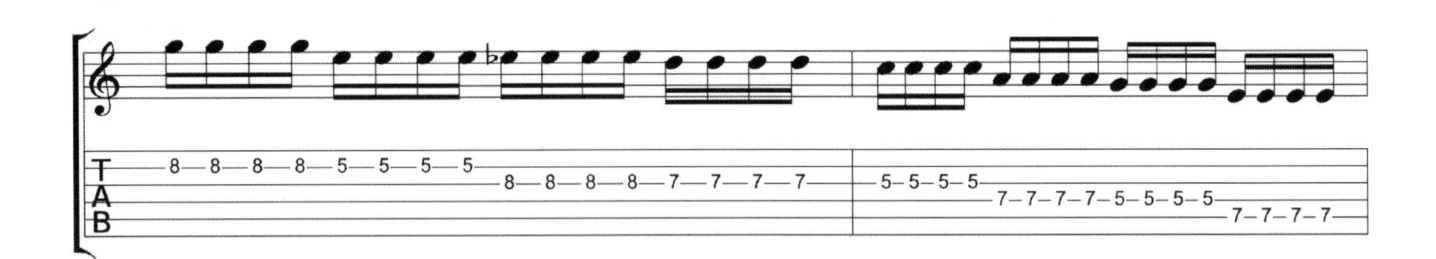

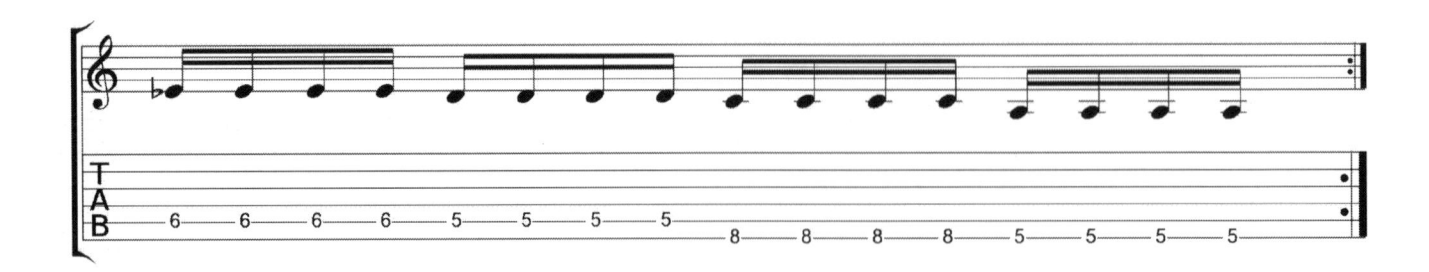

Play through the A Blues scale starting on the higher frets on each string.

Example 10e –

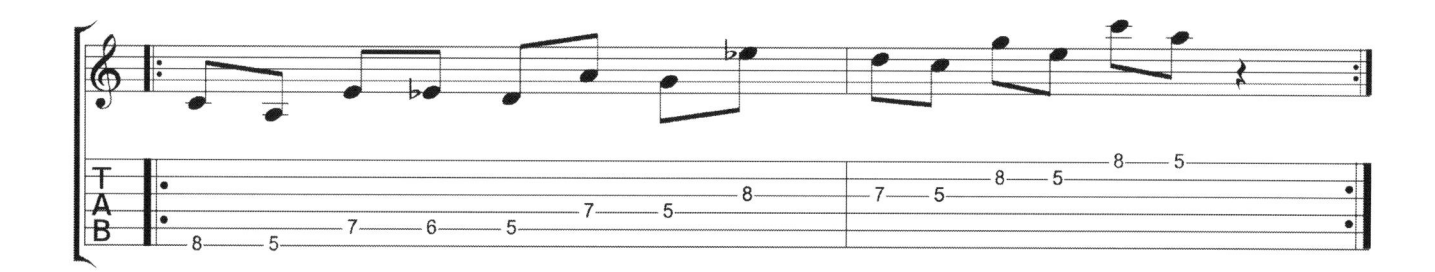

Work your way back through the A Blues scale shape but start from the lower fret on each string.

Example 10f –

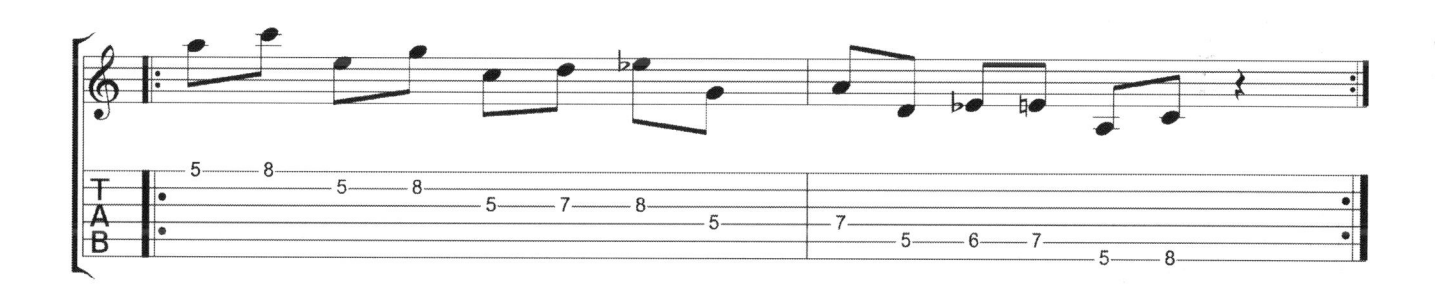

The next two examples introduce a string-skip within the A Blues scale shape. This helps you to add interesting musical jumps into your practice regime.

Example 10g –

Example 10h –

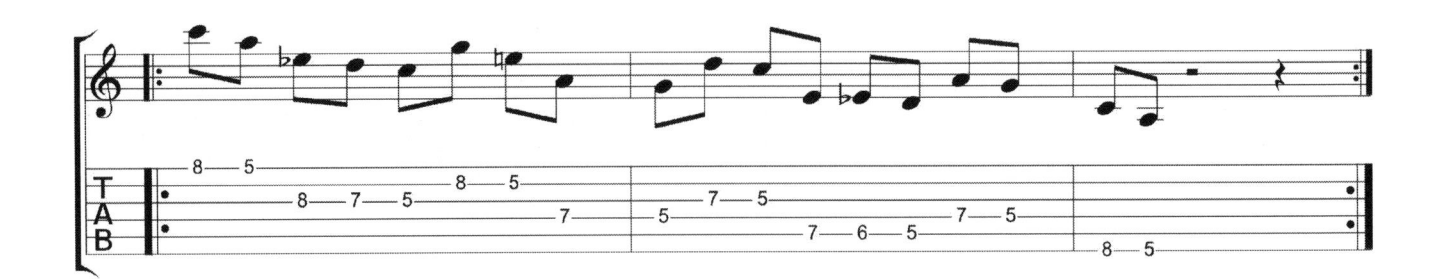

Another way to practice this scale is to combine groups of notes into patterns. Play the first three notes of the A Blues scale, then start on the second note of the scale and play the next three notes of the scale, and carry this pattern on throughout the whole shape.

Example 10i –

252

The final example in this chapter groups the A Blues scale into a pattern of four notes.

Example 10j –

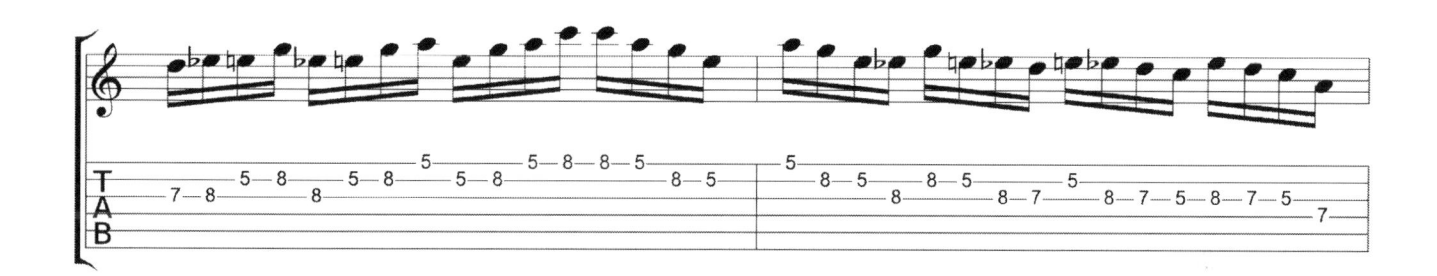

Don't rush into playing the A Blues scale licks and the full solo featured in the next two chapters before you have mastered all the examples featured in this chapter.

Practice these scale shapes with a metronome very slowly (at around 50 beats per minute) and only raise the tempo when you can play an example three times in a row. For a more musical application, play each example along with backing tracks one to four.

Pop Quiz

What notes are in the A Blues scale?

How many extra notes does the Blues scale contain than the Minor Pentatonic scale?

Name two famous guitarists that play the Blues scale.

Name three different ways you can practice playing a scale shape.

Answers on the final page!

Chapter Eleven – A Blues Scale Licks

Backing Tracks One to Four.

Now you have completed the A Blues scale technical exercises, it is time to learn some useful lick vocabulary built around this scale.

In this chapter, I have written ten A Blues scale licks based on the techniques seen throughout this book. These licks will include slides, bends and legato, so make sure you are confident with all those techniques before continuing.

The A Blues scale has one extra note than the A Minor Pentatonic scale; the note of Eb. I have made sure to focus on the Eb throughout these licks so you can get used to the unique sound of this brilliant scale.

In example 11a play the slide using your third finger. This will put your fingers in the right place for the rest of the lick.

Example 11a –

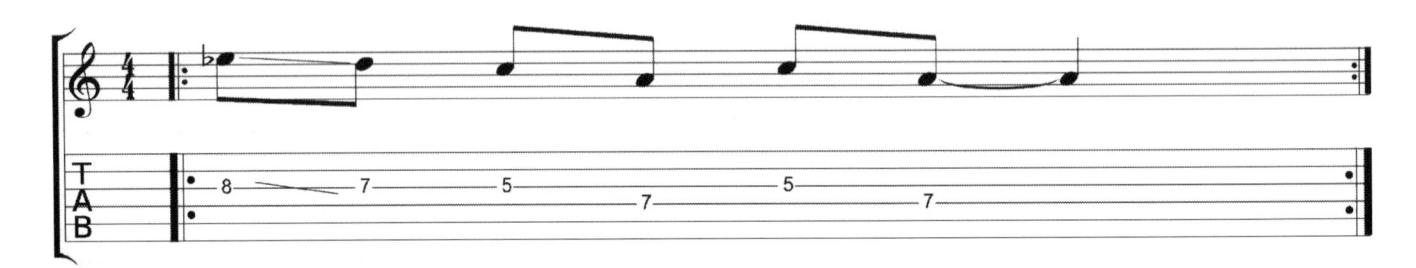

The third finger is used for all the slides featured in example 11b. Notice how bars one and three are the same, but bars two and four are different to create a 'call and response' blues lick.

Example 11b –

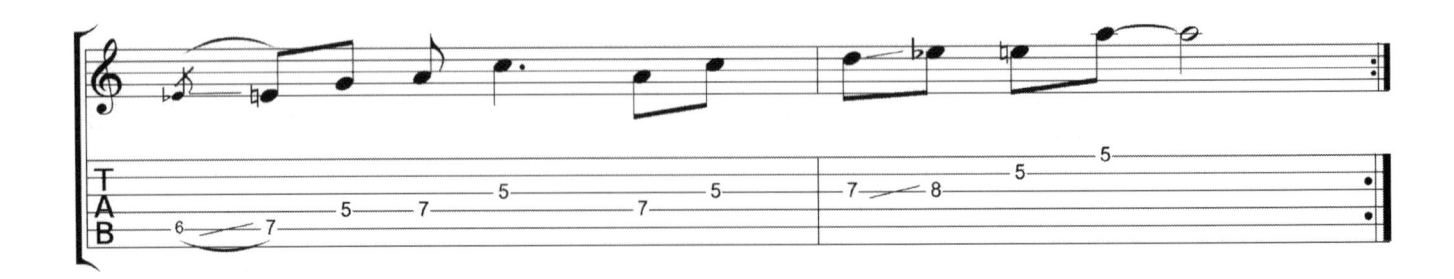

Use Backing Track Two, and start to build longer solo phrases by combining the licks featured in this chapter.

Example 11c –

Example 11d could act as a 'hook' or theme to a song or a solo because it is memorable and easy to sing.

Example 11d –

The rests between the notes give example 11e it's rhythmic, *syncopated* feel. Keep to the one-finger-per-fret technique when approaching this lick as it will work on the dexterity of all your fingers.

Example 11e –

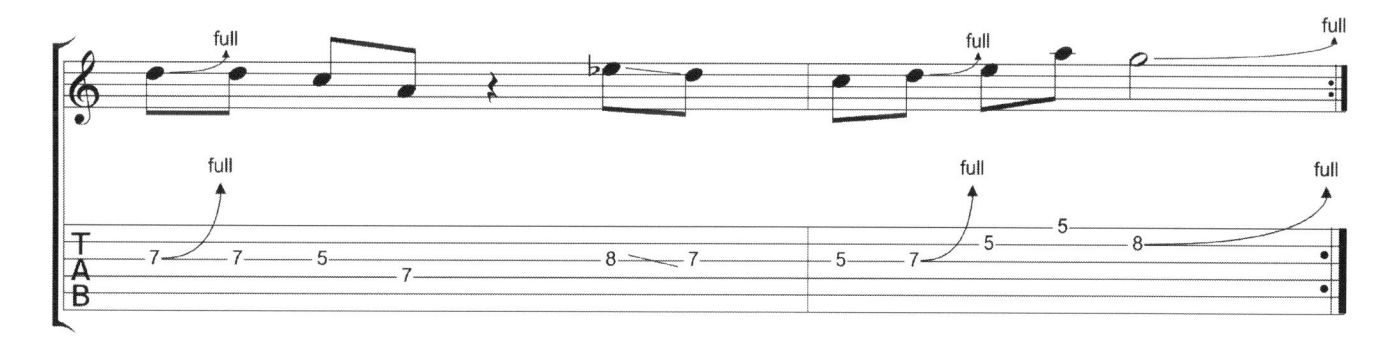

Double-stops can grab a listener's attention and sound bold and striking. This is shown in example 11f. By alternating between double-stops and single-note phrases you can add variety to your solos.

Example 11f –

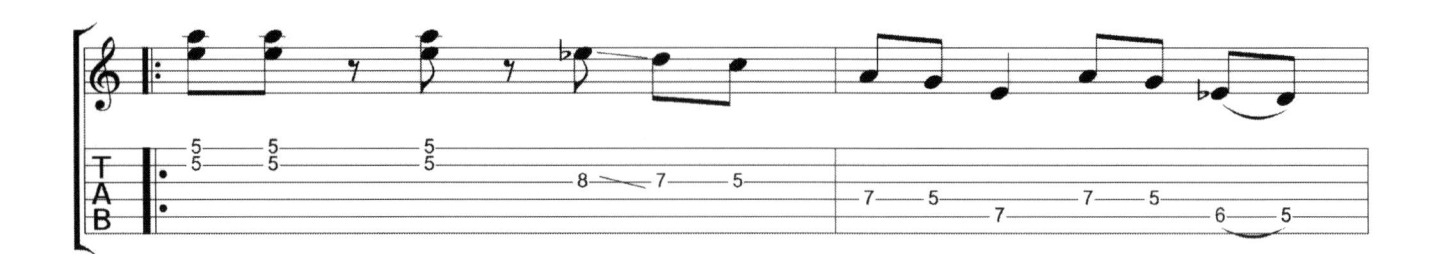

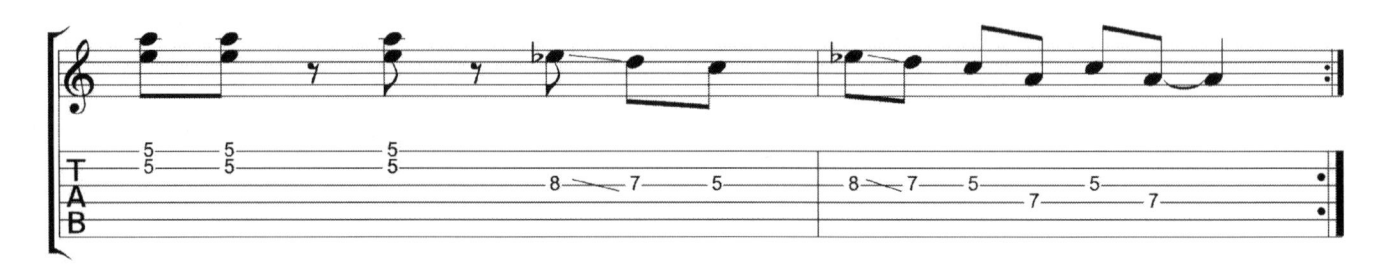

Add some string-skips into your licks as demonstrated in example 11g. Musical jumps stop licks sounding sequential and scale-based.

Example 11g –

Write your own lick based on the examples in this chapter. Two ways to do this are:

- Play the lick in reverse, starting from the end and working back to the beginning.
- Play the second bar before the first (or second half of the lick before the first half).

Example 11h –

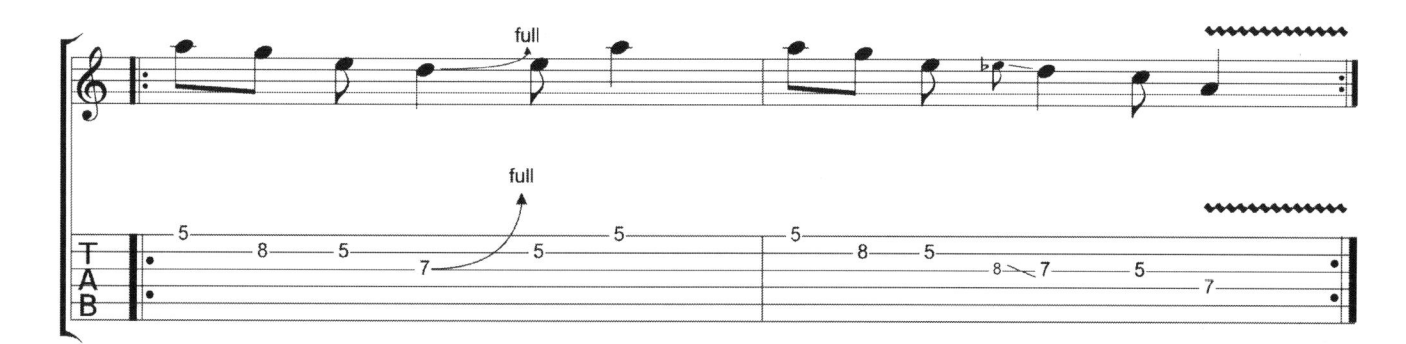

Example 11i –

The triplet rhythm seen in example 11i acts as the focal point to the lick. Count triplets using a three-syllable word such as el-e-phant. Triplets often give a bluesy feel to a lick, so keep that in mind when writing your own material.

Remember that having one lick memorised is more useful than *reading* ten licks from a book. There is absolutely no rush to complete the material here, so take your time and internalise as much as possible. Most importantly enjoy making music with it!

Example 11j –

Play and use these licks as much as possible in as many different settings as you can. Play them with a metronome, play them with the backing tracks provided with this book, jam with a friend and play them with songs that are in the key of A minor. Check out the list below for some good jam songs in this key.

Songs in the Key of A Minor

- Led Zeppelin - Stairway to Heaven
- The Beatles – While My Guitar Gently Weeps
- Red Hot Chili Peppers – Californication
- U2 – Electrical Storm
- Chick – Le Freak
- Lionel Ritchie - Hello
- Maroon 5 – Secret
- Bruno Mars – When I Was Your Man

Chapter Twelve – A Blues Scale Solo

Backing Track Three

Example 12a is a full solo that uses the A Blues scale and should be played over Backing Track Three.

This is my solo favourite in this book, and the Blues scale is my favourite lead playing tool.

As with all the other full solos, listen through to the track at least three times with headphones on before playing it. You can learn this solo in its entirety or pick out specific licks that appeal to you. Either way, make sure you play along with Backing Track Three, or even better jam with a musical friend!

As well as audio of my performance on this track, I have included a slowed down midi version so you can play along at a slower tempo.

Example 12a –

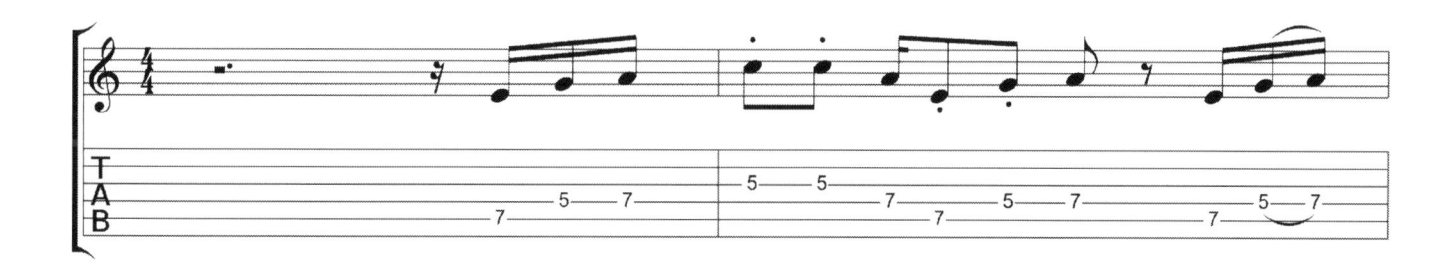

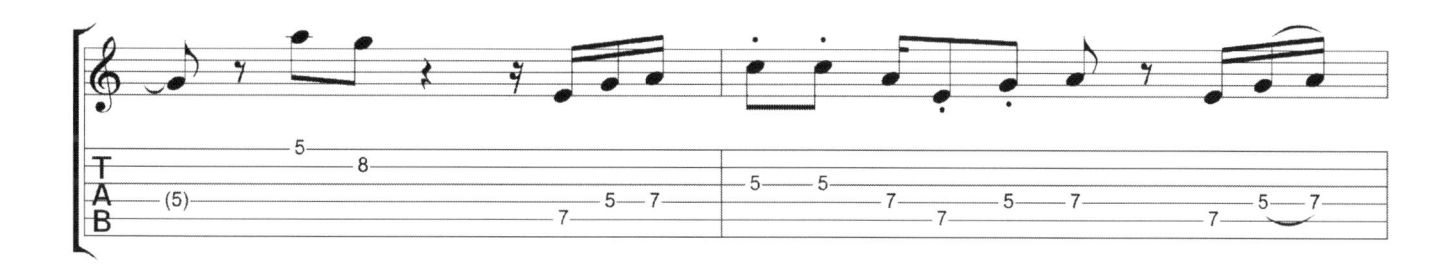

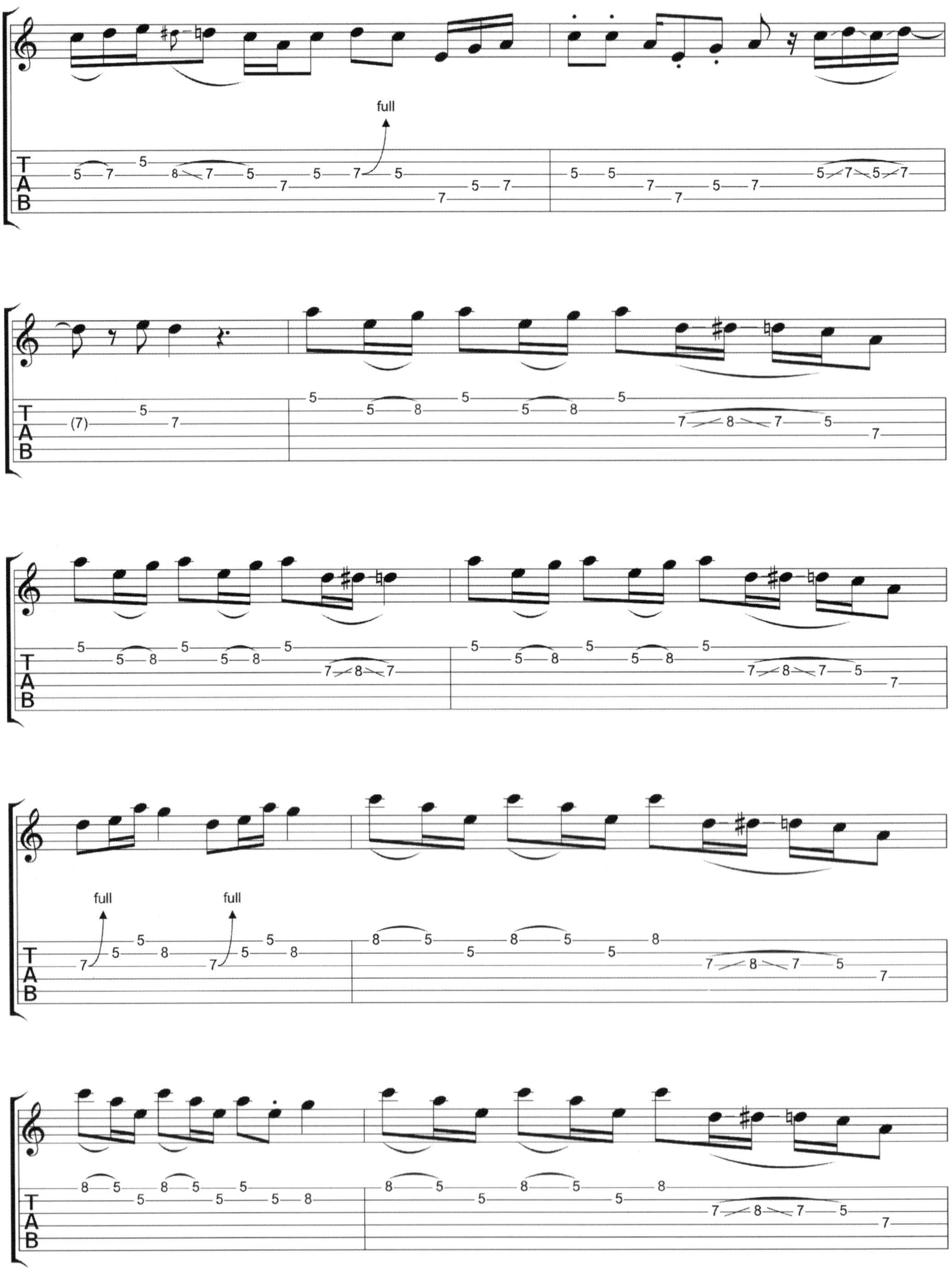
full
full
full

261

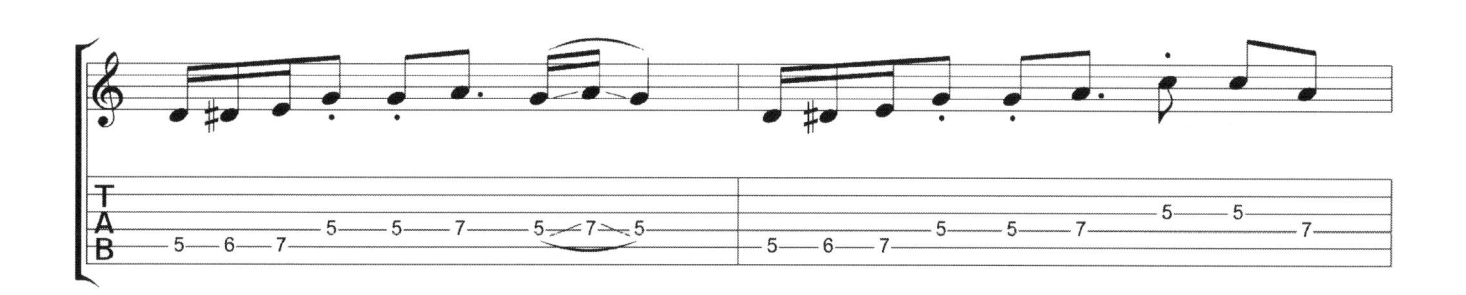

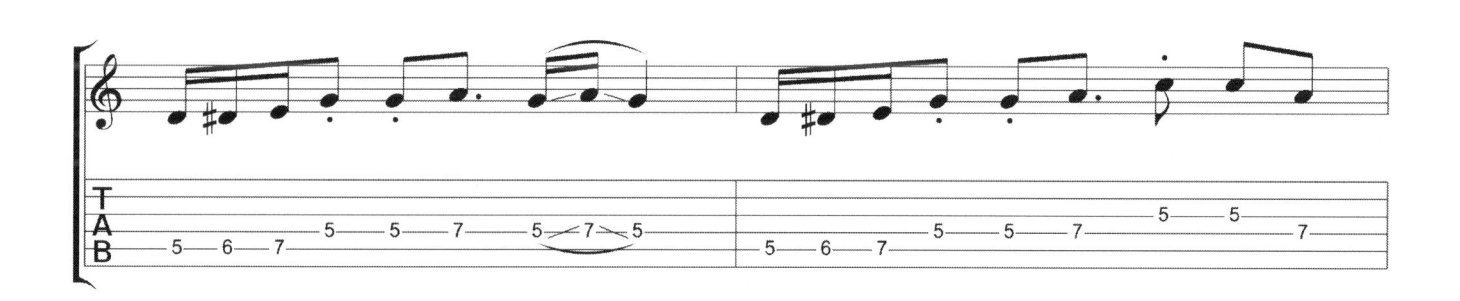

Now you have learnt the full A Blues scale solo, steal some of your favourite licks and play them over the songs mentioned at the end of the previous chapter.

When I first learnt to solo, I didn't have a teacher and I only knew the Minor Pentatonic and Blues scale shapes. I would play on every CD that my parents owned and figure out how to get my licks to work over as many different genres as possible. From Mozart to Michael Jackson, Bach to the Beatles, I spent time developing my lick vocabulary while using my ear as my guide.

Challenge

Setup a playlist with all the songs featured at the bottom of **page 74**. Press play and don't stop soloing using your A Blues licks until the final song has finished playing. Aim to vary your licks based on the genre and rhythm of the song you are playing, and repeat this exercise every day until it feels natural.

Once you feel comfortable playing along to these songs, record yourself. Even if it is just using a voice memo on your smartphone, this will serve as a good reference point for you to look back to later. Give it a title and a date for ease of reference.

Chapter Thirteen – The A Major Pentatonic Scale

The Major Pentatonic scale sounds happier than its minor counterpart and is synonymous with country, blues and rock, although it is very versatile and used in most genres. Slash, Chuck Berry and Eric Clapton are all associated with the Major Pentatonic sound.

The A Major Pentatonic contains the notes **A B C# E F#.**

The examples in this chapter will help you gain dexterity as well as fretboard fluency within the A Major Pentatonic scale.

You can play The A Major Pentatonic scale in the following way on the guitar:

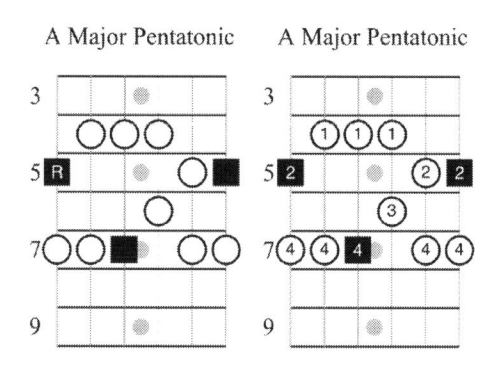

Play through the full A Major Pentatonic scale shape ascending and descending using alternate picking. Start the scale with your second finger so that you can follow the one-finger-per-fret rule. The second diagram above shows you the correct finger placements.

Example 13a –

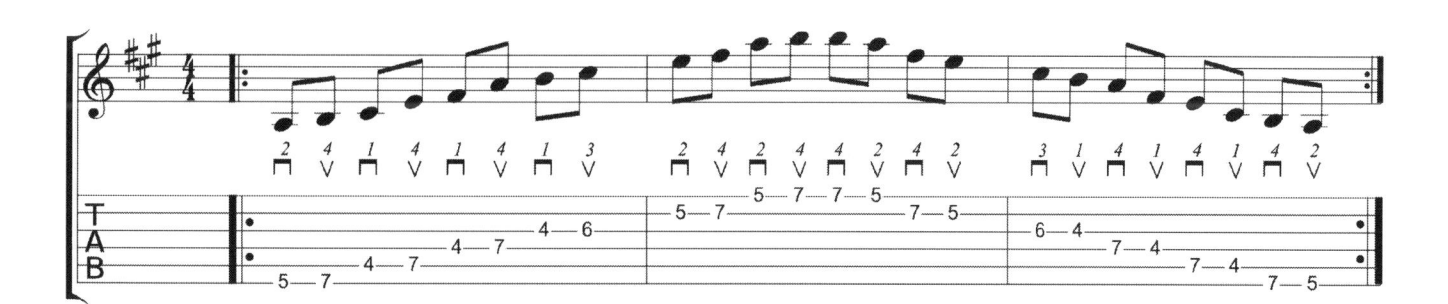

Double pick every note of the A Major Pentatonic scale in example 13b.

Example 13b –

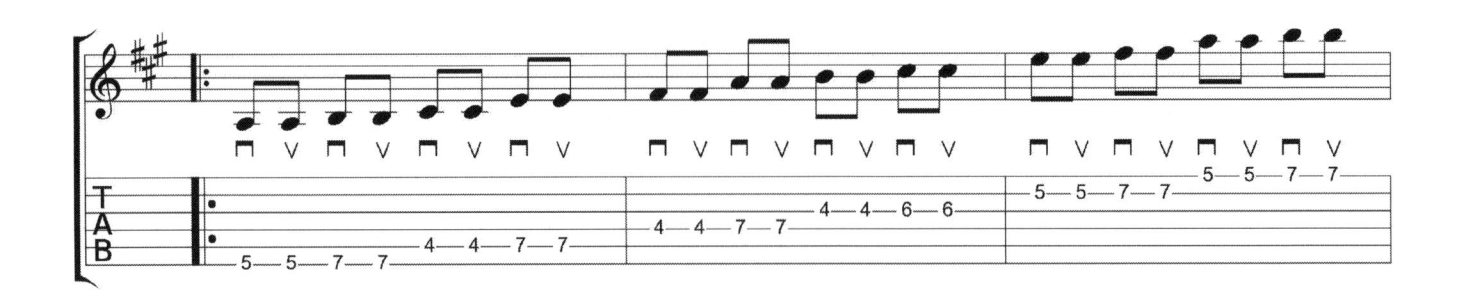

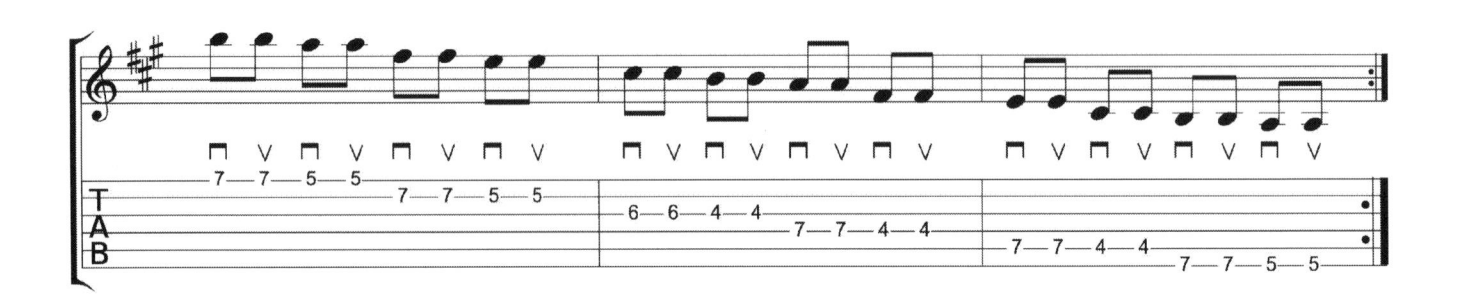

Example 13c demonstrates playing each note of the A Major Pentatonic scale three times using a triplet rhythm. Remember that you can use any three-syllable word to help you count a triplet, I prefer el-e-phant.

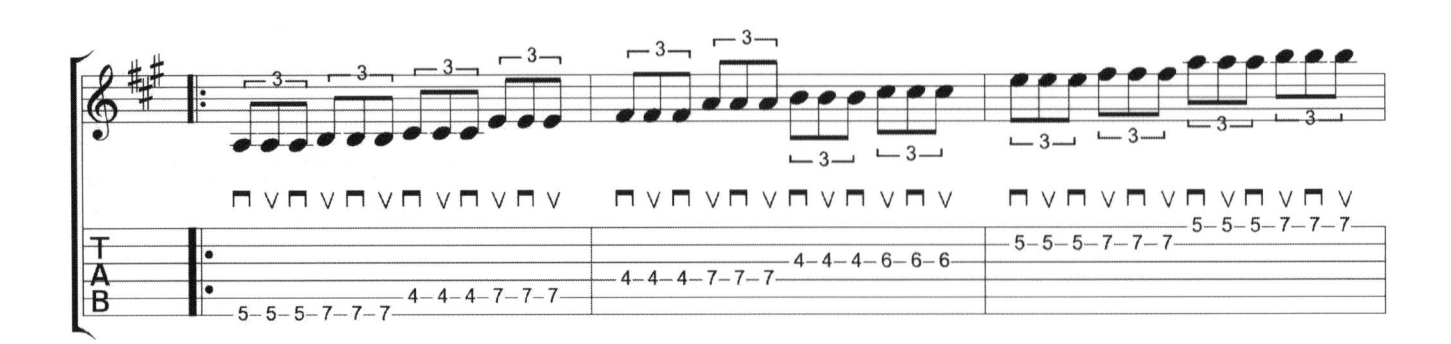

Example 13c –

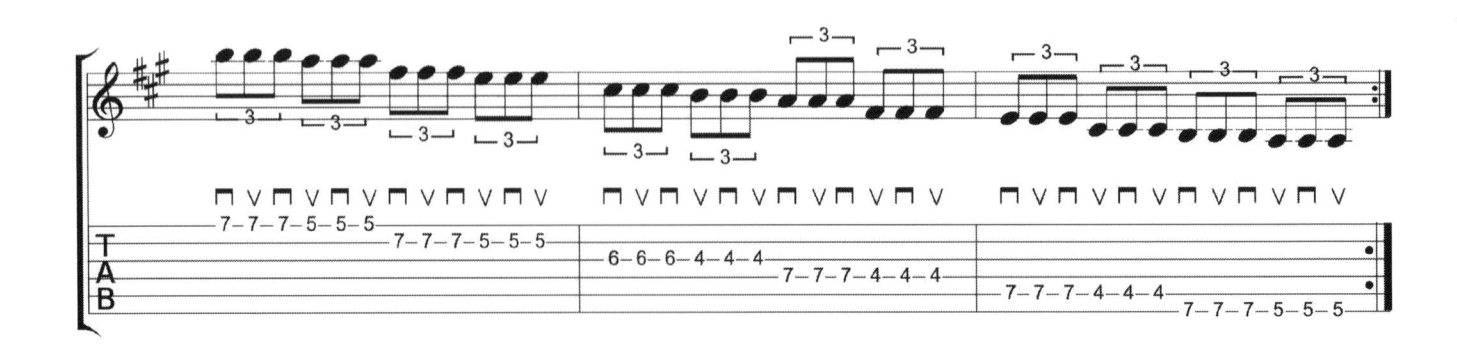

Now pick every note of the A Major Pentatonic scale four times.

Example 13d –

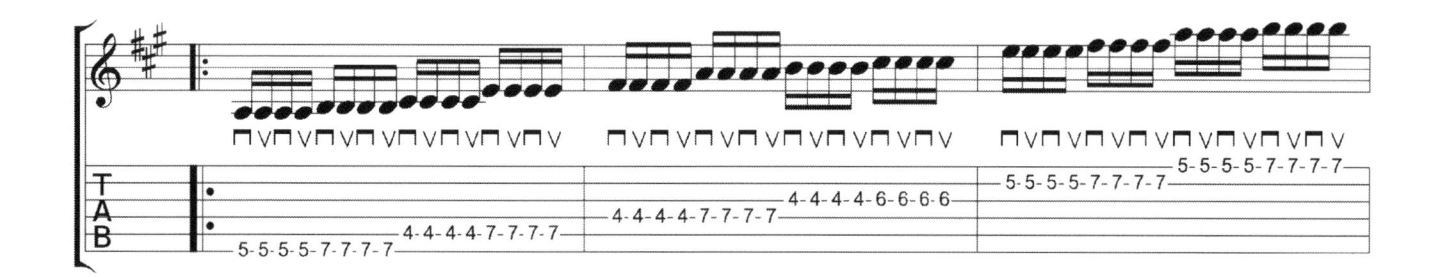

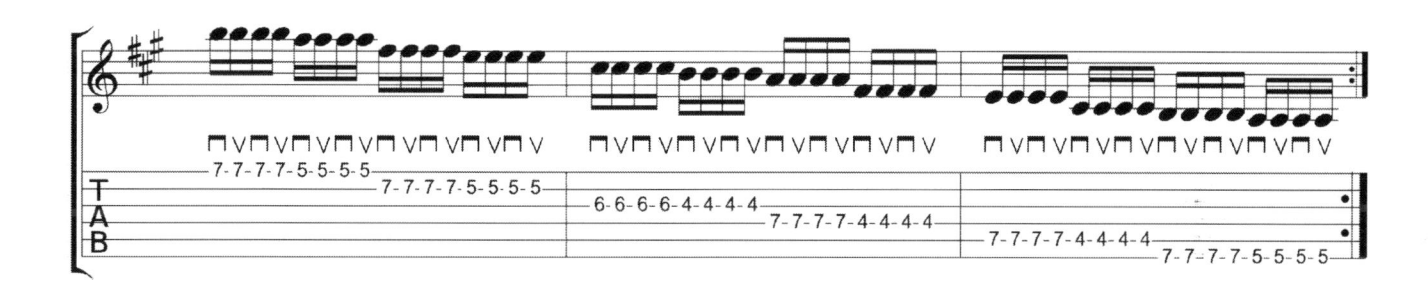

Start on the higher fret of each string and ascend through the A Major Pentatonic scale.

Example 13e –

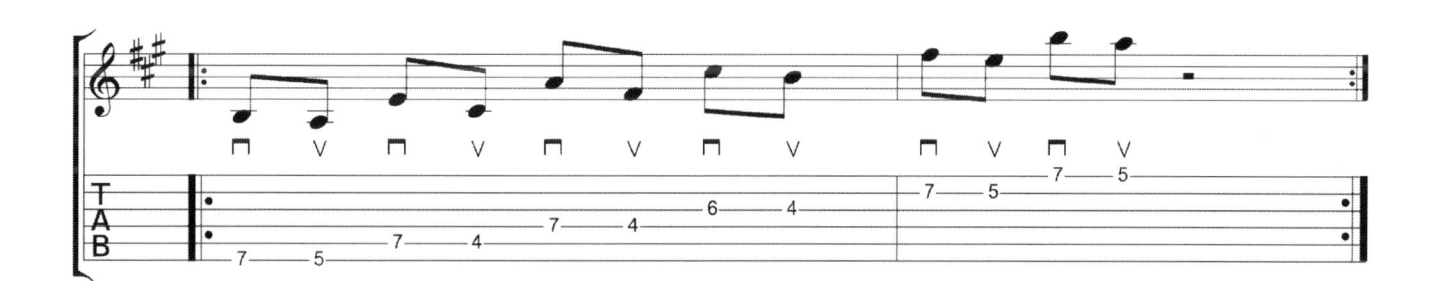

Descend through the A Major Pentatonic scale starting on the lower fret on each string.

Example 13f –

Example 13g shows how to ascend the A Major Pentatonic scale using string-skips.

Example 13g –

Now descend the A Major Pentatonic scale using string-skips.

Example 13h –

The next examples combine the A Major Pentatonic scale into groups of three-, four-, and six-note patterns. Practice these slowly and build up your muscle memory as these serve as great 'lick builders'!

Example 13i –

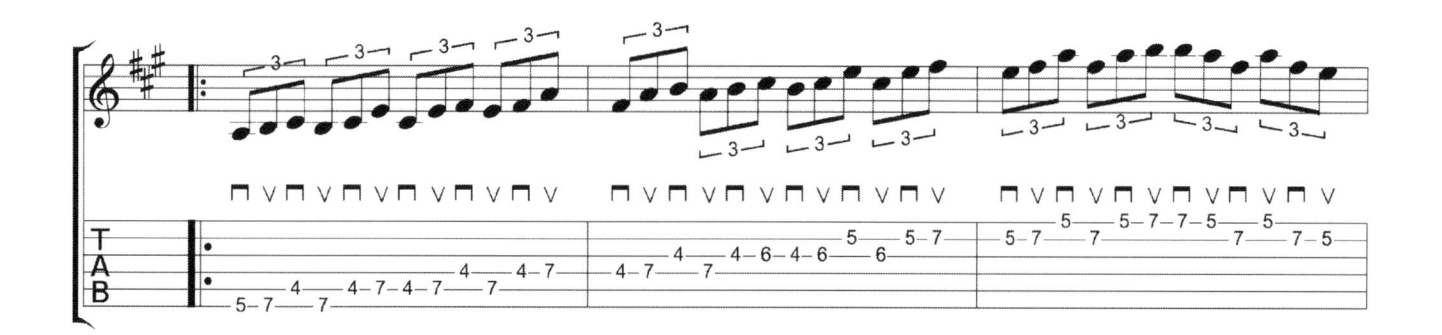

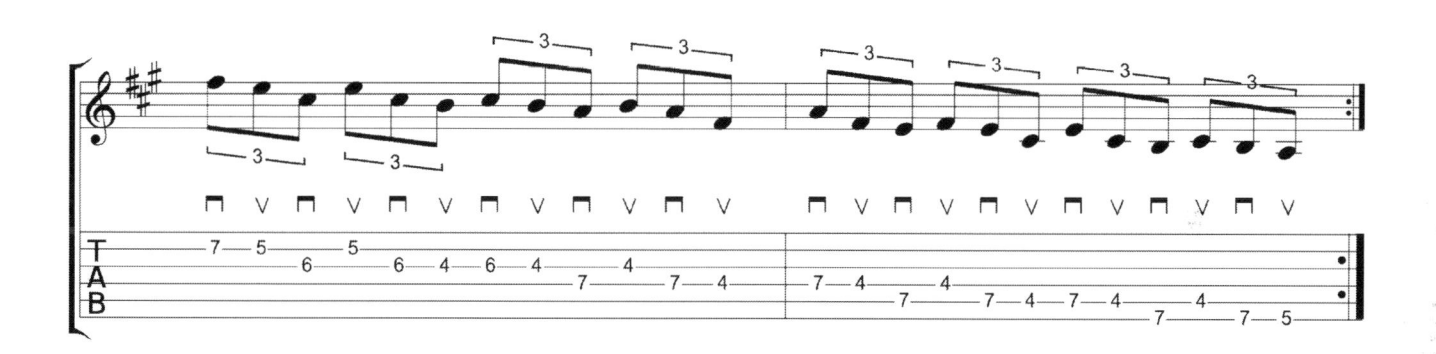

Example 13j –

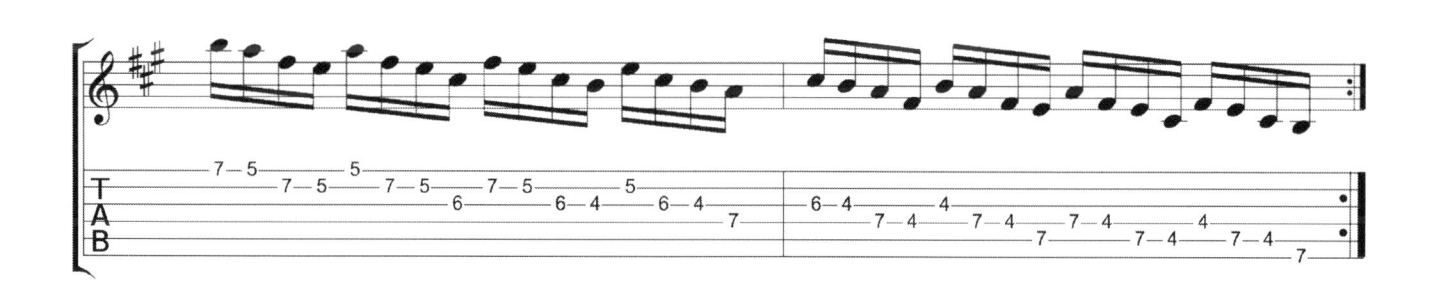

Example 13k –

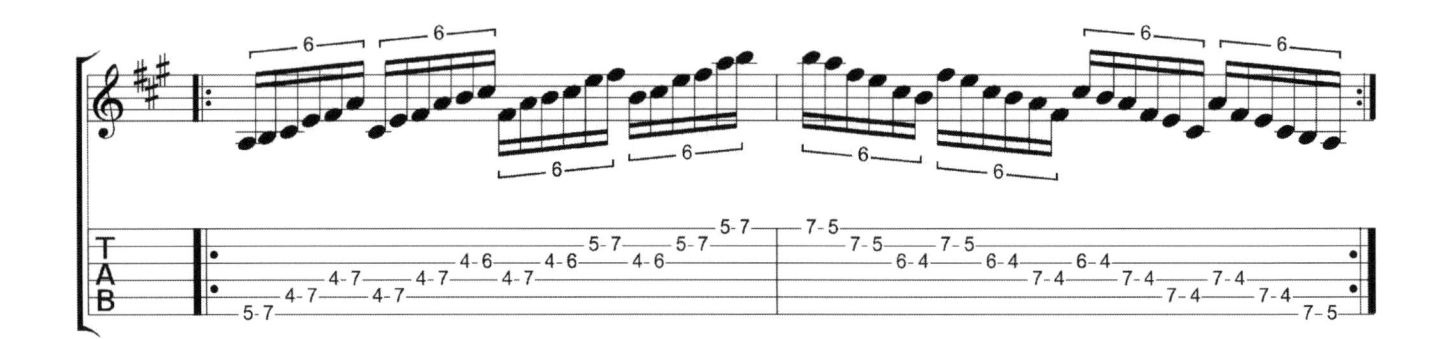

The final example in this chapter uses a 'skip-a-note' pattern. This is a useful exercise to help you break the habit of playing all the notes of the A Major Pentatonic sequentially.

Example 13l –

Pop Quiz

What are the notes in the A Major Pentatonic scale?

Name three guitarists who use the Major Pentatonic scale.

What genres of music is the Major Pentatonic scale synonymous?

How does the Major Pentatonic scale vary in sound from its Minor Pentatonic counterpart?

Answers on the final page!

Chapter Fourteen – A Major Pentatonic Licks

Backing Track Nine.

In this chapter, I have written five A Major Pentatonic scale licks that can be played with Backing Track Nine.

Be sure to practice these licks with a metronome and the backing tracks provided. Jam with a friend or solo along to the songs mentioned at the end of this chapter. Take time to internalise the licks and enjoy making your own solos from them.

The Major Pentatonic sound has a happier sound than its minor counterpart. In example 14a I have built a five-bar melodic solo around Backing Track 9 which has an expressive, vocal quality. Experiment with which finger feels most comfortable to perform the slides.

Example 14a –

Hammer-ons and pull-offs provide the backbone for this free-flowing A Major Pentatonic lick. Listen to the audio and emulate how I phrase this example.

Example 14b –

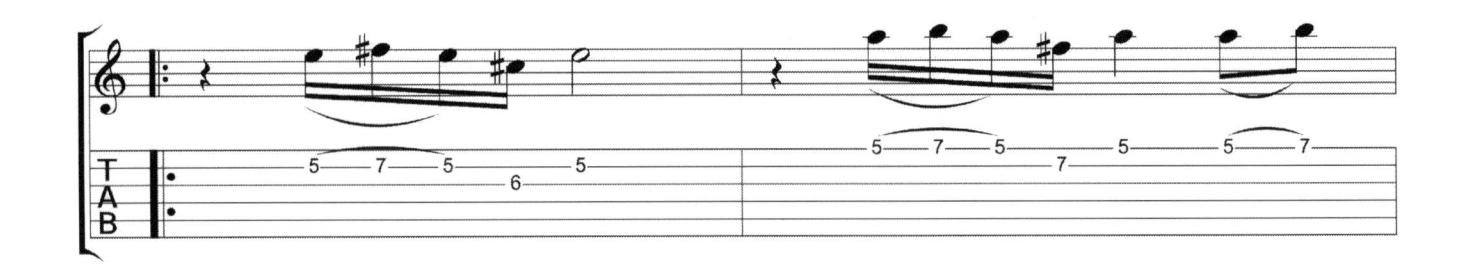

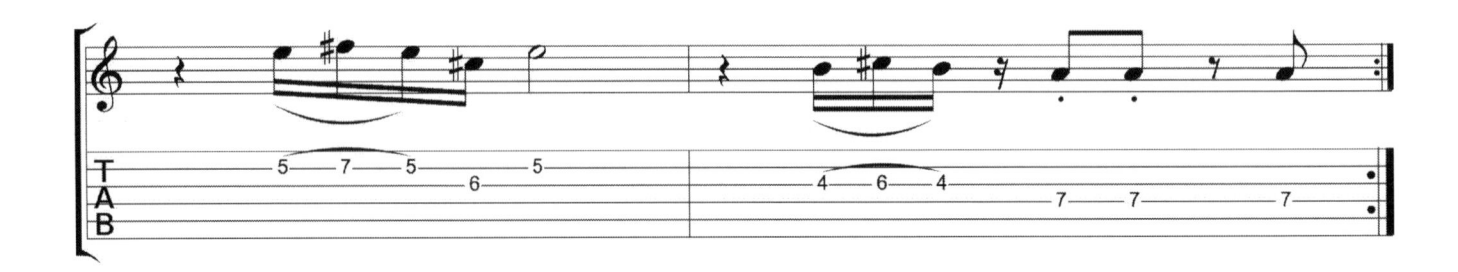

In example 14c, I demonstrate how to use long swooping slow bends using the A Major Pentatonic scale. The notation gives you a visual representation of each bend that I am playing.

Example 14c –

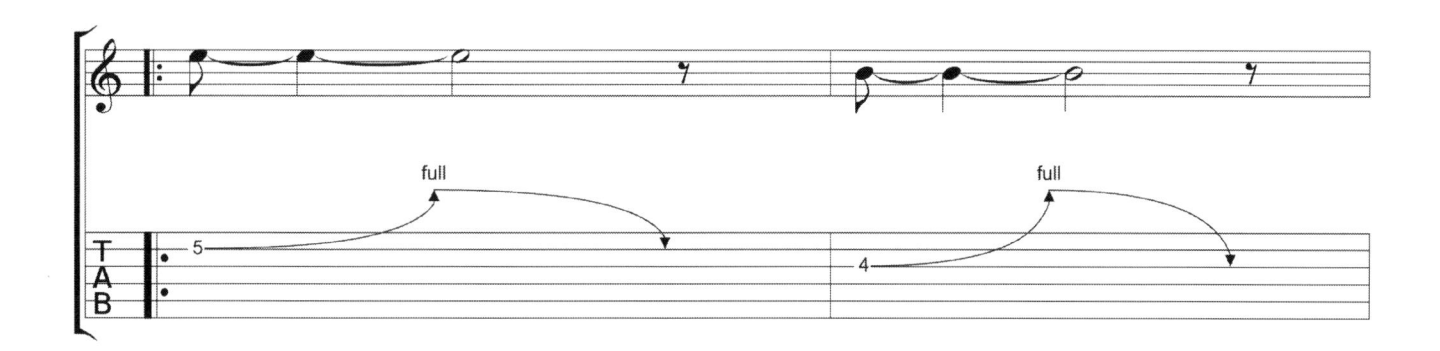

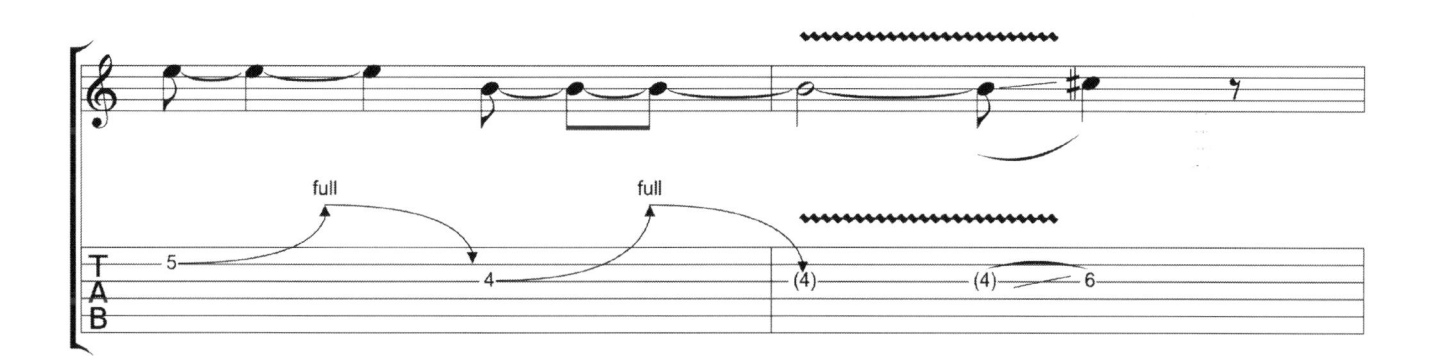

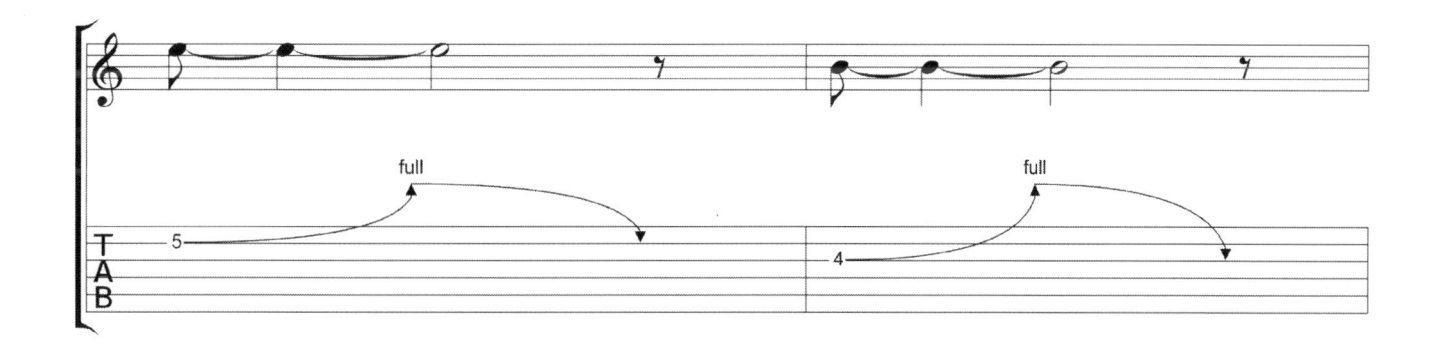

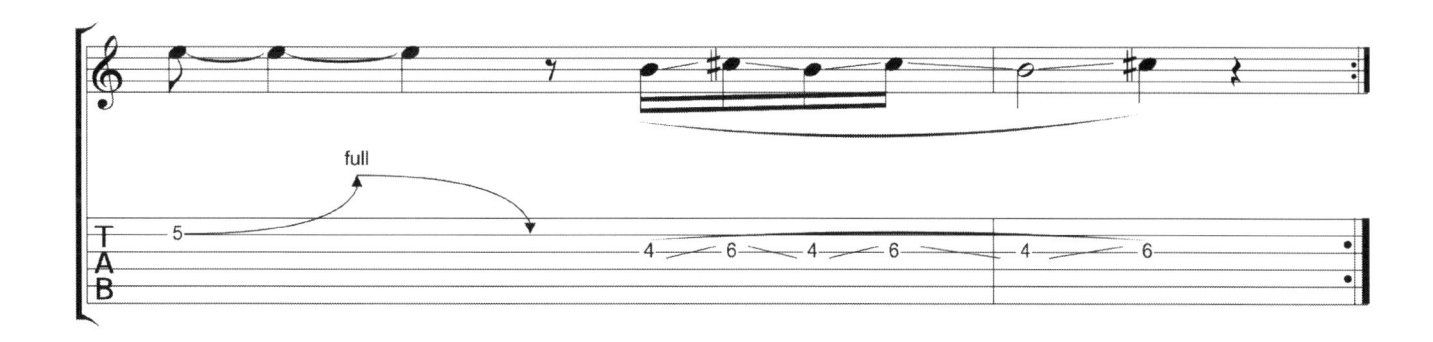

Simplicity can make for the most memorable lead guitar licks. Aim to let the hammer-on ring out while playing the note that follows.

Example 14d –

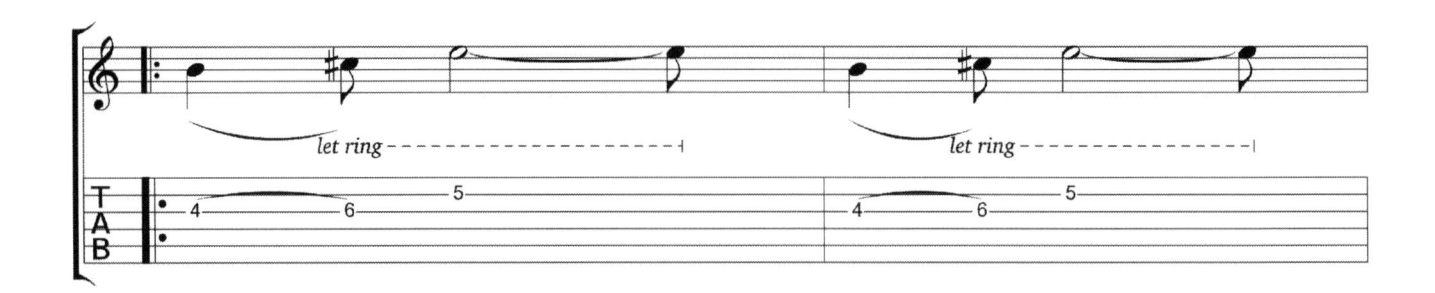

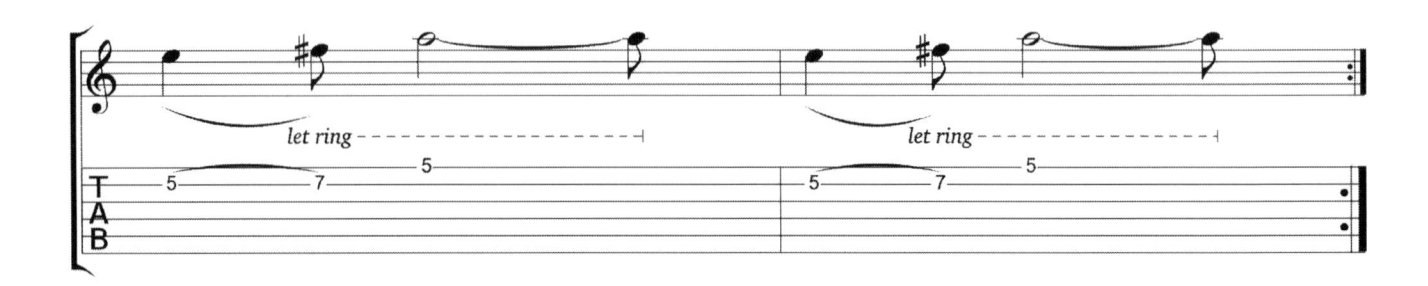

Jimi Hendrix loved to use the Major Pentatonic scale when improvising and playing solos. Check out the solo on the track The Wind Cries Mary for classic Major Pentatonic licks. Example 14e has a very Hendrix-style theme. Play the original double-stop pattern using your first finger and the second double-stop pattern using your first and second fingers.

Example 14e –

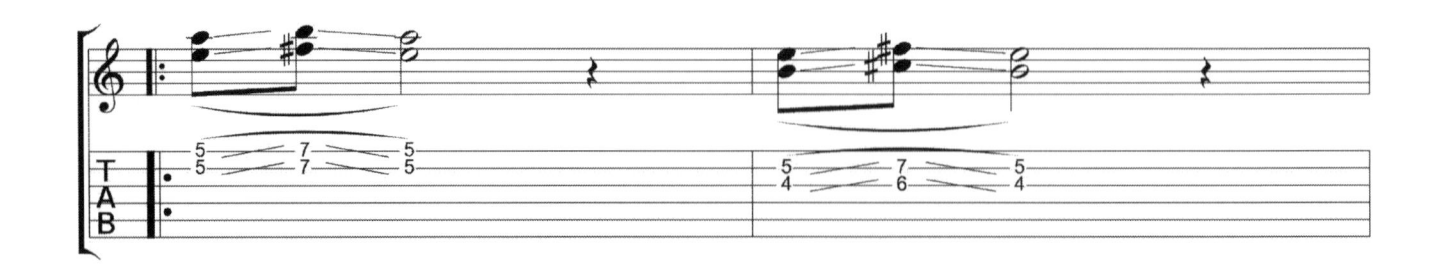

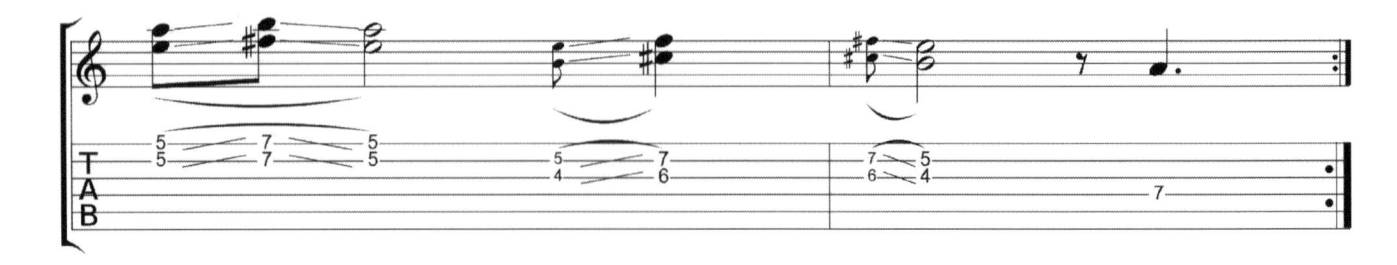

Songs in the Key of A Major

Jam along to these tunes using the licks given in this chapter.

Free – All Right Now

Eric Clapton – Tears in Heaven

The Beatles – Get Back

The Troggs – Wild Thing

Snow Patrol – Chasing Cars

Buy A Looper Pedal

One of the most useful tools I have ever bought in my guitar playing career is a looper pedal. It is the perfect jam companion and will always be the same level as you! I personally use a Ditto looper pedal in my practice regimes and lessons as I can quickly lay down a rhythmic idea or just a chord and then solo over it.

Alternatively, you can use the voice memo function on your smartphone to record a loop, and use that as your backing track.

Chapter Fifteen – A Major Pentatonic Solo

Backing Track Nine

Example 15a is a full solo that uses the A Major Pentatonic scale and should be played over the top of backing track nine.

Bars 9 – 14 will need to be practiced at a slower speed before bringing them up to speed. I have included the picking directions above each note of this section to tell you precisely how I approach playing this lick. This section has a classic rock sound and is similar to the end of the Free track, All Right Now.

All of the licks for the Major Pentatonic scale in this book are presented in the key of A, but it is crucially important that you spend time moving these licks and ideas around the fretboard to all twelve keys. Refer to **page 60** for how to find the root notes on the 6th string.

As always, I have included a slowed down midi version so you can play along at a slower tempo.

Example 15a –

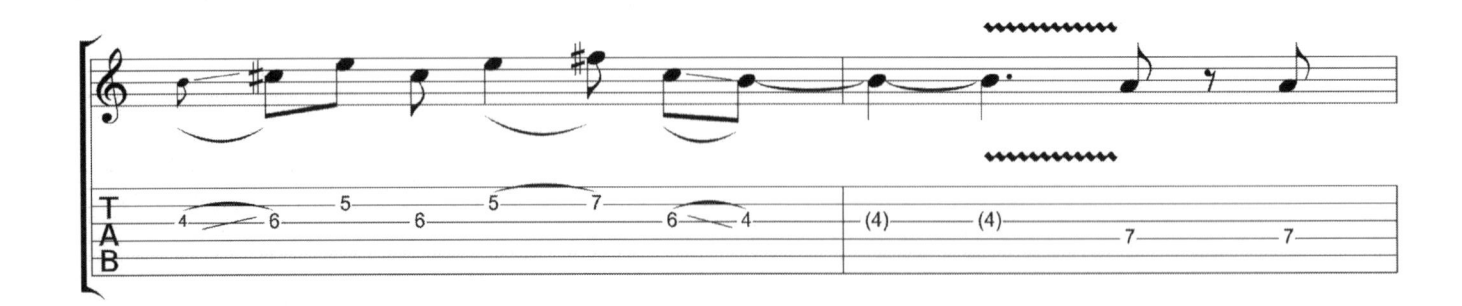

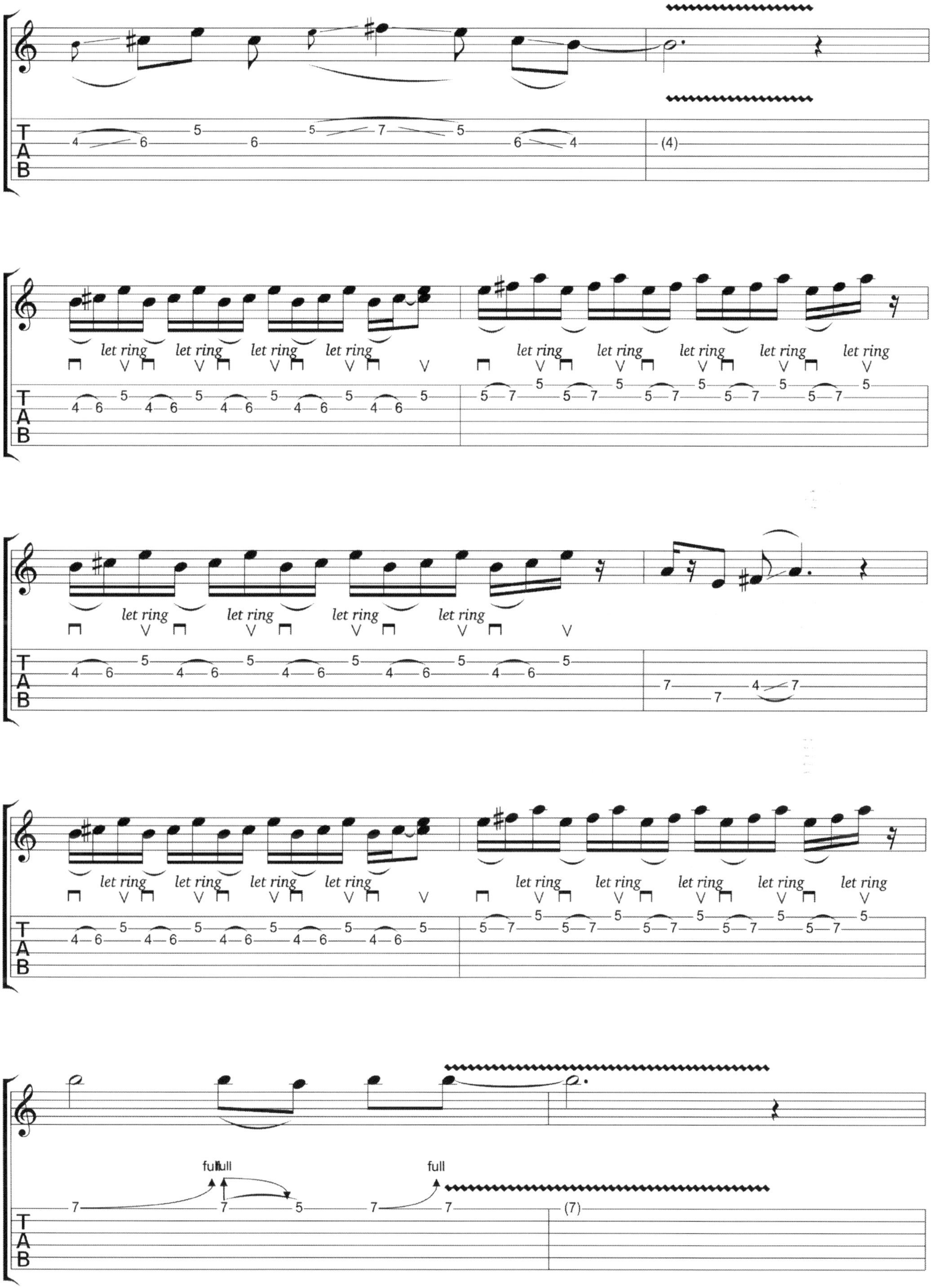
let ring
full
full
full

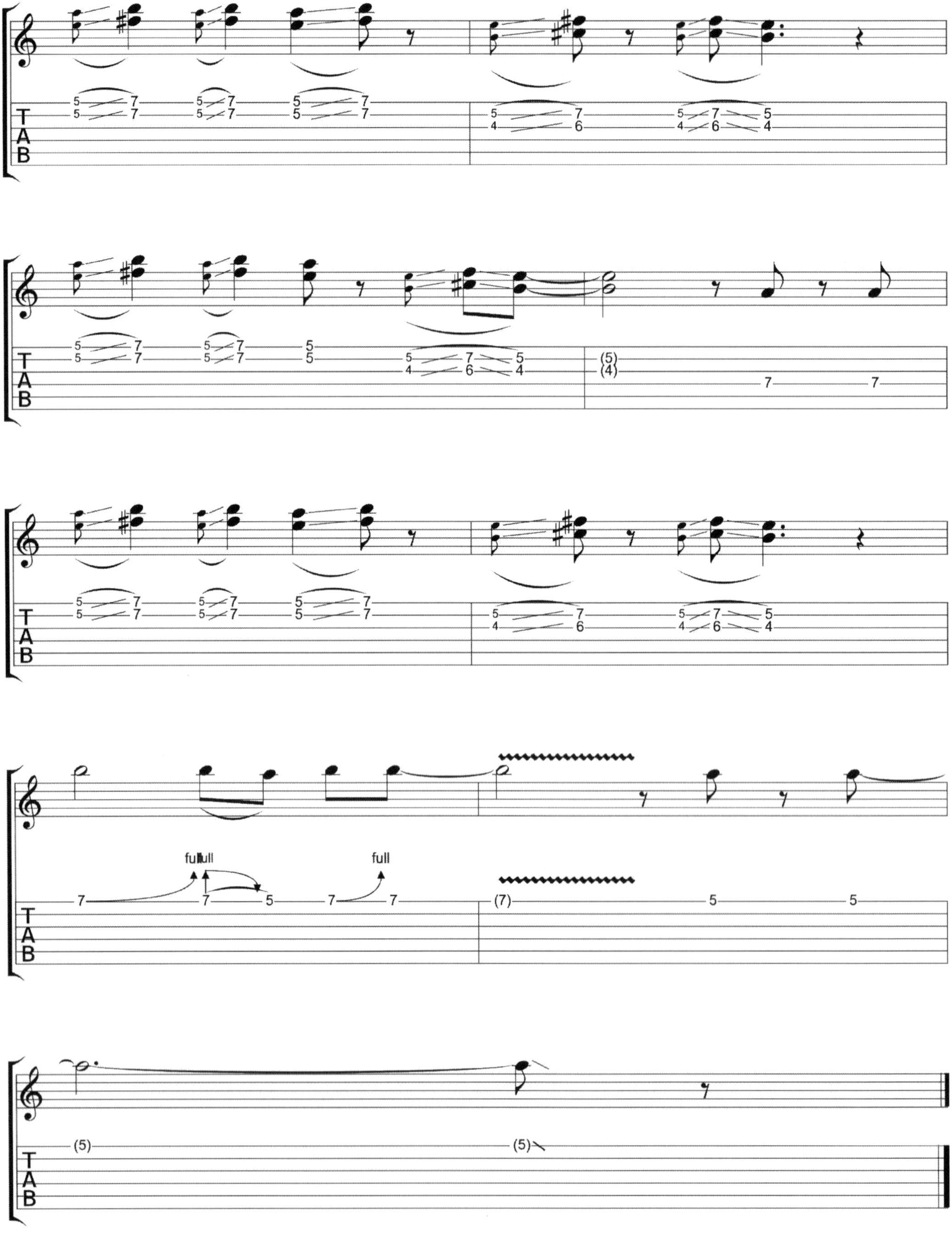
full full
full

Chapter Sixteen – The Four Note Soloing Challenge

Backing Track Three

Watch my Bonus Content Video Lesson for this chapter here:

www.fundamental-changes.com/ssbc

Although the scale shapes you have learnt should now feel comfortable to you, it can still seem daunting to create your own licks and solos with them. Enter the four-note soloing challenge!

The principal behind this challenge is simple: Pick a scale shape you know well, and restrict yourself to playing *only* four notes from that scale.

In example 16a, I have created a full solo based on just four notes of the A Minor Pentatonic scale. Shown below are the notes I have used to create this full solo.

A Minor Pentatonic

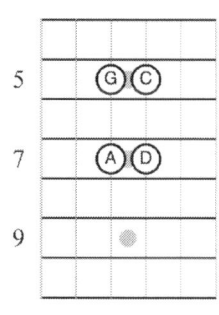

At first, the possibilities seem incredibly limited when dealing with just these four notes, but by applying bends, hammer-ons, pull-offs, slides and vibrato, the number of melodic options is vast.

Learn and study the solo I have created here before attempting to create your own solo using this four-note system. Steal as many licks as you can from this solo, and from all the earlier chapters based around the A Minor Pentatonic scale too.

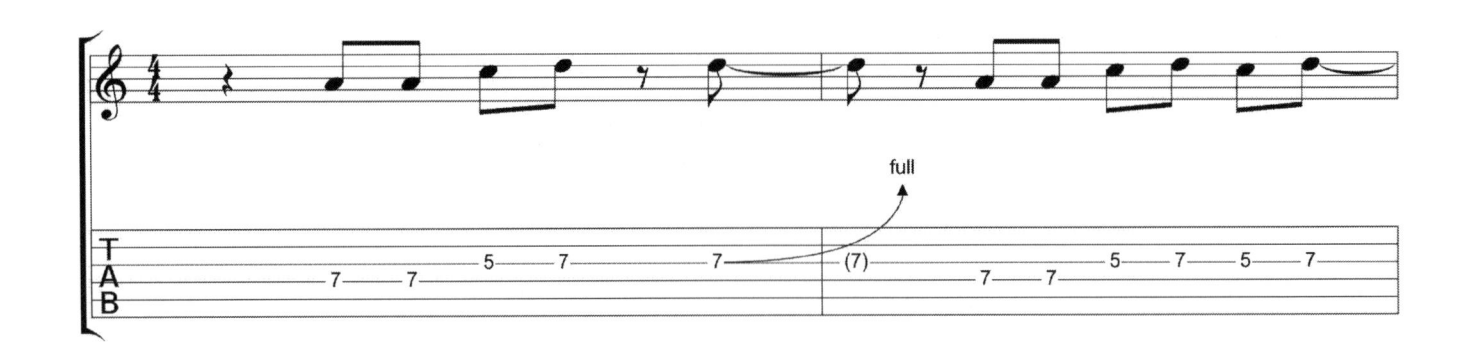

Example 16a -

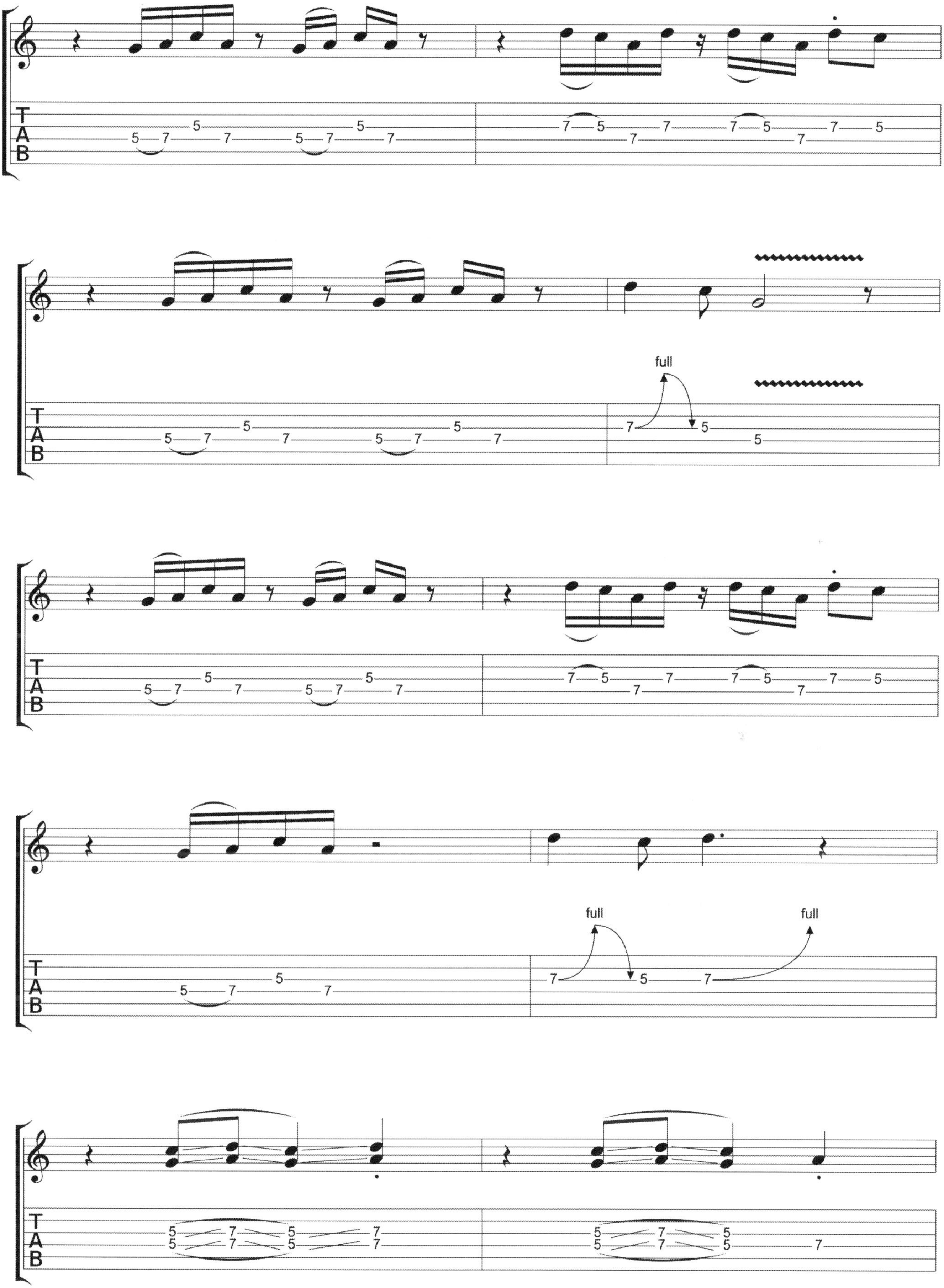
full
full
full

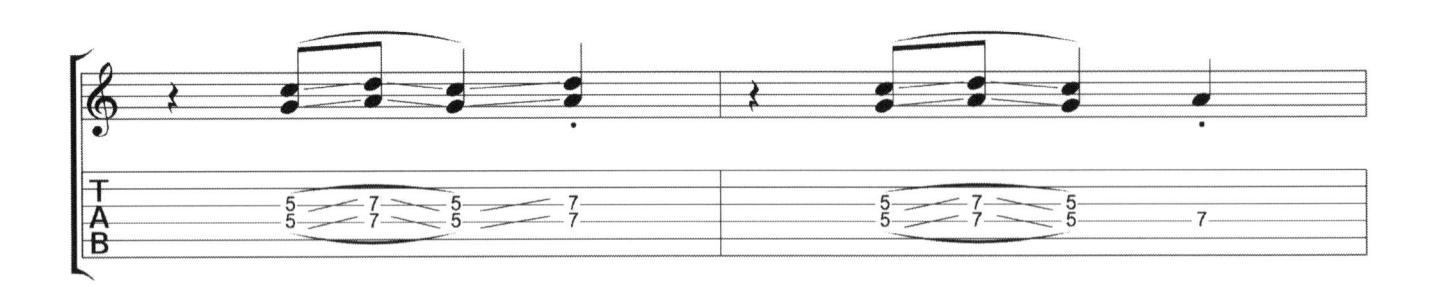

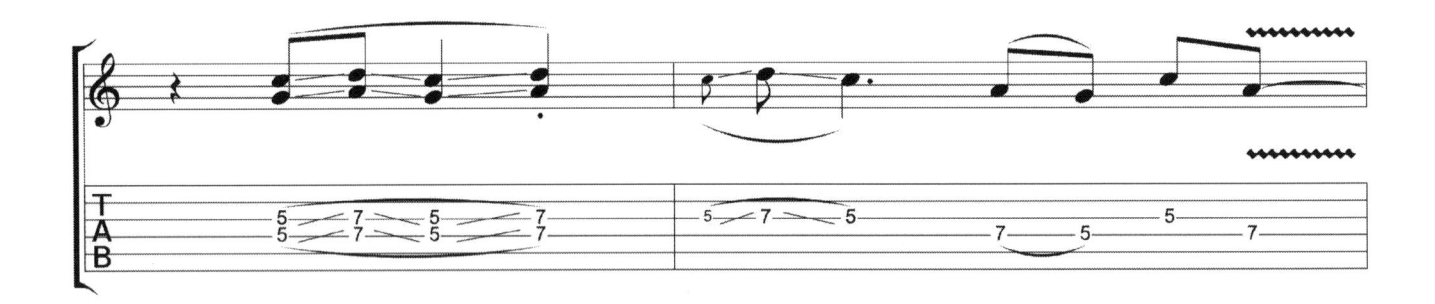

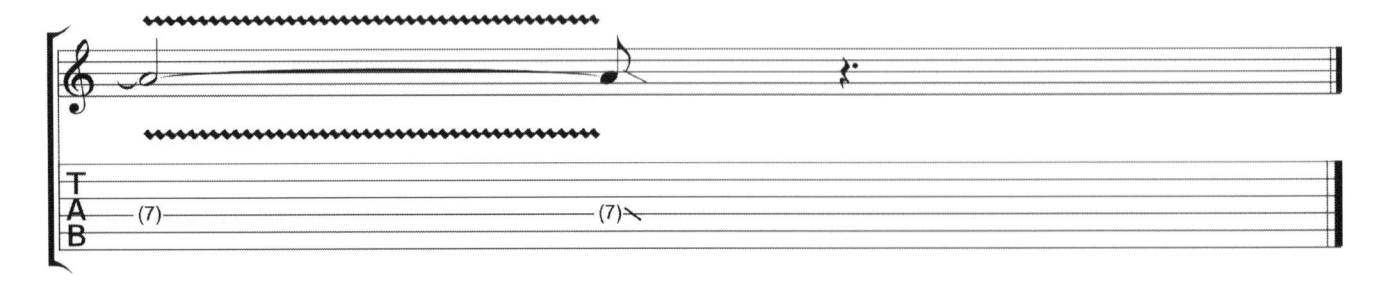

Once you have completed example 16a and feel comfortable creating your own solos using the four notes, you can apply this same strategy to *any* four notes from *any* scale shape.

For starters create a solo over backing track one using just these four notes from the highest part of the A Minor Pentatonic scale.

A Minor Pentatonic

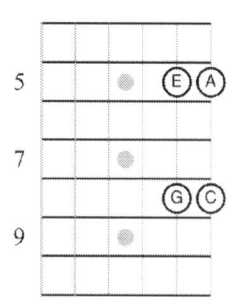

After you have completed the four note challenges with the A Minor Pentatonic scale, apply this idea to the E Minor Pentatonic scale, the A Blues scale and the A Major scale.

If you have created your own solo using this four-note soloing strategy, record a video of yourself playing and post it as a comment underneath the YouTube video featured at the start of this chapter.

Chapter Seventeen – 'In The Style of' Licks

Backing Track Five and Six

Jimi Hendrix, Eric Clapton, B.B. King, Stevie Ray Vaughan and David Gilmour are undisputable guitar legends. I have created five 'in the style of' licks in the key of E Minor, one for each of these artists.

Hendrix redefined electric guitar playing and changed the course of modern day soloing. Example 17a combines ideas from tracks like Hey Joe and Little Wing to form a blues-rock Hendrix-style lead line suitable for any backing track in the key of E Minor. As always, make sure you move all these licks to as many different keys as possible.

Example 17a – Hendrix

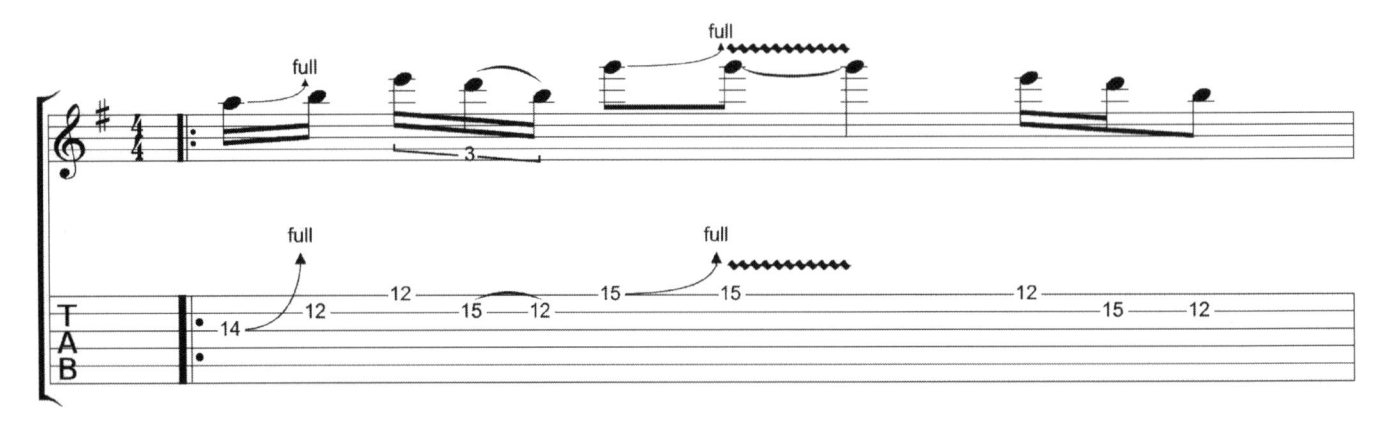

Triplets provide the basis for this blues-based E minor Eric Clapton style lick. Notice the combination of double-stops and single notes in this four-bar idea. I recommend checking out the lesser known track My Father's Eyes for a passionate Clapton song that's full of emotion.

Example 17b – Eric Clapton

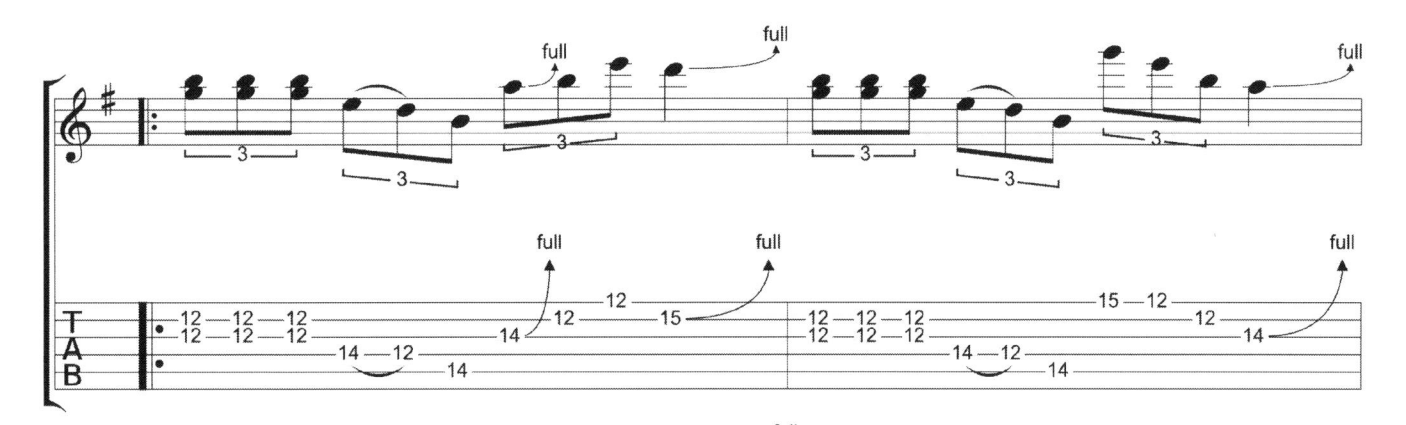

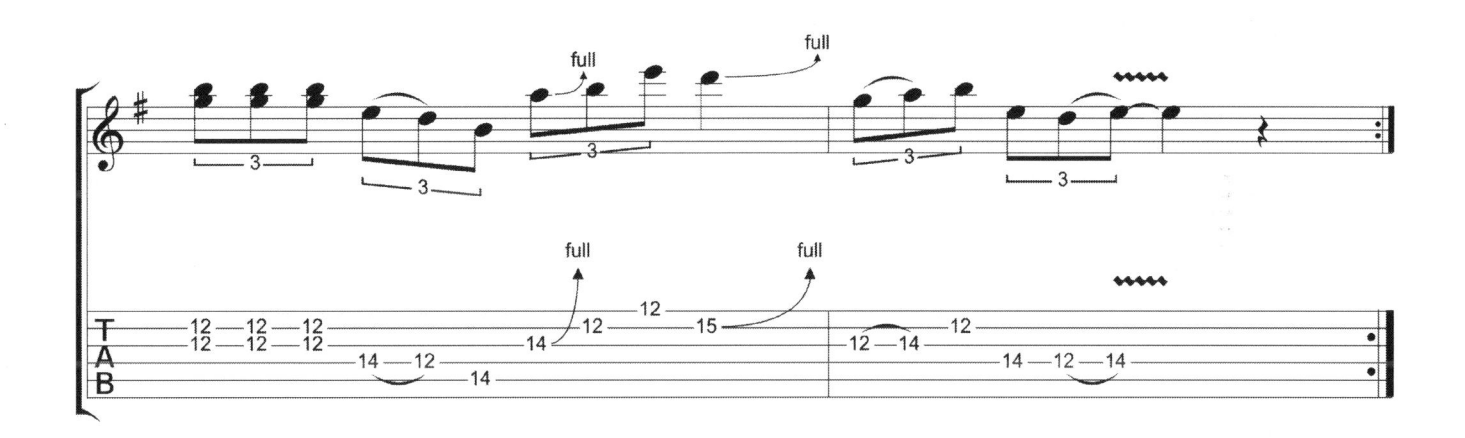

B.B. King could make just one note sing! His style is instantly recognisable; from his trademark vibrato to the beautiful touch, tone and expression in everything he played. Check out the classic track The Thrill is Gone for more licks in this style.

Example 17c – B.B. King

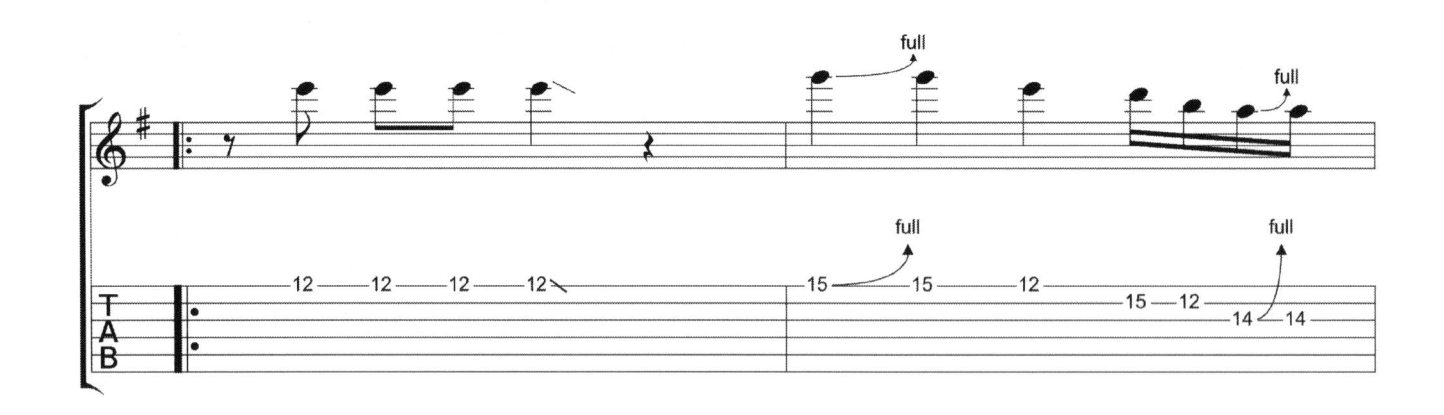

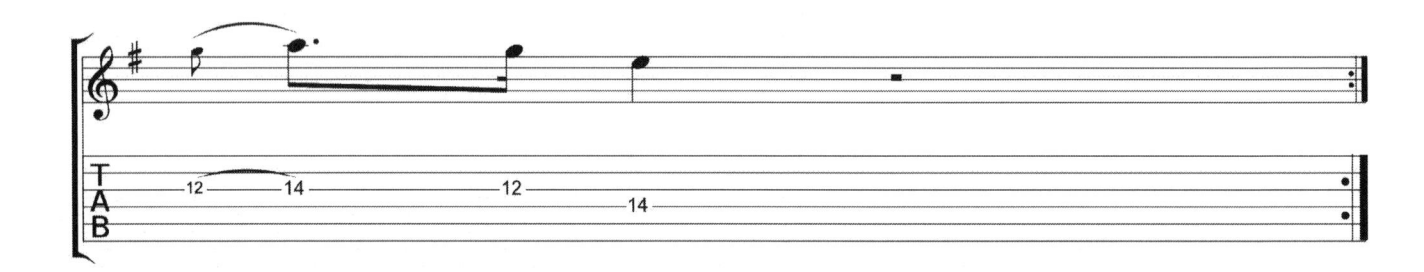

Stevie Ray Vaughan was of the most passionate players ever, combining his raw Texas Blues background with speed and prowess everywhere on the neck. Listen to the huge hit Texas Flood for more tasty SRV licks.

Example 17d – Stevie Ray Vaughan

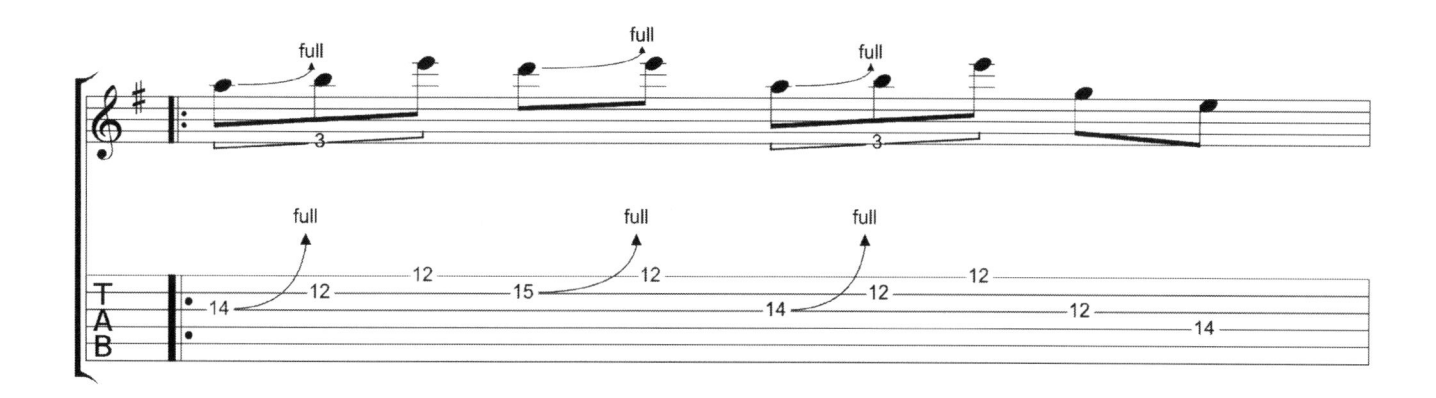

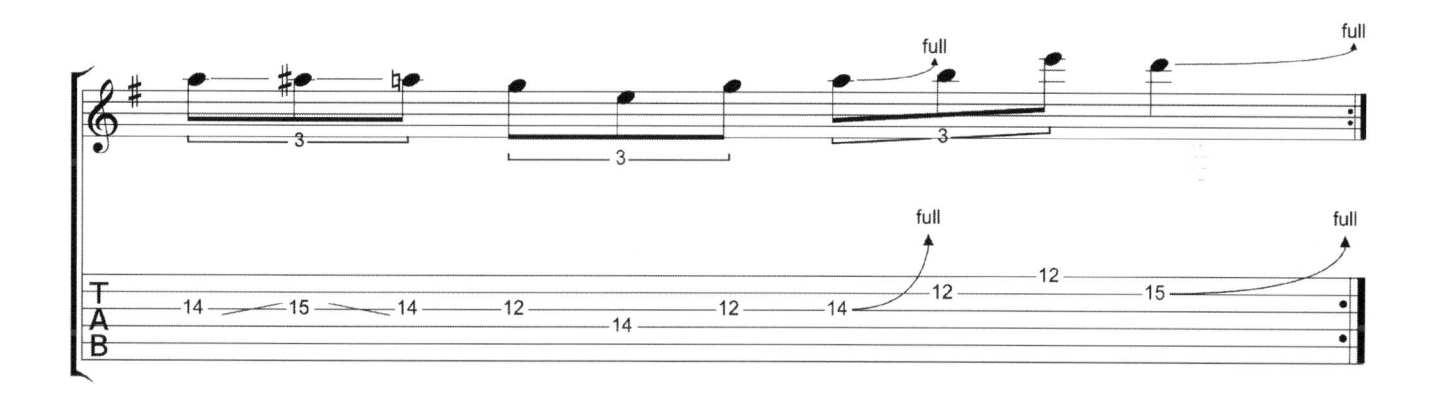

Famed for his time with Pink Floyd, David Gilmour is synonymous with the finest blues guitar licks around combining silky-smooth lead guitar and a classic Fender Stratocaster sound.

Example 17e – David Gilmour

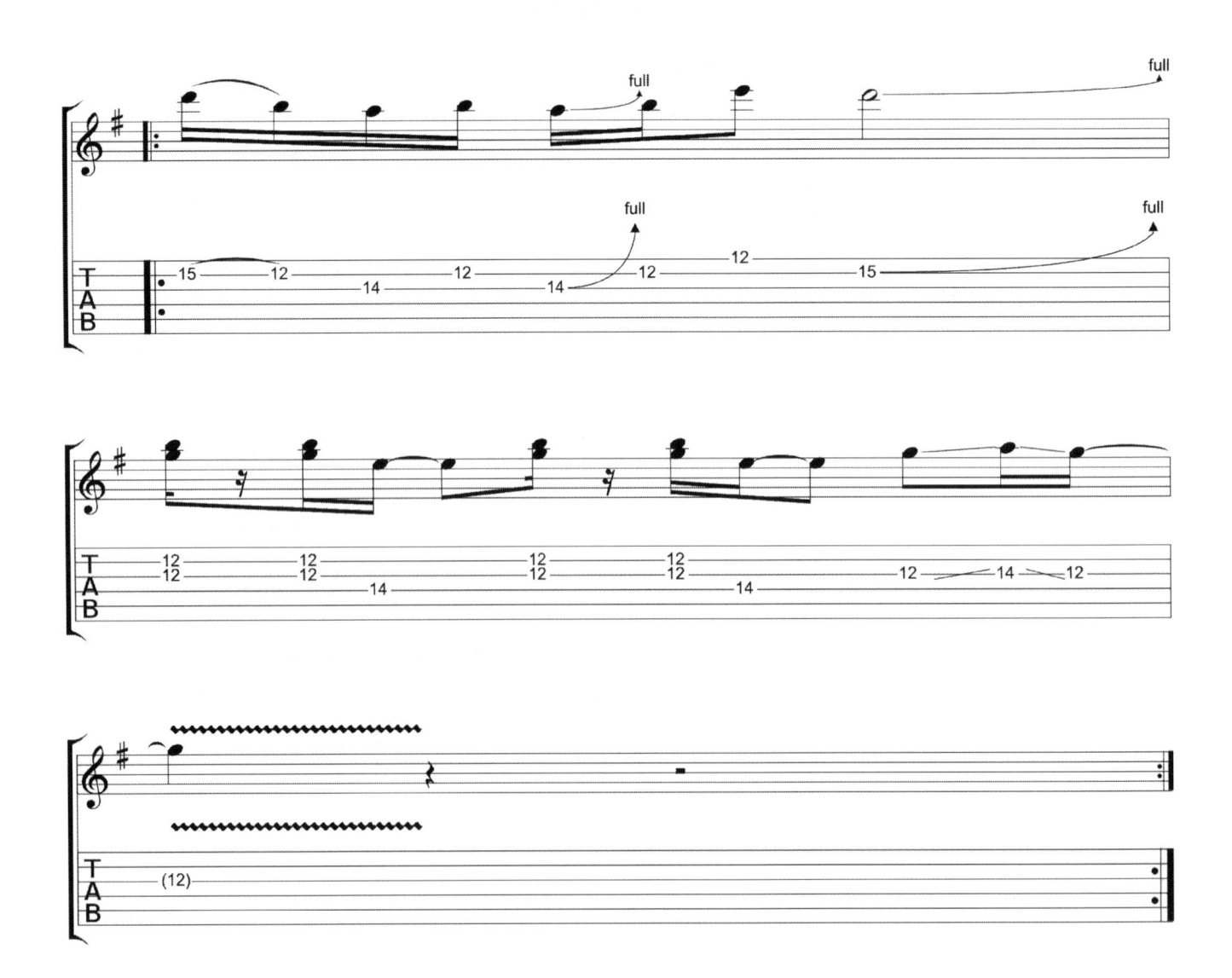

There is something incredibly satisfying about learning to play licks in the style of your guitar heroes and I have written a wide and varied selection of video articles based around guitar giants and how to play in their style.

Check out the **Fundamental Changes YouTube** channel for lots of free videos to push you to the next level in your guitar playing. **http://www.youtube.com/c/FundamentalchangesGuitar**

Conclusion

By now, you are probably swimming in a sea of new ideas and possibilities. I recommend you create your own personal video lick diary for reference. Film your licks, and if possible write them out in standard notation or tab. That way, when you look back in six months' time, not only can you see and hear how far your playing has come, you can revisit licks that you may have forgotten.

Practice what you don't know, not what you do! - This is quite simply the best advice I can give any musician. Use a metronome to help you master each example and use backing tracks to create a more musical approach to practicing.

An important goal should be to play with other people, so while you are developing your skills in this book find time to jam with other musicians. Playing with other instrumentalists is the best way to improve your musicianship.

Be sure to check out my other titles also released on the Fundamental Changes label:

My passion in life is teaching people to play and express themselves through the guitar. If you have any questions, please get in touch and I will do my best to respond as quickly as possible.

You can contact me on **simeypratt@gmail.com** or via the **Fundamental Changes YouTube channel**.

Discography

Here are some classic songs that contain either amazing solos or incredible lead guitar work throughout.

Albert King – Born Under a Bad Sign

Eric Clapton – Crossroads

Jimi Hendrix – All Along the Watchtower / Little Wing

B.B King – The Thrill is Gone

Leslie West – Mississippi Queen

Richie Blackmore – Highway Star (Deep Purple)

Billy Gibbons – La Grange (ZZ Top)

Larry Carlton – Kid Charlemagne

Carlos Santana – Samba Pa Ti

Eddie Van Halen – Eruption

Mark Knopfler – Sultans of Swing (Dire Straights)

Michael Schenker – Rock Bottom

David Gilmour – Another Brick in The Wall PT 2

Angus Young – You Shook Me All Night Long

Randy Rhoads – Crazy Train

Stevie Ray Vaughan – Pride and Joy

Yngwie Malmsteen – Black Star

Kirk Hammett – Master of Puppets

Joe Satriani – Always With Me, Always With You

Kurt Cobain – Come as You Are

Zakk Wylde – No More Tears

Dimebag Darrell – Cowboys from Hell

Slash – November Rain

Steve Vai – For The Love of God

The Scorpions – Rock You Like a Hurricane

The Surfaris – Wipeout

The Beatles – Something

Lynyrd Skynyrd – Sweet Home Alabama

Allman Brothers Band – Stormy Monday / Jessica

Toto – Rossana

Rush – Limelight

Tower of Power

The Doobie Brothers – China Groove

Ram Jam – Black Betty

Gary Moore – Parisian Walkways

Eric Johnson – Cliffs of Dover

Yngwie Malmsteen – Rising Force

Steve Vai – For The Love of God

Joe Satriani – Cryin'

Quiz Answers

P20

- A C D E G
- Melodic building blocks can act as the stepping stone to creating longer licks and eventually solos.

P25

- There are two types of slide, an upward and a downward.
- An upward slide is from a lower pitch to a higher one.
- A double slide is sliding between multiple notes using only one pick stroke
- Blues, Rock, Country, Jazz and Funk.

P35

- Bending is the technique of raising the pitch of a note by increasing the tension on the string.
- A semi-tone bend raises the pitch of a note by a half-step, or one fret.
- A tone bend raises the pitch of a note by a whole-step, or two frets.
- A tone bend is the most common in modern day electric guitar playing.
- David Gilmour, Jimi Hendrix and Carlos Santana.

P65

- E G A B D.
- Two notes played at the same time.
- Repeat certain licks throughout a solo.
- At least three times.

P71

- A C D Eb E G.
- One – the note of Eb.
- Angus Young and Joe Satriani.
- Multiple picks on every note, skip a string and groupings of notes.

P84

- A B C# E F#.
- Slash, Chuck Berry and Eric Clapton.
- Country, blues and rock.
- The Major Pentatonic scale sounds happier than its minor counterpart.

Printed in Great Britain
by Amazon